WA
AND THE
RISE OF
THE STATE

The Free Press
A Division of Simon & Schuster
1230 Avenue of the Americas
New York, NY 10020

Manufactured in the United States of America
10 9 8 7 6 5 4 3 2 1

Library of Congress Cataloging-In-Publication Data

Porter, Bruce D.
      War and the rise of the state : the military foundation of modern
politics / Bruce D. Porter.
      p. cm
   Includes bibliographical references and index.
   ISBN: 0-7432-3778-1
   1. Violence—History.   2. Politics and war—History.   3. War—
History.   4. State, The.   I. Title.
JC328.6.P67   1994
303.6—dc20   93-29346
                                                CIP

For information regarding special discounts for bulk purchases, please contact Simon &
Schuster Special Sales at 1-800-456-6798 or business@simonandschuster.com

DEDICATED TO SAMUEL P. HUNTINGTON
MENTOR, COLLEAGUE, FRIEND

Contents

Acknowledgments

Once upon a time, the study of war annoyed me to tears. As an undergraduate trying to master the details of European history, I found wars a great inconvenience, a bothersome interruption in an otherwise sensible flow of history. The historical narrative would shift abruptly to concentrate on battles and combat and death-dealing. Several pages later, history would resume. I know that many historians and social scientists share the frustration I felt then, for those who do not specialize in military history often display a tendency to gloss over periods of war quickly so as to get on with whatever line of narrative or argument they are pursuing.

In my case, frustration gradually gave way to bewilderment as I continued to study European history. I noticed that though the peaceful course of history indeed resumed after every round of hostilities, the end of every major war always seemed to mark the beginning of a new era. The prewar narrative did not in fact resume smoothly in the postwar period. Some kind of revolution had occurred in the interim, and a new world seemed to emerge from every war. I found this puzzling. Why should a war of only a few years duration inaugurate a whole new era? I began to suspect that the wars were more than mere interruptions in history, that they were grand causes of change in their own right. As the publication of this book demonstrates, the study of war ceased to annoy me from that time forth.

War and the Rise of the State was written under the auspices of the Olin Institute for Strategic Studies, which is under the Center for International Affairs, Harvard University, where I served from 1990 to 1993 as the Lynde and Harry Bradley Research Associate in Strategic Studies. The Center provided the ideal atmosphere for undertaking this study, while the unsurpassed resources of Harvard University's library system made the task an exceedingly pleasant one. The Bradley Foundation provided funding for the fellowship I held while writing

this book, and the Erhardt Foundation contributed funds to provide
me with a part-time research assistant during the summer of 1991. I
deeply appreciate the support of both foundations.

Writing a book is much like fighting a war. It takes enormous
amounts of time and energy, and it can only be accomplished by the
collective effort of many individuals. I am fully aware that any expression of gratitude made here will fall far short of what is called for, and
I am also mindful that the faults in this work are entirely my own, but
its merits owe much to my colleagues. In particular, I owe a great debt
to Samuel P. Huntington, the Director of the Institute and a long-time
supporter and friend. Professor Huntington encouraged me to join the
Olin Institute in 1990 and has been unstinting in his support of my
research effort from the beginning. His comments and suggestions on
the manuscript have been invaluable. Gratefully, this book is dedicated
to him. Stephen P. Rosen, the Associate Director of the Institute, has
also been a faithful supporter, and we have had many conversations on
war and state formation that have left me enlightened and stimulated.

Several colleagues read portions of the manuscript and provided
helpful comments and insights. Mindful that I am probably leaving
more than one reviewer out, I nonetheless wish to express gratitude to
Charles Cogan, Andrew Cortell, David Herrmann, Malcolm S. Forbes,
Jr., Stanley Hoffmann, Richard Hunt, Samuel Huntington, David
Kaiser, Eric Nordlinger, Paul Peterson, Kamal Shehadi, Janice Thompson, Charles Tilly, Adam Ulam, and Fareed Zakaria for the time they
took to read various chapters of the book. An anonymous reviewer for
The Free Press who specializes in Renaissance military history also
provided invaluable comments on Chapters 2 and 3. Two part-time
research assistants, Frederic Ruiz-Ramon and Jeff Cimbalo, helped me
verify much of the historical information and references herein. I feel
compelled to note a particular debt to Charles Tilly of the New School
for Social Research, not only for the bibliography and comments he
provided, but also for the invaluable intellectual path he cut in his own
classic works on war and the state.

Every writer owes a considerable debt to his or her publisher. The
editorial and production staff of The Free Press have been immensely
supportive and helpful throughout this endeavor. Joyce Seltzer
encouraged the effort in its early stages and Bruce Nichols, the senior
editor responsible for the project, was infinitely patient in pointing out
some rough places in the early drafts and brilliantly insightful in his
comments and editorial suggestions. The copy editor, Camilla Hewitt,
and production staff under Robert Harrington likewise merit nothing
but praise.

Last, but far from least, I am thankful for the support and encouragement of my wife, Susan, and my four children, David, Chris, Lisa, and Jennifer, all of whom found it curious that their normally peaceable father would be writing a book on so stormy a subject as war. They bravely put up with more than one war story and only occasionally asked when I would be finished.

I am painfully aware of the fact that any work purporting to draw generalizations about 500 years of history is bound to contain some errors, omissions, and misinterpretations. I am solely responsible for any such inaccuracies, my only excuse being that the fog of war grows denser with the passing of time. I do not believe, however, that any factual errors that may reside in the text will nullify its basic conclusions.

Prologue

THE PARADOX OF WAR

The army, in the words of the writer Robert Heinlein, is "a permanent organization for the destruction of life and property." Heinlein captures the essential paradox of every modern military establishment: that it employs large-scale and complex organization toward the ultimate end of physical destruction. War, the most violent of all enterprises, is also the most organized. In no other human endeavor—not in commerce, industry, education, religion, science, nor domestic politics—does collective action occur on such a large scale. And therein lies much of the burden and tragedy of modern politics, which for nearly five hundred years has been driven by the organizational imperatives of conflict.

The battlefield itself is Chaos Incarnate, the most wretched arena on earth, where death and devastation reign supreme. As William Tecumseh Sherman tersely observed and every soldier in combat knows, war is Hell. It is the "blood-swollen god" of Stephen Crane, the "brain-splattering, windpipe-splitting art" of Lord Byron, the "epidemic insanity" of Ralph Waldo Emerson. But if chaos and destruction are the hallmarks of battle, they are not the totality of war; quite opposite conditions prevail beginning immediately behind the front and extending backward to the seat of government. In the rear, order and regimentation reign. A complex logistics system procures and transports large quantities of equipment and supplies to the front. An encompassing bureaucracy trains and outfits reserve and relief forces. Hundreds of munitions factories manufacture the weapons and materiel of war, employing the most intricate and advanced technologies known to science. In a major war between industrial powers, large segments of the civilian population are mobilized for service in the armaments industry or in burgeoning wartime bureaucracies. A central government directs the whole of this vast effort, using extraordinary, and often extralegal, wartime authority to tax, regulate, confiscate, ration, conscript, and otherwise mobilize the resources required to wage the contest.

Thus, except at the front itself, war is a demonstrably organized, and *organizing*, phenomenon. Physicists measure the degree of disorder inherent in a given molecular system by its entropy. A high degree of entropy means a low degree of organization and order, while low entropy means a high degree of structure and organization. If human beings at war are viewed as atoms (and as such they are often treated during war), then war can be seen as an activity in which the negative entropy of the rear suddenly explodes into the extremely high entropy of the battlefront. No other human phenomenon, and few natural phenomena, display such a striking shift in entropy. Physicists also link entropy to time, and many combatants speak of a marked shift that occurs in the human perception of time during battle. This is not entirely subjective, for what would require years, decades, or generations in peacetime can happen during war in weeks, days, or even hours.[1] The intensity of military conflict unleashes or accelerates numerous forces for change, transforming industry, society, and government in ways that are fundamental and permanent.

From this Paradox of Organized Destruction flow other paradoxes of war. For example, by weakening or destroying traditional structures, or by compelling internal reforms, war may create conditions conducive to social change and political modernization. But "modernization" in this sense should not be taken to imply moral progress, for it may represent just the opposite. The tendency of social scientists until recently to commit the fallacy of associating "modernization" with progress only betrays the strong hold that evolutionary models have had on scholarship over the past century.[2] *Modernization*, as used in this book, simply means movement from medieval, traditional, decentralized, and personal forms of government to bureaucratic, rationalized, centralized, and impersonal forms. The modern is not necessarily superior to the traditional. Depending on the specific case, traditional forms may be culturally richer and offer greater scope for human liberty, while modern forms may be sterile and repressive. That war may serve a modernizing function says as much about the moral ambiguities of modernity as it does about the nature of war.

What then is the role of warfare in history? Liberal and progressive conceptions of history regard war as a transient phenomenon, an anomaly in the inexorable upward progress of civilization. Hegelian, Marxist, and fascist interpretations of history see war as a dialectical engine of that progress. Both conceptions disregard the tragic side of history. Wars are not mere intermissions in a human drama of relentless progress; their organizational residues are woven too deeply into the fabric of modern politics for that. But neither is war necessarily an engine of progress. It is instead a powerful catalyst of *change*, the direction of which is always morally problematic and often deleterious in effect. Regardless of whether a given war is just or unjust, defensive or offensive, positive or negative in its long-term consequences, military conflict tends to unleash the most primitive of human passions, often with enduring consequences for the moral fabric of the societies that wage it.

One consequence of European warfare from the Renaissance to World War II was an increase in the size and power of central governments. By imposing peace on violently divided societies, strong states helped avert the Hobbesian twin catastrophes of civil war and anarchy; unfortunately, the price of this dividend was too often the loss of political freedom. Here we confront yet another paradox of war: the military power required to defend against foreign aggression can easily be turned to internal repression. A government at war is a juggernaut of centralization determined to crush any internal opposition that impedes the mobilization of militarily vital resources. This centralizing tendency of war has made the rise of the state throughout much of history a disaster for human liberty and rights, a triumph of raw power abetted by conditions of large-scale violence. The Swiss economist J. C. L. Simonde de Sismondi spoke of this in a letter to a friend in 1835: "As war becomes more sophisticated it continuously increases governmental authority and decreases the power of the people."[3] The result may be what Harold Lasswell called "garrison states," political systems obsessed with national security, where perpetual war or the perceived threat of war leads to the concentration of all political power in the hands of an elite devoted to violence.[4]

Carried to an extreme, the logical culmination of increasing state power is the totalitarian state, whose rise in the twentieth century should have discredited forever that casual assumption of the Enlightenment that history was a linear march toward utopia. Not surprisingly, the intellectual precursors of totalitarianism included a diversity of nineteenth-century thinkers who glorified war as a wellspring of progress. The Social Darwinists saw war as a means of sifting the wheat of humanity from its weaker chaff. Their chief spokesman, Herbert Spencer, saw the triumph of the strong over the weak as "the decrees of a large, far-seeing benevolence." He argued that past competition among militant societies had weeded out weaker individuals and prepared the way for the emergence of a new industrial society led by men of high character, heirs of the militant conquerors of the past. In the decades leading up to World War I, various heirs of Social Darwinism—Arthur de Gobineau, Georges Sorel, Ernst Jünger, Oswald Spengler, Heinrich von Treitschke—rejected the liberal heritage of the Enlightenment and became increasing militant, racist, and imperialist in their pronouncements. Glorifying war, they inevitably came to glorify the state. Treitschke wrote of "the sacredness of war," and declared in words which prefigured fascism that "the grandeur of war lies in the utter annihilation of puny man in the great conception of the State."[5]

Another, pre-Darwinian lineage of the totalitarian mind traces back to the German philosopher Georg W. F. Hegel, who also saw war as an agent of progress ("As a result of war, nations are strengthened") and the state as the highest manifestation of Divine Wisdom working in History. Hegelian philosophy influenced both Social Darwinism and the development of Fascist doctrine in Europe, but its greatest impact was on Karl Marx and the rise of totalitarian ideology on the left. Marx identified class conflict as the engine of human progress, and Lenin wrote that class contradictions continue to exist in war, which for him was simply one of their manifestations.[6] But while the Nazi state took seriously the notion that total war and the total state would bring utopia, Lenin and Stalin were more expedient. Turning Clausewitz upside down, they turned politics into the continuation of war by other means, and the state into an engine not so much of actual warfare but of permanent military mobilization.

But the mobilization imperative of war does not always culminate in total state power; in certain circumstances it can actually foster democratization. This occurs when the state's demand for war-fighting resources gives bargaining leverage to the holders of those resources. Max Weber, despite his hyperbole, captures the crux of this process: "The basis of democratization is everywhere purely military in character . . . Military discipline meant the triumph of democracy because the community wished and was compelled to secure the cooperation of the non-aristocratic masses and hence put arms, and along with arms political power, into their hands."[7]

The right of the medieval Estates in England to give consent on matters of war and taxation (the latter invariably levied for war) was the foundation of the English parliament. The triumph of popular sovereignty in France was closely linked with the advent of the mass army. In the United States, white male suffrage made its greatest advances after the War of Independence and the War of 1812, and black male suffrage after the Civil War. Women in the United States and nearly a dozen European countries received the right to vote at the conclusion of World War I. It was not by chance that the one country in Renaissance Europe requiring active military service of all adult males—the Swiss Confederation—was also the only country with almost universal manhood suffrage. Perversely, it was also the last country in Europe to grant women the right to vote, not taking the step until 1971. The logic apparently was that if they didn't fight, why should they vote? One gun, one vote.

World War I, perhaps better than any other conflict, starkly illustrates the moral and political paradoxes of war. In the midst of its unrelieved carnage, the governments of France and Great Britain implemented extensive social, labor, and welfare reforms. In Britain, these included vastly improved infant and child-care programs, better maternity care, regulations on safety and hygiene in the workplace, free elementary education, public housing programs, and a new Ministry of National Health. In France, the state introduced minimum wages, rent deferrals for disadvantaged workers, stricter safety regulations in factories, and expanded medical services for workers. In both countries, trade unions made rapid strides during the conflict. Ramsay MacDonald, leader of the British Labour Party, though a bitter opponent of the war, acknowledged that it was doing more for the social agenda of the left in Britain than half a century of efforts by progressive reformers. Léon Abensour, an early historian of French feminism, claimed that French women made more progress during World War I than in fifty previous years of struggle. The irony that the bloodiest war in European history had advanced social reforms found expression in the title of a book by historian Deborah Dwork, *War is Good for Babies and Other Young Children*, a study of child welfare in England between 1898 and 1918.[8]

Dwork's whimsical title was obviously overdrawn in its implied optimism. In the total scale of human affairs, the social reforms of 1914–18 may be judged as mere societal sops by comparison with the mindless bloodletting of a war in which millions perished in order to move battle lines back or forward a few kilometers. Nor is it accurate to regard the violence and bloodshed of the war as having directly *caused* the social and welfare reforms of the period. War gives impetus to collective action and social organization, but it is not some purposeful agent of change that mysteriously spawns positive social goods from tragedy and destruction. The social reforms of World War I were not *direct* consequences of the war's violence; rather they were an *indirect* outcome—the result of human agency responding, even in a kind of moral backlash, to the senselessness and violence of the conflict. That is, they were an attempt to transcend the violence of the war, to distill positive reforms from the crucible.

A final paradox of war, one that is peculiar to democracies and especially to the American case, is what might be called the Liberal–Conservative Conundrum: liberal and reform-minded political leaders abhor war, but recognize the opportunity it presents for social reform; conservatives revere military institutions and traditions, but are often wary of actual conflict, sensing its potential for revolutionary change. In twentieth-century America, Democratic presidents have gone to war more readily and more often than their Republican counterparts. American political dialogue also reveals the irony of pro-military conservatives railing against Big Government, while forgetting that coercive taxation and bureaucratic organization are the *sine qua non* of funding and equipping armed forces in the industrial age. Conversely, anti-military liberals embrace the power of the state to accomplish social ends, but are not always mindful of the military origins of that power.

The manifold paradoxes of war penetrate to the very heart of the modern state—its capacity for mass organization. Medieval rulers could hire engineers to devise imposing war machines, but they had no conception of the bureaucratic state as the greatest war machine of all. The analogy of the state as a machine has been evoked repeatedly since the Renaissance, but rarely more effectively than by Mitchell Goodman in *The End of It*, which depicts the "immaculate contraption" of the U.S. Army in Italy during World War II:

> In Naples they had everything by now, a Big Business installed in old and new palazzi, equipped by the International Business Machines Corporation. You need a rifleman? Punch a button, a card falls out, orders are cut, he is put in a shipment, and shipped. From the training center to the grave: punch a card. Nothing is left out in this universal corporation, the vertical and horizontal corporation. All phases: Marketing, Transport, Supply, Legal, Archives. Insurance. Information. Public Relations. Entertainment. Medical, Surgical, Dental. Psychiatric. Graves Registration. . . .
>
> Palazzo after palazzo full of the corporation, grinding out waybills, due-bills, requisitions, contracts, memos, orders, procedures. It grew, as all the best corporations grow, until it was beyond the comprehension of any one man, and existed for its own sake.[9]

Goodman's portrait brings to mind the observation of H. G. Wells during World War I: "We have discovered that the modern economic organisation is in itself a fighting machine."[10] In the bowels of the vast war machines of modern states, some individuals thrive, finding fulfillment in collective effort; others suffer as mere cogs in the machine. The contradictions of modernity—its social fluidity and mobility on the one hand, its anomie and depersonalization on the other—reach their apex in the experience of war.

The machinery of the modern state is derived historically from the organizational demands of warfare, and states as we know them today trace their origins and development in large measure to the crucible of past wars. In the classic formulation of Charles Tilly, "War made the state, and the state made war."[11] Historians and students of politics have generally underestimated the role of organized mass violence in shaping politics as we know it today. There may be a reluctance to confront the military lineage of the modern state, for the implications of that lineage upset conventional notions about Western civilization on both the right and left wings of the political spectrum. But it is impossible to understand the nature of modern politics without considering its military roots, what Ernest Renan called "those deeds of violence which have marked the origin of all political formations, even of those which have been followed by the most beneficial results."[12]

How beneficial or otherwise those results have been, the reader may judge in the following pages. The organization of this study is as follows: Chapter 1 sets forth the theoretical underpinnings of the study; it defines key issues and identifies the principal effects of war on the state. Chapters 2 and 3 examine the rise of the early modern state from the Hundred Years' War to the Peace of Westphalia, with particular attention to the role of the Italian Wars and the Wars of Religion in shattering medieval structures and midwifing the passage to political modernity. Chapter 4 traces how the dynastic states of the eighteenth century became true nation-states as a result of the French Revolutionary and Napoleonic Wars. Chapter 5 examines the impact of industrialized warfare on the evolution of European states, with particular attention to the rise of the welfare state. Chapter 6 explores the military origins of totalitarianism in its Nazi and Soviet varieties, and Chapter 7 concludes with an examination of the American case. Isolated from Europe and Asia, and imbued from the beginning with an antimilitary, anti-statist spirit, America offers by far the most difficult test of the proposition that warfare and military power lie at the foundation of modern politics. It turns out to be but a partial exception.

The interconnections between war and the state are numerous and complex. Our attention in the following pages will range from Cromwell to Lenin, from the tax structure of sixteenth-century Castile to the social welfare system of Imperial Germany, from the demolition of private fortifications in central France under Louis XIV to the growth of the U.S. Bureau of Indian Affairs during World War II. Like most studies of war, this inquiry will undoubtedly raise more questions than it resolves, but that is the inevitable price of asking. "Ripeness is all," observed Edgar, son of Gloucester, in *King Lear*,[13] and as the historian Herbert Muller reminds us, it is enough, quite enough.

The Mirror Image of War

War is the father of all and king of all.

—Heraclitus, Fifth century B.C.

States make war, but war also makes states. The origins of the modern state, its rise and development, are inextricably linked with violent conflict and military power. There are few states in the world today whose existence, boundaries, and political structure did not emerge from some past cauldron of international or civil war. This is true of democracies as well as of dictatorships; of small states as well as of large. It is true of the venerable European states formed at the dawn of the modern era five centuries ago as well as of the fledgling nation-states that joined their ranks in the century after Waterloo. It is even true, in an indirect sense, of the scores of non-European states established since 1945: imperial conquests defined their boundaries, and the collapse of European empires after World War II made possible their political independence. The passing of the Cold War and the proliferation of ethnic conflict in Eastern Europe and the former Soviet

Union are having a similar effect today. What Heraclitus declared over two millennia ago remains valid yet: war is a grand progenitor of history, a catalyst of change that has done much to create the structures of power we know today.

This book is about the impact of war on the rise and development of modern states. It is concerned not with what causes war, but with what war causes—with how it affects the internal dynamics, structure, and power of the political systems that wage it. The following pages will argue that warfare and military rivalry played a fundamental role in the origin and development of modern European states, that the institutions of contemporary Western politics reflect the pervasive influence of organized violence in modern history. Since at least 1513, when Niccolò Machiavelli declared strong armies to be the foundation of all states, the link between the organization of physical force—the military—and the organization of political power—the state—has been a prominent leitmotiv of modern history.[1]

The following pages encompass the five centuries of history that range from the Hundred Years' War to the Yugoslav Civil War, the period commonly known as the modern era. Though only a fragment of the whole of human history, it was this era that witnessed the rise of the modern state and its proliferation as the dominant political organization throughout most of the world. Our attention will focus on the larger European world, including the United States. Europe was the birthplace of the modern state, and it remained the great breeding ground of states and the most active arena of world conflict until 1945. Though the proliferation of nation-states throughout the globe since World War II is also in part a legacy of imperialism and regional conflict, this study will not attempt to analyze in any depth the politics of states outside the Western world. In Europe, state and society developed in tandem over hundreds of years; outside Europe, in much of Africa, the Middle East, and Asia, the state remains largely an imported phenomenon, a set of institutions and a way of organizing politics that has never been fully accepted by traditional societies. A separate volume would be required to deal with the impact of war and European military institutions on political development in the extra-European world.[2]

Previous studies on the relationship between war and the state have focused primarily on international wars. This book will argue that civil wars played an equally crucial role in shaping states. By triumphing in civil wars, central governments established their authority and asserted the all-critical monopoly on violent force that Max Weber identified as the essence of the modern state. Though the suppression of popular revolts by military force may not be regarded as "civil war" in the strict sense of the term, such suppression was also a critical factor in establishing the authority of the early modern state, and such instances will be regarded as germane to this study when they entailed intervention by the central armed forces of a state, as opposed to local police or militia alone. (In the early period of European state formation, there was in any case little distinction drawn between military forces and police forces.)

The term "*war*" in the title of this book should be taken in the broadest possible sense. We will not confine our attention to periods of actual combat or focus only on the home front of states at war. The full impact of a war becomes manifest only after hostilities cease: it is then that combatant states must cope with paying off wartime debts, caring for returning soldiers, recovering from physical losses, and dealing with the internal repercussions of victory or defeat. It is essential, therefore, to look also at postwar trends and long-term effects. Further, even during periods of nominal peace, rivalry among states may impel them to undertake military preparations; these may have effects similar to actual conflict, particularly when they are intense and prolonged. And finally, since armies are products of war whose existence inevitably influences politics even in peacetime, we will consider how military establishments affect the internal political development of states over time.

What this book will *not* do is postulate a military dialectic of history. War is a profound agent of historical change, but it is not the fundamental driving force of history. Whatever causes war—economic factors, class conflict, human nature, modes of production, technological change, divine will—is by definition a more basic causal agent than war itself. No matter how ubiquitous or profound the effects of war may be, war itself is a derivative and secondary phenomenon, never a prime moving force. By the same token, war should never be seen as an exogenous force that acts on states and societies from without; it derives rather from within them. When we say that war causes a given political effect, we should keep in mind that this is only a convenient shorthand; what really happens is that state leaders, governments, military officers, armies, and populations, *in waging war and in coping with its myriad challenges*, cause those effects to occur. And finally, we should keep in mind that history is not just political, but involves the whole of human affairs—the arts, science, commerce, society, family, education, etc.—rich and complex spheres of life that often evolve in at least partial independence from the stormier worlds of war and politics.

THE IMAGES OF WAR REVERSED

Kenneth Waltz in his classic *Man, the State and War* sets forth three "images" of war, each being a different philosophical viewpoint on the origins of war.[3] The first image sees the cause of war in human nature; the second, in the internal structure of states; the third, in the international system. Since our concern is with the effects of war rather than with war's causes, it is necessary to reverse these images, to point Waltz's arrows in the opposite direction. Each of the three images has a mirror image: How does war affect human behavior?, How does war affect the internal structure of the state?, and How does war affect the international system? Sociologists and psychologists have studied the first of these mirror images extensively, while students of political science and international relations have examined many facets of the third. By comparison, the inverse image of the second image has been neglected. Only in the past two decades has interest in the subject begun to mount, stimulated by the work of Charles Tilly and a handful of other scholars.[4]

As early as the beginning of the century, the German historian Otto Hintze lamented this lacuna. In 1902 he wrote that students of politics frequently overlooked "the development of the state in relation to its neighbors." According to Hintze, a state's rivalry with foreign powers has as much bearing on its internal structure as does domestic competition among class and interest groups. To ignore this, he writes, is to wrench individual states from the context in which they were formed—to regard the state, wrongly, as an isolated entity whose development has no relation to its surroundings. In a later essay Hintze argued that "all state organization was originally military organization," and that the form and spirit of the modern state derived primarily from its organization for war.[5] Hintze's insights, regrettably, have not had the impact they deserve on contemporary political analysis. The causes of war continue to receive far more scholarly attention than its effects; the role of war as an independent variable remains neglected.[6] This neglect may stem in part from a hope or an assumption that concentrating on war as an outcome, and seeking to probe its causes, will contribute to reducing its incidence. Yet understanding the state as a creature of war may be equally relevant to achieving that end.

This book will examine three broad facets of the relationship between war and the state, three distinct mirror images of the second image: the role of war in the origin of the modern state; the influence of war on the evolution of states after their formation; and the impact of war on the power of states vis-à-vis their own societies.[7]

THE FIRST MIRROR IMAGE: WAR AND STATE FORMATION

Most of the world's landmass today is divided into states, and most of the world's population falls under the jurisdiction of political organizations that rightly can be called states. Their boundaries are the demarcating lines of political sovereignty; their interactions are the essential element of world politics; their governments are agents of power that control most of the world's military force. States are amorphous and fluid, never fully unified in purpose, and often badly fragmented by competing political factions, bureaucratic politics, and institutional conflict. Nevertheless, states do exist; they are not convenient fictions of political analysis and dialogue, as some would have us believe.[8] They come complete with "frontiers, capitals, flags, anthems, passports, currencies, military parades, national museums, embassies and usually a seat at the United Nations."[9] They conduct wars, engage in diplomacy, vote in international organizations, and appear in graphic color on political maps of the world. When we speak of France in a political context, we normally do not mean the people of France, the government of France, or even the country, geography, and terrain of France. We mean the state of France.

In contemporary political discourse, the term *state* conveys a dual meaning, though the distinction between the two senses of the word is often overlooked.

First, in the field of international relations as well as in traditional and vernacular usage, the state encompasses both a sovereign government *and* the geographically bounded territory, society, and population over which it presides. It comprises what Fred Halliday has termed *the national-territorial totality,* or in other words, that which is denoted visually on a map—the country as a whole and all that is within it, the territory, government, people, and society.[10]

Second, in much contemporary scholarship, including the "Return to the State" school of social science, the state is regarded as *an apparatus of power,* a set of institutions—the central government, the armed forces, the regulatory and police agencies—whose most important functions involve the use of force: the control of territory and the maintenance of internal order.[11] This conception of the state is largely Germanic in origin, with its roots in the writings of Max Weber. Weber defined the state as "a compulsory association which organizes domination," and argued that its principal characteristic was its monopoly on the legitimate use of force within its territory.[12]

These two conceptions of the state are not mutually exclusive; they merely represent different ways of looking at a complex phenomenon. In either conception, sovereignty is the indispensable attribute of the state, though the first tends to emphasize its external sovereignty within the larger international system; the second, its internal sovereignty and monopolization of coercive power. But it is important to keep in mind that despite the prevalence of the state as the organizing unit of politics today, states by *either* of these definitions simply did not exist in the medieval world. The state as we know it is a relatively new invention, originating in Europe between 1450 and 1650. Its emergence brought about what John Gerard Ruggie has called "the most important contextual change in international politics in this *millennium*: the shift from the medieval to the modern international system."[13]

Politically, the European medieval world was highly fragmented, consisting mainly of private estates and vaguely defined kingdoms. Jurisdictions overlapped, central authority was weak, and true sovereignty was nonexistent. Medieval warfare was a localized, small-scale affair that relied heavily on the valor of individual warriors and on technologies requiring only a low level of social organization. While the birth of the state was a complex phenomenon, involving many historical processes, it is significant that it took place at a time of unprecedented violence and chaos, during the era of religious wars unleashed by the Protestant Reformation. The intensity of armed conflict during this period precipitated what has been called a "revolution in military affairs," in which the size of armies, the cost of warfare, and the sheer firepower of military technology took a quantum leap forward. During this transitional era, the patchwork of feudal realms, duchies, independent towns, small principalities, and religious estates that made up medieval Europe was thrown into a crucible of military conflict that consigned many of its smaller parts to political oblivion. The rigors of military survival in such an era favored larger, more centralized political units that were able to control extensive tracts of territory, master complex military technologies, and mobilize the immense physical and human resources required for battle.[14] The result was the dawn of modernity and a revolution in political affairs that paralleled the military revolution. How it happened is the first object of our inquiry.

THE SECOND MIRROR IMAGE: WAR AND THE DEVELOPMENT OF STATES

It is not sufficient merely to make the case that war contributed to early state formation and the transition from medieval to modern politics. We must also confront the critical double question posed by Charles Tilly: "What accounts for the great variation over time and space in the kinds of state that have prevailed in Europe, and why did European states eventually converge on different variants of the national state?"[15] Tilly's attempt to answer this question ranges over a millennium and covers both the medieval and modern periods; his use of the term *state* encompasses premodern political systems that were not truly states in the modern sense of the word. Since our focus is on the modern period, we are primarily concerned with the rise of "different variants" of the national state. Put differently, our objective is to determine how war affects the development of states *after* their initial formation. Why did some states became absolutist monarchies, others constitutional monarchies, and others republics? How did dynastic states become nation-states? What accounts for the rise in nineteenth- and twentieth-century Europe of divergent political systems such as liberal democracy, the welfare state, and the totalitarian state?

Obviously the factors shaping state development and differentiation are multifaceted and complex, and war is only one of them. There are numerous theories of state development that emphasize alternative factors—modes of economic production (Perry Anderson); internal political dynamics (Samuel P. Huntington); the influence of the global system (Immanuel Wallerstein); collective rational choice (Mancur Olson, Bruce Bueno de Mesquita); or geographic and cultural factors (Stein Rokkan), to name some of the most prominent.[16] This book will neither advocate a unicausal theory of state development nor attempt a comprehensive theory, but it will argue that alternative explanations of state formation and evolution fall short empirically to the extent that they fail to take into account the pervasive role played by violent conflict.

One evidence of the link between war and state development is the correlation that exists between the political structure of states and the organization or "format" of their armed forces. Friedrich Engels noted this in 1855, and more recently, scholars such as Stanislav Andreski [Andrzejewski], Samuel Finer, and David Rapoport have described the phenomenon at length.[17] Andreski, for example, argues that military organization is a critical determinant of political organization, affecting the size and cohesion of states, their administrative hierarchy, and the extent of government regulation of a given society and economy. And Rapoport observes that military and political institutions are inseparable, a change in the character of one producing a corresponding change in the other.[18]

Our challenge is to probe the nature of those changes, to understand how wars, and the organization of states for war, have shaped the broad patterns of European history. Since the emergence of the first sovereign states in Europe, the state as an organizing form has passed through three stages of modernity, each one deriving in part from intense and protracted generalized conflict. The first such period of transformative war was the Era of Religious Wars connected with the Protestant Reformation, which culminated in the Peace of Westphalia and the emergence of the first secular sovereign states in Europe. From 1648 to 1789, the dominant form of European states was the *dynastic state*, whether constitutional or absolutist in nature. This early form of the modern state possessed limited internal and external sovereignty; it had acquired numerous features of political modernity but still strongly reflected its medieval origins and retained features of a private royal estate.

As the eighteenth century progressed, a string of great power wars stimulated rising nationalism across the continent and contributed in numerous ways to the outbreak of the French Revolution in 1789. The ensuing French Revolutionary and Napoleonic Wars (1792–1815) midwifed the passage to a second stage of political modernity, characterized by the rise and proliferation of the *nation-state* as the dominant political unit in Europe—a form of the modern state in which there was close identification between cultural nation and political state, and in which political legitimacy became linked to popular sovereignty. The nineteenth century was filled with endemic nationalist strife, as peoples sought to free themselves from larger empires and create new nation-states.

The third great period of transformative war in European history began almost a century after Waterloo and was primarily associated with World War I and II. Industrialized warfare, by virtue of the intense social and economic mobilization it entailed, ushered in a new stage of modernity, the rise of *the collectivist state*. This latest incarnation of the modern state was characterized by three distinct attributes: pervasive government intervention in the economy, mass participation in politics, and direct state responsibility for the welfare of its citizens. These three features of contemporary states superficially appear to be primarily of domestic origin, but they can be shown to have originated in large measure from the cauldron of the two world wars. The First World War was also a critical factor in the rise of the totalitarian states, primarily Nazi Germany and the Soviet Union, which can be seen as perverse mutations of the collectivist state and maladaptations to the demands of industrialized war.[19]

THE THIRD MIRROR IMAGE: WAR AND THE POWER OF STATES

The question of how war influenced the rise of different varieties of the modern state obviously cannot be separated from the issue of how power is organized in those states. Liberal democracies differ greatly in their organization of power from traditional autocracies; confederations from centralized states; totalitarian systems from absolutist monarchies. This issue is so fundamental, in both political and moral terms, that it calls for examination as a third mirror image in its own right. Our concern is not with the external military power of states, though war obviously affects this, but rather with their internal power. This includes both *repressive power*, the capacity to dominate by physical force, and *administrative power*, the more subtle capacity to influence, shape, and regulate society by administrative means short of physical force.[20]

Just as there is a balance of power in the international system, there is also an internal balance of power between the state and civil society. This internal balance of power demarcates the line between the public and the private—if a thing is public, it is subject to state authority; if it is private, it is not. Where that line is drawn determines the extent to which a given political system respects human rights and freedom. In liberal democracies civil society exerts considerable influence over the state, the sphere reserved for private activities is large, and the powers of the state are restricted. In autocratic systems the powers of the state are great and the scope of action of private individuals more restricted. In totalitarian systems the power of the state is immense and civil society is virtually under siege. At their extreme, totalitarian states attempt to abolish the sphere of the private and make everything—even conversations that take place at home or thoughts in the minds of citizens—a public matter subject to state authority.

Political philosophers have long recognized that war can affect the balance of power between state and society. James Madison stated it succinctly in 1795:

> Of all the enemies to public liberty, war is, perhaps, the most to be dreaded, because it comprises and develops the germ of every other. War is the parent of armies; from these proceed debts and taxes; and armies, and debts, and taxes are the known instruments for bringing the many under the domination of the few. . . . No nation could preserve its freedom in the midst of continual warfare.[21]

Or from Alexis de Tocqueville:

> . . . All those who seek to destroy the liberties of a democratic nation ought to know that war is the surest and the shortest means to accomplish it.[22]

Military conflict can aggrandize state power in several ways: by destroying traditional structures and sources of societal resistance that restrain central authority; by giving state leaders both the impetus and the moral justification for repressing factions, enlarging armies, and raising taxes; by fostering a sense of crisis and an acceptance of the violence that accompanies coercive rule. In this manner, wars throughout modern history have fostered authoritarian rule, undermined the civic order of traditional states, perverted consensual political processes within constitutional states, and threatened or destroyed established rights and liberties.

The tendency of war to aggrandize state power has led some scholars to suggest that heavy exposure to violent conflict makes states autocratic, while minimal involvement in war favors the rise of free political systems.[23] There is much truth to this, but there are exceptions also. If war only strengthened states, Europe today would be dominated by militarized, totalitarian behemoths. The intense social cooperation entailed in the waging of war may also have a democratizing effect, as shared sacrifice obliterates class barriers. The exigencies of war may compel autocratic leaders to make political concessions in order to ensure popular support. Mass military service may intensify demands for political representation and make it difficult for governments to deny their populations a say in political affairs. In general, the voice of the people is heard loudest when governments require either their gold or their bodies in defense of the state. Thus, while the religious wars of the Reformation destroyed medieval constitutionalism and helped forge absolutist monarchies in Western Europe, that absolutism eventually yielded in many instances to constitutionalism and democracy through a process of political bargaining between state leaders and society, in which issues of military service, taxation, and representation played a pivotal role.

THE MYRIAD POLITICAL EFFECTS OF WAR

War is a phenomenon of immense complexity. Thousands of factors bear on its outcome; innumerable variables interact in its unfolding; millions of individual decisions influence its course. As such, a war may rapidly transcend its original causes and become a powerful force for change in its own right, with myriad and diverse effects on the societies and states that are waging it. With respect to state development, those effects fall broadly into three categories: (1) formative and organizing effects; (2) disintegrative effects; and (3) reformative effects. A brief inventory of these effects, as they have been identified by political philosophers and students of war, will provide a useful foundation for the historical chapters that follow.

THE FORMATIVE AND ORGANIZING
EFFECTS OF WAR

In waging war states remake, reinvent, and reorder themselves. The intensity and challenge of war compel political leaders to undertake a whole range of activities that would be difficult or unthinkable in peacetime. This extraordinary activism of the state—its role as a catalyst of collective action—transforms not only the society and the economy, but the character of the state itself. Given effective political leadership and sufficient military power to avoid catastrophic defeat, states will tend to wax stronger during war.[24] They become more organized, more rational, more centralized—in short, better equipped not only to fight war, but to exert power and dominion at home. The formative and organizing effects of war—those effects that advance state formation and increase the power, authority, size, capabilities, or jurisdiction of the state—include those that follow.

Territorial Coalescence

The making of modern European states was foremost a process of "conquest and coalescence," in which militarily powerful states forcefully incorporated weaker political communities. In the fourteenth century, there were perhaps 1,000 or more separate political entities in Europe. By 1500, the number had fallen to under 500; by 1789, to under 350; and by 1900, there were only 25 left.[25] Most of this consolidation came about through deliberate acts of conquest and annexation, however disguised by rationalizing statesmen. As the nineteenth century's most articulate mouthpiece of nationalism, Ernest Renan, observed, "Unity is always realized by brute force."[26] War may also promote territorial coalescence by unleashing powerful forces of nationalism that override provincial loyalties, the most famous examples of which are the wars of Italian and German unification.

The Rallying or Unifying Effect

A kingdom at war may be a kingdom at peace. Unless a war is profoundly unpopular, the exigencies of military conflict promote *internal rallying*: state and society unite in the common effort; economic and political cooperation increase; factionalism and partisanship are diminished; consonance reigns. A distinguished line of political philosophers from Bodin to Hegel have observed that war unites nations, checks domestic strife, and consolidates the power of the state.[27] There are striking historical examples of this, when badly divided polities are suddenly united in war.[28] Mindful of the rallying effect of war, the leaders of divided states may be tempted to engage in *divergence*, promoting unity by resorting to foreign adventure—"to busy giddy minds with foreign quarrels" in the words of Shakespeare's Henry IV. Recent research suggests that deliberate diversion is not a common phenomenon, though it does occur on occasion. The Duke of Sully, chief minister of France under Henry IV, openly espoused its logic: "The true means of setting the realm at rest is by keeping up a foreign war, towards which one can direct, like water in a gutter, all the turbulent humours of the kingdom."[29]

The Centralizing Effect

Whether aggressive or defensive, war generally compels political leaders to centralize power in order to mobilize the resources necessary for its waging. This effect was critical to state formation in early modern Europe. Wars gave rulers both the incentive and the opportunity to concentrate power—and that power was the force that ultimately overcame the fragmentation of feudal society. Historically, efforts to centralize political power triggered resistance from regional and local power centers, or from groups and classes such as the peasantry or bourgeoisie. Because of this, the actual process of centralization almost always precipitated some measure of civil war. A trio of scholars observed this in an important study on the violent creation of political order:

> The entire historical process of creating a national state was a long and violent struggle pitting the agents of state centralization against myriad local and regional opponents. . . . As centralizing, war-making state builders increased their resource demands on their populations, the tax, food, and conscription riot often became the harbinger of much larger rebellions pitting nobles and peasants against the monarchical agents of national centralization.[30]

The victory of central governments in the resulting civil strife—whether this meant local insurrections, peasant uprisings, or the total division of the state—reinforced the centralizing processes that stemmed from external wars. Victory in civil wars was thus a crucial factor in the formation of centralized states, for only by establishing the unassailable fact of their authority could states assert the internal sovereignty that is characteristic of modern polities.

The Bureaucratizing Effect

The organizational challenge of modern war compels the rationalization of state administrations—the replacement of personal, traditional, and arbitrary methods of rule by impersonal, hierarchical, and bureaucratic methods. In early modern Europe, the Gunpowder Revolution accelerated the process of "going out of court," whereby daily administration was delegated from royal courts to impersonal bureaucracies. Since then, each successive round of war has made European governments more rationalized and less traditional in their structure. Military problems have begotten bureaucratic solutions.

Government Growth

In addition to rearing bureaucracies, war is a catalyst of their growth. There are many theories as to why government grows—the effects of industrialization, response to crisis, technological change, popular demand for services, etc.—but no theory explains bureaucratic growth as consistently as that of the impact of war and military rivalry.[31] At least until the 1950s, when welfare spending first began to overtake defense spending, the growth of most European bureaucracies took place primarily during war or as a result of military pressures. Even the widely cited Parkinson's Law ("Work expands so as to fill the time available for its completion") hints at the importance of military origins. The two agencies that Parkinson used to illustrate the relentlessness of bureaucratic growth were the British Admiralty and the Colonial Office—both occupied with defense and foreign policy. And in 1978, Parkinson recounted that the inspiration behind his famous Law was service as a staff officer in World War II. Citing the example of a private becoming a lieutenant colonel with a staff of 85 in only three months, he observed that in wartime "you can build in two weeks a bureaucracy which would take years to accumulate in peacetime, so you can actually watch the plants grow and proliferate."[32]

The Fiscal Effects of War

War makes death and taxes not only inevitable, but inseparable as well. If there is any universal law of state development, it may be that expressed by Thomas Paine in 1787: "War . . . has but one thing certain, and that is to increase taxes."[33] Throughout modern history, war or defense spending have consumed a large percentage of most state budgets, and in some instances over 90 percent. War has been the lever by which monarchs and central governments have imposed increasingly larger tax burdens on increasingly broader segments of society, thus enabling ever-higher levels of spending to be sustained, even in peacetime.[34] The capacity of capital-rich states to borrow large sums of money does not alleviate the fiscal effects of war, but only postpones them, since state debts ultimately must be paid off with future tax receipts.

The Ratchet Effect

In war, what goes up seldom goes down. The rapid growth of government and the massive tax increases that occur during war usually level off at postwar levels much higher than were in effect before the conflict. The result is permanent net growth in the size of the state and in the level of both spending and taxation. A recent historical analysis of spending and taxes in the United States, Japan, and several European countries has shown that this ratchet effect occurred after major wars not only in the industrial era but as early as the fifteenth century, and in every type of state.[35] One possible explanation for this is that societies will accept levels of taxation in a period of war that would be regarded as intolerable in quieter times, and that even after the crisis has passed this acceptance remains.[36]

War as an Opportunity for Leadership
Military conflict creates opportunities for leadership that otherwise do not exist. By accelerating the pace of change and imparting a certain malleability to human affairs, it enables strong political leaders—sometimes described as "state-makers"—to achieve goals and push through reforms that would be impossible to implement in peacetime. Numerous generals or statesmen who led their countries during great wars proved to be great architects of domestic politics as well: Gustavus Adolphus, William of Orange, Frederick the Great, Napoleon Bonaparte, Abraham Lincoln, Woodrow Wilson, David Lloyd George, Franklin Roosevelt, Charles de Gaulle, and even—in a country not his own—Douglas MacArthur.

THE DISINTEGRATIVE EFFECTS OF WAR

If war makes states, it also sometimes breaks them. While scholars have generally emphasized the tendency of war to strengthen states, the destructive forces associated with it may overwhelm and negate any organizing impetus it engenders. Carthage certainly received no developmental impetus from war. The *disintegrative or degenerative effects* of war are those that diminish, limit, or dilute the power, size, authority, or capacity of the state. Among this second category of effects are the following:

Total State Destruction
States can disappear without being plowed under and sowed with salt. As the previously cited figures on territorial consolidation indicate, European history is replete with such casualties of war—the city-states of Italy; autonomous subnational entities such as Aragon, Navarre, Burgundy, Brittany, Savoy, and Franche-Comté; and the 35 members of the German Confederation. The most tragic case of all was the disappearance of Poland from the European map in the wake of the Polish rebellion of 1794. It is true that most of these vanished political units never achieved the full measure of external and internal sovereignty that we associate with modern states, but their fate is as much a part of the history of European political development as the more successful state-building that took place within the survivors.

War as a Catalyst of Revolution
Arthur Marwick speaks of the "test of war" as the supreme trial of a country's social, political, and economic institutions.[37] If an estab-

lished regime fails that test entirely or insists on waging an unpopular war, the result may be popular revolution, either during or in the aftermath of conflict. French involvement in the American War of Independence helped set the stage for the French Revolution. The Napoleonic Wars subsequently spawned a host of nationalist insurrections across Europe. The French debacle in the Franco-Prussian War gave rise to the Paris Commune. Russia's defeat in the Russo-Japanese War helped provoke the Russian Revolution of 1905, and World War I paved the way for the Bolshevik Revolution of 1917 and the German revolution of 1918.[38] Numerous historians have postulated such a connection, and a recent statistical study of 177 wars demonstrates persuasively that violent regime changes do occur far more frequently right after wars than during peace.[39] The same is true of civil wars, which often break out immediately after international wars.

Diminished Capacity

A state can suffer immense damage short of total destruction or revolution. Defeat in war can destabilize government and paralyze administration. Human losses may result in a diminished labor base and pervasive, long-term psychological trauma. Territorial losses may mean a diminished state, while property losses may damage a national economy. If successful wars unite polities, unsuccessful wars may divide them. In short, even when it does not destroy, war may incapacitate and weaken states, reducing the ability of governments to govern effectively. This is why, even when revolution does not occur, a prolonged period of political and social crisis often follows defeat in war.[40]

Fiscal Collapse

A state that engages in costly defense spending or prolonged war, whether defensive or aggressive, may suffer long-term decline even if it is victorious—bankruptcy, after all, may have effects similar to those of military defeat. Over the long run, only those states will prosper that maintain a balance between their capacity to generate wealth and their expenditure of that wealth for military ends.[41] But since few states are able to sustain wars out of current revenue alone, wars almost invariably add to the public debt; historically, a vast portion of the public debt of European countries has accumulated during wartime. Debt does not necessarily weaken a state, and if the money is borrowed from domestic creditors, it may even strengthen it by increasing the public's stake in its survival. Access to credit may also give states an advantage in short wars by enabling them to mobilize more quickly. But the long-term effect of war-related debt depends entirely on the capacity of the state to service it through increased taxation after the war is over. Excessive, unserviceable debts will cause outside sources of capital to dry up and can lead to the decline or even the collapse of the debtor state.

THE REFORMATIVE EFFECTS OF WAR

War is an intensely revelatory experience that unmasks the defects of a given political system more starkly than peacetime processes could ever do. This has been termed the audit of war or *the inspection effect*, since pressure for reform inevitably mounts as large numbers of individuals see and "inspect" the flaws of their state.[42] Military defeat especially is a harsh schoolmaster, but the rigors of a victorious but difficult war may also force nations to confront the need for reform. Many of the great reforms of European and American history have occurred either during or in the immediate aftermath of great wars. War facilitates reform through the destruction or weakening of entrenched social strata and institutions, which typically act as barriers to reform, as well as through creating or energizing new political constituencies (veterans, widows, war heroes, taxpayers, etc.) with whom the state must bargain. The principal reformative effects of war are listed following.

The Integrative Effect
When war is fought as a cooperative endeavor of state and society, it tends to broaden the popular basis of the state and foster political integration. In ancient Greece, the full rights of citizenship in both Sparta *and* Athens (available to men only, of course) were closely tied to military service, and the same linkage persists in the modern era.[43] When aristocrats monopolized the means of war, they also monopolized the instruments of rule. As governments became increasingly dependent on bourgeois capital to finance their armies, the commercial and middle classes of Europe waxed in political influence. When great numbers of peasants and commoners entered mass armies, it became increasingly untenable to deny them a say in government. When total war demanded female labor in armaments factories, women too could not be denied political rights. Full rights of citizenship and suffrage have consistently derived from service in war.[44]

The Socializing Effect
War and military service promote socialization through the personal interaction, indoctrination, training, and sharing of the tasks and burdens that they invariably entail. This effect occurs in peacetime con-

script armies, but is most powerful during war, when larger numbers of conscripts experience common training and service. An interesting example comes from Israel, whose first prime minister, David Ben-Gurion, was faced with the challenge of forging a new state out of Jewish immigrants from around the world. In a speech to the Knesset in 1952, he said the following:

> We do not have hundreds of years [to build a nation], and without the institution of the military, a compulsory, educating, unifying institution, we will not become a nation in time. We cannot rely on an historical process only. . . . We must direct the historical process, speed it up, channel it to our goals. Through the Israeli Defense Force we can do in a short time things that would otherwise require dozens of years, and we cannot wait dozens of years.[45]

The quickest way to make a nation is to make an army.

The Social-Levelling Effect
Stanislav Andreski postulated that the higher the degree of societal participation in military efforts—the "military participation ratio"—the greater the degree of subsequent social leveling and political equality that would result. Such a leveling effect clearly occurred after the Napoleonic Wars and after the world wars of this century. The intense social cooperation demanded by war tends to erode class barriers, and the more protracted and intense the war, the greater this effect will be. On the other hand, Prussia and Russia under the Old Regimes managed to incorporate peasants and commoners into their armies for two centuries without yielding them significant political rights, and totalitarian states achieved mass mobilization for war by resorting to brute force, intimidation, and propaganda to nationalize and mobilize the masses. The deciding factor over the long run would seem to be not *whether* states fight wars, but *how* they fight them—whether the mobilization of human resources for war is largely compulsory or whether it relies on popular consent and support. Wars that are viewed as legitimate and that generate a high degree of patriotic fervor and enthusiasm will almost always strain existing class barriers.[46]

War as a Spur to Social Reform
A sense of national catharsis follows the conclusion of almost every major war, a sense of shared sacrifice, a desire to heal wounds and rebuild normal patterns of life, an awareness of the fragility of existence. This often translates into political pressures on the state to care

for the victims of war, improve domestic social and political conditions, and reward those groups who have sacrificed lives, family members, and property in battle. Only the promise of a better world can give meaning to a terrible conflict. Since, in the age of mass armies, the lower economic strata usually contribute more of their blood in battle than the wealthier classes, war often gives impetus to social welfare reforms.

THE MILITARY ORIGINS OF NATIONALISM

There is one effect of war that is of profound importance in European history, but that does not fit easily into any of the above categories and that, depending on its specific manifestation, may span them all. That effect is nationalism. When a state is seen by its population as embodying the aspirations of the nation, nationalism will strengthen the state and enhance its capacity to govern, particularly in times of war or crisis. On the other hand, multinational states, unless they can find a basis for their nationalism other than ethnicity or language, may be torn apart and destroyed by conflicting nationalisms. And finally, because nationalism is closely linked with the concept of popular sovereignty, it may serve as a reformative and democratizing force—the role it played in Europe from the French Revolution until World War I.

War itself is a powerful catalyst of nationalism. It infuses the collective consciousness of peoples with a sense of their national identity, while simultaneously linking that identity closely with the fate of the state itself. Nationalism in turn magnifies the unifying effect of wars, promotes a sense of shared destiny, and strengthens political bonds that might otherwise suffer centrifugal failure. The military origins of nationalism are reflected in the military rituals and symbolism that dominate national holidays, when military parades, fireworks, and many-gun salutes herald a nation's glory. Nationalism is also closely linked to the rise of the modern European languages, which came to transcend the status of vernacular dialects only when they became linked with states. A language is a dialect with an army.[47]

It is imperative to keep in mind that the violence associated with war does not in most cases directly cause the effects laid out above. They derive rather from the collective responses of human beings—state leaders, citizens, soldiers—to that violence and the challenges that it poses. We should not reify war or regard it as a willful agent of action in its own right, but rather view it as an impersonal phenomenon that serves to elicit human action, often in response to its terrors. By the same token, to the extent that positive effects derive from war—social leveling and democratization, for example—these originate in human efforts to cope with the violence of war, not in the violence itself.

WAR, THE STATE, AND THE BURDEN OF MODERNITY

Adam Smith's *The Wealth of Nations* is almost a work of holy writ for modern economic liberalism, yet it reflects also the moral paradoxes of military power and insecurity in the modern age. While most of the book praises the virtue of *homo economicus*, market economies, and an open international system, Smith in often overlooked passages also extols the value of standing armies, mass military training, and modern firearms for the preservation of civilization and order. The visionary who wanted government out of economic affairs very much wanted it *in* when it came to the defense of the "opulent and civilized" against the onslaughts of "the poor and barbarous nations."[48] The Father of Laissez-Faire acknowledged that military spending is inherently unproductive, that it may ruin states through excessive debt, that armies may threaten basic liberties, but he endorsed their necessity nonetheless—*something* must maintain the civil order essential to free commerce. Confronted with the reality of war, the consummate liberal is unmasked in these passages as the consummate conservative.

Commenting on the military revolution of seventeenth-century Europe, William McNeill elegantly summarized the mutually reinforcing link between military power and civil order:

> A well-drilled army, responding to a clear chain of command that reached down to every corporal and squad . . . constituted a more obedient and efficient instrument of policy than had ever been seen on earth before. Such armies could and did establish a superior level of public peace within all the principal European states. This allowed agriculture, commerce, and industry to flourish, and, in turn, enhanced the taxable wealth that kept the armed forces in being. A self-sustaining feedback loop thus arose that raised Europe's power and wealth above levels other civilizations had attained.[49]

In a similar vein, Max Weber saw discipline as one of the foundations of modern politics and argued, "The discipline of the army gives birth to all discipline . . . military discipline is the ideal model for the modern capitalist factory, as it was for the ancient plantation."[50] The discipline of the military provides discipline to the state, which in turn makes for a stable, peaceful, and prosperous society. Things could be worse.

Unfortunately, neither McNeill's concept of a self-sustaining feedback loop, nor Weber's vision of a disciplined state, nor Adam Smith's assertion that gunpowder fosters the preservation of civilization, can account for the tragic cul-de-sac into which military and state power led Western civilization in the twentieth century. It turned out to be but a short step from the discipline of the military to the discipline of the Gestapo, the discipline of the commissars, the discipline of the concentration camp. One man's civil order was another man's *gulag*. Totalitarianism is the final perversion of expanding state power, its essence captured in Mussolini's credo, "All for the State; nothing outside the State; nothing against the State."[51] Whatever the rhetoric or ideology—whether fascist, Nazi, Leninist, or Maoist—there has been a direct link between the glorification of war by totalitarian regimes and their prostration of all politics to the god of the state.

Nor in the end did the relentless pursuit of state power by Western states, whatever their form, lead to security: over 100 million persons died violently in the twentieth century either as victims of war or of state genocide, a toll that eclipses the total losses of all previous wars or massacres in all ages of human history combined. If flourishing commerce and industry are the positive fruits of the modern state, the bitter fruit—of which all partake, democracies and dictatorships alike-—is the pervasive insecurity caused by the existence of permanent, powerful armies. Human inventiveness, organization, and nature have led us into a trap between Scylla and Charybdis: without the state, internal anarchy or foreign oppression threaten; with the state, we risk internal bondage to keep at bay the anarchy of war, both civil and international. Yet having borne the burden of the state for five hundred years, we find that it has rarely fulfilled its twin promises of security and freedom.

The primacy of armed conflict in the evolution of the Western world is the essential tragedy of modern history. On the one hand, war has helped to create the oases of stability known as states; on the other hand, it has made of the state a potential Frankenstein monster, an instrument of unconstrained coercive force. The mirror image of war, like war itself, reveals both the best and worst of human nature. But regardless of whether war is just or unjust, positive or negative in its long-term effects, its ultimate price is always human life—and therein lies its inescapable tragedy. Unlike commerce, industry, or any other human endeavor, its cost is measured not merely in gold, but in blood as well. In its immediate manifestation, war is a terrible master, a destroyer above all else. "A man might rave against war," wrote F. E. Manning, "But war, from among its myriad faces, could always turn towards him one, which was his own."[52] This is the one mirror image of war we must never forget.

War and the Passing of the Medieval Age

A prince, therefore, should have no other object, nor any other thought, nor take as his own special art any other concern than war, its institutions and discipline; for that is the only art which belongs properly to one who holds ruling power.

Niccolò Machiavelli, *The Prince*

In 1337, a dynastic feud between Philip VI of France and Edward III of England precipitated the long series of conflicts that came to be known as the Hundred Years' War. This was an unfortunate choice of names, for the issues at stake were as old as the Norman conquest of England, and combat over them had occurred many times before 1337. Nor was the contest settled in 1453, the date historians traditionally give for the end of the war. It dragged on until 1559, when England ceded to France Calais, its last domain on the continent. It should have been called the Two Hundred Years' War or even the Four Hundred Years' War. Its significance lay less in shifting tides of territorial dominion than in the new methods of warfare and political administration introduced in the latter stages of the conflict, especially by France. Because of these, the long Anglo–French struggle effectively marked the beginning of the end of the medieval era in European history.

In the course of this interminable conflict, the kings of France and of England began to discover what Hugh Trevor-Roper has called "the secret of State." Without either realizing or intending it, they began erecting a "new apparatus of power," the political and military institutions that formed the basis of "the Renaissance State."[1] This new form of organization promised political and military power beyond anything attainable in the medieval era. For the real secret of the state, both then and for the next five hundred years, was its superior capacity for marshaling the resources of war. It was not a secret easily kept, however, tied as it was to universal imperatives of military technology and organization. By the mid-sixteenth century, both England and France had been eclipsed in might and prestige by an unlikely rival, Habsburg Spain, whose power also derived in part from the engine of the Renaissance state.

This chapter will examine how new military technologies and violent interaction between the larger medieval states contributed to the passing of the medieval age and the dawn of modern politics.[2] What follows is not an attempt, however, to posit a single cause for the origin of the Renaissance states. A multitude of factors contributed to their emergence: rising population; the growth of cities; expanding commercial links between key European centers; the growth of surplus capital and the development of early capital markets; evolving legal institutions, including the revival of Roman law; and the introduction of new technologies, with the invention of the printing press playing an especially important role. But war and military rivalry played a catalytic role in the overall process of state formation, accelerating other modernizing forces and providing both the opportunity and the incentive for strong leaders, "state-makers," to concentrate power in central governments. The passage from medieval to modern politics was the most important transformation in the nature of political power since the fall of the Roman Empire, and it bears close examination.

THE SHAPE OF POLITICS IN LATE MEDIEVAL EUROPE

The medieval or feudal period of European history spanned the years from the dissolution of the Carolingian Empire in the ninth century to the rise of the first centralized states some six centuries later. It was an era marked by the absence of cohesive central authority—a time when hundreds of small territories, cities, principalities, and estates functioned in relative independence and with little direction from any higher political authority. In the medieval world, as Joseph Strayer has observed, "the state did not exist. . . . The values of this kind of a society were different from ours; the supreme sacrifices of property and life were made for family, lord, community, or religion, not for the state."[3] Though some scholars apply the word *state* to medieval forms of government, they are misusing the term, adapting a modern concept to premodern forms.[4]

Centralized territorially based empires had existed in earlier millennia, but these too had disappeared from the political map of Europe after the dissolution of the Roman Empire. Catholicism provided a unifying ideology for Western Europe, but formed no cohesive political empire. Concepts integral to modern politics—such as sovereignty, bureaucratic administration, the public domain, and the secular state—were utterly foreign to a world in which power was fragmented, jurisdictions vague and overlapping, and structures of control weak. Political relationships were personal and highly localized, defined largely by ownership and tenancy of land. Taxation was rudimentary or nonexistent; income from private domains made up the vast majority of revenues. Modern diplomacy, with its embassies, ambassadors, and professional diplomatic corps had not been developed. Even the notion of a capital city did not exist. The lightly administered empires and kingdoms of the day had only minimal relations with each other and minimal control over their own territory and inhabitants. Thus in medieval Europe, in a sense far more literal than is the case today, the aphorism applied: *all politics was local.*[5]

The means of waging war were also highly localized in medieval Europe. Monarchs and princes did not enjoy a monopoly on military power, or anything remotely approaching one, even in their own territories. The military resources of the day were held in private hands, wielded by landed nobles, military orders, even ecclesiastical institutions. Large kingdoms were divided into patchwork enclaves of military power: into private armies, city walls, locally maintained fortresses, and powerful personal estates. As in all traditional societies, the aristocracy styled itself a warrior class, and war was the central purpose of its existence.[6] Being a landed class, the aristocracy saw territory as the source of all wealth and the natural object of their avarice; war for land was a profit-making venture. Sovereigns raised transient armies by relying on the fealty and support of this warrior class, especially those who maintained private stockpiles of weapons. Yet the aristocracy was a flimsy reed on which to base effective military power, for though theoretically obligated to fight for their sovereign, nobles often fought against him instead. The absence of standing armies left sovereigns vulnerable to such challenges, but ensured that violent conflict, though pervasive, was usually confined in space and waged on a smaller scale than would occur from the time of the Renaissance onward.[7]

The larger medieval kingdoms such as England and France possessed rudimentary administrations that assisted in the management of the royal household and lands. These were not organized like modern bureaucracies, and they had little formal hierarchy or clear division of labor. Virtually no distinction was made between the administration of the private "estate" or demesne of the king and what we would today call "affairs of state." Decision making centered in the Court, and office-holders did not constitute a separate professional class of any kind.[8] In short, the limited power that sovereigns had was based neither on military nor on bureaucratic power, but rested on tradition and prestige, the cultivation of seignorial fealty, and personal leadership.

From the twelfth to the fourteenth century, representative assemblies, or Estates, arose in virtually every country of Latin Christendom, usually as an outgrowth of medieval courts of justice. These institutions consisted of representatives from the various medieval "estates"—in this case, the term denotes the formally named interest groups of the Middle Ages such as the clergy, the nobility (magnates or lords), the gentry, and the towns. In England the Estates evolved into Parliament; in France, they formed the Estates-General; in Spain, the *Cortes*; in the Germanic lands, the *Landstände*; in the Netherlands, the States-General; in Sweden, the *riksdag*; in various parts of Italy, the councils. There were often several such assemblies in any one country, some regionally based, others more national in jurisdiction. The Estates were a critical element in the political and social organization of late medieval Europe, and the type of political system they formed—the *Ständestaat*, in the terminology of German historians—was an intermediate stage between feudalism and the early modern state. Their rise was closely linked with the rise of towns, which stood outside the traditional networks of lord–vassal relations and represented a source of independent power that required new forms of accommodation by the rulers.[9]

The *Ständestaat* was neither democratic nor broadly representative. The Estates excluded the peasant masses, and membership was usually based on status, appointment, and wealth rather than on election. But nor were the Estates weak, politically marginal, or transient, as they are sometimes portrayed. They were representative of the elite, politically active strata that composed them; they operated on the principle of majority voting; and they imposed significant limitations on the autocratic tendencies of their sovereigns, who were compelled to seek their consent to the levying of taxes, the promulgation of laws, and even the conduct of foreign affairs. This gave the *Ständestaat* a dualistic structure of power, with governing authority shared between the sovereign and the Estates. To the extent that the "medieval constitutionalism" embodied in this arrangement survived the strains of war, it provided a foundation for the later emergence of representative, democratic government in European states. However, where war was prolonged and intense it rarely survived, and autocracy resulted.[10]

The rise of the national state in both France and Spain was integrally linked with a withering of the privileges and power of these Estates. Over a period of two centuries, from approximately 1450 to 1650, the power-sharing order of the medieval era yielded to monarchical absolutism as the pressures of war, and the concomitant rise of standing armies and central bureaucracies, diminished royal dependence on the Estates. In England and Sweden (and for a time in subnational provinces such as Aragon and certain provinces of France) the Estates retained a measure of their traditional privileges, their tenacity providing a foundation for constitutional monarchy. But even there, the Crown had to restrict the power of the interest-group estates (especially the clergy and nobility) before modern state structures could emerge. Thus, while the rise of the national state brought certain benefits with it, we should not forget that in virtually all cases its rise was connected with the diminution of other independent sources of power. Potential seeds of authoritarian rule were planted at the very birth of the modern state.

THE CONTINENTAL PATH OF STATE FORMATION

The first rudiments of modern government originated in the course of the fifteenth century in a littoral triangle of the North Atlantic encompassing contemporary France, Spain, and England. A series of wars both within and among the three countries provided the catalyst for the emergence of the earliest state structures. In France, the centralizing effect of the Hundred Years' War favored the monarchy over regional power centers; it also gave rise to the first standing army in Europe, which subsequently enabled Louis XI to triumph over his aristocratic rivals. In England, the Wars of the Roses reduced the authority and depleted the resources of the nobility, enabling Henry VII to fill the resulting power vacuum to his advantage. In Spain, civil wars devastated Castile and Aragon prior to the joint accession of Ferdinand of Aragon and Isabella of Castile; the resultant anarchy facilitated centralization by the strong-willed couple. The subsequent conquest of Moorish-ruled Grenada then became the decisive event in the emergence of the Renaissance state in Castile. A century later, Francis Bacon eulogized Henry VII, Louis XI, and Ferdinand of Aragon as the "three Magi of kings" of their age. Later historians would refer to them as the New Monarchs. By building up military force and asserting royal authority, they reversed a long-term trend toward political decentralization across Western Europe.

With important variations from country to country, the process by which war stimulated state formation in the Renaissance consisted of five interrelated steps:

1. *an internal power struggle* between the center and the periphery of a given state;
2. *a shift in favor of the center* due to developments in military technology and organization that increased the cost and administrative complexity of waging warfare;
3. *a revolution in taxation*, as the rising fiscal demands of warfare, both internal and external, caused governments to make intensified efforts at revenue extraction;
4. *the rise of central bureaucracies* in response to the fiscal and administrative challenges of warfare;
5. *a feedback cycle* in which the increasing fiscal and bureaucratic power of states enabled them to field larger and more powerful armies, which meant larger and more destructive wars, which drove the whole process in a circular spiral upward.

We shall call this sequence of steps *the continental path of state formation*, since it was most characteristic of the large states on the European mainland. One critical point to note about the above sequence is that internal conflicts—civil wars, revolts, etc.—were as central to the process of state formation as external or international wars. State formation was as much a means for the resolution of internal conflict as for the waging of external war.

In Europe, state formation began as early as the Hundred Years' War, particularly in France, but its course was gradual and uneven, requiring over two centuries before the first genuinely sovereign states emerged on the continent. And England, as we shall see, diverged from the continental path in important ways. In order to understand the role that war and military rivalry played in this formative period of state development, we will examine to what extent the five steps outlined above operated in the three Atlantic kingdoms prior to 1494—the year France invaded Italy and triggered the series of conflicts known as the Italian Wars. This was the first post-medieval war, and the first general (i.e., first multiple axis) war in European history.

THE STRUGGLE BETWEEN CENTER AND PERIPHERY

The main axis of internal conflict in the Atlantic monarchies was between the monarchy (the center) and the landed aristocracy who were regionally based (the periphery). Because the monarchs were themselves of the aristocracy, this conflict was complex, often *sub rosa*, and tempered by bonds of fealty, religious faith, and the practical necessity of compromise. There was also a secondary axis of conflict between the monarchs and the large towns, whose growing size, wealth, and independence made them a factor of growing importance in the changing balance of power. But the nobility presented the main obstacle to central authority. The wealthier and more privileged nobles had private armies and large landed estates that operated as almost autonomous fiefdoms; their loyalty to the Crown was often tenuous. The rivalry between Crown and aristocracy gave monarchs incentive to acquire military resources both independent of and clearly superior to that of their noble peers. Only then would it be feasible to curb the nobles' traditional privileges and assert authority over the whole of national territory.

Each of the "New Monarchs" secured his or her preeminent status only after fighting bitter wars against aristocratic rivals. Louis XI's reign was marked by almost constant warfare with feudal lords, the foremost of whom was Charles the Bold, who waged a decade-long war (1467–77) aimed at carving out an independent Burgundian kingdom between a reduced France to the west and the Swiss Confederation to the east. In Spain, the marriage of Isabella of Castile to Ferdinand of Aragon provoked a struggle over the Castilian throne that lasted for a decade, with open civil war raging between 1475 and 1479. In England, Henry VII's victory at Bosworth Field ended the thirty-year-long struggle among the leading noble families known as the Wars of the Roses (1455–85). In all three countries, war-weariness facilitated the assertion of central authority as exhausted populations welcomed the advent of monarchs strong enough to enforce civil peace.[11]

The victory of the center in these civil wars was a vital first step toward the modern condition in which central authority enforces internal order. Without this assertion of royal prerogatives, the emergence of true state sovereignty would not have been possible. In France and Spain, the civil wars were also an important step in the consolidation of national territory that was integral to the formation of the modern state. (England by contrast was a unified territory long before the Tudor victory.) Louis XI's victories restored royal authority over the existing kingdom and added large tracts of territory; by his death in 1483, the boundaries of the realm approximated those of modern-day France. In Spain, the victory of Ferdinand and Isabella brought Castile and the provinces of Aragon together under one dynasty for the first time.

The civil wars weakened aristocratic opponents of central rule at a critical moment, when the organization and technology of warfare had already begun to favor centralized rule. The modernization of the French army that occurred near the end of the Hundred Years' War gave Louis XI the tool he needed to crush his aristocratic rivals; they regained some ground after his death, but not enough to reverse the trend toward stronger central rule. In Castile, the Catholic monarchs restored royal authority by revitalizing the *hermandades*, (brotherhoods) a militia force of medieval origin. The new *Santa Hermandad* became the backbone of royal power, "the most imposing military machine yet seen in the peninsula."[12] Municipally based and hence independent of the landed magnates, the *Hermandad* enforced a ban on private armies and even claimed the right of entry into the previously sacrosanct fortresses of the nobility, several of which it destroyed. In England, the restoration of royal authority by Henry VII did not entail the use of new or modernized military forces, but it was facilitated by the fact that the aristocracy had suffered serious economic losses as a direct result of the Wars of the Roses, and therefore its influence was severely reduced.[13]

The civil wars did not permanently end the friction between Crown and aristocracy. The aristocracy, with their private armies and financial resources, remained militarily indispensable—allies as often as rivals of the monarchs—but the wars shifted the internal balance of power toward the center. In Spain and France, the Crown began to govern with minimal reference to the Estates. Charles VII declined to summon the Estates-General for the last 21 years of his reign

(1440–61), setting a pattern that Louis XI and future French kings would try to follow. Ferdinand and Isabella governed Castile without summoning the Cortes from 1483 to 1497. English kings, however, took a different approach, seeking to curb the power of the great barons by forming a tacit alliance with the lower estates in Commons. The Wars of the Roses strongly reinforced this royal–bourgeois alliance when Henry Tudor received support from numerous middle-class professionals whose economic interests were threatened by the wars of the nobility.[14] This alliance gave the monarchy a broader revenue base and a counterweight to the landed interests, but only at a price: by relying on bourgeois support, rather than building up military forces of their own, English kings reared the constitutional edifice that constrained them. This was an important way in which England diverged from the continental path of state formation.

THE INCREASING COST AND COMPLEXITY OF WARFARE

Changes in military technology and tactics from 1350 to 1500 greatly increased the cost of fielding effective armies. Rising costs, in turn, favored larger countries and more centralized governments, which alone could afford and manage the new warfare. The principal revolution was in the increasingly successful use of gunpowder in siege and field artillery. The crux of the matter as far as state formation was concerned was this: artillery was generally too expensive for the nobility to purchase, and hence tended to become a monopoly of the Crown. The superior military technology of the day both gravitated to and reinforced the political center. Already in the fourteenth century France had established a king's office for artillery; its budget increased tenfold between 1375 and 1410.[15] Under Charles VII, the brothers Jean and Gaspard Bureau engineered critical technical advances in French artillery, which played a crucial role in France's securing of Normandy from 1449 to 1453, particularly in the last engagement at Castillon. The budget for artillery nearly quintupled again under Louis XI, enabling further acquisitions and technical breakthroughs that contributed to the defeat of Charles the Bold in the Burgundian War.[16] In Spain, the Catholic monarchs used artillery to great effect in the conquest of Granada, while in England cannon were used in the major battles of the Wars of the Roses. One of Henry VII's first official acts as King was to appoint a new royal master of ordnance and expand the staff under him.[17]

The development of the handgun, even its first crude incarnation

as the arquebus, also shifted power away from the nobility by accelerating the trend toward using large numbers of infantry as the mainstay
of land armies. Foot soldiers had been important in high-medieval
warfare, but from the mid-fourteenth to the mid-fifteenth century
infantry had lost ground to mounted cavalry, a seignorial monopoly.[18]
The handgun once again made the common foot soldier as valuable in
battle as the self-equipped noble cavalryman—the *caballero*, the *cheva-
lier*, the *Landesknecht*—whose deeds until then had been the very stuff
of lore. The handgun eroded the military monopoly of the nobility
and hence threatened their social status; many of them instinctively
recognized this and regarded the new weapon as an invention of Satan.
Man for man, infantry also cost less than cavalry, and the handgun
made it practical to deploy large numbers of them in battle.

The Gunpowder Revolution in both artillery and handguns thus
dramatically shifted the internal balance of power in late medieval politics:

> By royalizing warfare, on the one hand, and by proletarianizing it, on
> the other, the gun helped to tip the balance of power within each
> European state away from the nobility and in favor of the crown. The
> process was gradual and complex, and its rate varied in the different
> parts of Europe. But the long-range effect was everywhere the same:
> gunpowder technology curbed, and finally extinguished the freedom
> of landed magnates to exercise significant independent, organized mil-
> itary and political power.[19]

As the new technologies advanced, chivalric warfare became obsolete.
War lost its glory in the eyes of the nobility as the importance of individual warriors diminished. War was no longer a contest of personal
skill and valor; now it was a test of political organization and fiscal
strength.[20]

The most important military innovation of all was not technological
at all, however, but organizational. It was the rise of permanent professional armies in France and Spain, the first such formations since the
Roman legions. As in many facets of state development, France led the
way. In 1439, an *Ordonnance* (edict) of Charles VII reserved the right of
levying troops to the Crown alone, establishing in principle a royal
monopoly on armed violence—though in practice numerous fortifications and large stocks of weaponry remained in noble hands. An *ordonnance* of 1445 created what has been called the first standing army in
Europe, companies of 500 horsemen stationed in various provinces of
France. Though these companies were recruited from the nobility, they

became a standing professional force far superior in ability to the cavalry raised by traditional feudal levies.[21] The last stages of the Hundred Years' War saw this modernized French army, equipped with the finest artillery of the day, defeat English forces that remained largely medieval in their structure and equipment.

Though the Spanish *Hermandad* might be regarded as a kind of standing domestic army, it was neither suited nor intended for service abroad. The modern Spanish infantry originated later in connection with the campaigns against Granada. To defeat the Moors, Ferdinand and Isabella assembled a peninsula-wide army with both medieval and modern components: royal troops under direct command of the Crown, forces from the Church and Military Orders, the private armies of the nobility, and the *Hermandad* itself. This army grew to over 50,000 troops, an almost unprecedented size for the era, and its royal component became the nucleus of the Spanish infantry, which was to become the preeminent military force of Europe in the sixteenth century.[22]

The rising military power of the French and Spanish monarchs enabled them to enforce internal order more effectively, quell rebellion, and to assume something resembling sovereignty over large tracts of territory. As the size and importance of their infantry forces grew over the next fifty years, the nobility's role in warfare became increasingly subordinate to the direction of the monarchs.[23] This marked the beginning of a long process of co-optation by which the aristocracy of continental Europe gradually relinquished their own military fiefdoms in exchange for service in the officer corps of the standing armies of the monarchs. England, as usual, remained the exception. Henry VII in 1489 did attempt to raise an open-ended subsidy for a standing force of 10,000 archers, but failed dismally.[24] The English Crown remained dependent on the nobility for effective land power and did not field a standing army until over 150 years later. It was a lacuna of profound significance for the constitutional development of the English state.

THE REVOLUTION IN TAXATION

In medieval kingdoms, revenue from the royal domain was usually far more important than taxation per se, while the feudal levies paid by peasants to manorial lords were part of an economic system that was largely independent of any national administration. The rising cost of warfare in the late medieval period was the foundation of the modern "tax state," for it compelled monarchs to seek new sources of revenue and gave them the moral imperative needed to demolish the feudal barriers to centrally levied taxes.[25] The result was a veritable revolution in the nature of government revenue. Income from the royal domains declined in importance as taxation, both direct and indirect, became the dominant source of central revenues. "Extraordinary" revenues, which originally could be used only during wartime, tended to become both regular and permanent. And in France and Spain, though not in England, the role of the Estates in approving taxes dwindled as the monarchs successfully imposed certain taxes without seeking their consent. The culmination of these developments was a marked increase in central revenues, with the real per capita increase in the late fifteenth century nearly 200 percent for England and France, and as high as 1,000 percent or more for Spain.[26]

The fiscal expansion of the French state advanced in waves, each impelled by a new financial crisis, each crisis precipitated by a new war. The right of French monarchs to raise permanent, national taxation was first established under Charles V (1364–80) early in the Hundred Years' War, a development Christopher Allmand has characterized as "momentous," arguing that it was unquestionably brought about by the needs of the war.[27] More radical changes occurred following the raising of the siege of Orléans by Joan of Arc, which emboldened Charles VII to reimpose indirect national taxes without consulting the Estates-General.[28] As France won territory from the English, Charles simply imposed the new tax system on each reconquered region, in a "revenue mill" forged by conquest: taxes supported the army, which conquered new lands, which he compelled to pay more taxes, which supported a larger army, and so forth. From 1440 until his death in 1461 Charles levied an annual *taille*—a direct tax apportioned according to the number of soldiers each province owed the war effort—unilaterally and without consent, suppressing the nobles' resistance to this step (the "Praguerie revolt") by force. With some hyperbole, Martin Wolfe has described the tax revolution of Charles VII as "one of the decisive steps in the history of Western civilization."[29] Certainly it was a milestone in the emergence of the sovereign state in France.

The growing tax powers of the Valois monarchy incited numerous revolts by the French aristocracy and towns against Charles's successor, Louis XI. Yet, ironically, these revolts forced Louis to raise taxes to even higher levels in order to wage what amounted to perpetual civil war. Total revenues doubled during his reign, while income from the *taille* alone increased 300 percent just between 1470 and 1484. Another indication of growing central power was the numerous obligations imposed on the towns of France—including forced loans and requisitions of foodstuffs and supplies, most of which went to support the army. The revenue extracted under Louis XI reached between .41 and .48 *livres tournois* per capita, a figure not exceeded until after the French Wars of Religion.[30] This remarkable statistic belies the notion of the early Renaissance state in France as having only weak extractive power, while showing that civil war can promote centralization and fiscal expansion as much as, or more than, international conflict.

The Spanish conquest of Granada cost as much as 80 million *maravedis*, a sum that would have been impossible to raise without new sources of revenue.[31] The Catholic monarchs reorganized the traditional financial departments of Castile early in their reign and again in the early 1490s, when the fiscal demands of the *Reconquista* became onerous. Revenue grew spectacularly—by a factor of over 28 in the thirty years from 1474 to 1504.[32] The monarchs even attempted to tax the nobility, and while this as yet proved impossible (medieval strictures still remained in force), they did develop or revitalize numerous sources of revenue that did not require Cortes approval, such as the *alcabala*, a kind of sales tax.

In contrast to the continent, England did not undergo a revolution in taxation. The principle of taxation by consent had been established as early as the Model Parliament in 1295, when the Crown was desperate for money to wage wars in Scotland and France, while the representation of the Commons had become permanent by 1337.[33] War was almost the sole rationale that would persuade Parliament to grant new monies to the Crown, and virtually all preambles to parliamentary grants justified them solely on military grounds.[34] This constitutional constraint made it difficult for Henry VII—who needed middle-class and urban support against his noble rivals, but who faced no serious threats from abroad—to introduce new forms of taxation.

The Tudor king concentrated instead on coercive means of revenue extraction designed to weaken his aristocratic rivals: forced loans; bonds of recognizance mandating good behavior or forfeiture; the prosecution and fining of nobles who retained private armies; acts of attainder and forfeiture. Of the sixty-two peerage families that flourished during Henry VII's reign, three fourths were either under attainder, bound by recognizance bonds, or otherwise at the mercy of the Crown.[35] Henry also reorganized the Exchequer, restoring financial order to the royal administration, which had fallen badly into disarray during the Wars of the Roses.[36] By efficient management, he more than doubled his annual income. It was £113,000 by the end of his reign, though this remained less than Edward III and Richard II had received a century earlier and far less than the incomes of his counterparts on the continent. The early Tudor regime was regaining lost ground, not breaking new.[37] Its fiscal structure remained more medieval, hence more constitutional and consensual, than its continental counterparts.

ADMINISTRATIVE REFORM AND BUREAUCRATIZATION

Demand for war-fighting revenue was the primary impetus behind the creation of early state institutions. Administrative bodies grew up devoted to managing the ever-more-complex financial, military, and legal affairs of the monarchs. Though minuscule by contemporary standards, these began to assume the form of permanent bureaucracies. Inevitably a portion of the revenues raised by these bodies went not to the army but back to the bureaucracy, whose organizational prowess was then applied both to raise additional money and to build up military forces. In the classic formulation of Max Weber: "At the beginning of the modern period, all the prerogatives of the continental states accumulated in the hands of those princes who most relentlessly took the course of administrative bureaucratization."[38] The loyalty of these early bureaucracies remained entirely personal, dedicated to the King rather than to the still vaguely defined "state" or the public interest per se.[39]

The historian Bernard Guenée sees the growth of the French bureaucracy as the most distinctive feature in the development of the French state in the late medieval and early Renaissance period.[40] In addition to noble *officiers*, who typically purchased their posts as a patrimony, the bureaucracy included increasing numbers of professional administrators or *commissaires*, many of whom were not of high birth. A similar process took place in Castile, where the fiscal requirements of the Catholic monarchs led them to overhaul their antiquated financial administration and reorganize the Council of Castile. Significantly, the nobility received no voting rights in the new Council.[41] The Castilian administration increasingly recruited professional lawyers or *letrados*, often from classes below the nobility. They formed the core of a permanent bureaucracy outside the royal household, a powerful tool against the magnates and a force for political centralization in its own right. (The need to train a steady stream of new recruits for the Castilian bureaucracy also gave impetus to educational reform—by the time of Philip II, the percentage of Spanish males attending universities was the highest in Europe.[42])

Again by contrast with the continent, early Tudor England did *not* develop a bureaucratic administration. Henry VII's reorganization of the Exchequer was hardly "bureaucratization," for his administration remained entirely household in nature and medieval in style, and he showed no interest in rationalizing it. Henry's reign did see the centralization of royal revenues under the Chamber, a more efficient organ than the Exchequer, but the Chamber was decidedly nonbureaucratic. England's isolation from the winds of continental warfare simply made a well-administered but medieval form of government feasible for longer than it was in France or Spain. While France and Spain built up large standing armies and appointed salaried royal officials in their provinces, Henry created in England neither a salaried civil service nor a standing military force to back it up.[43]

THE FEEDBACK CYCLE: LARGER ARMIES, LARGER WARS, STRONGER STATES

When historians speak of the "Military Revolution" of the Renaissance, they generally have in mind the exponential increase in the size and firepower of armies that occurred in the sixteenth and seventeenth centuries. But already before 1500 the Gunpowder Revolution had brought about a smaller but no less significant quantum leap, at least on the continent. The size of the French army under Louis XI reached as high as 80,000 in wartime, while Spanish forces fielded against Granada grew from around 10,000 men in the early campaigns to over 50,000 men by the end. Paradoxically, the existence of such concentrated military power made the Valois and Spanish monarchs both more secure and less secure. They were more secure against internal rivals, for though their new military power did not prevent challenges to their authority—and rising taxes may have actually stimulated such challenges—the same power made them less likely to succeed. The buildup of centralized military power was thus an important step on the long path toward establishment of internal state sovereignty. At the same time, the large army of one state only threatened the security of the other, thus giving both monarchs further incentive to expand their military forces—which in turn enhanced their internal power, enabling them to extract the resources required for further military expansion. What Joseph Schumpeter said of a later era applied here as well: "created by the wars that required it, the machine now created the wars it required."[44] The Sisyphean cycle of modernity was already beginning to turn in the fifteenth century.

The events of this early period reveal an interesting pattern that recurs throughout much of modern history: major foreign wars were almost invariably followed by rising internal tension and often by civil war. This is because war starkly reveals the internal problems of a state (the "inspection effect" noted in Chapter 1), but simultaneously exert a unifying effect that masks those internal cleavages until the war ends. After the Hundred Years' War, internal strife broke out almost immediately in both England (the Wars of the Roses) and in France (the Burgundian War, and other struggles between Louis XI and regional lords). Since power accrues to the center most strongly during wartime, the periphery often sees in the cessation of hostilities an opportunity to reassert its autonomy. But since there was never a clear division between military power and police power—between the means for waging external war and those for crushing internal rebellion—revolts against states lately steeled in war usually failed; the state's armed forces crushed them.

The wars of this early period also saw some of the earliest manifestations of a national feeling that transcended provincial and feudal loyalties. Inevitably this protonationalism came to center on the monarchs, whose power and capacity to rally the nobility constituted the bulwark of communal security and strength. In the course of the Hundred Years' War, particularly in its later stages, large segments of the French population came to identify the triumph of the Valois monarchs as the triumph of France itself. The royal army became their own army; the king was now seen as responsible for their protection. (The war apparently did not have the same effect on the enemy English population, which was less attached to the disputed territory, regarding it primarily as a dynastic possession, not a national one.)

In Spain, the decade-long conquest of Grenada also stimulated early manifestations of Spanish national feeling.[45] Castile led the campaign and provided the bulk of military forces, but Aragon, Catalonia, and Valencia also contributed troops, money, and equipment. The war thus welded together the Christian population of Iberia in a highly evocative military campaign that was "the crucible of the monarchy."[46] The *Reconquista* also brought two-thirds of the Iberian peninsula and four-fifths of its population under Ferdinand and Isabella, while simultaneously strengthening their hand vis-à-vis the nobility. Though the latter contributed forces to the war, the success of the royal army in the Granadan campaigns, and the role of the Crown in orchestrating the entire campaign, demonstrated the superiority of centralized government in mobilizing military power.[47] The rising national feeling in Spain, coupled with its burgeoning army, bureaucracy, and treasury—all paralleled by similar developments in France—set the stage for a Habsburg–Valois showdown and the first general war in European history.

THE CONSTITUTIONAL PATH OF STATE FORMATION

From the above, it should be clear that England diverged in several critical points from the continental path of state formation. It pursued instead what we will call *the constitutional path*, in which the bureaucratic and centralizing effects of war were muted, and no revolution in taxation occurred. One reason for this was the existence of a well-established middle class with which English monarchs could ally in their efforts to counter the landed power of the nobility. Middle-class representation in the Commons meant that the constitutional arrangement of the medieval era actually *facilitated* monarchical efforts to counter this landed power—hence the Crown had no incentive to crush the Estates. Eventually, the Commons would wax so strong as to directly rival the monarchy and provoke the greatest civil war in English history, but in the early Tudor period that day was still far off. The second factor that preserved constitutional government in England was its insular isolation. Secure behind the Channel, England had no engine of constant war to drive the process of centralization and state formation.

THE DAWN OF MODERNITY: THE ITALIAN WARS

The modern age of European politics can be said to have commenced in September 1494, when France invaded the kingdom of Naples, touching off the first of the Italian Wars. Ostensibly Charles VIII wanted only to enforce a dynastic claim, but his September invasion marked the crossing of a Rubicon between the medieval and the modern age, as the Europe-wide contest that followed surpassed in scope and significance any previous medieval conflict. Historians may dispute the newness of the New Monarchies,[48] but the fact remains that the first major war between them was a wholly new phenomenon, as their contemporaries realized. The modern features of the Italian Wars did not emerge from nowhere but were the logical result of the developmental trends that had taken place over the preceding half century, as we have just seen.

France entered Italy with an army of over 25,000 troops, including regular French infantry and crossbowmen and large numbers of Swiss mercenary pikemen. It brought with it the best artillery ever made: 140 superbly crafted bronze 50-pound cannon on wheeled carriages and 200 smaller bombards, the technical fruit of the Hundred Years' War and of subsequent innovations during the war with Burgundy. This field artillery required hundreds of soldiers and technicians to support it, as well as some 8,000 horses to transport the guns and supply wagons. The Italians had some cannon of their own, but they had never seen such technically advanced artillery, nor any kind of cannon deployed in such large quantities and with such smoothly orchestrated mobility. The organizational complexity of fielding, supplying, and feeding an army of that size equipped with such heavy weaponry could not have been mastered by any wholly medieval state. It was a first demonstration of what could be accomplished with bureaucratic organization. The city-states that faced it were overawed: Florence and the Papal States yielded after token resistance; the Neapolitan fortress of Monte San Giovanni was devastated by the French cannon in only eight hours, though it had once withstood a siege of seven years.[49]

France's inexorable southward march alarmed its neighbors and precipitated the formation in Venice of the first multipower alignment in European history. Fearing they would be cut off, the French withdrew, fighting their way out of Italy in the Battle of Fornovo; by 1498, Spanish forces under Gonzalo of Córdoba had taken Naples for Ferdinand. But France had only just begun. Over the next six decades, under three kings, it invaded Italy six times. In the medieval era, wars were usually fought between contiguous domains; now the geographic scope of conflict expanded. For the first time, multiple power centers joined in the same contest. Venice, the smaller Italian city-states, certain of the Germanic states, and England all became involved at one time or another, though France and Spain remained the central axis of conflict. The accession of Charles V to the Spanish throne in 1516 greatly magnified the geopolitical import of the conflict, as Charles became simultaneously king of Castile, Aragon, Naples, Sicily, Sardinia, and of the Spanish territories in the New World; three years later he acquired the Austrian Habsburg realms and the throne of the Holy Roman Empire. Determined to block the hegemonic aspirations of an empire stretching from Vienna to Peru, France fought Spain across the face of Italy for sixty-five years, their interaction profoundly affecting the evolution of the international system in Europe and the internal development of every European state.

The Habsburg–Valois conflict was played out in many parts of Europe—Navarre, Burgundy, the Germanic lands—but the Italian peninsula was the main battleground throughout. The violence wreaked on Italy devastated its countryside and destabilized its city-states, which became hapless pawns in a vast chess game beyond their playing abilities. Resisting feebly, shifting alliances opportunistically between the invading powers, they gradually lost their independence, political stability, and military self-respect. Hostilities ended in 1559 with the signing of the Treaty of Cateau-Cambrésis, not because one side had gained a decisive advantage, but because both sides were exhausted and financially drained by wars that had spanned a lifetime. Spain had demonstrated its military superiority on many occasions and emerged from the wars as the hegemon of Italy and the strongest military power in Europe. But France had also won its share of battles and demonstrated that complete Habsburg ascendancy was impossible. Artillery, meanwhile, continued to revolutionize warfare: at Ravenna in 1512, a single cannon ball felled 33 men; in Novara in 1513, cannon fire killed 700 men in three minutes.[50]

The Italian Wars drove vigorous processes of centralization and state formation in both France and Spain. The wars also generated new currents of distinctively modern political thought. Indeed, Donald Begot argues that modern political consciousness was first born in the early stages of the Italian Wars, beginning with the invasion of 1494.[51] In 1513, the year of the Battle of Novara and the high point of the Holy League's efforts to expel France from Italy, Niccolò Machiavelli published *The Prince*, the first of several classic works of political thought published across Europe over the next six years: Claude de Seyssel's *Monarchy of France*, Erasmus's *Education of a Christian Prince*, Thomas More's *Utopia*, Guillaume Budé's *Institution of the Prince*. These "men of 1494," as they have been called, were preoccupied with statecraft, diplomacy, and war; all of them reflected a newly modern outlook on the nature of politics.[52] In this sense, the intellectual foundations of modern politics, and its institutional origins, derived in part from the tumult of the new warfare.

WAR AND STATE FORMATION, 1494–1559

The effect of the Italian Wars in breaking down medieval structures and promoting state formation on the continent is best illuminated by looking separately at the post-1494 political development of France and that of Spain. We will then turn to England and see how its constitutional path of state formation took it on a very different trajectory.

THE HABSBURG–VALOIS WARS AND STATE FORMATION IN FRANCE

The wars with Spain depleted the French treasury and forced Francis I (1515–1547) to undertake administrative reforms. Yet his reforms never resolved the fiscal dilemma, since other contenders were also boosting their military spending. France was caught in a cycle of escalating violence, which its own efforts at taxation and military spending only served to propel upward; hence a fresh military crisis loomed every few years. This unremitting fiscal pressure forced centralizing reforms on a government whose inclinations were still largely medieval, but whose aspirations required the organizational accoutrements of a modern state.[53]

Two reforms in particular arose from France's involvement in the wars. In 1523, as it was mobilizing troops for a fresh campaign in Italy, Antoine Duprat, the king's chancellor, established the first central treasury of the realm, the *Trésor de l'Épargne* or Treasury of Savings. The acute fiscal crisis caused by the earlier wars motivated him, as well as an awareness that France's past military setbacks had stemmed in part from a failure to pay troops. The formation of a central treasury was a critical step in the emergence of a distinction between government (public) and royal (private) spheres of money management, a recognition of the fact that French tax revenues were no longer just the private income of the king but the lifeblood of a permanent, transcendent French government.[54] The second major reform, the Edict of Cognac, followed in 1542 in the middle of the Fourth Italian War. It divided France's four financial districts into sixteen new districts, each under an official of the Crown. This Edict merged all types of revenue under one administration and enlarged the authority of the Central Treasury to collect taxes.

Under the impetus of these reforms, regular tax revenues in France increased from 5,000,000 *livres* in 1515 to over 9,000,000 *livres* by 1546, of which military expenditures still consumed over half. But even while regular tax revenue was increasing at about 2 percent per annum, prices were also rising slowly, wiping out much of the gain. This has led some scholars to argue that the growing power of the French state was largely an illusion. Although it is true that the technical and administrative shortcomings of the age imposed limits on the absolutist tendencies of the French monarchy, regular revenue alone does not tell the whole story. To maintain its forces in the field, the monarchy also extracted "extraordinary" revenues from various sources, including special "military levies" imposed on the cities and Estates for support of the French army. In Dauphiné alone, such levies reached as high as 382,000 *livres* in a single year (1538). For purposes of state formation, the amount of revenue was in any event less significant than its source: in a sharp departure from the medieval pattern, more than 90 percent of regular revenues came from sources clearly recognizable as taxes, rather than as income from the personal royal domains. Under Henry II (1547–1559), the Crown also began to borrow substantially from sources inside and outside of France for the first time, enabling the military and bureaucratic expansion of the state to progress ahead of actual receipts.[55]

The French bureaucracy and army also grew rapidly as a result of the campaigns in Italy. Between 1494 and 1559, the average annual size of the armies fielded by France at least doubled, to some 50,000 troops. The growth of the artillery service was particularly significant: by the accession of Henry II, some 275 gunners in service consumed 500,000 pounds of gunpowder annually, 25 times the corresponding amount a century earlier. As for the central bureaucracy, by the Battle of Marignano (1515), it employed at least 5,000 officials (and perhaps as many as 8,000), and their numbers continued to grow rapidly under Francis I. This was due in part to the creation and sale of hundreds of offices, a source of revenue that reached 900,000 *livres* per annum during his reign, or about 18 percent of ordinary revenues. But requirements of scale also played a role, for as the activities of the central government expanded, it became impossible for the royal household administration alone to supervise them.[56] Bureaucratization had become essential to governing.

The prolonged Habsburg–Valois struggle served as a powerful stimulus to French national consciousness. One evidence of this was the Villers-Cotterêts decree of 1539, which mandated French as the official language of the courts and the bureaucracy. This official declaration of a vernacular *lingua franca* marked the beginning of three centuries of efforts by French governments to harness language in the service of political centralization.[57] The decree came only one year after the end of the Third Italian War, at a time when another war already threatened. Other developments also signaled a rising national awareness in France: the term *state* entered the French vernacular during the period of the Italian wars; Guillaume Budé and Claude de Seyssel propounded political theories justifying royal absolutism; Francis I became the first French king to be called "Your Majesty," a title previously reserved for emperors.

By 1559, France manifested a level of national consciousness that clearly transcended traditional feudal loyalties, and it had the largest bureaucracy in Europe, an order of magnitude larger any other country except Spain. The emerging French state still retained numerous practices and institutions that were medieval in nature and it was, like all other Renaissance states, severely limited in administrative capacity. The nobility dominated local government and continued to resist central intrusions into its affairs; internal sovereignty in the modern sense still lay beyond the horizon. But the power of the monarchy vis-à-vis alternative political bases was increasing, and the passage from medieval to modern politics was under way.

THE HABSBURG–VALOIS WARS AND THE STATE IN CASTILIAN SPAIN

The empire of Charles V was a loose association of several principalities. He governed them separately and was known by a different title in each; his person was the only common thread. Given the communications and transportation limits of the day, there was never any prospect that this sprawling conglomeration would evolve into a unified state, nor did Charles establish a central administration to govern it. His was a purely dynastic empire, stitched together by marriage and inheritance. Even Greater Spain should not be regarded as a unified state, since the province of Aragon retained a separate administration. Our attention will focus therefore on Castile, the core of this vast imperium and the only Habsburg realm that clearly had entered on a path of political modernization.

Castile's role as the heart of an imperial dynasty complicated and ultimately retarded the process of state formation in Spain. Under Charles V, Spanish territory was hardly threatened, and then only by Moorish sea raiders from the Mediterranean. Revenues raised by the Crown went to support Habsburg armies fighting in imperial wars far from Spanish borders and often remote from Castile's direct interests. This reduced the developmental force of protonationalism, retarded the process of state formation, and meant that the largest standing army in Europe was not always available for quelling internal troubles at home. Even the fiscal benefits Castile received from the empire, such as the inflow of precious metals from Spanish America, proved to be a mixed blessing: they caused rapid price increases and led the government to become dependent on outside income rather than developing an effective administrative and taxation system at home. As the center of an empire, Castile's political energy was directed outward. The emperor was absent from Spain for long periods, including fourteen years at the end of his reign; he left the daily routine of governing to viceroys and lesser officials, who lacked the authority to undertake needed reforms.

Despite the dilution of modernizing forces by imperial preoccupations, centralization continued to advance in Spain. As in France and England, the resolution of a serious internal conflict—the revolt of the Comuneros in 1520–21—helped consolidate the authority of the Crown vis-à-vis a new source of resistance to its power: the towns. Whereas the greatest challenges to state authority under Ferdinand and Isabella had come from the landed aristocracy, the Comuneros were municipally based. Though there was a brief possibility that the rebellion would make common cause with certain of the great estates of the nobility, the rising radicalism of the Comuneros cost them all their noble support, and a royalist army decisively defeated the rebel forces at Villalar. Castilian liberty was thoroughly crushed, and the Crown was not challenged again for over a century. This was a clear instance of how a military victory by the center over an internal challenger served to confirm the rising internal sovereignty of the state.

With Castile secure, Charles V concentrated on building up the armed might of the Habsburg Empire, with forces that may have numbered as many as 148,000 near the end of his reign.[58] This was the largest force in Europe, though scattered over immense distances and composed of diverse components under separate commands. In addition to the ceaseless war against France, Habsburg armies waged campaigns against Protestant heretics in Germany and "infidel" Turks in the East. Not surprisingly, the dominant factor shaping Castilian political development was the ceaseless search for warfighting revenue:

War and ever increasing taxes seemed to be the lot of the emperor's subjects. . . . Every letter that passed between the emperor and his viceroys, every memorandum presented to him by his ministers, was directly or indirectly concerned with problems of finance; for only ready money would keep in the field the emperor's armies, keep afloat his galleys, the instruments on which, in the last resort, all his policies and the very existence of his empire depended.[59]

Castile was essentially on a permanent war footing throughout the Italian Wars. The resultant fiscal pressures led to the creation of a Council of Finance (*Consejo de Hacienda*) and the overhauling of Castile's antiquated financial administration. The Castilian bureaucracy employed several thousand officials by 1559, but unlike the French equivalent, large parts of it were devoted not to fiscal administration but to imperial affairs, including management of the growing empire in America. The fact that much of the bureaucracy saw itself as representing not the Spanish state but rather the larger empire inhibited the emergence of a sense of public domain in Spain, and was one reason state development there lagged behind that in France.[60]

Further reforms, particularly of Castile's antiquated and inequitable taxation system, might have put the Castilian state on a more enduring basis. But access to bullion from America, as well as borrowed capital from banking centers in Antwerp, Augsburg, and elsewhere, enabled Charles to sustain his empire without initiating any modernizing reforms at home, even in the midst of war. During his reign, total Spanish revenue from foreign loans nearly equaled normal internal income from other sources.[61] As the obligations of the Crown rose, nervous bankers raised their interest rates: from 17.6 percent in 1520–32 to 49 percent and even 67 percent after 1552. The rising cost of borrowing funds coupled with the tax exemptions of the Aragonese realms and a tax revolt in Ghent forced Charles to rely ever more heavily on Castile for revenue.[62] But the emperor, preoccupied with imperial affairs, still paid insufficient attention to the economy of his crown jewel, which began a slow slide toward fiscal collapse and eventual irreversible decline. In the Spanish case (contrary to Charles Tilly's theory of capital being a critical factor in successful state formation) access to capital did not foster political development, but only hindered reform and hastened the decline of the state.[63]

WAR AND THE CONSTITUTIONAL PATH OF STATE FORMATION, 1494–1559

England became embroiled in various phases of the Habsburg–Valois wars, but only intermittently and for reasons that had little to do with Italy. England joined the war against France from 1511 to 1514, and again from 1521 to 1526, before briefly allying with France against Spain. Hostilities with France broke out again in 1544–46, 1549–50, and 1556–58. England also fought at least five separate wars with Scotland during the period in question, in most of which France aided the Scottish side. Henry VII and Henry VIII also faced several internal rebellions, the most serious of which were Perkin Warbeck's Rebellion (1495–99), the Pilgrimage of Grace (1536), and the East Anglian revolts. With the exception of these, the wars of the Tudor kings prior to 1559 were not fought in the main on English soil, and none of them seriously threatened the survival of the monarchy. Peace and territorial security tempered the process of state formation in England. The wars that did occur spurred administrative reforms, stimulated national consciousness, and enhanced central authority, but they were not sufficiently intense or prolonged to destroy the medieval constitutional structure of England, in which Parliament remained an integral component of the state.

When war with France broke out in 1511, the expenses of the Crown multiplied tenfold to nearly 700,000 pounds, with over 90 percent of this being military expenditures.[64] The fiscal situation worsened in the campaigns of the 1520s, when Parliament resisted providing grants, forcing Henry to rely on loans and special sources of revenue. The sweeping administrative reforms of Thomas Cromwell in the 1530s (characterized by G. R. Elton as a "revolution in Tudor government") occurred in peacetime, but were carried out largely in response to the financial crisis precipitated by the wars with France.[65] The Cromwellian reforms accelerated the process of "going out of court"; from 1530 to 1542, in every domain of government, household methods of administration were replaced by impersonal, rationalized, and bureaucratic methods.[66] Though not all these reforms survived Henry's reign, they marked the first real break with medieval government. The size of the English administration, however, still remained a full order of magnitude smaller than that of France.

It is significant that the reform of English administration took place in the same decade as passage of the Acts of Appeals and Supremacy and other anti-Papist statutes. The English Crown's break with the Church of Rome and the resultant dissolution of the monasteries (itself an important source of revenue, without which the later wars against France would not have been feasible) represented a decisive assertion of state sovereignty—the triumph of secular over religious authority, of national over universal loyalties. The Henrician Reformation hastened the development of a distinct English political identity, and—by dramatically increasing the level of tension between England and the continent—gave strong impetus to English defense spending. Coastal fortifications alone consumed an average 29 percent of the Crown's regular income from 1539 to 1547, as the King's ministers led efforts to repair and arm coastal fortresses, prepare beacons, and build blockhouses. Coastal inhabitants and local militia participated in these efforts enthusiastically, reflecting the emergence of a new national consciousness.[67]

Fiscal pressures mounted sharply during the last Henrician war with France (1544–46), which cost over £2,000,000 and left the English treasury nearly bankrupt.[68] Despite such pressures, the administration of military affairs was one of the last to go "out of Court," in part because Henry VII saw himself as a warrior-king and insisted on managing it himself. But near the end of his reign he established an Ordnance Office and Naval Board outside the Court, and put the ordnance under a professional military officer for the first time. Recognizing the technical inferiority of English artillery, he imported gunnery experts from France and Italy so as to reduce his dependence on continental foundries.[69] The Naval Board was essential to management of the rapidly growing Tudor navy, which by the time of Henry's death had reached a peak of 53 well-armed warships with a total displacement of roughly 10,000 tons.[70]

The rise of the Tudor navy was a pivotal factor in England's political development. The English aristocracy were neither trained for naval warfare nor interested in it; nor could any English magnate have afforded to deploy a private navy. English naval power arose instead in tandem with overseas commercial interests and the merchant marine; it was from the beginning a mainly bourgeois undertaking, free of feudal vestiges. As mercantile capitalism flourished in England and the monarchy came to rely on middle-class support in its effort to dominate the nobility, the expansion of the Royal Navy followed in logical tandem. Naval power simultaneously strengthened and tempered English state formation. Since only the Crown could afford to procure warships, the more England relied on naval forces for security, the more it would rely on the central government. But as Otto Hintze observed in 1906, land forces give a military cast to states, while sea power is only "a mailed fist," unsuited for use against internal enemies.[71]

Rising naval strength compensated for the weakness of England's land forces, which fell progressively behind those of the continent, where the intensity of the contest over Italy drove both technical and organizational modernization. Without a standing army, England could not hope to stay competitive. The Tudors maintained small numbers of regular troops to man frontier garrisons and serve as royal bodyguards, but under Henry VIII these numbered less than 4,000. Feudal contract armies, royal musters of the militia, and foreign mercenaries—all traditional medieval sources of manpower— provided the remainder of England's land forces. Without the private forces of the nobility, the Crown effectively had no army: in the war against France in 1513, the nobility provided 80 percent of English forces; in 1544, 75 percent. Although by 1559 this quasi-feudal system had given way to a more centralized militia system in which the Crown commissioned its own recruiting agents rather than relying on royal letters to noblemen, this was still a long way from formation of a permanent army.[72]

Because England lay isolated from the winds of continental warfare, it was perhaps inevitable that its path of political development would diverge in important ways from its rivals on the continent. Given the small size of the English bureaucracy, the weakness of the English army, and the dependence of the monarchy on Parliament for financial support, it is misleading even to speak of "Tudor absolutism." Yet this picture of a restrained and limited Renaissance state in England should not obscure the very real achievement of the Tudor monarchs in imposing—by acts of livery and maintenance, forfeiture, and the banning of private armies—a measure of centrally enforced order on a once violence-prone English society. As an island kingdom, medieval England had enjoyed territorial unity and a high measure of external sovereignty; under the Tudors, the internal sovereignty of the state increased as well. According to Lawrence Stone, "the greatest triumph of the Tudors was the ultimately successful assertion of a royal monopoly of violence both public and private, an achievement which profoundly altered not only the nature of politics, but also the quality of daily life."[73] It was under Henry VIII that the word *state* first acquired its modern sense of body politic or supreme civil power; *state* had already been in use for a hundred and fifty years, but only as a synonym for *estate*.

TWO ALTERNATIVE PATHS: THE SWISS CONFEDERATION AND THE CITY-STATES OF ITALY

The course of state development in the large monarchies of the Atlantic littoral presents a rather one-sided picture of how war affected politics in the Renaissance era. A more balanced appraisal necessitates a look at two other Renaissance polities, Switzerland and Italy, whose political trajectories diverged sharply from the continental and constitutional paths that we have outlined here.

SWITZERLAND AND THE COALITIONAL PATH TO STATE FORMATION

The Swiss Confederation was a unique phenomenon in late medieval and Renaissance Europe. It was the antithesis both of the New Monarchies, where centralizing forces held sway, and of its fellow Germanic principalities in the Holy Roman Empire, which were still mired in feudal disarray. The Confederation had neither a central bureaucracy nor a state administration at the national level during the first five hundred years of its existence. Yet it not only fielded effective armies, but displayed an internal cohesion and stability that set it apart from the more transient military leagues of the era. Politically decentralized but socially cohesive, it was a sovereign state without a state apparatus, "an asylum for republican ideas in the midst of monarchical and feudal Europe."[74] The success of its formula is seen in its survival as an independent state to the present day.

The formation of the Swiss confederation and its emergence as an independent state followed a radically different path from that of the Atlantic monarchies. Its path of state development might be termed *the coalitional path of state formation*. It had five essential elements:

1. *the absence of a serious internal power struggle* between centralizing and local forces.
2. *a war of independence* from a larger empire that forged a military alliance between geographically linked provinces.
3. the formation by these provinces of *a representative assembly* responsible for foreign and military affairs.
4. *a decentralized approach to administration*, with taxation not

centralized but remaining the responsibility of the provinces, and with a local administration predominant in most spheres.

5. *the existence of long-term threats to security* that molded a sense of national unity and helped maintain the coalition even in peacetime.

The result of this developmental path was a highly decentralized, non-bureaucratic state that nevertheless proved capable of fielding formidable military power when necessary.

Troubled by Habsburg encroachments on their traditional privileges, the cantons of Uri, Schwyz, and Unterwalden formed an Everlasting League in 1291, promising mutual assistance "within the valleys and without, with all might and strength, against any and all who inflict on any of them violence, trouble, or injustice."[75] Significantly, this alliance was spearheaded by councils of burghers and free peasants, not by aristocratic families; it was moreover a genuinely equal alliance of cantons, with no single dominant center in control. At Morgarten in 1315, the Confederation defeated an Austrian army of nearly 10,000 men, despite being outnumbered seven to one. The victory had a strong unifying effect, solidifying the Confederation and making it a magnet for surrounding towns and rural districts that also resented Habsburg domination. Between 1332 and 1353, Lucerne, Zürich, Glarus, Zug, and Bern joined the Confederation. Swiss territorial unity was thus not the result of conquest but of voluntary confederation.

The Swiss Confederation fielded a militia force dominated by burghers and peasants; it was not a feudal army and it owed fealty to no aristocratic family. The format of the Swiss militia proved to be highly significant for the country's political development, for in the course of the fourteenth century, the Confederation won victories over Austrian troops at Laupen (1339), Sempach (1386), and Näfels (1388), in each case defeating feudal armies dominated by nobles. This class dichotomy on the battlefield discredited the already weakened aristocratic elements in the Confederation, whose ties to the imperial House of Habsburg were suspect. Consequently, the Swiss nobility declined rapidly in power and influence, and the rural districts gradually purchased or confiscated its lands and property. The absorption of these lands created the territorial continuity that was essential for the formation of the Swiss state. The demise of the landed aristocracy also infused the Confederation with a remarkably modern sense of egalitarianism; by 1485, most of the towns and cantons of the Confederation had abolished serfdom. Power gravitated to the burghers of the towns and the farmers of the rural cantons; the Swiss acquired a reputation as born enemies of nobility.

In Switzerland as elsewhere in Europe, the French invasion of Italy in 1494 marked a crucial turning point in political development. It exacerbated tensions between the Confederation and the southern German members of the Holy Roman Empire, because the Swiss refused to pay imperial taxes or recognize the authority of the imperial Reichstag. The eventual outcome was the brief Swabian War of 1499, in which the Swiss routed every Imperial army sent against them despite being heavily outnumbered in most battles. Though the Peace of Basel that ended the war did not technically recognize Swiss sovereignty, independence was its de facto effect. The victory also resulted in the Confederation becoming a magnet for neighboring small domains seeking security. Five additional towns or rural districts joined in 1501, giving it the form that would endure until Napoleon forced the conversion of the Confederation into the Helvetic Republic nearly three hundred years later.

In its form of government, the Confederation was highly decentralized, governed largely at the canton level by democratic *Landesgemeinde* in the rural districts and more oligarchical councils in the towns. The wars of the Swiss Confederation had virtually no bureaucratizing effect, at least not at the national level, where no administrative apparatus of any significance emerged. Instead of forming a central government, the thirteen cantons sent representatives to a national assembly, the Federal Diet in Bern. This Diet was responsible for conducting foreign and military affairs, mediating disputes between cantons, and issuing regulations affecting commerce and public safety across the Confederation. Individual cantons were not bound to accept the decisions of the Diet, but a tradition of yielding to majority votes developed, at least on issues of military and foreign affairs. The viability of this confederative structure presupposed a high degree of internal unity; in fact the absence of serious internal cleavages in Switzerland prior to the Reformation is one reason why the centralizing effect of external warfare was muted in the Swiss case. A critical step of the continental path of state formation—a competitive struggle between center and periphery—was missing; this meant that there was neither incentive nor political justification for imposing order by centralizing power.

The Confederation's decentralized structure did not lead to military weakness. Man for man, the Swiss fielded the most effective fighting force of any state in the early Renaissance. Early in its history, the Confederation adopted universal military service for all able-bodied males beginning at age fifteen. Those who could not serve paid an obligatory war tax, while anyone caught shirking military duty was subject to having his house destroyed—republican government did not preclude the exercise of repressive power when national security was at stake. Military service took place not in a federalized standing army but in locally based militia units. One military historian observes that whereas the Swiss continued to rely on militia forces, their militia units were permanent, drilled regularly, and remained cohesive throughout the life of their members. This enabled them to retain some of the cohesion of professional armies and to far surpass the average feudal levy in fighting capability.[76] In short, the Swiss found a way to derive many of the advantages of a standing army without the usual accoutrements of political centralization and a bloated bureaucracy. The socializing effect of militia service also imparted a unity and coherence to the Swiss political system that its highly decentralized political structure could not otherwise have produced.

Disastrous defeats at Marignano in 1515 and Pavia in 1522 and 1525 shattered the myth of Swiss invincibility. The pike proved to be no panacea against artillery and the arquebus, and now even the Swiss began to add gunpowder weapons to their arsenals.[77] Individual cantons continued to pursue mercenary opportunities, but Swiss disasters in the Italian Wars moved the Confederation nearer to the posture of neutrality that it would eventually adopt as formal policy. Yet if the military ascendancy of the Swiss did not endure long in the modern era, the Confederation itself did; even the cleavage of the Reformation proved insufficient to pull it apart, despite serious internal schisms. Conceived in war, it was perhaps the most remarkable political and military phenomenon in Renaissance Europe. Switzerland's alternative path to sovereignty—egalitarian, democratic, decentralized—demonstrated to Europe that centralized monarchy was not the only form of government capable of defending borders and maintaining the public peace. Montesquieu, two hundred and fifty years after the Swabian War, lauded the inherent superiority of federal republics and help up the Swiss Confederation as a model. Only a federal republic, he argued, can defend itself externally without becoming corrupted internally. "Composed of small republics, it enjoys the goodness of the internal government of each one; and, with regard to the exterior, it has, by the force of the association, all the advantages of large monarchies."[78]

WAR AND POLITICAL DISINTEGRATION: THE ITALIAN CITY-STATES

The Swiss Confederation survived as an island of freedom in a rising ocean of absolutism because its cantons were united in determined

resistance to outside rule. A quite opposite fate befell the city-states of
Italy. Devastated by the Habsburg–Valois struggle over their territory,
and unable to forge a lasting coalition, they lost both independence
and internal stability. Their experience sheds light on the disintegrative effects of conflict: on how military inferiority and catastrophic
defeat can retard political development and impede the formation of
modern state structures.

In the course of the fourteenth and fifteenth centuries, five strong
and relatively independent political units had emerged in the Italian
peninsula: Milan, Florence, Venice, the Papal States, and Naples. For a
time, they enjoyed the best mercenary armies and the most advanced
military technology in all of medieval Europe. The intrapeninsular
diplomacy of these city-states in the half century prior to 1494 constituted the first European balance-of-power arrangement, the "Concert
of Italy," which was the precursor of the modern state system of
ambassadors, embassies, and diplomatic protocol.[79] The commercial
spirit, advanced culture, and political sophistication of these city-states
set them apart from the other small principalities and kingdoms of
medieval Europe; Leopold Ranke regarded them as the first modern
states. Their failure to create a unified Italian state, however, left them
vulnerable to the new warfare of their larger neighbors. As Michael
Mullett observes, no Joachimist prophet was needed to see that balka-
nised Italy in the 1470s and 1480s was headed toward disaster: "It was
an unstable alliance of competitive states . . . whose squabbles were
likely at any moment to bring into the peninsula the vast, predatory,
destructive forces of the highly organized transalpine or transmediter-
ranean national monarchies."[80]

Within individual city-states, centralization and state formation
occurred on a small scale. In Venice, for example, various military
conflicts—the War of Ferrara, endemic wars with Genoa, and the
Long War against the Ottoman Empire—had spurred political development and contributed to the familiar cyclical process of taxation,
administrative centralization, and military procurement. By the fifteenth century Venice possessed both a bureaucratic administration
and a taxation system with certain modern features, and it had used its
abundant wealth to acquire formidable military power, mostly by
retaining mercenary soldiers, the *condottieri*. Mercenary armies in
other parts of Italy were often poorly managed, and easily turned
against their paymasters, but in Venice the army was well administered
and could easily have become a true standing army. Florence and
Milan lagged behind the Venetians in military power, but they too had
established officialdoms of a recognizably early modern type by the
mid-fifteenth century.

The municipal scale of political development in the city-states was one factor that exposed them to the degenerative impact of war: no one city-state was large enough to cope with the superior military power of the French invaders. In effect the city-states had coalesced prematurely, and hence on too local a scale, to wage the new warfare. A second factor was their failure to organize an Italy-wide defensive effort. Such an effort might have culminated either in a peninsular state under a dominant center (possibly Venice) or in a confederation with the potential to solidify eventually into a larger state—i.e., it might have followed either the continental or the coalitional path of state formation. But instead, intrapeninsular schisms precluded military coordination. Myopic preoccupation with the balance of power *within* Italy caused the city-states to overlook the real threat from outside, to see in the French invasion only an opportunity to weaken rival neighboring cities. Typically, each city-state tried by diplomatic maneuver to shift the burden of its defense to some other city, often by intriguing with the invaders. They did not reckon on the magnitude of military power that would come down on Italy, nor on the length and intensity of the wars. Nor did they realize until too late how far behind Italy had fallen in military technology and tactics.

The rivalry and intrigue among the peninsular city-states only encouraged foreign intervention and prolonged the Italian Wars. As the interminable fighting continued, its cumulative effect on Italian agriculture, industry, and politics was devastating. Large tracts of the countryside and almost all the major cities of Italy were left in ruins, including Rome, which was sacked by unpaid Habsburg troops in 1527. Human suffering and loss were immense. "A civilization that had been four centuries in the making now suddenly faced naked superior force. The centers of authority took the heaviest concussions, and a vast instability was sensed."[81] One of the degenerative effects of the war was the destabilization of governments that once had been stable and had functioned effectively. Violent or sudden changes of regime took place at a dizzying pace, as depicted in Table 2–1. The wars thus had a debilitating effect on Italian political development and were a major reason why a unified Italian state under a single government did not emerge for three more centuries.

Tragedy and irony mingled in the case of the Republic of Florence. The irony was that the wars indeed enhanced the power of the Florentine state; the tragedy was that this power became almost wholly repressive in its expression. The Medici-dominated government was overthrown in 1494, and Florence entered a period of political instability that culminated in the overthrow of republican government and the establishment of tyrannical rule. This sorry outcome did not result

**Table 2–1.   Violent or Sudden Changes of Government in Italian
City-States, 1494–1559**

Florence: 1494–95, 1512, 1527, 1530
Milan: 1499, 1500 (two changes), 1512, 1513 (two), 1515, 1521, 1522, 1524 (two changes)
Naples: 1495 (two changes), 1501, 1503
Cities under Venice: 1509 (two changes in some cases)
Rome: 1527
Bologna: 1506, 1511, 1512
Urbino: 1502 (three changes), 1503, 1516, 1521
Pisa: 1494, 1509
Savoy, Piedmont: alternating rulers between 1494 and 1559
Romagnol cities: numerous changes between 1499 and 1530
Genoa, Pavia, Brescia, Novara, Cremona, Parma, Piacenza: numerous changes between 1499 and
1540s

Source: Adapted from Lauro Martines, *Power and Imagination*, p. 296.

because Florence made no effort to defend itself. The city spent enormous amounts of money during the wars, burdening its citizens with
numerous new taxes, forced loans, and fines that enhanced the waxing
power of the city government and paved the way for despotism. But
only a small portion of Florence's expenditures in any given year were
devoted to supporting its own troops.[82] Like others of the city-states,
Florence sought by diplomatic maneuver to evade conflict and to
transfer the burden of war to other peninsular states and armies. The
result was that Florence yielded control of its foreign policy to the
Papacy, mortgaged its sovereignty, and lost its internal freedom. The
Fortezza da Basso, erected in the 1530s ostensibly to defend the city
against invaders, became instead a symbol of despotism.[83]

     Machiavelli, himself a Florentine state secretary and diplomat, was
a dismayed observer of the Italian collapse. He attributed it to the
weak leadership and lack of spirit of Italy's princes: "Never imagining
in times of peace that things might change . . . when evil times befell,
they could think only of flight and not of how they might defend
themselves."[84] Since it is impossible to replay history, it is impossible to
know if a concerted defensive military effort by the city-states might
have prevented the disaster that befell them. Italy had a competent and
proud military tradition, as well as the finest engineers in Europe;
Leonardo da Vinci, Michelangelo, Albrecht Dürer, and other great
minds all applied their talents to the Italian cause, but their efforts
were to no avail. Neither technology nor genius could compensate for
the absence of a central state, with its capacity for large-scale organiza-

tion. And no state could coalesce without strong political leadership, the absence of which made the Italian cause hopeless. Warfare may unleash impersonal forces that favor political centralization and state formation, but only flesh-and-blood political leaders can take advantage of those forces. State building requires state-makers.

William McNeill observes that beginning in the fourteenth century the geographical proximity of the European states facilitated the rapid spread of new military technologies; this in turn intensified war, made transcontinental hegemony impossible, and encouraged state formation.[85] A prime example was the success of the beleaguered Italian city-states in designing fortifications that could withstand repeated artillery fire. Utilizing a combination of defensive trenches, artillery for defense, and specially designed walls backed by loosely compacted earth to absorb cannon fire, the new star-shaped fortresses—a design known in French as the *trace italienne*—came too late and proved too costly to save the city-states from disaster.[86] But mercenary soldiers quickly spread the design to the rest of Europe, where it became a technical impediment to Habsburg ascendancy just at the critical historical moment when Charles V threatened to forge a single European empire. By precluding continental hegemony, the new technology fostered the coalescence of political power at the geographical level of the state.

A more felicitous fruit of transnational information exchange was the effect of the Italian Wars in spreading the cultural glories of the Italian Renaissance to the rest of Europe. When the heterogeneous mercenary armies of France disbanded, the troops dispersed in every direction across Europe, carrying news "of a warm, sunlit land inhabited by a people who lived a life of cultivated refinement . . . but who—perhaps for that very reason—were too disunited to defend themselves against a determined invader."[87]

In the final accounting, Western civilization derived an immeasurable benefit from the fact that Italy spent its finest creative energies not on impregnable bastions and standing armies but on seemingly more fragile works of Renaissance art, architecture, and culture; these have continued to enrich Western civilization long after the importance of star-shaped citadels has faded into obscurity.

CONCLUSION: THE MILITARY ROOTS OF MODERN POLITICS

An iron triangle of arms, capital, and bureaucracy was forged at the very birth of the modern state. It has been with us ever since. In a self-perpetuating cycle, the need to wage war impelled rulers to accumulate capital in order to fund bureaucracies; these in turn extracted more capital, which bought armies, which made possible greater wars. Each war in turn pushed the cycle to a new level of destruction, as well as to higher levels of power accumulation (see Figure 2–1). In this manner, war undermined the feudal structure of medieval Europe. The French historian Bernard Guenée observes the following of this formative period:

> War had thus forced States to resolve financial, administrative and political difficulties. Their structure had been profoundly altered by it. . . . For only the richest and most powerful States could afford to levy, pay, equip, and supply an army, and this army then enabled them to crush all internal resistance and to threaten their neighbors. Italy's misfortunes at the end of the fifteen century stemmed solely from [her division] into States which were each too small to maintain an effective army.[88]

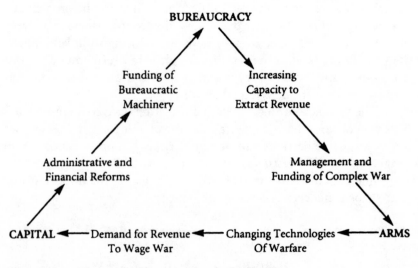

Figure 2–1. The cycle of war and state formation

The crude dictates of survival in the Renaissance era meant that only the larger, wealthier states could ride high on the tide of military advancement.

Douglass North has offered an analogy from economic theory to explain the transition from medieval politics, with its multiplicity of small states, to the modern era of large centralized states. He compares this transition to what occurs in an industry with numerous small firms when a technological change is introduced that makes the optimal size of a competitive firm much larger than before.[89] The small firms must increase in size or go bankrupt. As the weaker ones go out of business, the industry becomes an unstable oligopoly, where a reduced number of larger firms engage in cutthroat competition for market share. In many respects, medieval principalities were indeed like small business firms, each of them the private domain of one ruler. The increasing cost and complexity of warfare created a new economy of scale that favored larger states and made control of large tracts of territory more feasible. The structure of Europe accordingly became that of an unstable oligopoly—one reason perhaps why conflict was so intense in the century after 1559.

The debacle of the Italian city-states shows the difficulty of such small "firms" surviving unbridled war, whereas the case of the Swiss Confederation indicates that economy of scale was not an absolute condition of survival: a small state could survive if its territory was defensible and its population highly cohesive. The Swiss case also demonstrates that Max Weber was wrong in his assertion that the modern state is absolutely dependent upon bureaucratic administration.[90] Centralized bureaucracy, with its inevitable dysfunctions and tendency to enhance state power, is not the inevitable destiny of states in the modern age, nor an inexorable outcome of state formation. Geography, human agency, leadership, and national character are crucial, if elusive, variables that can influence the manner in which war shapes the political course of a given people.

With respect to human freedom, the three paths of state formation led to widely divergent outcomes. The continental path led toward absolutist rule, the crushing of local privileges, and the withering of once sacrosanct liberties. The constitutional path led to a lesser degree of centralization and left intact a medieval structure of traditional freedoms and consent by assemblies. The coalitional path produced hardly any central state and forged the most free system of all; it was the sole path that led to early republican government. In short, the degree of state formation was inversely proportional to the degree of human liberty that prevailed. But the Italian case shows that where no cohesive center develops and the polity is disunited as well, anarchy and state dissolution result—hardly a propitious outcome either. The delicate balance between despotism and anarchy rests on the precarious fulcrum of state organization for war.

By 1559, of course, the processes of state formation and modernization had barely commenced. Though certain features of modernity had begun to materialize in Europe—territorial sovereignty, geographically fixed government, bureaucratic administration, and a growing distinction between public and private domains—no state could as yet be described as truly modern, even in the basic sense of nonmedieval. None was fully sovereign within its territory; the basis of every state remained dynastic and partly religious in nature; governmental administrations retained much that was medieval in character; a feudal society remained entrenched in most countries. The Valois and Habsburg monarchs may have risen above their medieval status as *primus inter pares*, but they were as yet a long way from ruling as *rex imperator*. Nevertheless, the passing of the medieval age was proceeding inexorably, and its demise was in large measure a consequence of advancing military technology and the upheaval of war. The roots of political modernity were military in their nature and origin.

The thesis that war gave birth to the modern state is accepted by many historians, but not by all. One prominent scholar of Renaissance military history, J. R. Hale, has argued that war was only marginally a political issue in early modern Europe. But Hale weakens his case by narrowing the term *war* to include only international conflicts—not military rivalry, internal strife, or civil war. He argues instead that defensive preparations, not actual war, led to the rise of state institutions—an untenable distinction in an era filled with constant strife. At one point, Hale argues that Spain's record of continuous warfare was not as important as the struggles over the consolidation of the traditionally divided Iberian peninsula, the adventure of trans-Atlantic empire, and "the strain of religious-racial conflicts," as if all these did not involve some measure of war. He argues that artillery did not centralize power, but admits that "the emphasis on cannon and gunpowder in the records of state intervention is striking." If there is a case against the primacy of war in state formation, this is not it.[91]

Most scholars of the early modern state acknowledge the role of war and state rivalries in its emergence, but offer other explanations as well. J. H. Shennan emphasizes the evolution of political and judicial philosophy.[92] Gianfranco Poggi points to the rise of towns, of city-based production, and the general commercialization of the economy.[93] Charles Tilly stresses the role of urbanization and emerging capital centers. Immanuel Wallerstein and Perry Anderson, writing from a Marxist perspective, emphasize the primacy of economic factors.[94] Yet while identifying a wide range of factors all of these scholars affirm the importance (and many affirm the centrality) of warfare in the origin of the modern state.[95] Certainly the rise of the state was not a unicausal phenomenon, but war was a catalyst that intensified the effect of other factors. A valid alternate theory would have to postulate causal factors that would be fully operative *even in the absence of war*. And its proponents would need to find actual examples in the Renaissance era of centralization, bureaucratization, and the breakdown of medieval institutions occurring in the absence of war or in ways clearly unrelated to war. They will search for a long time.

The Military Revolution and the Early Modern State

Many princes have lost their countries and ruined their subjects by failing to maintain sufficient military forces for their protection, fearing to tax them too heavily. Some people have even fallen into slavery under their enemies because they have wanted too much liberty.

Cardinal Richelieu, *Testament Politique*

During the century from 1559 to the end of the English civil wars, Europe experienced the most intense and unremitting warfare of any period in its history before or since. Not until the twentieth century would the world again witness slaughter on so vast a scale. Yet World War I and World War II lasted a total of only twelve years, while in the century after the Treaty of Cateau-Cambrésis (signed in 1559), Europe was engulfed in almost constant war. The French Wars of Religion raged for 36 years (1562–98); the Dutch revolt against Spain (1559–1648) spanned two generations and came to be called "The Eighty Years' War"; the bitter religious and political strife of the Thirty Years' War (1618–48) pulled almost every European power into combat on an unprecedented scale and devastated the Germanic lands. The English Civil Wars (1642–60), a protracted French–Spanish war (1648–59), and the Northern War (1655–60) capped off this century of conflict. But this list of major wars paints at best a partial picture, for this was also the era of Spanish–Portuguese rivalry, of English–Scottish and English–Irish conflict, of endemic war between Russia and Poland, of the attempted invasion of England by the Spanish Armada, of the Battle of Lepanto and other encounters between Christian Europe and the Ottoman Empire.

Historians have called this era of upheaval the Age of Power, the Crisis of the Seventeenth Century, the Transformation of Europe, the Age of Religious Wars, the Era of the Military Revolution. It was the great bridge between the medieval and the modern world, an era in which war was not merely an extension of politics but the very essence of politics, both at home and abroad. The violence of the era had political consequences on three different levels. At the level of the continent as a whole, the religious wars shattered the medieval vision of Europe as a unified Catholic imperium and made impossible the hegemony of any one kingdom or religion. At the local level, war undermined the princely particularism of feudal society and, by stimulating major concentrations of armed power, reversed the tendency of Europe toward territorial fragmentation. Between these two levels, a new political unit took shape—the sovereign state, the only organization capable of mobilizing the human and material resources necessary for modern warfare. The coming of the state was the culmination of trends going back as far as the Hundred Years' War, as the previous chapter has shown.

A CENTURY OF TRANSFORMATIVE WAR

A triad of historical forces gave the century from 1559 to 1660 its powerfully transformative quality. The first element of the triad was a *military revolution* in the technology, tactics, and scale of war. The second was acute *ideological conflict*, namely the intellectual, social, and political tensions unleashed by the Protestant Reformation. The third was a *hegemonic struggle* for domination of the continent, the Habsburg bid for supremacy in Europe. A similar conjunction of forces has occurred only two other times in European history—from 1789 to 1815 and from 1914 to 1945—and in both cases it was also associated with radical transformations in the nature of European states.

THE MILITARY REVOLUTION

The Gunpowder Revolution examined in the last chapter was only the beginning of a much larger revolution in military affairs, which culminated in the massive bloodletting of the Thirty Years' War. There were several components to this revolution: a quantum increase in the firepower of armies; advances in tactics, training, and strategy intended to exploit this firepower; the proliferation of star-shaped citadels of *trace italienne* design, resulting in lengthy siege wars; a dramatic increase in the size of European armies; and finally, the growing complexity and administrative burden of war. Each of these elements had important implications for the development of European polities.[1]

Rising Firepower
More than any other factor, the rapid proliferation of handguns and siege cannon was the genesis of the Military Revolution. We have already seen in the last chapter how gunpowder weapons rendered smaller political units and provincial lords—anyone who relied on walled castles and cavalry forces for defense—highly vulnerable to attack. Rulers who did not already have the new weaponry, and who could afford it, scrambled to get it; those who already possessed it enlarged their stockpiles severalfold. The costs and organizational effort of procuring and maintaining large stocks of artillery, or of deploying large infantry formations armed with muskets (a Spanish innovation in the 1550s), spurred the centralization of political power across western Europe.

Advances in Tactics, Training, and Operations
Effective use of artillery and handguns required tight command and control, better tactical coordination among military subunits, and improved logistics. Maurice of Nassau, the great Dutch commander, pioneered numerous tactical innovations, such as coordinated volleys and line formations, that necessitated strict command procedures as well as constant practice and drill. Drawing on the vocabulary and methods of the ancient Roman legions, he produced the first illustrated drill manual, while John II of Nassau founded the *Kriegs- und Ritterschule* at Siegen in 1617, one of Europe's first military academies. Via countless mercenary networks, the Dutch methods of drill and

command spread to other European armies. Gustavus II Adolphus of Sweden adopted them enthusiastically, and in doing so created the first modern army administration in Europe, complete with standardization of equipment, organized pay and supply services, and the capacity to conduct combined arms operations. The modern command army thus emerged on the stage of Europe, highly disciplined and conceived as a pliant instrument of state authority. The success of this type of hierarchical organization would make it an attractive template for organizing all kinds of large-scale human endeavors in the future, from civil service bureaucracies to industrial factories to totalitarian states.

Advances in Fortifications

The century of the Military Revolution was one of siege warfare, with large armies conducting prolonged sieges against well-engineered and heavily defended fortresses. The painstaking, plodding nature of siege warfare partly accounts for the extraordinarily long wars of the era, the Eighty Years' War being the quintessential example. The high cost of the new star-shaped bastions was a factor in the consolidation of centralized states, since only very large or capital-rich states could afford to construct them. Siege warfare also encouraged a division of labor within military organizations, as technical experts and engineers played a growing role in the service of army and state. Maurice of Nassau created a whole hierarchy of officials to oversee engineering projects and even established a chair of fortification at Leyden University. There was intense competition between Spanish and Dutch fortification engineers; technical advances made by one country were rapidly copied by the other and diffused across Europe by the mercenary officers serving in the Netherlands.[2]

Growth in the Size and Cost of Armies

The size of European armies deployed in wartime rose more or less steadily from 1400 to 1559, then took a dramatic leap in the century that followed. The increase after 1559 is depicted in Table 3-1.[3] The armies of this era were raised largely by commercial contract and contained large numbers of foreign mercenaries; their allegiance was purchased and did not necessarily flow from any higher loyalty to state or nation. But this does not alter the fact that they represented specific states and defended their interests. The high cost of contract armies, and their growing size, invariably meant higher expenditures for the state, with their concomitant higher taxes. Theodore Rabb has estimated that the per capita tax burden in Europe at least *quadrupled* between 1520 and 1670. But it was not just the growth of armies that escalated the costs of war; the cost of outfitting each individual soldier also increased. In 1596, one of the ministers of Philip II estimated that for an equal number of men, three times as much money was needed as had been spent by Charles V; by 1630, the cost per soldier had climbed to perhaps five times the amount of a century before.[4]

Table 3–1.   Size of European armies, 1559–1660 and 1700

YEAR	CASTILE/ SPAIN	FRANCE	ENGLAND	SWEDEN	UNITED PROVINCES
1555	150,000	50,000	20,000		N/A
1595	200,000	80,000	30,000	15,000	20,000
1621				18,000	
1625	150,000				
1631				83,000	
1635	300,000	150,000		180,000	50,000
1652		70,000			
1655	100,000	100,000	53,000	50,000	
1700	50,000	392,000	87,000	100,000	100,000

Source: Data from Rasler and Thompson, *War and State-Making*, p. 66; Michael Roberts, *Essays on Swedish History, The Swedish Imperial Experience*; Charles Firth, *Cromwell's Army*, pp. 34–35.

The Administrative Burden of War

Changes in the technology, tactics, and scale of war increased its overall complexity and made the administrative aptitude of governments a critical factor in achieving success in battle. The Military Revolution thus precipitated a Bureaucratic Revolution: governments formed war offices; civilian bureaucracies sprang up to manage military production and supply; finance departments, reeling from the spiraling costs of war, faced drastic overhaul and rationalization. On the average, the size of central state bureaucracies probably quadrupled during this era. Bureaucracy in turn enhanced revenue extraction and arms procurement, in the familiar fiscal-military cycle outlined in the preceding chapter. As Michael Roberts has observed, by 1660 the modern art of war was born, with its large armies, command discipline, authoritarian states, submergence of the individual, and troubling conjunction of finance capital and technology. "The road lay open, broad and straight, to the abyss of the twentieth century."[5]

THE CRISIS OF THE REFORMATION

Technical and tactical advances in warfare, profound though they were, do not alone account for the transformation that Europe experienced in the century after 1559. The vast political changes of this era are incomprehensible without taking into account the great cleavage of the Protestant Reformation and the intensity of violent conflict that it unleashed. The Reformation was the most consequential historical event between the fall of the Roman Empire and the French Revolution, and its greatest impact occurred from 1520 to 1660, concurrent with the Military Revolution.[6] Contemporaries of all classes were far more conscious of the transformations wrought by the Reformation than of the changing nature of war, though the two were intertwined.

By accentuating the social and political schisms of Europe, the Reformation imparted a fervor to warfare—an ideological and emotional intensity—that partly accounted for the scale and brutality of conflict from 1559 to 1660 and that undoubtedly accelerated the Military Revolution itself. Religious tension exacerbated warfare not only between states but *within* states, making the entire century one of endemic civil war. As in the preceding century, civil war broke out most often at the conclusion of large international wars. The religious basis of these civil wars often concealed other underlying and long-standing conflicts, such as the irrepressible rivalry between the nobles and their monarchs, who usually managed to end up on opposite sides of the theological chasm. The civil wars of the century were critical to state formation, for as internal violence mounted it became increasingly clear that only strong, centralized governments could overcome the deep divisions of their societies and impose order on fractured polities. In effect, the sovereign, secular state was "invented" as a solution to the wars of religion.

According to David Held, the whole fabric of medieval thought had to be shattered before the state could emerge as the highest claimant on human loyalty. More than any other event, the Reformation accomplished this, prompting new ways of thinking about political authority.[7] As the ultimate rebellion against established authority, the Reformation inevitably gave impetus to other forms of rebellion, including class struggles in which religion played only a marginal role. Numerous peasant uprisings were fueled in part by the antiauthoritarian spirit unleashed by Luther, Calvin, and Zwingli (the largest of which, the Peasants' War, ended in the slaughter of over 100,000 German rebels). Yet, paradoxically, though the Reformation kindled rebellion against authority the long-term effect of the religious wars was to *strengthen* political authority at the national level. As the supranational authority of emperor and Church declined, the *state* grew stronger at the expense both of particularist centers of power and of aspirants to universal hegemony in Europe.

The primary exception to this pattern was Germany, where the devastation of the Thirty Years' War seriously damaged the prospects for national unification and central rule. That war, however, was not only a religious conflict but the grand climax of the Habsburg bid for mastery in Europe, the third or hegemonic element of the triad of forces that shaped politics in this century.

THE HABSBURG BID FOR EUROPEAN ASCENDANCY

For a century and a half after 1500, the threat of Habsburg hegemony loomed over Europe. Charles V in particular aspired to establish a universal Catholic empire as a way to bottle the genie of the Protestant Reformation and restore the spiritual unity of the medieval world. Even after his abdication in 1556 split the dynasty into two halves— Spain and the western domains under Philip II, the Holy Roman Empire and eastern Habsburg lands under Ferdinand I—the rest of Europe still feared that a coordinated drive by the two wings of the dynasty might successfully dominate the continent. Implausible though this outcome may appear in retrospect, France, England, and the Scandinavian countries were determined to avert it, as were the German princes (both Protestant *and* Catholic) who owed allegiance to the Austrian emperor, and equally the rulers of the Dutch provinces whose new sovereign resided in Madrid.

Virtually every war of the century unfolded against this backdrop. During the Eighty Years' War, the Dutch received frequent support from both England and France, who sought to weaken their Habsburg rival. France repeatedly went to war against Spain, their shared Catholicism notwithstanding. The scope of alliance formation against Habsburg power reached its apogee in the Thirty Years' War, known to contemporaries as "the Great War." Prior to the twentieth-century war of the same reputation, it was the closest thing to total war Europe ever experienced, a crucible of modernization that helped melt the institutions of medieval government into new political forms.

The war evolved in three primary stages, with each successive stage drawing additional parties into conflict in a classic spiral of escalation that eventually drew all of Europe into the maelstrom.[8] The conflict began in 1618 as an encounter between the rebellious Protestant states of Bohemia, Silesia, and Moravia and a resurgent Counter-Reformation under Ferdinand II of Austria. When the former offered their allegiance to Frederick V, Elector Palatine, Ferdinand responded with massive force, assisted by Duke Maximilian of Bavaria. The imperial forces under the command of Tilly made rapid advances, and in 1620 routed the rebel forces at the Battle of White Mountain, before going on to occupy the Palatinate and depose Frederick.

With the issue of the Bohemian Crown settled, the war should have ended. Instead it entered its second or "German phase," as Ferdinand and Maximilian carried their crusade into the northern Protestant territories of Germany. The progress of the imperial armies alarmed not only Protestant England and Scandinavia, but *Catholic* France and Venice as well; all feared that Ferdinand's victories in Germany would encourage him to pursue Habsburg ascendancy over all of Europe. In 1625, the emperor retained the services of a military entrepreneur, Albrecht von Wallenstein, a resourceful Bohemian with a gift for military organization, who quickly raised an army of 30,000 to supplement Tilly's forces. In 1625–26, the combined imperial forces routed a Protestant counteroffensive by Christian IV of Denmark. By 1628, Wallenstein had increased his army to 125,000 men, occupied most of Denmark, and gained control of the Baltic coast. Alarmed by the advances of this "popish league," Sweden prepared for war.

From here, the war entered its third stage, becoming a transcontinental conflict of vast significance, indeed the first "world war" in history. The fear of Habsburg ascendancy galvanized France into action. Richelieu was determined to thwart the European ambitions of the Habsburg empire, utterly heedless of the consequences for the Catholic Church. The French agreed to subsidize the Swedish army to the amount of a million *livres* a year. For more than a decade prior to this crisis, King Gustavus Adolphus had undertaken a vast political and military reform in Sweden, exploiting the lessons of statecraft and war learned by Atlantic monarchs during the previous century. Having never played much of a role in European affairs before, Sweden in 1630 suddenly "burst upon the European firmament like some new star."[9] The Swedish army decisively defeated Tilly at Breitenfeld and in short order rolled back the Habsburg gains in Germany, despoiled Bavaria, and prepared to invade Austria. But in 1632, Gustavus Adolphus perished in battle against Wallenstein at Lützen, and the Swedish army soon suffered reverses.

The colorful Wallenstein has received inordinate attention from historians; some even claim that he grasped the nature of power in the seventeenth century better than Olivares or Richelieu.[10] In fact, he was an anachronism whose limits became clear barely a year after Lützen, when Ferdinand charged him with treason and imperial agents murdered him. Military genius and entrepreneurial brilliance aside, Wallenstein failed to comprehend the changing nature of politics in his era. He was merely one of a long line of German military entrepreneurs whose art—the raising of private armies for profit—was rapidly being outmoded by permanent military establishments under state administration. Never again would a privately raised army play a pivotal role in European warfare.

The importance of state-controlled armies became evident beginning in 1635, when the war, its religious origins largely forgotten, widened to encompass all of continental Europe. France declared war against the entire Habsburg axis—Austria, Spain, and the Spanish Netherlands—while continuing to subsidize Sweden's forces in Germany. For thirteen years Europe's largest armies fought across the face of Germany, waging campaigns of a geographical scale and complexity that would have been inconceivable in the medieval era. Not yet able to fully master the fiscal and logistical challenges of waging war on so large a scale, the occupying armies ravaged the land and terrorized the inhabitants as they sought to provide for their soldiers. Millions perished. The Military Revolution had progressed beyond the capacity of states to master its management, with consequences so terrible that fear of a similar war contributed to a new restraint in warfare throughout the ensuing century.

In 1648, after four years of complicated negotiations at which virtually every state in Europe was represented, the Peace of Westphalia ended the war. It was the first grand settlement in European history, covering every important issue of the war and endorsed by all the major powers of the day.[11] It actually consisted of two agreements, the Treaties of Osnabrück and of Münster, which ratified a revised version of the formula agreed on at Augsburg over ninety years earlier: each prince would regulate the conduct of religious affairs on his territory; religious tolerance was encouraged, and princes were enjoined not to impose a specific faith on their subjects. This formula ended the religious wars that had plagued Europe for over a century and ensured that henceforth the state would be a secular entity and that religion would never again play a dominant role in international affairs. (The papacy had no doubt about the implications: Innocent X denounced the Westphalian treaties as "null, void, invalid, iniquitous, unjust, damnable, reprobate, inane, empty of meaning and effect for all times."[12]) The settlement also recognized the independence of the Dutch Republic and the Swiss Confederation, confirmed territorial concessions to France, and fixed territorial boundaries that endured with only minor variations for over two hundred years.

The Peace of Westphalia is often viewed as marking the birth of the modern European state system and the formal recognition of the concept of state sovereignty. But this is far more evident in retrospect than it was at the time. The German principalities that won the right in the Treaty of Münster to declare war, impose taxes, and form alliances independent of the Holy Roman Empire, had hardly attained to the status of sovereignty as we understand it today. In fact, it was not until 1660 or even 1670—after Louis XIV of France had subdued the *Fronde*, demilitarized the French countryside, and fortified his national borders—that the first fully sovereign state in Europe can be said to have emerged. The Thirty Years' War did not render Europe modern overnight, but it accelerated the modernizing forces already unleashed by the Military Revolution and the Reformation.

WAR AND STATE FORMATION IN THE AGE OF POWER

In order to understand how war influenced state formation in the era of the Military Revolution, we will first return to the kingdoms of the North Atlantic littoral, which we last left poised on the brink of the modern world. The triad of military, ideological, and hegemonic forces outlined above caused far-reaching changes in these westernmost states, which had earlier led Europe in the process of modern state formation. War had stimulated the centralization of power, the proliferation of bureaucracy, and the concomitant weakening of regional and seignorial power centers.[13] France continued to pursue the continental path of state formation, while England remained on a constitutional path, albeit with some centralizing tendencies. Spain, by contrast, had now entered a Golden Age, the pinnacle of its power and glory, before going into rapid decline, a casualty of the degenerative effects of war.

After attending to these venerable states, we will turn our attention to a pair of newcomers to the ranks of aspiring sovereignty: the Kingdom of Sweden and the United Provinces of the Netherlands, both of which dazzled the world of seventeenth-century Europe with their military accomplishments despite their diminutive size. They offer further examples of the constitutional and coalitional paths of state formation examined in the last chapter. Finally, we will look at the tragic case of Germany, where the massive violence of the Thirty Years' War caused political degeneration, with deleterious effects that continued to reverberate right into the twentieth century.

CIVIL WAR, FOREIGN WAR, AND STATE SOVEREIGNTY: THE CASE OF FRANCE

From 1562 to 1598, France experienced the degenerative effects of war on a massive scale. It is no accident that the French Wars of Religion broke out shortly after Cateau-Cambrésis: the Habsburg–Valois conflicts had exerted a unifying effect on France that had sublimated tensions growing beneath the surface, including mounting aristocratic resentment of the high taxes and debts the wars had produced. Radiating outward from Geneva, the rising force of Calvinism exacerbated the crisis. At the onset of the civil wars, only about 10 percent of France's 20 million inhabitants were Huguenots, but among the nobility, the ratio was nearly 40 percent. Calvinism became a gage with which leading provincial nobles—the Montmorency and Bourbon families in particular—challenged the primacy of the French Crown. Religious motivations notwithstanding, the war was at bottom a renewal of the historical rivalry between the Crown and the provincial nobility, a classic struggle between center and periphery.

Historians have identified at least eight distinct wars within the "Wars of Religion," but there were only three periods (1562, 1567–69, and 1587–89) during which large-scale military engagements occurred.[14] Assassinations, atrocities against civilians, and guerrilla raids predominated; famine and economic disruption took the lives of tens of thousands. The conflict at times assumed the form of a war of secession by the southwestern regions of France, where Huguenots dominated, but most of the larger battles were fought over Paris, revealing these wars to be primarily a struggle for control of the political center. The Bourbon candidate, Henry of Navarre, finally took Paris in 1594, but only after the assassination of his rivals, the repulsion of Spanish troops who intervened from the Netherlands, and a politic conversion to Catholicism. The new monarch, now Henry IV, required four more years to restore civil peace to France. This he accomplished in part by declaring war on Spain, a textbook example of diverting internal tensions into external conflict.[15] The France divided by war was thus reunified by war. Peace with Spain was signed in 1598, the same year the Edict of Nantes formally ended the religious fratricide.

The rapid reconstitution of the French state after 1594 illuminates why civil wars do not necessarily impede state formation, and sometimes even accelerate it. During the years of civil strife, the centralized taxation system originally put in place by Francis I become a prize of battle as rebellious provinces, lords, and towns captured segments of it for their own purposes. Troops from both sides enforced revenue collection, diverting funds to private armies and fiefdoms and sometimes triggering local tax revolts. Evidence that the partitioned tax system continued to function comes from French state records showing that total revenue from the *taille* actually *increased* from 1562 to about 1588, in the midst of the war, though not all these funds reached the Central Treasury in Paris.[16] As Martin Wolfe put it, monarchical institutions were maintained vertically but were broken up horizontally. Yet when the religious wars ended, the French central government was able to weld the tax system back together rapidly. Its vertical integrity and operational continuity during the war made reconstruction of its shattered shards eminently feasible after 1594.[17]

The key to this successful reconstitution was the tenacity of the French bureaucracy, which continued to operate throughout thirty-six years of violent strife and even grew in size as new offices were created and sold to raise revenue. The venality and corruption of the French bureaucracy were notorious, and it suffered from religious factionalism; yet a series of devoted secretaries of state kept the machinery of government running despite the disruptions of the Wars of Religion. Many of the top officials who had served during the war continued service under Henry IV, including Nicholas de Neurfille, Sieur de Villeroy, whose *fifty-eight years* of government service, most of it as a secretary of state, extended from the reign of Francis II to that of Louis XIII![18] The tenacity of this state apparatus helped make possible the reintegration of the French taxation system and the restoration of a strong monarchy after the wars. A similar pattern manifests itself throughout French history—after the *Fronde*; after the French Revolution; after the Revolution of 1848, the Paris Commune, and the Second World War. Periods of revolution or war, however tumultuous, have always been followed by reconstitution of the state and reassertion of the central bureaucracy. This pattern shows the tendency of *structure*—entrenched political and bureaucratic institutions—to predominate over *process* in the long run. This may be part of the answer as to why the centralizing effects of war have tended to outweigh its disintegrative effects throughout history.

The half century after the Edict of Nantes saw the consolidation and strengthening of the French state under the leadership of a series of powerful monarchical officials—the Duke of Sully, Cardinal Richelieu, and Cardinal Mazarin.[19] Like the Count-Duke Olivares of Spain, Thomas Wentworth of England, and Axel Oxenstierna of Sweden, they typified a class of person that did not exist in the medieval era: powerful ministers who rose to the pinnacle of the state apparatus by strength of competence and will, rather than by their high birth or inherited wealth alone. Mazarin's low birth and foreign parentage particularly displeased the *Frondeurs* of the French nobility, who found it difficult to accept this erosion of the traditional linkage between power and pedigree.

Integral to the consolidation of the French state that occurred during the tenure of these ministers was the long but ultimately successful struggle of the Crown against its myriad internal adversaries: first, the Huguenots, whose resistance to royal authority erupted anew under Louis XIII, only to be finally crushed in the siege of La Rochelle (1628); second, the widespread tax revolts that occurred after France intervened in the Thirty Year' War; and finally, the *Fronde* of 1648–53, the defeat of which essentially confirmed the unassailable authority of the monarchy for over a century to come.[20] Absolutism arose in France when the central government demonstrated its military superiority by triumphing in what amounted to continual civil war.

An unabashed centralizer and disciple of absolutism, the Duke of Sully became chief minister to Henry IV by virtue of his service during the civil war as a gunner, engineer, and administrator. His tenure (1599–1610) illustrates how military rivalry and defensive preparations can promote state formation in ways similar to the effect of actual warfare. At enormous cost, Sully expanded the French navy and oversaw construction of nearly fifty bastions and fortified points from the Ardennes to Marseilles. He devoted particular attention to revitalizing the French artillery, his panacea for "all the maddening maladies of the state." Appalled by the condition of French gunnery, he dismissed incompetent officials, enlarged the service, and initiated direct government production of arms at the Paris arsenal; by 1610, he had added at least one hundred large siege cannon to the army's inventory. The annual expenditures of the French government increased over 60 percent from 1600 to 1610, in addition to which it accumulated reserves of over 15 million *livres*, intended as a war chest for possible hostilities against Spain or Austria. To achieve such levels of expenditure, Sully overhauled the financial machinery of the state: improving accounting procedures, enhancing the central secretariat, and creating a more rational hierarchy with clear lines of authority.[21]

If the religion-based cleavage of the Reformation dominated Sully's day, the imperatives of the Military-Bureaucratic Revolution and the struggle against Habsburg hegemony defined the era of Cardinal Richelieu as chief minister of Louis XIII from 1624 to 1642. War was the dominant feature of his tenure. France fought several smaller wars from 1624–32 before beginning its massive intervention in the Thirty Years' War in 1635. From then until 1659, the French were on a war footing continually, and the familiar cycle of taxation, military expenditures, and bureaucratic expansion rolled on at a faster pace than ever. France had as few as 12,000 men under arms in 1629; but during the war years, it maintained between 150,000 and 200,000 troops continually in the field.[22] The Military Revolution made this an expensive proposition, and the existing fiscal system of France, though modern by the standards of the day, broke down under the strain. The state went heavily into debt, and all three types of taxes—indirect, direct, and extraordinary—were increased. Revenue from the *taille* alone skyrocketed after 1635 and more than quadrupled within a decade. As always, the increase fell largely on the peasantry, who bitterly resented it. The consequence was tax rebellion on an unprecedented scale.[23]

France had experienced popular uprisings before, but never of the frequency and scale seen under Richelieu. There were major uprisings in Saintonge, Lower Normandy, Guienne, Sologne, and Boulonnais, as well as the more famous Croquant uprisings of 1637 and 1643.[24] Historians have cited a host of causes for the rebellions, but three stand out: resistance to encroaching centralization, resentment toward the army and its frequent abuses, and opposition to the burden of wartime taxation. The fact that taxation was administered through a venal system of tax farmers and local officials did not alter the reality that the central state stood behind these tax collectors and was the prime mover of the rising levies. It was no coincidence that the insurrections largely took place between 1630 and 1660, the period of transition to absolutist rule; the revolts were a barometer of the pain caused by the assertion of central power. And though royal authorities sometimes retreated in the face of spirited local resistance, the state always returned like a relentless incoming tide.

Several historians of Marxist inclination have portrayed these tax revolts as a form of class struggle. Yet there were numerous examples of nobles or gentry leading the uprisings; for though the burden of taxation ultimately fell on the peasantry, higher taxes also threatened the feudal income of landowners. The tax revolts were a kind of low-intensity civil war, with virtually all social classes opposing the infringing power of the military-bureaucratic center. In the Dauphiné, for example, agrarian unrest and urban tax revolts occurred in 1625–26, 1641, and 1642, but the provincial Estates also protested the *taille* increases strenuously, leading the Crown to suppress the Council of the Nobility and forbid meetings of the Second Estate. The Dauphiné thus became the first autonomous province (*pays d'état*) to lose its privileged status.[25]

The main vehicle for extending state power into the interior of France was a system of royal agents known as provincial *intendants*, an institution born in and perpetuated by war.[26] Desperate for revenue but frustrated by rampant tax resistance at the local level, Richelieu greatly expanded their number and authority. In addition to overseeing tax collection, the *intendants* helped enforce order in the provinces. They had close ties with the French army and assisted in the recruitment of troops, the oversight of military accounts, and the maintenance of fortifications. There was a logic to this, since the army played a growing role in enforcing central taxation as the Richelieu era progressed. Some *intendants* even commanded special companies of *fusiliers* dedicated to tax collection.[27] The rising military power of the state thus directly strengthened its capacity to extract the revenue that upheld it.[28]

Resentment of the rising power of the state led to the outbreak of the *Fronde* in 1648, the last serious challenge by the provincial Estates and the nobility to the centralizing measures of the Crown. One of the main demands put to Mazarin by the *Frondeurs* was for the abolition of the *intendants*, despised symbols of central authority. As civil war spread across France, provincial insurgents usurped local tax collection, and state revenues plunged catastrophically, much as had happened in the Wars of Religion. This time, however, royal victory came much sooner. The bottom line was that the opponents of the government were incapable of raising military forces sufficient to match the French army. The "Governmental Revolution" of Louis XIII and Richelieu, as it has been called, and the military power that it forged, made possible a decisive royalist triumph.[29] The specter of renewed civil war also persuaded many of the nobility and propertied classes that there was no alternative to a strong monarch; the logic of the Hobbesian compact was inexorable. Though France remained troubled for many years after the *Fronde*, the absolutist trend continued apace, and the Bourbon monarchy faced no major crisis again until the French Revolution. What is more, France decisively defeated Spain in a long war in 1648–59 to emerge as the strongest power in Europe and the archetype of post-Westphalian modernity. Forged in conflict, the secular centralized bureaucratic state had prevailed both at home and abroad.

One other facet of the development of the French state calls for attention. This was the systematic destruction of hundreds of privately-owned fortifications and walled strongholds throughout central France, a process sometimes known as "the demilitarization of France." Even in 1600, after Henry IV had restored royal authority, there remained in France many private fortifications that could still serve as centers of brigandage or of resistance to central rule. They could also be costly to the state, as royal forces were obliged to occupy various citadels to ensure that these citadels did not fall into enemy hands. Under Henry IV, the policy had been established that "no places should be fortified but the frontiers,"[30] and as many as two dozen citadels were destroyed in his reign. Richelieu continued this policy, advising Louis XIII that "all fortresses not on the frontier must be razed; we should keep only those at river crossings or which serve as a bridle to mutinous great towns."[31]

The policy of demolishing private fortifications in central France reached its apogee under Louis XIV. Marshal Sébastien Le Prestre de Vauban, the brilliant engineer who ranked second only to Louvois as a military leader under the Sun King, created a virtual demilitarized zone in central France by destroying or neglecting to maintain six hundred or more fortresses or walled cities in that area. Even the fortifications around Paris were demolished in 1670.[32] This policy was aimed at curtailing the penchant of the French aristocracy for war and ensuring that internal challengers would have no bases from which to operate. It was an unprecedented assertion of the military supremacy of the Crown, an important step in establishing the state's monopoly of the legitimate use of violence.

Vauban also built a massive network of border fortifications that enhanced France's security and proclaimed its emergence as a territorially-based state bounded by well-defined geographical frontiers.[33] The dual accomplishments of razing fortifications in the interior and enhancing them on the border were essential steps in the emergence of true state sovereignty for France. The domestic tranquility that demilitarization brought to the French heartland, after the periodic ravages of civil war and brigandage, was one of the undeniably positive fruits of the modern state, its coercive excesses notwithstanding. War made the state, and the state made peace.

CIVIL WAR AND CONSTITUTIONAL SURVIVAL: THE CASE OF ENGLAND

While absolutism arose in a France beset by constant bloodshed, constitutionalism survived in an England sheltered from the winds of war. From the accession of Elizabeth I to the outbreak of the Civil Wars in 1642, England enjoyed over eighty years of relative peace, at least by comparison with the unrelieved carnage on the continent. The only serious military threat it faced during this period was the attempted invasion of the Spanish Armada in 1588, the turning point of a long naval war that ended in 1604. England fought other overseas wars in this period—twice against France (1562–63 and 1627–30) and once more against Spain (1625–30), but neither adversary ever threatened English territory and no large-scale ground combat took place. One effect of this was that the English monarchy remained subject to constitutional limitations of medieval origin that elsewhere in Europe disintegrated under the compulsion of violence.

The relative tranquility of the Elizabethan and early Stuart years had a marked effect on both Crown and aristocracy, and on their rivalry.[34] During the extended peace from 1562 to 1588, the barons had little opportunity for military service, and by the turn of the century most private fortresses were in decline. The Earl of Leicester maintained modern and well-equipped fortifications, including siege cannon, at Kenilworth, but he was almost the sole exception to the trend, and he never challenged the Queen's authority directly. By the time Charles I summoned the Long Parliament in 1640, eight decades of only sporadic warfare meant that few of the aristocracy retained any practical knowledge of how to fight. Sir Walter Raleigh observed that while in earlier times a typical nobleman might have had enough in his armory to equip several thousand men, there were by his own day few who could arm fifty.[35] On the other hand, small arms were distributed widely among the propertied classes, whose interests were focused in Parliament.

The declining military importance of the English aristocracy stemmed also from the late Tudor shift to reliance on naval power as the primary line of defense against invasion. Elizabeth's accession to the throne took place in 1558, the same year Calais was lost to France forever. The loss of England's last toehold on the continent forcibly confirmed its status as an island power. Naval expenditures accordingly increased to levels much higher than under the earlier Tudors, particularly after Elizabeth received word of the Spanish naval victory at Lepanto. The Crown did not totally neglect land forces—from

1558–61, for example, it made large purchases of arms for the militia—but sea power came first. In the 1570s, regular naval expenditures amounted to an average 11,175 pounds per annum; in the 1580s, 27,481 pounds; in the 1590s, 48,538 pounds.[36] Such high outlays were feasible because, in the absence of war, trade was flourishing and state revenues were rising. But at the same time, those increasing revenues had the effect of allaying any internal pressure for fiscal or structural reform.

England's reliance on a naval defense strategy and prolonged years of insular isolation and peace thus saddled the Stuart monarchy with fateful weaknesses that became painfully apparent during the first Civil War. Peace had caused "administrative arthritis," in the words of one historian, who has noted that since the Stuarts never faced a realistic threat of invasion, they never had a good excuse to implement unpalatable fiscal innovations.[37] While on the continent the Military Revolution precipitated sweeping administrative, fiscal, and military reforms, the English monarchy found it difficult to modernize its medieval ways. Under Charles I, the total number of paid officials was under 3,000, and most of those were attached to the royal household; only 900 or so could be considered professional civil servants, a figure far smaller than in France.[38] This suggests one answer to the long-standing historical debate over why the French monarchy prevailed with relative ease over the *Fronde*, while the English monarchy suffered abysmal defeat against a Parliamentary uprising just a few years later. Extensive involvement in continental warfare had steeled the institutions of the French monarchy, but not the English ones. After the Peace of Westphalia, Mazarin had large numbers of troops available to deploy against the *Frondeurs*, whereas the absence of a standing army in England now left Charles vulnerable to his adversaries.[39]

Like so many civil wars in European history, the proximate cause of the English Civil War was military defeat.[40] In the second Bishops' Wars with Scotland (1640), English troops fared abysmally, in part because the Short Parliament had denied the Crown sufficient funds to field a decent army. Bankrupt after the defeat, the King was forced to convene Parliament once again, but the Long Parliament (1640–1653), like a magnifying glass, focused to a white-hot point the resentments of disparate social groups against him. Parliament's most persistent demand throughout the crisis—control of the armed forces—went to the heart of a basic question: which institution, monarchy or Parliament, would govern England in the future? The latter's victory in the ensuing civil war meant that Parliament would be that institution, confirming a long-term shift in power that even the Restoration of the Stuarts hardly interrupted.

Because the civil war represented a breakdown of the long-standing alliance between the Crown and the Commons, and because the wealth possessed by the latter had risen to several times that of the aristocracy as a whole, this conflict has often been interpreted largely in class terms—a reconciled monarchy and nobility allied against an economically resurgent bourgeoisie. Yet as in France, a significant portion of the nobility joined the rebellion, as many magnates retained their traditional opposition to central rule, while several dozen members of the Commons defected to the king. It is also important to recognize that the economic fissures coincided with and reinforced the pre-existing religious and regional divisions, as the South and East (London, the port cities, the manufacturing towns, and the Puritan population) sided with Parliament, while the North and West (the Catholic and Anglican population, and the agricultural districts) remained with the monarch. Given the numerous and deep cleavages of the English polity, it is not surprising that restoration of the monarchy was possible only after a period of military rule. Only armed force could contain such powerful centrifugal forces and reconstitute a viable center.

The first war, of 1642–46, saw the division of the country into contending military zones with separate administrations, taxation regimes, armies, and navies. Both sides began the war with a severe shortage of arms and in possession of antiquated, run-down fortifications. It was a conflict of small skirmishes and sieges with the largest battle, at Marston Moor in 1644, involving less than 50,000 men. But total mobilization figures were more impressive. At the peak of the fighting, there were as many as 150,000 men in arms, nearly one in eight of all adult English males. In order to sustain such numbers and close an eighty-year gap in military technology, both sides imposed draconian taxation and conscription regimens. Parliament, for example, imposed income taxes as high as 20 percent on the propertied classes as well as heavy excise duties. Both sides imported from the continent veteran officers who had experienced the new warfare at its most ferocious in course of the Thirty Years' War. The historically belated result was the first modern war in English history.

In 1645, Parliament established the New Model Army under Oliver Cromwell. Organized along continental lines, led by gentry officers, and highly trained, this disciplined force easily routed the King's forces at Naseby, bringing to an end the First Civil War. But beginning with the formation of the General Council of the Army in 1647, the New Model Army emerged as an independent third force in English politics. Still unpaid, and alienated by the Presbyterian leanings of Parliament, it refused to disband and became increasingly politicized. The phenomenon of the Levellers in the army, who agitated for universal manhood suffrage and an egalitarian republic, underscores the democratizing penchant of modern armies and suggests that further radicalization of the military would have been possible—perhaps even taking England down a path similar to the French Revolution. But the Scottish invasion and onset of the Second Civil War (1648–51) nipped army radicalism in the bud, though the conservative temper of seventeenth-century English society and the religious basis of the civil wars might have averted a more radical path in any event. As it was, the army did undertake the most blatant military intervention in the history of English politics, "Pride's Purge," in which it arrested or expelled half of the members of Commons, leaving the Rump Parliament that executed Charles in 1649.[41] For the first time in modern history—but hardly the last—the machine designed to wage war on behalf of the state turned like a Frankenstein's monster on its makers.

Contrary to the intuitive thesis that civil wars weaken states, the period of the Commonwealth and Protectorate (1649–60) suggests that unless a civil war causes the total dissolution of a state, the victory of *either* side will result in a stronger—i.e., more authoritarian—central government. Because civil war is essentially a zero-sum game, a rebellious faction that captures the political center may feel threatened and so may impose a despotism harsher than the one it has overthrown. England under Cromwell was ostensibly a republic, but in reality it was a military government permeated by military values and garnished with a sprig of theocracy. Garrisoned throughout the country and divested of aristocratic preference, the New Model Army became the most powerful and most modern organization in England, with a clear command structure, merit promotion, a national basis for recruitment, regular pay, and uniforms. It proved more effective than its Stuart predecessors in trade wars with the Netherlands (1652–54) and Spain (1655–58). Cromwell's brutal campaigns against rebels in Ireland and Scotland reflected the almost fanatical militarism of his rule, but in the longer perspective of history they appear as important steps toward the eventual territorial unification of a larger British state.

At home, Cromwell taxed by decree and appointed regional military commanders, Major Generals, with immense authority to intervene in local affairs. But even under Cromwell England did not slide into full-fledged absolutism.[42] The Lord Protector did not abolish the old representative institutions, and he did not establish a fully rationalized, powerful, self-perpetuating bureaucracy capable of becoming the core of either a royal or a personal dictatorship. He relied on the Protectorate Parliament for new revenues, and acquiesced in its opposition to the regional commanders. When Parliament called for a reduction in taxes and in the size of the army, Cromwell responded by disbanding several regiments, thereby reducing the total land forces of the three British kingdoms to only 30,000 men. But large investments in warships meant that total military expenditures still never dropped much below 90 percent of the budget; even at this, per capita taxation in England was at only one fourth of the rate that autocratic Prussia would attain in 1688.

The English Civil Wars are a prime example of how the Reformation divided states in the short term but strengthened them over the long run, by forcing the resolution of long-standing issues and establishing the nation as the focus of the population's loyalty. Indeed, the revolution against Charles I and civil wars that followed were the breeding ground of modern English nationalism. Though on the surface Restoration England reverted rapidly to its ante-bellum form, the civil wars also left behind a legacy of modernization, with felicitous effects on the development of England's political system. The restored Stuart line acquired a more efficient taxation system, a rationalized administration, and the beginnings of a standing army organized along continental lines. After the Restoration, itself an act of military intervention in politics, there was widespread recognition that the Tudor militia system had provided inadequate protection for the monarchy. Venner's Rising in 1661 persuaded Charles II to cancel the planned demobilization of the army. Two regiments were retained permanently, and by the end of his reign the army stood at 9,000–10,000 men. Under James II, it reached 20,000. This was small by continental standards, but it was a milestone in the political and military modernization of England. The army that had destroyed the English monarchy had now become its main bulwark.[43]

THE FISCAL BURDEN OF IMPERIAL WARFARE: THE CASE OF SPAIN

The reign of Philip II, from 1556 to 1598, marked the pinnacle of Spain's Golden Age. Spain's armies were the largest and best equipped in Europe, its culture flourished, and its vast empire in the New World was the envy of other European monarchs and the source of a seem-ingly endless stream of precious metals. Yet a little more than half a century later, Imperial Spain emerged from its long wars with France, England, the Netherlands, Portugal, and the Ottoman Empire as a power in rapid decline, a "shipwreck of a nation that appeared to be abandoned by its God."[44] It had lost the United Provinces and been forced to cede Artois, Roussillon, and parts of Cerdagne to France. Its economy was in severe recession, its treasury bankrupt, its Aragonese provinces in revolt, its army depleted. And this was only the beginning of misfortune: after another long war, Spain was forced to recognize Portugal's independence in 1668; in 1678, it lost Franche-Comté to France, and by 1714, it had also lost Milan, Naples, Sardinia, the Span-ish Netherlands, and certain of its possessions in the Caribbean. By 1705, its army had shrunk to 50,000 men, one eighth of that wielded by its arch-rival France.

The Eighty Years' War was the most costly of Spain's imperial endeavors and the most crippling to the Spanish state. But Spain in the Age of Religious Wars also fought numerous conflicts with England and France, interminable Mediterranean campaigns against the Turks, even a war with the Vatican. It twice intervened in the French Religious Wars, and it attempted to aid Austria against the Protestant princes of Germany. Spain also faced rebellions in the Iberian peninsula—the uprising of the *moriscos* (1568–71), the revolt of Aragon (1591–92), the simultaneous revolts of Catalonia and Portugal beginning in 1640—as well as in Italy, where Sicily and Naples revolted in 1647. In addition to land warfare, Spain engaged in constant naval campaigns from the Mediterranean to the English Channel, from the North Atlantic to the Caribbean. Embroiled in blood on every side, the Spanish empire pre-sented a textbook case of imperial overextension.

The consequences of Spain's excessive commitment were painfully apparent on numerous occasions. It was no coincidence that the Dutch Sea Beggars captured Den Briel less than six months after the Battle of Lepanto; much of the Spanish fleet was still in the Mediterranean, while the Army of Flanders was off in France in support of the Catholic cause! Similarly, Spain's intervention on behalf of the French Catholic League in 1590 diverted forces from the Netherlands and made possible the capture of Breda by the States-General, the first major Dutch victo-ry in more than a decade. The Catalonian revolt of 1640 gave Portugal an opportunity to rebel, as Spain had too many troops abroad to cope with two simultaneous revolts in Iberia. It is hard to differ from the verdict of Robert Watson, who in 1783 wrote of Imperial Spain that "her power corresponded not with her inclination."[45]

The case of Spain suggests that while some war may strengthen states, too much war will weaken them, even when the destruction of battle largely spares their home territory. The cause of Spain's downfall was fiscal collapse, which short-circuited any formative effects of the conflict. The roots of that collapse can be traced back to Charles V, who bequeathed to his son massive debts and a tradition of relying on outside credit that had served Spain poorly. The first bankruptcy occurred not long after his abdication, when in 1557 Philip II suspended payments to Spain's creditors, sending shock waves through the banking centers of Europe.[46] Eventually, in what would become a gimmick beloved of Spanish finance, the defaulted debts were converted into *juros*, long-term annuities bearing a low interest; this, however, only postponed the inevitable reckoning. Spain's financial picture brightened in the 1560s as the flow of American gold bullion increased, but precious metals never amounted to more than a quarter of Spanish state income.

The costs of war escalated dramatically after 1568, the year Holland and Zeeland rebelled and the revolt of the *moriscos* began in Andalusia. The latter revolt, which took 60,000 troops to suppress, provoked deep if ultimately unfounded fears of Turkish collusion with the rebels. The victory at Lepanto only briefly assuaged these concerns, and expenditures on galleys and coastal fortifications, as insurance against possible Turkish raids in the western Mediterranean, increased throughout the decade. Meanwhile the Army of Flanders grew to over 67,000 troops by 1572, with Spain eventually sending some 9,000 men a year to fight the Dutch. Shortly before the Armada, Spanish military outlays took a quantum leap upward and remained on a high plateau for some fifty years, even during the Twelve-year Truce with the United Provinces.[47] Spending on artillery and small arms nearly tripled, but contrary to the image of Spain as primarily a land power, there were also years between 1587 and 1623, when its naval spending exceeded that for land forces.[48]

The crushing costs of war bankrupted the Spanish crown twice more under Philip II (1575–76 and 1596), while Philip III and Philip IV declared *de facto* bankruptcy an additional six times—in 1607, 1627, 1647, 1652, 1656, and 1662! To maintain credit, the Crown converted most defaulted loans into *juros*, the total obligations of which grew inexorably, consuming the majority of state revenues by 1654; of the remaining budget, perhaps *90 percent or more* went to the military. Insolvency hobbled Spanish war efforts and undermined the fiscal foundations of the Castilian state. The bankruptcy of 1557 forced Spain to sign the Treaty of Cateau-Cambrésis; the bankruptcy of 1607 obliged its agreement to the Twelve-year Truce with the United Provinces; the bankruptcy of 1647 hastened acceptance of the terms at Westphalia; the bankruptcy of 1662 hobbled its efforts to keep Portugal. But the most dramatic effect of imperial Spain's insolvency was the extended series of mutinies in the Army of Flanders from 1570 to 1607. On at least forty-six occasions, Spanish garrisons in the Low Countries refused to fight and sometimes even betrayed their forts to the Dutch in order to force the Crown to pay them; its payroll obligations were often months in arrears. In most cases Spain eventually did pay up, but often only after irreparable damage had been done to its military position.[49]

Spain's insolvency was a symptom of an even more fundamental weakness: its failure to adapt its outmoded institutions to the fiscal and managerial requirements of the Military Revolution. To put it bluntly, the Spanish leaders never got their act together. As in France, the pressures of incessant warfare forced Spain to greatly expand the size of its bureaucracy, so much so that by 1650 there were thousands of officials employed. But unlike France, Spain never undertook the political, financial, or taxation reforms associated with modernization. The Spanish rulers failed to develop a central banking system, a competent financial administration, or a tax structure that was even remotely equitable, though various counselors, Olivares in particular, argued that such reforms were imperative if Spain was to sustain its military power.

The government of Castile at the highest level remained conciliar in form and, instead of being run by professionals, was dominated by courtiers, grandees, and clerics. There was complete confusion of judicial and executive functions, with no central organ attending specifically to the administrative affairs of state. The preoccupation of large segments of the Castilian bureaucracy with imperial affairs, including the administration of the vast empire in the New World, also drained bureaucratic energies and hindered centralization. During the pivotal decade of the 1580s, when Spain's military exertions reached their apex, Spanish officials attempted some modernizing reforms: the Council of War was divided into two secretariats and given a professional staff, and the system of *juntas* emerged, giving somewhat greater flexibility to Spanish administration. But these reforms, and later attempts made in the 1590s and under Olivares, largely failed to transcend the semifeudal legacy of Charles V.[50]

The failure to reform the irrational taxation system of Castile was especially disastrous. Aside from loans, bullion, and ecclesiastical taxes, the principal sources of Castilian revenue were the *alcabala*, a general sales tax; the *servicio*, an annual grant from the Cortes that eventually became permanent; and the *millones*, a tax on foodstuff and other basic items of consumption. All three taxes fell disproportionately on the peasantry and lower classes, who were least able to afford them. Attempts to reform or replace the tax system failed. The *alcabala* more than tripled between 1562 and 1574; this brought the Castilian towns to the brink of a tax revolt, which forced a brief reduction. But after the resumption of hostilities against the Dutch in 1621 Olivares devised numerous additional taxes, nearly doubling the burden on the Castilian taxpayers by 1642. Such increases showed little regard for the long-term impact on Castile's economy, to whose ruin they contributed.

The traditional privileges of the Aragonese realms of Spain (Aragon, Valencia, and Catalonia) further complicated fiscal reform. It was extremely difficult to raise money in these principalities, where powerful *cortes* steadfastly defended their ancient rights, including the right to approve virtually all new taxation. The burden of taxation hence fell primarily on Castile, which from 1621 to 1640 raised some 38 percent of the total revenue of Habsburg Spain, versus only 1.1 percent from the Aragonese lands.[51] Olivares proposed a Union of Arms as an interim step toward full integration of the Aragonese realms, and after the English attack on Cadiz in 1625, he attempted to take advantage of the rallying effect of war to win support for this initiative. Despite strenuous efforts, he failed to overcome the opposition of the local *cortes* to the plan. Outside of Spain, other Hapsburg realms generated large sums of revenue, but in most cases, these were less than the costs to Spain of holding those territories in the face of rebellion or outside aggression. It fell to Castile to shoulder the burden of imperial wars far from its territory and well beyond its means. As Alamos de Barrientos moaned at the beginning of Philip III's reign, Spain offered the strange spectacle of an empire in which the principal kingdom subsidized its subordinate parts![52]

One early sign of Spain's decline was the collapse under Philip III of its military recruitment system. From the time of Charles V, Castile had run a centralized recruiting system that largely bypassed municipal governments and ignored the traditional role of the *Señoría* in raising armies. Though the system was notoriously corrupt, it ensured central control and kept the nobility at arm's length. But under Philip III, Castile reverted to a quasi-medieval system of recruiting, relying on the landed nobility, towns, and private contractors to raise troops. Not surprisingly, given the close link between the military and political order of any state, this resulted in a power shift: the nobility, whose

martial role had languished for two generations, re-emerged as indispensable to the defense of Castile, not only in recruiting, but in leadership and command as well. In southwest Spain, regional defenses
reverted entirely to the control of local magnates. The *cortes* of Castile
also made somewhat of a comeback in assertiveness and power.[53]
Clearly, centralization under the pressure of war is not a one-way
process.

After 1659, when the Peace of the Pyrenees stripped it of key possessions, Spain never again played the part of a great power. But a footnote to the sorry tale of its decline is in order. During the War of the
Spanish Succession (1701–14), Philip V, the Bourbon heir over whose
claim to the throne the war was fought, abolished the constitutions of
Aragon, Valencia, and Catalonia, and by force created a unified Spanish state. Spain emerged from that war with its new dynastic line
secure, its government and laws unified, its army again respected. In
the wake of that war, Spain also overhauled its administration and
finances, introducing a comprehensive tax that righted the long-standing imbalance between Castile and the Aragonese realms.[54] The irony
was supreme. The Spanish empire had been built up by marriage and
might until 1559; it was then undone by a century of incessant warfare.
Yet in the end, it re-emerged as a stable and unified state, thanks in
part to a war fought in alliance with its once bitter rival France. War is
a fickle midwife.

THE CONSTITUTIONAL PATH OF THE SWEDISH MILITARY STATE

During the Thirty Years' War, King Gustavus Adolphus succeeded in
harnessing vast segments of Sweden's society and productive capacity
in the service of what one scholar has described as an archetypal "military state."[55] Yet despite intense involvement in the war, Sweden, like
England, followed a constitutional path of state formation that upheld
representative institutions, even while modernizing its administration.
The parallels between the two countries do not end there. In medieval
Europe Sweden, like England, was an exception to the general pattern
of political fragmentation, maintaining a territorially unified state
throughout most of the Middle Ages.[56] In the Land Law of 1350, the
powerful landed magnates of Sweden had won from the Crown rights

surpassing anything found in the Magna Carta, rights they successfully defended for nearly two centuries thereafter. As a result, the monarchy became hopelessly weak vis-à-vis both the nobility and the Catholic Church, which functioned almost as a state within a state. With so weak a central government, Sweden could not easily defend itself and fell under the domination of Denmark.

Sweden's war of independence against Denmark (1520–23) under the charismatic Gustavus I Vasa laid the foundations for a united, independent state under a strong monarchy. Gustavus Vasa's reign (1523–60) was reminiscent of that of Henry VII in England, inasmuch as he restored the authority of the monarchy and collaborated with the Swedish parliament, the *riksdag*, in curtailing the power of the nobility. Gustavus Vasa's monarchy was so much stronger than its predecessors that he, like the early Tudors, has sometimes been described as "absolutist," but this is a misnomer. Not only did he rely on the *riksdag* and accept the tenets of medieval constitutionalism, but his administration remained almost entirely household in style. Gustavus Vasa did depart from medieval patterns in one major way, however; he created a system of nationwide conscription that enabled Sweden to field Europe's first truly national army, a fighting force more reflective of its society than perhaps any other military force of the day. Its success in doing so may have stemmed partly from the fact that Sweden's peasantry had always been freeholders, never subject to feudal serfdom.

It was not until the reign of Gustavus II Adolphus (1611–32), however, that the Swedish state cast off its medieval garments and donned more modern raiment. During his reign, Sweden was at war almost constantly with Denmark, Poland, or Russia; beginning in 1630, its intervention in Germany pitted it also against the more formidable adversaries of the Austrian Habsburg empire. By 1633, Sweden's annual war budget had reached over 4 million *riksdaler*—a colossal sum for a country with a population of only 1.12 million people. (This was more than *four times* the amount of the Älvsborg ransom imposed by Denmark in 1613, an indemnity Sweden had paid only by imposing a heavy tax on every Swedish adult, including the king, for a period of six years.) Yet Sweden not only managed to raise such sums, it did so largely out of domestic income. Foreign loans and subsidies covered only a small portion of its regular military budget.[57] How was this possible?

The answer is that Gustavus Adolphus, with the assistance of his chancellor, Axel Oxenstierna, had undertaken the task of converting Sweden from a medieval kingdom into a modern state. Their effort was a deliberate, unabashed attempt to borrow the administrative and political formulae for military success developed by France, Spain, and England, the efficacy of which had already been demonstrated on European battlefields. It was a crash program of political modernization that in a little over twenty years brought about the same transformation in the Swedish state that had taken more than a century to accomplish in the Atlantic monarchies, while simultaneously boosting the Swedish economy—a program without which Sweden never could have sustained the rapid escalation in the cost and size of its armed forces that took place after 1620.

The Chancery Ordinance of 1618 converted the Swedish chancery into a modern bureaucracy staffed by professional civil servants. The treasury was reorganized into a true department of government controlled by central auditing. An effective system of bookkeeping followed in 1624. On the strength of these new fiscal institutions, the Swedish monarchy implemented new taxes on land, consumable goods, and agricultural products. It justified the new taxes on grounds of military necessity and won support for them in the *riksdag*, even though they violated the traditional fiscal immunities of the nobility.

In 1626 a second Ordinance further rationalized the Chancery along collegial (departmental) lines, while in 1630, two new *collegia* were formed—a War Office and an Admiralty—to manage the complexities of raising and equipping military forces. The warrior king also overhauled Sweden's system of local government, dividing the country in 1621 into fixed geographical districts, administered by provincial governors, *ståthållare*, with clearly defined functions and authority, including responsibility for overseeing tax collection and military recruitment. The imperatives of war thus propelled the Gustavian reform campaign even into the hamlets and countryside of Sweden.

The political reforms of Gustavus Adolphus were no less impressive than his modernization of the Swedish armed forces. Gustavus Adolphus retained Gustavus Vasa's concept of a national conscript army, but made it more effective by introducing innovative tactics and equipment, and implementing a system of training based on the Dutch methods developed by Maurice of Nassau. Gustavus Adolphus developed the salvo method of fire, merged his administrative with his tactical army units, and divided his army into thinner lines, smaller battalions, and more maneuverable brigades. These innovations made the Swedish infantry the most effective attack force of its day. In 1621, a code of strict military discipline and justice, the Articles of War, was instituted; coupled with a regimen of training, it helped make the Swedish army a disciplined fighting force that rarely mutinied. In

1620, the Crown expanded the conscription base, declaring all Swedish males from 16 to 60 eligible for service; the first standing provincial regiments in Europe thus came into being, some of which remain in place today. The Swedish army grew steadily: by 1621 it numbered nearly 18,000 men; by 1629, 26,000; by late 1630, over 42,000; in 1631, 83,000. During the Thirty Years' War, it reached a peak of over 180,000 troops; it included a large mercenary component but was officered almost exclusively by Swedes.

As we saw in the last chapter, the acquisition of artillery played an important role in the consolidation of the first Renaissance states, and was a critical component of their unprecedented military power. The lesson was not lost on Gustavus Adolphus. Under his leadership, Sweden began an intensive program of artillery development and production. This effort stimulated the development of Sweden's iron and copper industries, whose output was needed both for weapons production and for wartime revenue.[58] By 1630, Sweden had become the only European country entirely self-sufficient in the production of armaments; by the 1650s, it was exporting up to 1,000 artillery pieces a year![59] The Swedish regiment-piece, a highly mobile three-pounder with a rapid rate of fire, proved superior on the battlefield to anything Sweden's opponents had. This was not merely a technical achievement, but a triumph of state administration as well.

It is tempting to ascribe Sweden's meteoric rise to the charismatic leadership of King Gustavus Adolphus. Certainly without him Sweden's modernization would have taken place more slowly. But it was the pressures of war that drove the reforms of Gustavus and Oxenstierna, as shown by the fact that the reforms continued after the monarch's death. In 1634, two years after his passing and in the midst of the war in Germany, the Form of Government was promulgated, which codified the structure of the Swedish state as a constitutional monarchy with clearly defined legislative and judicial branches, an administrative center in Stockholm, and a professional staff of salaried civil servants. Almost overnight (historically speaking) Sweden had made the transition from a medieval to a modern state.

One puzzle of Swedish history is the survival of constitutional monarchy and representative institutions despite the extraordinary violence of the Thirty Years' War and other conflicts which elsewhere fostered absolutism. After all, there was not a single year between 1600 and 1660 that Sweden was not at war. Brian Downing tries to explain it by arguing that the Swedish war effort entailed only a low degree of domestic mobilization. This conforms with a long-standing tendency of historians to minimize the sacrifices of Sweden in the war, both because when the Swedish army reached its peak, mercenary soldiers constituted some 82 percent of its ranks; and because as the war progressed the army supported itself largely by living off the German countryside, imposing a harsh military administration on occupied territories.[60]

Unfortunately, the high mercenary component in the Swedish army has blinded many scholars to what was really achieved: 18 percent of a 180,000-man army represents some 32,000 troops, which for a country as diminutive as Sweden (approximately 1.12 million inhabitants in 1630), represented a military participation ratio of nearly 3 percent of the population—an extraordinarily high figure for any era, and an unprecedented achievement for the seventeenth century. (Under Charles XI, the ratio would rise even higher.) No other country of the day came anywhere close. To put this figure in perspective, if the United States today were to field a similar percentage of its population, it would have armed forces of over 7 million persons! In terms of numbers, Sweden fielded the first mass army in Europe, a hundred and sixty years before the *levée en masse* of Revolutionary France.[61]

In terms of human resources, then, Sweden's sacrifices to wage war were immense. Given the war's protracted nature, the Swedish countryside suffered severe losses. Bygdeå lost 38 percent of its male population aged between 15 and 30; other parishes also suffered a high toll. Such human losses no doubt caused more pain than the fiscal burden of war, but this was not small either. French subsidies and exactions from occupied territory eventually paid for about 96 percent of the costs of maintaining forces in Germany, but other military costs—armaments, warships, home defense, and sundry garrisons—claimed over 35 percent of the state's budget. What is more, as the government strained to meet its recruiting goals, it was forced to alienate Crown lands to the nobility as compensation for their recruiting efforts or to pay officers' salaries. This also meant a serious loss of revenue, forcing the Crown to resort to loans and extraordinary taxes to finance its military machine. Though Sweden had a good record of paying back its loans (unlike so many regimes of the era), this too was accomplished only by stern discipline at home. Sweden ended the war in Germany with its population depleted and war-weary, its revenue base squeezed dry, and debts that entailed further sacrifices to pay off. This was hardly the profile of a state touched lightly by domestic mobilization.[62]

There are better explanations for why constitutionalism survived in Sweden. The fact that the war was not fought on Swedish soil limited its potentially degenerative effects. Sweden's broad-based method of conscription encouraged social-leveling effects that were manifested immediately after the war in popular demands that the lands and revenues alienated to the nobility now revert to the state, so as to spread the burden of taxation more equitably. (Not until the rise of fascism three centuries later would any European state figure out how to field a mass army without making concessions to its population.) Finally, despite numerous wars abroad, many of an imperialist nature, Sweden never fought a civil war in the seventeenth century, or for that matter, at any time thereafter in its history. Full-fledged absolutism seems to arise most easily when states are intensely involved in *both* foreign and civil wars. Seventeenth-century England was torn by internal strife and fought two major civil wars at home but avoided major land warfare abroad. Sweden was embroiled in Scandinavian turmoil throughout the seventeenth century but, perhaps partly for that reason, entirely avoided internal revolts—parliamentary, peasant, or otherwise. At the end of the Thirty Years' War and again after the First Northern War— in accordance with the historical pattern that the end of war aggravates domestic conflict—it suffered high levels of social discord, but these never escalated into civil war.

The Danish–Swedish War of 1675–79 was followed by nearly half a century of monarchical dominance in Sweden, the era of "Carolinian absolutism." Unlike the Thirty Years' War, the Danish–Swedish war was partly fought on Swedish soil, creating a sense of threat that caused power to flow strongly to the center. This in turn gave rise to a politics typified by monarchical domination of the *riksdag*, the keeping of a standing army in peacetime, and the relative independence of the Crown in foreign affairs. But even at the peak of the Carolinian ascendancy, when the Declaration of Sovereignty of 1693 declared Charles XI "an absolute, all-commanding and governing sovereign king," Sweden preserved enough of its constitutional structure intact so that it readily reasserted itself after 1718. The immediate cause of that reassertion was Sweden's defeat at Poltava by Peter the Great, which discredited the war machine of Charles XII and generated reform pressures that, after his death, led swiftly to the restoration of full constitutionalism. Swedish imperialism could not survive the trauma of defeat, while Swedish absolutism could not endure the long-term levelling effects of the mass military service that made its imperial power possible.

THE DUTCH REVOLT AND THE COALITIONAL PATH TO STATE FORMATION

All four countries above—France, England, Spain, and Sweden—had this in common: the imperatives of war and the Military Revolution resulted in both enlarged central bureaucracies and standing armies. In Sweden and England, these processes were more limited than in France and Spain, but they occurred nonetheless. The Dutch Republic followed an entirely different path. Though it was a child of war, born of the same bitter and remorseless conflict that unraveled the Spanish empire, it acquired neither a central bureaucracy nor a standing army in two generations of intense warfare. The Eighty Years' War (1568–1648) forged a sense of Dutch nationhood where there was none before and created almost by accident a sovereign polity from a diffuse and discordant alliance of expediency. For more than a decade after the Dutch Revolt began, it had neither a fixed center nor a coherent political platform. Its leaders had no intention of forming a new state. Yet their war with Spain culminated in the establishment of a state that was undeniably modern in form, though neither monarchical nor centralized. Like Switzerland, it followed the coalitional path of state formation, becoming an anomalous republic in an absolutist age. Its rise contradicted the maxim penned by Sun Tzu two millennia earlier: "There is no instance of a country having benefited from prolonged warfare."[63]

Prior to 1559, the Low Countries, though not as fragmented as the Germanic lands, formed neither a united nor an independent polity.[64] Charles V in 1548 had brought them under a single administrative umbrella governed by a Spanish-appointed governor in Brussels, but they remained divided in numerous ways, including customs and trade barriers, widely divergent monetary and legal systems, and linguistic differences. The provinces were governed by stadholders drawn from thriving noble families of either Walloon or Germanic origin. In conformance with the late medieval pattern, the provinces all had representative assemblies, *États* or *Staten* (States), who every three years would send delegates to a central States-General. The States-General was not an executive body, but it did provide some basis for a growing sense of commonality among the provinces. The States themselves were dominated by urban oligarchies, a function of the long-standing dominance of town and village government in the Netherlands.

As in Switzerland, the rise of an independent state in the Netherlands stemmed from rebellion against Habsburg rule. The Dutch Revolt was actually several revolts rolled into one: a revolt of Protestant burghers against Catholic rule; a revolt of fiercely independent towns and provinces against central government; and a revolt of a rising Dutch identity against rule by a power increasingly seen as "foreign."[65] Prominent among Dutch grievances against Spain were the high taxes imposed on the Dutch by Philip II to finance his war with France, so the Revolt also assumed the form of a large-scale tax rebellion. The Dutch rebels lost almost all their early battles—but the rebellion refused to die, fueled by resentment of the Inquisition, of the atrocities committed by the Duke of Alba, and of the Tenth Penny tax levied in 1572. In the summer of that year, rebel "Sea Beggars" captured the port of Den Briel in southern Holland, a bridgehead that they expanded to embrace the seven northern provinces. The rebellious provinces initially had no intention forming an independent state, but repeated failures to achieve reconciliation with Philip II led them to form the Union of Utrecht in 1579 and to declare their independence in 1581. The Union was intended as an alliance rather than a state constitution, but it is usually regarded as the birth of the Dutch Republic, since it commenced the confederated war effort from which arose a sense of shared political destiny.

Early in the war, the States-General recognized the need for a single military command and created the position of Captain-General, which was first held by William of Orange, "the Silent," and after his assassination in 1584 by his son, Maurice of Nassau, whose innovations in infantry tactics were discussed earlier. The creation of a single army under a unified command was a critical step in the formation of an independent state, though the army of the Provinces could hardly be described as a national army. For one thing, individual regiments were raised in, supplied, and funded by individual provinces; their efforts were coordinated only at the highest command level. Rarely in history was a victorious war fought by an army so decentralized. The provincial regiments, moreover, comprised only a portion of the total military force; the wealthy Dutch relied heavily on foreign mercenaries, especially in the early stages of the war.

The war forged a unified but highly decentralized state, a rudimentary republic with barely any central administration. It did not at all fit the standard Weberian conception of the state as a centralized bureaucratic entity, yet it proved both enduring in form and unquestionably modern in spirit. The institution binding the Dutch together was a parliamentary rather than a bureaucratic organization, and aside from the States-General, the only central institutions that operated during the war were the Council of States (legally the central executive of the union) and the Chamber of Accounts. Both bodies had little independent authority and between them developed only the scantiest of bureaucracies, vastly overshadowed by those of Amsterdam and the provincial governments. At the end of the longest war in European history, the Dutch central government employed no more than 300 persons!

Though the northern provinces of the Netherlands were initially less prosperous than the southern ones where Spanish rule continued, they nonetheless had formidable wealth, which increased as wealthy Huguenots emigrated to the north from Antwerp. Some scholars have cited the indigenous wealth of the Dutch and their capacity to obtain international credit on the basis of that wealth as the main reason why the Netherlands were able to win the war with Spain and yet emerge with a constitutional system intact.[66] Certainly the importance of the Dutch fiscal ability to rent military power, and rent it quickly, cannot be denied. But as in the case of Sweden, the degree of internal resource mobilization by the Provinces was much higher than is generally recognized, and individual Dutch towns—many of which withstood sieges for years, suffering great privation—sacrificed far more than gold alone. Moreover, wealth means nothing in war unless it can be mobilized, and even access to credit only postpones the reckoning of the tax man.

The cost to the Dutch of fighting Spain escalated from an average of under 5 million *guilder* annually in the 1590s to 10 million *guilder* annually by 1604–1606. In a war of attrition and siege, fortifications consumed an enormous part of their budget, often only slightly less than was spent on maintaining the field army. When hostilities resumed in 1621, costs escalated further, reaching the unheard-of sum of 18.8 million *guilder* annually by 1640. This was an enormous fiscal liability for the Dutch population, far beyond the borrowing capacity of the state, and necessitated taxes far more punitive than the infamous Tenth Penny that had helped to provoke the revolt in the first place. The resulting tax hikes by Holland and the other provinces triggered demonstrations and rioting in at least six cities. Like the ever-insolvent Spanish, the Dutch also sometimes had difficulty meeting their military payroll, particularly in the difficult years of 1624–25, when the soldiers' pay was as much as four months in arrears.[67]

If credit did not work military miracles, then what did? What enabled the Dutch cities and provinces to prosecute successfully one of the longest wars in European history and yet retain their republican institutions and a high degree of regional and local autonomy? Why did centralizing forces not gain the upper hand, as was typical in seventeenth-century Europe? Several reasons come to mind. First, the Dutch Revolt was a war fought specifically in defense of local commercial and religious privileges and against the centralizing forces embodied in the Spanish state. Jealous of their traditional privileges, Amsterdam and the Dutch provinces fought to ensure that the military power needed to fight the war would *not* translate into centralized political power. This accounts for their visionary "failure" to establish a central taxation system. Each province or city collected its own taxes and sent funds to the States-General to support the war effort.[68] Because taxation was local, thus decentralized, the fiscal pressure of war strengthened local, not central, government.

Second, the Dutch revolt developed not only as an alliance of provinces, but as an alliance between the Dutch nobility and the urban bourgeoisie. The former provided military experience and leadership; the latter, financial resources. In this sense, it differed radically from the struggles between monarchy and aristocracy in other countries of Europe, where monarchs often allied with the towns and commercial interests against the nobility. The role of the Dutch nobility in the Revolt is not diminished by the fact that their success was possible only with support of the urban commercial patriciate who came to dominate Dutch internal affairs both during and after the war. The fact is that without the military leadership, skills, and resources of the great noble families—Orange, Hoorn, Egmont, Nassau—the war could never have been fought in the first place.[69] Seen as a conflict between the Spanish monarchy and the Dutch nobility (it was of course much more than that), this was one of the few European political struggles in which the nobility prevailed!

Finally, as in Sweden, the Dutch provinces managed to avert civil war among themselves. Sir William Temple wrote in 1672 that they should be called the "Disunited Provinces" because of their constant bickering, yet the Provinces managed to retain sufficient solidarity for military success and the survival of their representative government.[70] One important source of that internal unity was the war itself, as shown by the fact that during the Twelve-year Truce (1609–1621) with Spain, the provinces came close to civil war, as they did again in 1649–50, shortly after the conflict ended. Many Dutch leaders, in fact, opposed the truce with Spain, precisely because they feared that the provinces would dissolve their ties without an enemy. Even at the peak of the war, they experienced a chronic political crisis at the center, with the authority and jurisdiction of the States-General constantly in question. But in the end the very fact of the war's interminable duration made for a unifying effect that overcame internal jealousies. The enormous sums of wealth that were borrowed from domestic lenders to wage the war also bound a whole generation of bourgeois creditors to the success of their Union.

An important military factor in the shaping of the Dutch Republic was its intrepid use of naval power to win battles, capture Spanish wealth, and generate phenomenal trading income. Though until the naval Battle of the Downs in 1639, the decisive battles of the war were fought on land, the urgent need of the Dutch to replace markets lost or curtailed in Iberia compelled them to strenuous efforts at shipbuilding, which in turn greatly boosted the Provinces' seafaring commerce. The Dutch became the most dynamic trading nation in the world, establishing commercial outposts in such distant places as Archangel, New Amsterdam, and Nagasaki. This explosion of overseas commerce, seen by contemporaries as near-miraculous in its scope, was vital to funding the Dutch war effort, enabling revenues to increase without oppressive measures. It suggests a sea-oriented variant of William McNeill's military-commercial "feedback loop": naval expansion boosts national overseas trade, which in turn increases tax revenues and makes possible further naval expansion.[71]

Incomprehensible to foreigners, who constantly predicted its eminent collapse, the Dutch polity that emerged from the conflict with Spain was "a peculiar jumble of medieval remains, Renaissance invention, and contemporary improvisation."[72] It was not a democracy in the modern sense of the word, but was nevertheless one of the freest countries in Europe, and one where the rule of law was generally upheld. Like the earlier case of Switzerland, its establishment demonstrates that even when war unifies, it need not centralize nor overly bureaucratize. By forming defensive alliances of a confederative or federal structure, it is possible under certain circumstances for a people to win independence from foreign domination while yet remaining free from the power and reach of the native central bureaucracies that typically flourish and extend their power during war.

GERMANY AND THE DISINTEGRATIVE EFFECTS OF WAR

The case of Germany provides a poignant finish to our examination of the most war-wracked century in European history, because here, as in the earlier case of Renaissance Italy, war resulted only in political decay and dissolution. In the seventeenth century, Germany was a loose conglomeration of over two hundred principalities, duchies, margravates, ecclesiastical states, and imperial free cities, among which were scattered hundreds of semiautonomous manors, estates, and knightly orders that vowed allegiance to the emperor alone. The political fragmentation of the Germanic states made them acutely vulnerable to invasion by the highly organized states on their borders, with their large-scale centrally controlled armies—a vulnerability that translated into immeasurable catastrophe in the Thirty Years' War. That war left Germany weaker and more divided than ever before, thus opening a vast political and military vacuum in Central Europe. It was a vacuum only partially filled by the rise of Brandenburg-Prussia, the one German state that clearly emerged stronger after the war. The logic of political development in Europe ought to have led to a unified German state by 1700 at the latest; instead, this happened only in 1871. Even the word *state* entered the German language later than English or the Romance languages.[73] It was a postponement for which all of Europe eventually paid an inordinate price.

Never had Europe witnessed suffering and destruction on a scale so vast as occurred in Germany in the latter years of the Thirty Years' War. It was not pitched battles that caused the devastation, for deaths due to combat were only a minor factor in the total sum of casualties. The states of the era still could not master the logistical challenge of mass conflict, so armies survived in the field by pillaging and terrorizing the civilian population. Magdeburg was besieged ten times before being sacked in 1631, with over 20,000 of its inhabitants massacred. Other cities and villages suffered multiple sieges or military occupations; many went heavily into debt from paying marauding armies not to attack. By the end of the war, thousands of villages were depopulated, their inhabitants fled to safer regions or to the haven of walled cities. It became difficult to sow and harvest, and mass starvation took many lives, as did epidemics of typhus, dysentery, scurvy, and the plague. The German lands fell into a nether world of utter depravity where brutality, torture, rape, and even cannibalism became commonplace. Historians once estimated that the Germanic states had lost as much as 33 percent of their urban and 40 percent of their rural populations. Recent studies suggest that the losses were closer to 15 to 20 percent. This still amounts to a loss of nearly 4 million lives, more than in any other European war prior to the twentieth century.[74]

The physical and human losses of the conflict crippled the economy of the Germanic states and weakened them politically and militarily. But they alone do not account for the German failure to achieve unification as an integrated nation-state. Most of the demographic loss was made up by the early eighteenth century, and the economy of the German estates and villages recovered rapidly after the war. Germany remained fragmented, however, and little modern-style state formation occurred outside of Brandenburg-Prussia. Even in wartime a political, as opposed to linguistic or cultural, basis for German unity did not really exist. The Holy Roman Empire had no central administrative apparatus. The religious divide between the Protestant North and the Catholic South made any effective cooperation between them problematic, though an abortive attempt to unite their efforts was made at Frankfurt in 1631. Nor, even within each religious camp, was there a dominant urban center around which Protestant or Catholic unity might have been forged. Hence, though most German princes recognized by 1631 the urgency of creating a "third force" to protect German interests against foreign invaders, such a force was never established.[75]

The German princes also failed to form an alliance that might have solidified into a confederation. The Swiss cantons, after all, also had no clear center but still found the leadership necessary to form a defensive coalition. In Germany, by contrast, the Protestant Union formed ten years before the war hardly functioned once the conflict began. A Leipzig meeting of Protestant princes in 1631 attempted to coordinate united resistance against the emperor's encroachment on their rights but resulted in little action. As princely particularism triumphed over the common defense, Germany became the trampling ground for armies from all over Europe; it was a stunning reprise of what had occurred in Italy during the Italian Wars. Even absent a larger alliance, individual German principalities might have aided one another against outside enemies, but this rarely happened; vacillation and opportunism characterized Germany's political elite throughout the war years.[76] Grand historical forces aside, it seems obvious that absent a will to wage a determined fight, involvement in war alone will hardly induce state formation.

Near the end of the war, one German state—Brandenburg-Prussia—found that will and consequently emerged larger and stronger from the conflict.[77] With over a million subjects, it was among the largest of the Germanic states, a potential rival to Bavaria and Saxony in political influence. During the first twenty-two years of the war, the vacillating and weak George William was its ruler, his army an ill-disciplined rabble of criminals, vagrants, and incompetents. When he died in 1640, foreign troops occupied large tracts of Brandenburg; the war had decimated its villages; its population was less than half its prewar size. Yet only eight years later, when the Peace of Westphalia was negotiated, Brandenburg played an influential role in the talks and received numerous territorial concessions in the final settlement.

This turnabout in Prussian fortunes followed the accession of Frederick William, the "Great Elector," one of the remarkable leaders of his time. He immediately set about remedying Prussia's fundamental shortcoming: its military weakness. Purging the army of troublesome officers and feckless troops, he converted it into a small, disciplined fighting force, which by 1648 had grown to 8,000 men. It was this accomplishment that earned him grudging respect in the peace negotiations. Rejecting the logic of mercenarism, the Great Elector enlisted only his own subjects and paid them decently, ensuring their loyalty on both patriotic and pecuniary grounds. In effect, he adapted the Military Revolution from his nemesis, Sweden, and in doing so laid the foundations of an army that would become the most disciplined fighting force of modern Europe, and of a state that would become the hub around which Germany would eventually unify.

CONCLUSION: THE TRANSFORMATION OF EUROPE

From 1559 to 1660, relentless war transformed the face of western Europe. By compelling an unparalleled degree of political organization, the wars of the era spawned the basic institutions of modern politics—territorial sovereignty, centralized government, bureaucratic administration, permanent military establishments, separate public and private domains, a secular state, an international system of states—features of politics that we take for granted today, but which were largely unknown in the medieval era. In substantial measure, *modernity derived from the pressures of war*, at least in the sphere of politics. This is a sobering conclusion for anyone enamored of the rationality, enlightenment, and progressive course of Western civilization. Europe never did tame the violence permeating the medieval world, but only pushed it outward to the perimeters of the political system—to the borders and the relationships *between* states—where it has continued to rage throughout the modern era.

In Chapter 2 we observed that large states were better equipped than small ones to endure the violence of the Renaissance age. This chapter has pointed out limits to that comparative advantage of size. Given the communications, transportation, and technical limitations of the day, large empires were not well suited to mastering either the Military or the Bureaucratic Revolution. The Holy Roman Empire had almost no central administration and no army solely its own; it began to disintegrate under pressure from smaller, more organized states. The Spanish empire as a whole was too vast to govern effectively; it unraveled under the centrifugal stress of large-scale violence. Thus, it is too simplistic to say that the emergence of the modern state was a process of larger political units crowding out smaller ones. The tiny fiefdoms and principalities of the medieval era could not field effective armies after the Gunpowder Revolution and so perished; but large empires also could not wield effective power over the whole of their territory, and they too fell apart. The modern state emerged in the middle of the size range as the political unit best suited in scale and organization to field modern armies.

The assumption of the full powers of the throne by Louis XIV in 1661 and the emergence of a powerful sovereign France in the heart of western Europe marked and symbolized the transformation of Europe that had taken place in the blood-drenched century from 1559 to 1660. Our focus on that transformation should not obscure the persistence of the medieval in post-Westphalian Europe. In Eastern Europe, modernizing processes were barely stirring, while in the West there remained sundry pockets of substate autonomy: private fortresses, free cities, magnates whose fealty and resources monarchs could not command. The aristocracy still dominated local government as well as the ranks of central bureaucracies and officer corps.[78] But though the emerging states of Europe were much less centralized than their descendants would become, the inexorable trend was toward *the centralization of the means of violent coercion.* National governments were coming to control the primary military assets of their countries and to determine how those assets would be used both internally and externally. Even the predominance of the nobility in the army and in the bureaucracy represented in large part a cooptation, even a domestication, of their class by the monarchs. As to the civil wars, tax revolts, urban insurgencies, and baronial rebellions that marked the century, the simple reality is that those challenges to monarchical authority *almost always failed.*[79] Militarily superior, the state triumphed in the end.

Given the imperatives of the Military Revolution, the real wonder of the age was not the rise of the state, but the survival of constitutional and representative systems in England, Sweden, Switzerland, and the Dutch Republic. The fact that three of these states were naval powers, oriented seaward, may partly account for their relative freedom—an explanation often advanced in the case of England. But England's constitutionalism may have owed less to its being a seagoing power than to its being an *island power.* Secure behind the Channel, Tudor monarchs had no incentive to build a standing army or a bureaucratic state to support it. How do the other three fit into this schema? In a sense, they too enjoyed certain attributes of "island powers." The Swiss Confederation stood isolated in an Alpine stronghold; Dutch terrain was ideal for defense, with abundant rivers, swamps, and lowlands to confound the Spanish infantry; Sweden was on the periphery of Europe, its heartland rarely invaded (and when it was, in 1675, a form of absolutism soon followed). Perhaps a common thread in the rise of constitutional monarchies and republics was simply "defensible territory." Where war threatened less, it fostered less oppressive rule.

In all four of these states, representative assemblies of medieval origin survived the winds of war; in this sense they experienced less modernization than their absolutist contemporaries. Being less modern, they were actually more free—a dichotomy that says much about the moral ambiguity of modernization. Like absolutist states, constitutional and republican states had to levy high taxes in wartime; they too paid enormous sums to acquire the means of defense. The difference was that they, through consensual processes, enlisted the support of large portions of their populations in the common defense, including those groups that had no aristocratic background. James Harrington wrote in *Oceana* in 1656 that government could be based either upon the nobility or upon the army. These countries pointed to a third way: defense based on a wider political compact. In England, the essential party to that compact was a rising middle class of merchants and city-dwellers who allied with the monarchy against the feudal landed interests; in the Netherlands, it was the urban-based and commercially oriented bourgeoisie, whose wealth was the sinews of the Dutch war for independence; in Switzerland, it was a combination of burghers and peasants, the vast majority of the population; in Sweden it was a free peasantry, enlisted in the first mass conscript army in Europe. In this sense, all four states transcended medieval politics, where the nobility had been both the hegemons of local politics and the sole warrior class.

The decline of Spain—which fought too much—reminds us again that war can break states as well as make them. Paul Kennedy's notion of imperial overstretch causing internal exhaustion and decline seems à propos here. Yet it is fascinating, and possibly significant, that the three western European countries who experienced the degenerative effects of war most harshly in the sixteenth and seventeenth centuries emerged in the twentieth century as the main standard-bearers of fascism, with all its glorification of War and the State writ large. The causal links between the Italian Wars and Mussolini, between seventeenth-century Castile and Franco's Spain, or between the Thirty Years' War and Hitler's rise, are admittedly distant and attenuated. But perhaps there is a calculus in the subconscious of nations that seeks to compensate for the humiliation of defeat by the exaltation of war and martial values, however delayed the compensation may be. The scars of Mars run painful and deep, and heal but ever so slowly.

War and the Rise of the Nation-State

Now every French citizen is a soldier, and a willing soldier at that!

> —Jacques Pierre Brissot de Warville,
> Address to the French Legislative Assembly,
> December 29, 1791

Vive la Nation!

> —French war cry at Valmy, September 1792

By 1660 the cake of state was baked in France, and the recipe was in demand across all Europe. The institutions of feudalism were inexorably declining; the claims of Church and empire to universal political supremacy were irretrievably lost. The state had emerged as the logical unit of politics, superior to all other forms of organization in its capacity to generate armed force, the currency of power. While the majority of European kingdoms and principalities retained their medieval form in the first decades after the Westphalian settlement, traditional politics could not and did not long endure the shock of military encounters with the armies of France or Sweden, the two states where the military revolution had proceeded furthest. Modern warfare unleashed modernizing pressures with a vengeance. Via numerous transmission channels, including unabashed borrowing and imitation, the military engine of state formation began to operate in yet untouched regions of Europe, both West and East. Eventually, carried abroad by the trading companies, steamships, and bayonets of imperial powers, the bureaucratic state would proliferate throughout the earth. Wherever the gun went, the filing cabinet followed.

The proliferation of sovereign states took place in three main waves of historical development. From 1648 to 1789, state formation took place almost exclusively within Europe, with absolute monarchy the most common form. The states of this era, with the exception of a few anomalous republics, retained a dynastic basis and were not actual *nation-states* as the term is understood today. Though the borders of a given European state might approximate those of a specific linguistic or cultural community, the sense of community at the national level was only weakly felt, and the identification of nation with state was weaker yet. The European state was now more than a private dynasty, more than a cluster of feudal realms, but it was not yet widely perceived as the political incarnation of a sovereign people. European trading companies and colonists established settlements and outposts throughout much of the world during this period, but of these only the British colonies of North America successfully formed an independent state prior to the French Revolution.

The second great wave of state formation occurred in the wake of the French Revolutionary and Napoleonic Wars, which unleashed powerful forces of nationalism all across Europe. Originating in war and propagated by invading armies, this nationalism transformed dynastic states into true nation-states, widely identified in the popular imagination as the embodiment of the national community of the populace. Nineteenth-century nationalism produced a new arithmetic of state formation: multiplication by division, as multinational empires split into a host of new states (Greece, Belgium, Romania, etc.), and addition by subtraction, as wars of national unification welded disparate principalities into unitary states (Italy, Germany). This period essentially ended after the First World War, which precipitated the final disintegration of the Austro-Hungarian and Ottoman empires, creating a boomlet of new nation-states on the periphery of Europe.

The third—and still continuing—wave of state formation took place outside the borders of Europe and overlapped with the second, as the organization of the bureaucratic state proliferated throughout the globe. The New World led the way with the birth of the United States, followed by the Spanish and Portuguese colonies throughout Latin America winning their wars of independence. In the last quarter of the nineteenth century, the European imperial powers embarked on a feeding frenzy, annexing over 10 million square miles of territory, including most of Africa, and bringing 84 percent of the word's terrain under European dominion. By blood and by iron, the imperial states exported Western military technology and administration into virtually every part of the world, stimulating political reforms and modernization even in the most venerable of ancient empires, albeit at an enormous cost to human life. The cumulative effects of the two World Wars then shattered the overseas empires of the European powers, leading to their withdrawal from Africa and Asia and the rise of scores of new sovereign states, the majority of the membership of the United Nations today.[1]

Extra-European state formation remains an unfinished process, for though new sovereign states have emerged in much of the globe, many of them remain but administrative overlays on traditional societies and could not fairly be characterized as unitary nation-states. Nor can the process of state formation be said to have ended even in Europe, for between 1989 and 1993 alone, in consequence of the breakup of the Soviet empire and the war in Yugoslavia, no less than *fourteen* new states made their debut in Europe.* More are certain to follow. Whether the breakup of former Communist states is simply a continuation of the nineteenth-century pattern in which nationalism is destiny and every linguistic community seeks to form its own state, or whether it represents a fundamentally different and fourth stage of state development, remains as yet difficult to say.

WAR, ARMIES, AND EUROPEAN STATE FORMATION, 1660–1789

Our primary concern in this chapter is the passage of Western politics to a new incarnation of modernity, that of the nation-state. But

---

* The list, for the curious, is as follows: Ukraine, Belarus, Estonia, Latvia, Lithuania, Moldova, Georgia, Armenia, Azerbaijan, Slovenia, Croatia, Bosnia-Herzegovina, Macedonia, Slovakia. Serbia, Montenegro, and Kossovo together make up what is left of Yugoslavia—not a *new* state. Five Central Asian states also emerged—Tadjikistan, Kazakhstan, Uzbekistan, Kirgizistan, Turkmenistan—but these are generally considered Asian rather than European.

though the French Revolutionary and Napoleonic Wars were the mid-
wives of this passage, understanding it fully requires that we return to
the period shortly after Westphalia (1648) and consider what happened between then and 1789. The eighteenth century was an era of
rapid state proliferation that paralleled the rise of modern nationalism. In the course of the century, a pentarchy of powers—France, Austria, Prussia, Russia, and England—came to dominate European
affairs. Only England, furthest to the west and secure behind the
Channel, retained the representative system it had inherited from the
medieval era. The three eastern powers, by contrast, lacked natural
borders and suffered from territory poorly suited for defense. Exposed
and vulnerable in a world of rising military power, they pursued the
continental path of state formation; like France, they became absolutist states with centralized bureaucracies, large standing armies, and
royal dominance of the nobility.

Before looking at how war reared these absolutist giants, three general features of the period should be mentioned. First, the absolutism
of the day was neither absolute, total, nor totalitarian. Though Louis
XIV in 1692 issued an edict proclaiming his universal lordship over all
territory in France, the communications and transport realities of the
day severely limited his power to penetrate French society. Also,
numerous societal sources of resistance to monarchical power persisted in Enlightenment Europe; of these the nobility remained predominant, despite the ground it had lost to royal power in the preceding
two hundred years. Although a Louis XIV might overawe the French
nobility for a time, the *parlements* reasserted themselves under Louis
XV, rejecting an income tax proposed to finance the War of Austrian
Succession and waging a bitter dispute in Brittany over the right of the
central government to build roads for defense. The traditional barriers
to absolutism were weakest in Russia, where the *oprichniki* of Ivan IV
("Ivan the Terrible") in the sixteenth century had executed over 10,000
boyars and converted the nobility into a service class with minimal
corporate privileges. The same barriers were strongest in Habsburg
Austria, where the landed class remained powerful and the sprawling,
multinational character of the dynasty made central control intrinsi-
cally more difficult.

A second feature of the era was the limited nature of war. The
horrors of the Thirty Years' War had persuaded European leaders of
the enormous destructive potential of the new warfare. The wars of
the eighteenth century were consequently shorter, less destructive,
and more mindful of the need to avoid civilian casualties. Several
factors contributed to this. An increasingly sophisticated system of

interstate diplomacy mediated disputes, signaled intentions, and maintained equilibrium. The Swiss jurist Emerich de Vattel codified rules of war in 1758 that were more restrictive, and more widely accepted, than those proposed by Grotius over a century earlier. The logistical and commissariat system developed by the Marquis de Louvois, the French secretary of state for war under Louis XIV, spread to all the larger states of Europe, enabling armies to supply themselves from large food depots and permanent magazines rather than by looting the civilian population. The new conventional wisdom held that armies should remain within five days' march of their bases; this obviously tended to limit the scope and size of battles. Frederick the Great epitomized the eighteenth-century attitude toward war when he opined that the civilian population should not even be aware that a war was taking place.[2]

A third general characteristic of eighteenth-century Europe was the prevalence of mercantilist economic policies. Because mercantilism and "enlightened despotism" are so often invoked as capturing the spirit of the age, it is important to recognize that they derived at least in part from the requirements of war. European monarchs had always known that money was needed to wage battle, but in the eighteenth century it began to dawn on them that the capacity to generate revenue was linked to the condition of their countries, that the cows had to be kept healthy and plump if they were to be milked regularly. Whatever the enlightened despots may have thought of the *philosophes* of the Enlightenment, whatever genuine altruism or concern for the public welfare they may have felt, their economic policies were aimed foremost at enhancing the state's capacity for war-fighting. Jean Baptiste Colbert, whose name is most closely associated with mercantilism, put it simply: "Trade is the basis of finance, and finance is the sinew of war."

In short, notwithstanding Frederick the Great's vision of battle not interfering in civilian lives, war continued to exert a profound influence on the internal affairs of states from 1660 to 1789—less from its violence and destructiveness than from its organizing and formative effects at home. The urgent need for funds to cover the large debts run up in the Seven Years' War (1756–63) motivated many of the most prominent and loudly hailed domestic reforms of the Enlightenment era, and the most spectacular manufacturing achievements of the century were largely military in nature. It was hardly the liberality and vision of Enlightenment philosophy alone that transformed Prussia into the fourth-largest manufacturing country in the world by the death of Frederick the Great in 1786.[3]

MILITARY CONFLICT AND DOMESTIC REFORM

France emerged from its defeat of Spain in 1659 as the ascendant power in Europe. Louis XIV carried the logic of the absolutist state to its culmination, forging the largest war machine and administrative apparatus of any European power. The number of troops at his disposal reached a peak of 392,000 during the War of the Spanish Succession (1701–14), with a standing *peacetime* army of 150,000—as many as Richelieu had wielded at the peak of the Thirty Years' War. Even the French navy in 1689 was briefly the largest in Europe, with more ships of the line than England's. The military reforms of Vauban and Louvois elevated the French army beyond the Military Revolution of the seventeenth century, converting it to an efficient, well-trained fighting force with a strict chain of command, promotion based on merit, fixed pay scales by rank, and standardized uniforms. Louvois established a network of supply depots, created a reserve system, integrated the artillery with the regular army, and instituted military hospitals and a pension system for disabled veterans, the first in Europe. By the end of the Sun King's reign, the French army was in many respects closer in spirit and form to the European armies of today than to the army of Richelieu.[4]

With its splendid court and unparalleled army, France became the prototype of European state formation, its institutions widely seen as incarnating the secrets of military success, its innovations shamelessly copied. Shifting alliances and the tendency of the European states to maintain a shifting balance against French power made it impossible for France to assert continental hegemony—indeed, France's battlefield record was always less impressive than the peacetime promise of its army. But European *perceptions* of French military superiority enabled the French language to conquer the courts of Europe, while French arts, letters, and drama asserted a kind of pan-European cultural hegemony as well.

From 1660 to 1789 France was a central player in every major European conflict involving multiple powers, with only one exception—the Great Northern War of 1700–1721. Table 4–1 lists the major multilateral wars of this period and the key antagonists; again and again, the large powers allied with or faced off against France. No other power played such a pivotal role in alliance politics; no other state fought with and against so many other major powers so frequently. This constant military interaction with the most advanced military power on the continent inevitably had a profound effect on the thinking of other state leaders and the evolution of their internal

Table 4–1.   Major European Conflicts, 1660–1789.

DATE	WAR	PRINCIPAL CONTENDERS
1688–97	War of the Grand Alliance	France vs. England, United Provinces, Spain, Sweden, Austria
1700–21	Great Northern War	Sweden vs. Russia, Poland, Saxony and Denmark
1701–14	War of the Spanish Succession	France and Spain vs. Austria, Britain, and the United Provinces
1733–38	War of the Polish Succession	France and Spain vs. Austria and Russia
1740–48	War of the Austrian Succession	France and Prussia vs. Austria and Britain
1756–63	Seven Years' War	Austria, Russia, France, Sweden and Spain vs. Prussia and Britain
1778–83	War of American Independence (in Europe)	Britain vs. France, Spain and the United Provinces

policies. Even in the small principalities of Germany—Bavaria, Saxony, the duchy of Württemberg, and the electorates of Mainz, Cologne, and Trier—French subsidies and military support had the effect of strengthening the power of princes and central governments à-vis their respective towns and estates.[5]

Prior to 1648, European state formation had been driven largely by circumstance; only in Sweden was there a conscious attempt to forge a modern state by borrowing from the military and political institutions already extant on the continent. This changed in the eighteenth century, which witnessed several deliberate "top-down" efforts at forming centralized bureaucracies and standing armies on the French or Swedish models. Military defeat or perceptions of threat motivated most such efforts. Prussia embarked on its first modernizing reforms in response to the devastation of the Thirty Years' War. The First Northern War (1655–60) lent momentum to the process. As the Great Elector declared on its eve, "The military preparations of all our neighbors compel us to follow their example."[6] Russia's defeat at the Battle of Narva in 1700, when a brigade of 8,000 Swedish soldiers trained in the art of continental warfare routed 35,000 Russian soldiers, impelled Peter the Great on a determined reform course. Austria's defeats at Mollwitz (1741), Hohenfriedberg (1745), and Soor (1745) in the Silesian Wars sent shock waves through the Austrian establishment and spurred its first serious modernizing reforms.

In the case of Austria, Maria Theresa's principal advisors, Counts Friedrich Wilhelm von Haugwitz and Wenzel Anton von Kaunitz, recognized that the loss of Silesia had occurred primarily because Austria, unlike Prussia, was not internally organized to make effective use of its resources. Between 1748 and 1763, Haugwitz and Kaunitz undertook a far-reaching reform program: the army was enlarged and restructured along modern lines; an antiquated structure of government was replaced by a more rational, bureaucratic administration; taxation and military recruitment quotas were imposed on the landed nobility. Additional military reforms followed the Seven Years' War. The Theresian reforms undermined the Austrian estates and reduced the weight of the *Länder*, consolidating Upper and Lower Austria into a modern, centralized political structure (though the rest of the Habsburg realms remained under more traditional forms of rule).[7]

The reformative impact of war is particularly instructive in the Russian case. By the time Peter I, "the Great," assumed the full powers of the throne in 1689, the Romanov dynasty had long since reestablished the primacy of the Tsar over Russian society, briefly lost during the Time of Troubles. In this sense, Russia was already "absolutist," but it was a thoroughly medieval despotism, untouched by the modernizing trends in the West. And though Russia had fought intermittent wars with Poland, Sweden, and Turkey during the seventeenth century, its approach to war remained medieval. This changed rapidly under Peter the Great, during whose thirty-five-year reign Russia was completely at peace for only 25 *months*.[8] Two events in particular spurred the new Tsar's obsession with reform. The first was Peter's Grand Embassy to Western Europe in 1697–98, an extended tour during which he inspected the industry, weaponry, craftsmanship, and political institutions of France, Holland, Germany, and England; he returned home determined to modernize Russia, especially in military technology. His second epiphany was Russia's defeat by Sweden at Narva, which Peter recognized as deriving not only from Sweden's superior military forces but also from the administrative-political machinery that produced and supported them. Narva marked the beginning of twenty-one years of war with Sweden, during which time Peter literally rebuilt the Russian state in order that it might wage war on a par with the Western powers.

He began by replacing an antiquated recruiting method with a system of general conscription applied to all classes. Regular annual levies were made, with up to 30,000 men added to the ranks every year; the Russian army increased to 113,000 men by 1708. Instead of troops disbanding during peacetime, regiments were made permanent and the Crown assumed direct responsibility for their maintenance. The Tsar also launched a crash program of naval armament, which by 1703 put the first small Russian fleet in the Baltic; by the end of his reign, the

Russian navy numbered 48 ships of the line, over 800 galleys, and 28,000 men. Peter also modernized his military administration, eventually creating a General Staff, a Commissariat, a Ordnance Office, an Artillery Office, and Naval and Military Colleges.

In 1707, a Russian victory at Lesnaya indicated that the Petrine reforms were beginning to pay dividends. But the decisive Russian victory at Poltava the following year proved to be a powerful catalyst for reform, having an even greater impact on Russian internal affairs than the defeat at Narva. By persuading Peter that his reform course was on target, it spurred sweeping political and administrative innovations. Before Poltava there had been only two Petrine ukases (Acts) dealing with governmental organization; after Poltava, there were hundreds, a veritable flood of reforms, as Peter overhauled his financial and taxation system and reorganized the Russian state administration along more rational lines. Defeat as a catalyst of political reform is a common phenomenon; the post-Poltavan reforms show that victory sometimes has a similar effect as well.

The Russian historian Vasili Klyuchevsky maintains that overtaking the West militarily was the undeviating goal of the entire Petrine reform program, even of those administrative innovations that were not directly military in nature.[9] This obsession was passed on to his successors as well, catapulting Russia on a three-centuries-long course of Herculean efforts to keep pace with Western military advances. Because the Western powers interacted far more closely with one another in commerce, diplomacy, and war—and because of the more rapid progress of capitalism, and later industrialization, in Western Europe—the West achieved rapid rates of technological innovation that Russia found difficult to match. The effort to catch up was a constant *leitmotiv* of Russian history from the time of Peter the Great onward. In attempting to match the West while rejecting Western values and refusing to liberalize Russian society, Russia only reinforced its autocratic course; state-driven innovation was substituted for social initiative, and despotism became an instrument for containing the social forces unleashed by modernization.[10]

THE MILITARY LOGIC OF THE ABSOLUTIST STATES

The rise of the state invariably meant the political subjugation of autonomous classes or groups by the center. Just as the growing power of the French state under Richelieu and Mazarin triggered revolts by both lords and peasants, the rise of the absolutist state in Prussia, Rus-

sia, and Austria met with strong internal resistance. During the First
Northern War (1655–60), the Great Elector demanded large grants
from the Brandenburg estates; when they resisted, he imposed a land
tax by force and ceased to consult the Estates. In 1662, faced with an
incipient revolt in East Prussia, he marched 2,000 troops to Königs-
berg and compelled the *Junkers* (nobles) of the Prussian Estates likewise to yield to his authority. Later in the decade, when the Prussian
Landtage (Estates) were dithering over tax payments, the execution of
a recalcitrant noble quieted all resistance.

In Russia, Ivan IV ("Ivan the Terrible") had broken the back of
noble resistance a century before Peter the Great, but the latter faced
revolt from a different quarter—the elite military corps known as the
Streltsy, who resented his early reforms aimed at improving the discipline of the corps. Regarding the *Streltsy* as a traditional, quasi-
autonomous social and military order that had to be subjugated, Tsar
Peter brutally crushed the revolt, executing over 1,000 insurgent
troops. He then integrated the *Streltsy* gradually into the reformed regular army. Peter's ruthlessness contrasts with the more indirect
approach of Maria Theresa, who sought to persuade the Austrian
Estates to provide long-term grants and used compulsion only on rare
occasions—as when Carinthia was forced to make contributions in
support of her army. Though the Austrian Estates lost some of their
independence, they were never crushed or abolished, while non-Aus-
trian realms of the empire, such as Hungary and Bohemia, retained
considerable autonomy. The failure to achieve a truly integrated state
may be one reason why the larger Austrian empire proved nonviable
in the long run. Like Spain's in the previous century, Austria's imperial
possessions vitiated its central state formation.

It is striking that once the structure of absolutism was in place, neither France, Prussia, Russia, nor Austria experienced serious internal
challenges to absolutist rule again until 1789. Louis XIV faced a brief
revolt in Brittany in 1675, and he required 20,000 troops to subdue the
Camisard Revolt in 1702–1704; thereafter, the French state enjoyed
domestic tranquility until 1789. With the single exception of
Pugachev's Revolt (1773–74), a peasant uprising on the steppes of the
Volga far from Moscow, Russia also experienced no further serious
violence. The internal equilibrium of the Old Regimes rested upon the
familiar triad of army, taxes, and bureaucracy. Central power was
upheld by military force, which was organized and funded by bureaucracies, which collected taxes that funded both the bureaucracy and
the military, both of which in turn enforced tax collection. It was a circular arrangement that amply justifies Charles Tilly's description of

the modern state as a kind of protection racket. The most vital leg of this triad was the standing armies of the absolutist monarchs, which made successful rebellion almost impossible for over a century.[11]

Prior to 1600, the French army had rarely exceeded 25,000 troops in peacetime or 50,000 in wartime, a ratio equivalent to a small fraction of 1 percent of the population—and of course even less if the foreign mercenary component in the Army is taken into account. The ratio nearly tripled under Richelieu, but still remained under 1 percent; under Louis XIV, during the War of the Grand Alliance, it reached nearly 2 percent with a high complement of foreign mercenaries.[12] The growth of the Prussian army was even more impressive, as well as more indigenous, rising from a peacetime strength of 18,000 in the 1660s and 1670s to 40,000 in 1713, to 83,000 in 1740. Much of this growth can be credited to Frederick William I (1713–40), who was nicknamed "the royal drill sergeant" and who dressed in uniform during much of his reign. Declaring 50,000 soldiers worth more than 100,000 ministers, he slashed the Prussian bureaucracy so as to free up funds for the army. His successor, Frederick the Great, by 1755 had again doubled the size of the Prussian army; by his death in 1786, it numbered 200,000 men and was generally acknowledged as the best-trained, best-equipped army in Europe. Some 20 percent of Berlin's population of 100,000 were soldiers, and the Comte de Mirabeau was describing Prussia as not a state with an army but an army that happened to possess a state. By then, it had achieved a military participation ratio of 4 percent, double that of Louis XIV and roughly *five times* what Richelieu had mobilized in the Thirty Years' War. It was a ratio higher even than France attained after the *levée en masse* of 1793. In purely quantitative measure, the mass army had arrived in Europe even before the French Revolution.[13]

On the strength of the Theresian reforms, the Austrian army increased rapidly, reaching a level of 108,000 troops by 1754 and climbing to 200,000 at the peak of the Seven Years' War. Four decades earlier, the Russian army had also undergone rapid growth, reaching 200,000 by the end of Peter the Great's rule in 1725 (not counting 100,000 Cossacks and mercenary troops).[14] But though this was a large force in absolute terms, in relative terms as a percentage of population, it reflected a much lower level of human mobilization than in either Prussia or France, and that level remained lower even after the size of the Russian army reached 500,000 by the end of the century. This alone would explain why the Russian military—though it was a conscript force drawn from every class of society and every district of the country—did not emerge as an independent political actor or a catalyst of social leveling in the eighteenth century. But how are we to explain the case of the Prussian army? Normally we would expect a high military-participation ratio to stimulate egalitarianism and demands for political participation, but the Prussian soldiery remained docile and exerted little overt leveling influence within German society. Why?

The answer may lie in the high degree of social discipline demanded by the Prussian state—a characteristic that persisted throughout its history and that carried over into the Imperial and Nazi periods as well. Quaint depictions of "enlightened absolutism" aside, the fact is that Prussian rulers ran an exceedingly authoritarian, austere regime, which demanded strict fulfillment of duty and virtually total submission of their citizenry to the needs of the most militarized polity in Europe.[15] Prussian justice was less arbitrary and less physically cruel than in Russia, but through the constant invoking of discipline and duty the Fredericks instilled in their populace an extraordinary degree of internal obedience to the state. By infusing Prussian society with a martial political culture, they neutralized the potentially deleterious side effects to autocracy of a large standing conscript army.

The maintenance of large standing armies was an expensive proposition for all the absolutist states. The Theresian financial and taxation reforms doubled Austrian state revenue to 40,000,000 florins, of which a lean 35 percent was supposed to cover army expenses. In fact, the Seven Years' War cost Austria some 260,000,000 florins, of which 44,000,000 were spent in a single year (1760), more than the entire annual revenue of the state. Under Frederick the Great, fully 80 percent of state revenue went to the army. Under Peter the Great, military spending more than quintupled, regularly absorbing 80 to 85 percent of revenues and sometimes (1705) as much as 96 percent! It is no wonder that the absolutist states have been described as little more than "machines for making war."[16]

As a percentage of state revenues, French military spending in peacetime never quite achieved the heights of Prussian spending, but the levels were impressive enough, contributing to the eventual fiscal and political ruin of the Bourbon monarchy. A statement of royal finances in 1680—when France was at peace—shows military expenditures equalling some 47,487,000 livres, nearly 49 percent of total spending. But this does not include some 11 livres in debt repayments, the vast bulk of which were accumulated during earlier wars. Together, the two military components consumed over 60 percent of the French budget. And this was in peacetime; the percentage inevitably escalated

sharply during wars, when only massive borrowing staved off insolvency. By 1786, shortly before the Revolution and also a year of peace,
the ratio of military spending in the total state budget had risen to 74
percent.[17] The french state might have adopted as its motto a new
Cartesian imperative: "I fight, therefore I am."

Such high levels of military expenditure forced all the absolutist
regimes to impose unprecedented levels of taxation, enforced in every
case by military power. Machiavelli in *The Discourses* had written that
money was not the sinews of war, but rather good troops, since "gold
does not find good soldiers, but good soldiers are quite capable of
finding gold."[18] Never was this more true than under the *anciens
régimes*, when military terror enforced the writ of the tax collector and
armies served as tools of repression as well as of expansion and
defense. In 1724 Peter the Great imposed a "soul tax" on every adult
male in Russia; it remained the primary source of state revenue until
1886. The army enforced collection of the tax by brute force, its
inevitable abuses spurring the flight of the populace beyond the ever-
more-distant frontier. In France, military garrisons based in the countryside enforced the tax-collecting writ of the *intendants* and the
corrupt tax farmers. On occasion, French troops even confiscated
household utensils and farming implements from the peasantry—
their only means of livelihood—when cash could not be obtained.
Since the bulk of these revenues went into the support of the army,
France was literally heeding the Old Testament injunction of the
prophet Joel to beat its plowshares into swords.[19]

Bureaucracy, the third leg of the absolutist triad, flourished under
the pressure of war. At Versailles, the Grand Monarch Louis XIV
added numerous councils and commissions to his administration,
seeking to turn the bureaucracy into a pliant instrument of state policy; the term *minister* was first applied to state secretaries during his
reign. In Prussia, during the Third Dutch War (or Franco-Dutch War)
of 1672–79, the *Generalkriegskommissariat*, originally formed during
the First Northern War, became independent of the privy council and
acquired vast powers of taxation and financial administration. After
the war, the *Kriegskommissariat* became a juggernaut of centralization.
Its rapidly expanding hierarchy of officials acquired authority over
every facet of public life, from manufacturing to municipal administration. Brandenburg-Prussia became subject to a tightly unified civil-
military administration that had been set up originally mainly to fund
and supply the army. In the course of the next century, this Prussian
administration became the nearest thing in Europe to a classic Weberian bureaucracy: an efficient, faceless civil service devoted to the inter-

ests of the state and largely free of the corruption that plagued other absolutist regimes.

Peter the Great's post-Poltavan reforms had an immense impact on Russia's administration, resulting in virtually a "cult of bureaucratic institutions" with offices created to supervise and oversee virtually every physical structure or activity in the country from individual barracks to private homes. Under a system of Colleges (departments) modeled after Sweden, Peter put in place a top-down, hierarchically-ordered bureaucratic machine, the central ranks of which more than doubled between 1717 and 1723 alone. The Tsar also introduced a formal Table of Ranks slotting virtually the entire nobility into a bureaucratic pecking order that was divided into military, civil, and judicial services. Admittance to given Ranks was based on merit, and did not exclude commoners; this began to erode the hereditary structure of the nobility. (It is interesting to note that some 270 years later, when the post-Soviet Russian Federation undertook to reform its bureaucracy and create a modern civil service, the leading reform proposal envisioned a system modeled on Peter's Table of Ranks.)[20]

Austria, as usual, did not go quite as far as its neighbors. Though it, like Prussia, established a *General-Kriegs-Commissariat* responsible for supervising the military and the economy, it was a less centralized, less effective, and less powerful bureaucracy than its counterpart. The strategic implications of this were not obvious at the time, but the weaker Austrian administration would prove consistently unable to mobilize military resources as effectively as the Prussian bureaucracy. Even in the mid-eighteenth century, the trends were emerging that would culminate in Prussian, rather than Austrian, dominance over Germany.

ALTERNATIVE PATTERNS: BRITISH CONSTITUTION-ALISM, POLISH DECLINE

War did not invariably beget absolutism after Westphalia. Though after France, Great Britain was the most militarily engaged power of the eighteenth century, it retained and even strengthened its constitutional structure. The partitioning of Poland also reflects a different pattern, reminding us again that war can have disintegrative as well as formative effects.

The main objective of William of Orange when he captured the English throne in 1688–89 was to mobilize England's full military potential in the struggle against Louis XIV; Consequently, between

Table 4–2.   British Military Expenditures, Wartime Peaks and
Peacetime Lows, 1688–1783. (Index = British pound, £)

MAJOR WARS	WARTIME PEAK	PEACETIME LOW
War of the Grand Alliance	£11,000,000	£3,000,000
War of Spanish Succession	15,000,000	5,000,000
War of Austrian Succession	12,000,000	6,000,000
Seven Years' War	21,000,000	10,000,000
American War	28,000,000	24,000,000

Source: John Brewer, *The Sinews of War*, p. 39.

1688 and 1714 the English state was almost constantly at war with
France. During this period, virtually every branch of the government
expanded in response to the pressures of war and empire, and Great
Britain of necessity assumed many of the political features of the large
continental states, including high rates of taxation, a standing army,
and a well-administered professional bureaucracy.[21] War continued to
drive British state development throughout the following century. The
period from the Glorious Revolution to the American Revolution saw
five sharp jumps in the size of Great Britain's army, navy, bureaucracy,
military expenditures, tax receipts, and national debt—coinciding
respectively with the five major wars in which France was a principal
adversary. Military expenditures, for example, would soar during a
war as the army and navy expanded vigorously; afterward, expenditures would drop, but never to prewar levels. The result of this "ratchet
effect" was cumulative net growth from war to war (see Table 4-2).
The mushrooming of Britain's debt—from a negligible amount in
1688 to over 242 million pounds in 1784—likewise occurred almost
entirely during wartime.[22]

Sustaining such immense military expenditures required an efficient taxation system. The English after 1688 developed one of
Europe's finest: legally uniform, rationally organized, and relatively
uncorrupted. Astonishingly, constitutional Great Britain in the eighteenth century achieved per capita revenue income nearly twice as
high as that of autocratic France! In the century after Charles II,
Britain's aggregate net tax revenue increased tenfold, reaching 20 million pounds by the time of the French Revolution. Such a robust tax
base gave its creditors confidence, enabling it to borrow money more
readily and at lower interest rates than its continental counterparts. All

this belies the notion of Great Britain as a lightly administered, lightly taxed "weak" state. How was this possible?

The historian John Brewer postulates that the answer lies in the domestic support generated by constitutional government. Precisely because Britain was *not* absolutist—because the British Commons zealously scrutinized proposals for taxation, because it held royal officials responsible for how funds were accounted for and spent, because there were counterweights to monarchical authority—British institutions acquired a public legitimacy that the arbitrary methods of absolutism could never achieve.[23] Taxation by representation made it feasible to sustain higher levels of taxation and elicit greater national sacrifice in war than was possible through military-bureaucratic coercion. Edmund Burke in 1775 spoke of the "liberal obedience" that derived from constitutional government as the foundation of the British army and navy.[24] The British case again illustrates that while war affects every kind of state in far-reaching ways, the manner in which a people organizes itself for defense is a critical variable in determining how their political system evolves at home, as well as how it copes in an anarchic international environment.

Eighteenth-century Poland offers an example parallel to Italy and Germany of the disintegrative effects of war. The extremely weak political institutions that emerged in Poland during the medieval period— an elective monarchy, the *pacta conventa* limiting royal power, the infamous *liberum veto* that allowed even a single delegate to dissolve the Diet and nullify its will—made it very difficult for a strong central Polish government, even a constitutional one, to develop. With no semblance of central authority and with its institutions mired in the worst of feudal particularism, Poland stood little chance in competition with states where the Military-Bureaucratic Revolution was in full swing. Its vulnerability became obvious in the First Northern War (1655–60) and the Russo-Polish wars of 1654–56 and 1658–67, when internal divisions played into the hands of foreign enemies, resulting in diplomatic setbacks and territorial losses.

These seventeenth-century losses portended the three partitions of Poland at the end of the eighteenth century, all of which resulted from specific wars. But the real defining catastrophe for Poland, the event that crippled the state and made it incapable of resisting foreign encroachments, was the Great Northern War of 1700–21. During this war Poland, much like the Germanic states in the Thirty Years' War, became a hapless battleground for the armies of neighboring states. The restraints on violence against civilian populations that had been accepted in Western Europe after 1648 still had not penetrated to the eastern half of the continent.[25] The bitterly fought war caused Poland's population to plummet by at least a million persons, mostly from disease, while the financial extractions of the Russian, Swedish, and Saxon armies sometimes amounted to more than the entire annual revenue of the state. Polish villages were plundered mercilessly; famine, epidemic, and depopulation followed.

Poland never recovered from the effects of this war. Without a central locus for reform efforts, defeat only widened its internal fault lines. In the War of Polish Succession (1733–38), the Polish Crown became a pawn of foreign armies and Poland was left a virtual satellite of Russia. Upon a revolt of Catholic nobles in 1768, Russian troops invaded, setting in motion the train of events that culminated in the First Partition. Shocked by the loss of one third of their population and territory, the Polish Diet agreed to abolish the *liberum veto* in 1788; four years later, it made the throne hereditary. All this was too little, too late. Factionalism prevailed again, as reactionary Polish lords rebelled against the new order, giving Catherine II of Russia ("Catherine the Great") another excuse to intervene. The Second and Third Partitions (1793 and 1795) divided what was left, erasing Poland from the map of Europe for over a century.[26] It was the most spectacular casualty of conflict among the hundreds of political entities that disappeared in the modern era. Unlike them, however, Poland would get a second chance after World War I, when the states that once partitioned it had themselves been decimated by war.

WAR, REVOLUTION, AND THE GENESIS OF THE NATION-STATE

From whence sprang the full-blooded nationalism that swelled to such heights of intensity in the French Revolution, that inspired soldiers and citizens to swear oaths to *patrie* and *nation*, that fired the French armies at Valmy and eventually propelled them across the face of all Europe? Why did nationalism become the most powerful political force of the nineteenth century, the forge of states, and why does it remain such a potent force in Europe and much of the world today? If we are to understand the passage of the state into the second stage of its modernity, the stage primarily associated with the nation-state, it is necessary first to consider the origins of nationalism.

We think of the nineteenth century, particularly the period between 1815 and 1880, as the Age of Nationalism, when a well-articulated ideology of nationalism emerged for the first time, a political doctrine that held that states should coincide geographically with nations—and that every nation large enough to constitute a sovereign state had the right to form one.[27] The voices of this classical nineteenth-century nationalism included Jeremy Bentham, Friedrich von Schlegel, Friedrich List, Ernest Renan, Karl Theodor Welcker, Jules Michelet, and Giuseppe Mazzini; its statesmen-executors were Giuseppe Garibaldi, Camillo Benso di Cavour, Louis Kossuth, and Otto von Bismarck. But nationalism is more than just a doctrine of state formation, and its origins predate the Restoration era. Nationalism is also a powerful collective emotion fixated on the mystical and mythical image of *the nation*. It is a kind of modern tribalism or political religion capable of eliciting strenuous exertions, supreme sacrifices, and deeply felt hostility— above all in war and in connection with war. For while nationalism is widely recognized as a cause of war—stimulating nationalist insurrections within states and bitter feuds between them—war is also a progenitor of nationalism. Its modern form developed in parallel with the rise of modern warfare and the modern state; from the beginning it was closely and inextricably intertwined with both.

As a collective passion rather than a political doctrine, nationalism—or what is perhaps more properly termed *protonationalism*—can be traced in European history at least as far back as the Hundred Years' War. Joan of Arc did not implore the Dauphin Charles to retake Normandy from the English. She told him to drive the English out of *France*—and this was over three hundred years before the French Revolution, in an era in which personal loyalties are regarded by historians as rarely transcending village, province, and Church.[28] Machiavelli, ever a harbinger of modernity, displayed a remarkably precocious sense of nationalism in his appeal to the Medicis of Florence to form a *national* army, free of all mercenary influence, to liberate Italy from the invasion of foreign powers.[29] The Spanish *Reconquista* likewise awakened national consciousness across the Iberian peninsula. There is nothing like warfare to sharpen communal identity and create a sense of the "otherness" of enemy peoples.

Though there is much evidence of the nationalizing impact of conflict during the two centuries between Agincourt and Westphalia, the Protestant Reformation and the religious passions it unleashed initially *slowed* and *muted* the development of protonationalism into modern state-centered nationalism. It was not only that particularist and religious loyalties were so intense; it was also that the religious wars divided the newly emerging states *internally* almost as sharply as they divided them from one another. The civil wars of the Reformation era—the Schmalkaldic War, the French Wars of Religion, the English civil wars—aggravated internal schisms and complicated, at least in the short term, the investment of national feeling in the emerging centralized states. The fact that the newly centralized states endured these strains and did not break up is an indication of their growing power and tenacity, but so long as the religious wars continued, nationalism could not coalesce around secular political institutions and the states could not become nation-states. The Puritan revolution against Charles I, in its evocation of the rights of the English people vis-à-vis royal authority, is sometimes regarded as the first manifestation of true nationalism in Europe, but the strong religious sentiments it embodied, and which continued to divide England after the Restoration, precluded English nationalism from acquiring either the intensity or the modern quality that continental nationalism would later assume in the French Revolution.[30]

Only after the passions of the religious wars subsided could national feeling come to fix on the state as its primary locus. Nationalism did not create the modern state; rather the modern state stimulated the rise of nationalism. As absolutist states grew in power—as religious and feudal claimants on loyalty retreated, as the borders of Europe were increasingly recognized as the frontiers of states rather than as dynastic property lines, as advances in warfare made the bureaucratic state the only tenable bulwark of security—human loyalties naturally began to stray from Church and village. The national feeling that had existed in unfocused form for centuries came in the course of the eighteenth century to be centered increasingly in the state. This can be seen as early as 1683 in Leibniz's satirical *Mars Christianissimus*, in which he complained of Louis XIV's France that "they already scorn our nation," in Spinoza's claim that devotion to country was the highest form of piety, in Herder's call for Germans to "spit out the green slime of the Seine" (i.e., the French language). The Marquis d'Argenson observed in 1754 that "never before were the names of Nation and State evoked as often as today. These two words were never pronounced under Louis XIV, and one hardly knew what they meant."[31]

The wars of the eighteenth century were the lunar gravity driving the incoming tide of nationalism. Precisely because they were limited wars, not fought for some supranational empire or supreme cause, but only for the narrow interests of the state, they strengthened perceptions of the state as the primary claimant on loyalty. During a war, human loyalty tends to migrate to the highest level at which the current collective military efforts are organized, and after 1648 that level increasingly became the state; armies became seedbeds of nationalism in their own right. Though mercenary forces still constituted a sizable portion of national armies, moving with ease from one paymaster to another, the percentage of native-born soldiers increased steadily as the century progressed. By 1789, 75 percent of the French army were French subjects. When Austria occupied much of Galicia in the First Partition of Poland, the idea of raising regiments for the Austrian army from the occupied territory was suggested—what would have been routine practice even fifty years earlier. Field Marshal Franz Lacy, an adviser to the Regent, Joseph II, argued against the plan on the grounds that "a national spirit is taking a general hold, especially among the common people. We may therefore expect the Poles to be as attached to their fatherland as the Silesians."[32]

There are in fact many war-related sources of nationalism, and all of them were at work in the eighteenth century. One was the unifying effect of frequent wars; faced with a common external enemy, the community of the nation tends to rally, and now for the first time there were coherent central governments to rally around. (As the sociologist George Simmel argued, a perception of mutual threat invariably promotes group cohesion—even at the level of a nation!) Another factor that helped solidify the budding nationalisms of eighteenth-century Europe was the integrating effect of military service on soldiers—for example, by promoting usage of a single dialect and by diluting parochial attachments. Finally, when faced with the prospect of death in battle, the human mind inevitably seeks some higher meaning—and in wars where religion played little or no role, the myth of the nation offered one answer. Frederick the Great sought to inculcate his soldiers with a passionate Prussian patriotism that was closely akin to modern nationalism. His writings speak of the "spirit of the army," while his war cry at the Battle of Zorndorf—"Come, children, die with me for the fatherland!"—was only a short step from the *Vive la nation* of Valmy.[33]

There were also nonmilitary factors in the rise of nationalism, of course, such as the increasing availability of the printed word in vernacular languages and the published writings of the Enlightenment philosophers, above all Rousseau, who gave philosophical undergirding to the concept of popular sovereignty.[34] But just as the French invasion of Italy in 1494 had given rise to the "generation of '94" in political philosophy, so also did the wars of the eighteenth century— particularly the American War of Independence—stimulate nationalist thinking. The rationalism of the Enlightenment was not the only source of the nationalism articulated by Rousseau, Johann Gottfried Herder, Edmund Burke, Vicomte de Bonald, Thomas Jefferson, and Thomas Paine; their writings were also a response to the drumbeat of current events.

The crisis of the *anciens régimes* came about in part because dynastically based states could not fulfill the nationalist aspirations that their very existence had stimulated. Though the autocratic state was the locus of collective efforts during wartime, it was unable to offer its subjects anything beyond security; it could not fill what Michelet called "the immeasurable abyss" left by the Enlightenment. For the autocratic state to do that, it would have to represent the interests and aspirations of the nation, not merely those of the ruling dynasty. The incompatibility of dynasticism with nationalism was the fundamental contradiction that destroyed the *ancien régime* in France. That contradiction also accounts for the schizophrenia of nineteenth-century nationalism, which fixated on the state as the embodiment of nationalist aspirations, the Sovereign of the General Will, yet sought to overthrow established monarchical states everywhere.

After 1789, nationalism became a revolutionary force that challenged the legitimacy of any government that did not derive its sovereignty from the nation; it rejected traditional nonnational sources of legitimacy, such as the divine right of kings or dynastic property rights, as usurpations of the popular will. Nationalism insisted that the state become the nation-state, that its wars become the wars of the nation and not of any private cause alone. It happened first in France, where the rivulets of eighteenth-century nationalism became suddenly a raging torrent that overflowed French borders and flooded the continent.[35]

MILITARY FACTORS IN THE ORIGIN OF THE FRENCH REVOLUTION

If the French Revolution burst upon Europe like some vast cosmic fireball, it was not because of its radicalism alone (Rousseau was well known), nor its internal turmoil (another *Fronde*), nor even its regicide (Charles I of England was not forgotten). It was because Revolutionary France sent massive numbers of troops pouring outward across its borders as if dispatched to remind the world that a true revolution, and not a mere revolt, was in progress. To the *philosophes* of Europe, the Revolution was the realization of a century of intellectual ferment; to the people of France, it was a grand struggle over who would govern. But to the established order of Europe, it was an urgent,

profound military threat that focused minds marvelously on the
source of its irrepressible energy: the fusion of nation and state.

Few events in modern history were so complex in their origins and
progressions as the French Revolution of 1789–99. A host of social,
economic, political, and ideological factors entered into its making,
and in emphasizing its military side this chapter obviously paints an
incomplete picture. But the specifically military factors that entered
into its making help explain why Revolutionary France rapidly became
embroiled in wars with its neighbors, why the French state was so easily seized by Napoleon, and why France was at war for the better part of
twenty-three years after 1792. As Simon Schama has argued, the military aggressiveness of France after 1792 was neither accidental nor
antithetical to the spirit of the Revolution, but was the logical culmination of almost everything it represented.[36]

What were the military elements that contributed to the coming of
the French Revolution? The first was the direct impact of the American War of Independence. Deeply humiliated by its defeat in the Seven
Years' War, France after 1763 actively encouraged—via agents, propaganda, and diplomacy—an American independence movement as a
way of striking back at Great Britain. Under the American–French
alliance of 1778, the French made strenuous efforts on behalf of the
American cause, efforts that were wildly popular with the educated
French public. The French fleet fought the British in the West Indies
and around the world; in 1781 alone, when the French navy cut off
Cornwallis at Yorktown, French naval spending was *five times* its normal annual amount. Moreover, though the Marquis de Lafayette and
other French officers initially went to America more for glory, adventure, and vengeance against the British than for any high-sounding
commitment to liberty, they returned brimming with idealism; the
American revolution had radicalized them in advance of their own.
Lafayette and the Comte de Rochambeau are best known, but at least
thirty-six other prominent Frenchmen played leading roles in both the
American and the French revolutions. Among the aristocratic elite
back home, the war also quickened the rise of nationalism, both
through its ideological influence and by fanning intense anti-British
feeling.[37]

A second war-related factor was the fiscal crisis of the Bourbon
monarchy. The immediate cause of this was the enormous outlays of
the American War, which compounded the burden of French war
debts that had piled up since Louis XIV. The Seven Years' War, in particular, had exacted an immense toll on the French state. Between 1753
and 1764 (years for which good data are available) France's debt nearly

doubled, from 1.36 million *livres* to 2.35 million. Servicing this debt required more than 60 percent of total state expenditures per annum.[38] The American War, over 90 percent funded by loans, added another 1.20 million *livres* of debt—the straw that broke the Treasury's back.[39] In Chapter 1, we identified an "inspection effect" of war—how it reveals to a people and a polity their most serious defects. The American War did this for the *ancien régime*, painfully revealing the defects of its antiquated and inequitable taxation system—defects that a venerable series of aristocratic critics, including Marshal Vauban in his *Dixme Royale* (1707), had recognized as portending trouble for the monarchy. Whatever the larger causes of the French Revolution, its *immediate* cause was this fiscal crisis brought on by the American War.[40] In a France where every social class already despised the corrupt taxation system of the Farmers-General, and where the nobility had a long tradition of resisting direct taxation, the Crown's intent to raise new revenues provoked spirited resistance from the *parlements*— almost a replay of the *Fronde* of 1648—and compelled Louis XVI to summon the fateful Estates-General to Versailles. The French Revolution, like the earlier American Revolution, began as a revolt against taxation made necessary by the cost of war.

A third, and ultimately decisive, military factor in the French Revolution was the politicization of the French army and the erosion of the Crown's monopoly of armed power. By the late 1780s, even before the Estates-General convened, some 3,000 troops were deserting annually, and in 1788–89, there were numerous incidents—at Rennes, Béarn, Toulouse, Besançon, and Grenoble—of officers or soldiers resisting orders to suppress local disturbances.[41] By the time of the storming of the Bastille (an operation spearheaded by over a hundred soldiers from the French Guards and the line army) the Crown rightly felt it could no longer trust the 20,000 troops ringing Paris. Nor did the army fall into line when the National Assembly asserted control over many facets of its administration after February 1790. Like the Long Parliament before it, the Assembly discovered how difficult it was to control an army that had tasted power. Desertions and mutinies multiplied, and there were massive defections to the salaried National Guard formed by municipal authorities in Paris. By July 1790, more than one third of line army units were experiencing serious insubordination, usually involving confrontation between soldiers and officers. The Minister of War declared that insubordination was creating a "military democracy" and driving the aristocratic officer corps into exile. When the monarchy was overthrown in the revolt of August 1792, the senior army commanders, even those of royalist sentiment, almost unanimously concluded that their troops would not support a march on Paris to restore the King. By then the French elite were beginning to understand what dozens of monarchs, dictators, and General Secretaries would eventually learn: that it is impossible to isolate a large standing army from larger currents of social change, and that once the army is lost the state is lost as well.

REVOLUTIONARY EXPANSIONISM AND THE MILITARY ORIGINS OF THE TERROR

The military factors discussed above do not alone explain the intense nationalism and militarism that emanated from the Revolution. Why did the Revolution turn outward, and why did France become a militarized and militarily expansionist state so swiftly after its army had nearly collapsed?

Part of the answer lies in the close connection between France's earlier wars and the development of French nationalism. Following the humiliation of the Seven Years' War, a deeply felt *ressentiment* toward Great Britain brooded among the French elite. Victory in the subsequent American War did not assuage this anti-British feeling but only gave French nationalism an increasingly militant and triumphalist tone. And though Austria had fought in alliance with France in the Seven Years' War and remained nominally an ally, anti-Austrian sentiment was also strong. (This was reflected for example in the popular opprobrium heaped on Marie Antoinette, whose Austrian birth and ties with the Austrian court made her exceedingly unpopular—especially after 1785, when during a minor diplomatic crisis with Austria she persuaded her husband to moderate the French position.) In short, French nationalism on the eve of the Revolution had come to define itself very much in *antiforeign* terms, and this xenophobic brand of nationalism gained rapid momentum as the Revolution proceeded. Camille Desmoulins expressed its essence in *La France libre* (1793): "The foreigners are going to regret that they are not French. We shall surpass these English, so proud of their constitution, who ridiculed our servitude."[42]

The French decision to declare war against Austria in 1792 is often portrayed as a reaction to the Declaration of Pillnitz, as the launching of an ideological crusade for the Rights of Man against the tottering despotisms of the Old Regimes of Europe. It was nothing of the sort. The Declaration of Pillnitz was a carefully hedged, largely symbolic gesture that stirred little response in Paris. Furthermore, Austria had no real interest in waging war. Joseph II had *reduced* his army by

25,000 men before going to Pillnitz, and his advisers had *welcomed* the Constitution of 1791, which they assumed would render Louis XVI a less formidable opponent. By contrast, the Girondists in the National Assembly agitated vigorously for war throughout the fall and winter of 1791 and the spring of 1792, as a way of diverting attention from France's internal problems and consolidating their own position at home. The ideological impurity of their motives is shown by their zeal to have *Prussia*—despotic, militaristic Prussia—as an ally of France against Austria. The King also wanted war, thinking that it would enhance his own power or, failing that, would result in foreign intervention that would end the Revolution. His was the classic error of traditionalists and conservatives everywhere who think war will enhance their position—it usually undermines it. In short, France went to war not in a flush of idealism but rather urged on by radicals and a miscalculating monarch, both of whom hoped to exploit the dynamic of war for their own purposes. But once declared, the fact of war itself intensified French nationalism and gave rise to national myths that endure even today.[43]

This should not be taken to minimize the significance of the Declaration of the Rights of Man in setting France apart from the rest of Europe. The statement in Article 3 that all sovereignty resides in the Nation marked the formal fusion of nation with state and was itself an important step in the evolution of French nationalism. But in the fury of the Revolution, the ideal of popular sovereignty became inextricably joined with the reality of a xenophobic nationalism before which the more liberal nationalism of the Declaration retreated. Once the Nation went to war against its enemies, the Nation's army inevitably became the focal point of national aspirations and the embodiment of nationalist fervor. The images of war, blood, and battle that permeate the verses of "La Marseillaise," and its repeated refrain—"*Aux armes, citoyens*"—perfectly capture the ascendancy of the military element in the nationalism of the Revolution. Nor was it just the volunteers and the National Guard that manifested the new nationalism. The regular units of the Fifth Artillery in March 1792 petitioned the Assembly not to increase army salaries, as they preferred to fight for liberty, not pay. And at Valmy, when the power of French nationalism first reverberated on the battlefield, it was the regular line army and particularly the artillery, whose bourgeois officers had not left the service, that carried the brunt of the fighting.[44]

Well before the *leveé en masse*, the nationalization of the French army had begun. Three key events altered its character and made it more representative of the nation.

First, beginning in 1790 and with accelerated tempo after the royal flight to Varennes, over 2,000 noble officers fled France and were replaced by NCOs or National Guard officers. By early 1793, nobles constituted only 15 to 20 percent of the officer corps; by mid-1794, only 2 to 3 percent of captains were of the nobility, while 67 percent were artisans or bourgeois and a remarkable 22 percent were peasants.

Second, a series of recruitment drives enlisted large numbers of new soldiers. In the summer of 1791, the Assembly called for 100,000 volunteers from the National Guard; in April 1792, after declaring war on Austria, it called for an additional 83,600 volunteers. Fully 68 percent of this latter group were peasants, compared with only 15 percent in the line army of 1789. The volunteers served in separate units, but beginning in 1793, when the National Guard was gradually amalgamated into the line army, many became regular soldiers. In February 1793, the Assembly announced a third levy of 300,000, of which at most 180,000 were raised, largely by conscription and largely from the peasantry. In addition to elevating peasant representation, the recruitment drives gave the army greater geographic balance.

A third step in the nationalization of the army occurred in August and September of 1792, when the Assembly discharged the Swiss and the Royal Liégeois Regiments of the Army—alien citizenship having become *prima facie* grounds for doubting loyalty. By February 1793, only about 4 percent of the French army were foreigners.[45]

The proclamation of the *levée en masse* of August 1793 was a desperate measure forced on the Committee of Public Safety by the Republic's precarious military situation. After Valmy French armies under Dumouriez and Custine had advanced rapidly into the Austrian Netherlands and the Rhineland; in February 1793 the Assembly, flush with victory, had declared war on Great Britain and the United Provinces. The conscription measures announced that month triggered massive domestic resistance, above all in the western provinces. By March of 1793, the French armies abroad were suffering stark reverses, and the First Coalition had been formed. By June, the Vendée was embroiled in full-scale civil war; anti-Republican insurrections were occurring across Brittany, Anjou, and Poitou; the "Federal Cities" of Lyons, Bordeaux, Marseilles, and Toulon had revolted; Prussian armies had defeated the French in the Rhineland; and a British-Hanoverian army had triumphed in the Austrian Netherlands. It was in this context of stark threat—at the ever-powerful conjunction of simultaneous civil and international war that either destroys states or enormously enhances their power—that the Committee of Public Safety assumed full dictatorial powers, leading in short order to the *levée en masse* and the Terror.

The *levée en masse* marked the consecration of the Army as the embodiment of the French Nation. Rousseau in *The Government of Poland* (1772) had advocated a people's army in which every citizen would serve as a soldier. In the same year the Count de Guibert published an *Essai général de tactique* advocating a citizen army and predicting that if any nation ever coupled such an army with a plan of aggrandizement, it would overwhelm Europe (though he doubted it would actually happen). In the 1770s and 1780s, numerous other French *philosophes*—Montesquieu, Joseph Servan, the Abbé Mably— came out in favor of a citizens' army. The newly formed National Guard, with its patriotic élan and bourgeois officer corps, was viewed by many as just such an army, particularly after the obligation to serve in it was made universal, at least in theory. But the *levée en masse* went further. It attempted to create not merely an army of citizens, but a *nation of soldiers*, mobilized and dedicated to the military cause of the state. Article I of the decree of August 23, 1793, says it all:

> From this moment until that in which the enemy is driven from the territory of the Republic, all Frenchmen are permanently requisitioned for service in the armies.
>   Young men will go forth to battle; married men will forge weapons and transport munitions; women will make tents and clothing, and serve in hospitals; children will make linen into bandages; and old men will be carried to the public squares to arouse the courage of the soldiers, while preaching the hatred of kings and unity of the Republic.[46]

Formally, the decree conscripted all able-bodied men between the ages of eighteen and twenty-five into the army. All told, it raised nearly 300,000 fresh soldiers, almost twice as many as the Assembly had raised the previous spring, bringing the size of the French army to approximately 750,000, an impressive 2.9 percent of the national population. In social composition, the levy was almost a mirror image of the French nation, drawing fairly on all classes.[47]

The much vaunted nationalism of this enlarged French army was hardly a spontaneous phenomenon. From the beginning, the state fostered and manipulated the nationalism that sustained it. Jean Baptiste Bouchotte, Minister of War at the time of the *levée*, targeted his troops with a vigorous propaganda campaign, distributing over 7,000,000 copies of twelve revolutionary journals. The government also distributed patriotic songbooks and organized revolutionary *fêtes* for the soldiers. In this and other respects, the mass mobilization of 1793–94 portended the manipulation of nationalism that would become commonplace in the twentieth century. The economic sphere showed impressive achievements that also derived in part from the energy of nationalism. The large metallurgical factories of Le Creusot and the armaments factory at St.-Etienne were flooded with state contracts. Thousands of improvised workshops manufactured muskets, gunpowder, and other materiel. Church bells from all over France were melted down to make cannon. Engineers, chemists and other scientists offered their services, developing, among other things, a new method for manufacturing saltpeter.[48] The first true nation-state in possession of the first mass citizen army formed a national engine of war like none Europe had ever seen before.

The domestic strain of war—especially the civil war in the West—was the primary cause of the Terror, which began one month after the *levée en masse*. While ideological fanaticism may account for the Terror's cold amorality, neither ideological nor economic factors can explain why it happened. Statistical evidence of war as the driving force and rationale is found in a classic study by Donald Greer on the incidence of the arrests and executions carried out by authority of the Committee. Fully 74 percent of all the executions took place in the seventeen *départements* embroiled in the civil war—the Vendée and other provinces of the West, and the Rhône valley, where the Federal Cities were situated. Outside of Paris itself (which suffered 16 percent of the executions), the remainder of the carnage was concentrated largely in the frontier provinces, where enemy forces threatened and opportunities for treason were rife. Where neither civil war nor foreign army threatened, the Terror was a minimal event.[49]

Greer's statistics further suggest that the civil war in the Vendée and elsewhere—what Robespierre termed the threat of an "internal Coblenz"—was a larger factor in causing the Terror than the threat from abroad. The two were linked, however, for the deployment of much of the French army abroad or on the frontiers forced the revolutionary government to rely on terror and other unorthodox methods to contain the insurrections at home. The tightly drawn military-bureaucratic dictatorship of the Committee of Public Safety imposed draconian price controls, instituted war taxes, and dispatched specially formed *armées revolutionnaires* (urban militia consisting mostly of unemployed *sans-culottes*) from Republican-controlled cities into the countryside to enforce economic controls and to requisition grain and equipment for the army. Eventually numbering nearly 40,000, the *armées*—"Terror on the move" in the words of Richard Cobb—facilitated the domination by the modernizing cities over the traditional agrarian society and the penetration of the revolutionary state into the countryside.[50] In terms of forging a unitary French nationalism, the Republican victories in the civil war were at least as crucial as any military successes abroad, for the provinces that revolted were the most medieval, the least secular, the least "modernized," and the least integrated sections of France; their victory would have called into question the basic ideological legitimacy and cohesion of the newly incarnated centralized nation-state.

Would the Revolution have perished without the Terror, as Saint-Just claimed? Theda Skocpol, for one, argues that it probably would have, since only an immense concentration of power could have held France together in 1793–94. And since the Revolution *in toto* acted as a "gigantic broom" that swept away the "medieval rubbish" of seignorial and particularist privilege and paved the way for industrial capitalism to emerge in France, both the Revolution and the Terror were integral components of political and economic modernization.[51] So long as "modernization" is not confused with moral progress, this is at least an arguable perspective, one that finds resonance in much of contemporary scholarship. But the tendency of Western historians and social scientists is ever to read progress backwards into history. Preoccupied with history's "evolution," we are easily blinded to its tragedies. The remorselessness of the Terror, the unspeakable atrocities committed by Republican forces in the Vendée, the harshness of the Committee's "de-Christianization" vendetta are stark reminders of the ambiguous nature of political change in the modern era and the ever-present potential of war to corrupt and debase human nature. By concentrating absolute state power, war corrupts absolutely.

THE NAPOLEONIC TRANSFORMATION OF FRANCE

Given the close linkage between war and state formation, it can hardly be regarded as coincidental that both the Puritan revolution in England and the secular Revolution in France culminated in military rule. In conditions of anarchy and strife, the army often emerges as the one social organization with sufficient discipline to seize power and govern. The parallel of a single charismatic military officer assuming dictatorial powers in each country is also no accident, given the tendency of military organizations to concentrate power in a single leader, and most often in that general acknowledged by his peers as greatest in war. When Napoleon Bonaparte came to power in the *coup d'état* of 18 Brumaire 1799, France had been at war for over seven years, and the

Corsican was a national hero. Beneath the froth of regime changes in Paris, the French state had become an immense military machine. It was only logical that a general head up this machine, especially given the widespread yearning for a restoration of public order. The regrettable inclination of historians has been to devote far greater attention to his foreign exploits than to his domestic achievements—and rarely to relate the two—yet the latter not only proved more enduring, but had a greater imprint on French life down to the present than all the unstable experiments and innovations of Assembly, Convention, and Directory before him.

As First Consul and later Emperor, Napoleon consolidated the three main gains of the Revolution: rationalization, centralization, and secularization. All were characteristics of modernity; all derived from the inexorable calculus of the military state. Prior to his coming, the architects of the Revolution had undertaken two principal rationalizing reforms: the abolition of the feudal rights of the old *pays d'états* and the privileged cities, and the division of France into 83 geographically more or less equal *départements*, in turn further subdivided into districts, cantons, and communes. These reforms ostensibly made France a unified nation, equally administered in all its parts, though the tumult of civil war, terror, and upheaval in Paris made this a rather theoretical proposition. Napoleon kept this basic structure intact but instituted a system of centrally appointed prefects, subprefects, and mayors that converted it from an edifice of republican rationalism into a top-down hierarchy of centralized power. This military propensity to centralize and rationalize carried over into almost all aspects of state administration, whether in the First Consul's creation of the Bank of France in 1800, his reorganization of the judiciary under the Court of Cassation, the formation of a centralized Ministry of Police over the *gendarmerie*, or the transfer of responsibility for tax collection from municipal officials to a system of inspectors and assessors supervised by a general director in Paris. Central auditing, rigorously enforced, enabled the Napoleonic revenue system to yield a balanced budget in the year X (1801–1802) for the first time in many years.

With respect to the aggrandizement of state power, two ministries played major roles: the Ministry of the Interior and the Ministry of Police. Their efforts were closely coordinated at the center and often overlapped. The Ministry of the Interior attempted to regulate, to a degree of detail that became ever more minute as time passed, every facet of French life—agriculture, commerce, roads, bridges, mines, education, arts, public works, scientific establishments, and the National Guard. It was also responsible for that highly intrusive, ever-dominant fact of young male existence under Napoleon, conscription, and between 1800 and 1815 the French state drafted a total of at least 2 million men. As the nineteenth-century historian Gabriel Hanotaux observed, the French Empire was "an empire of recruitment" before all else.[52]

The Ministry of Police under Joseph Fouché turned France into the most efficient police state yet seen in Europe, the severity of its measures justified in part by the unceasing threat from foreign enemies, especially Great Britain, and the need to enforce the Continental System, which sought to ban all European trade with the latter. The Ministry enforced censorship of the press, conducted surveillance of suspected persons, and employed a system of passports and identity cards intended to make it easier to distinguish between foreigners and citizens. The French system of passports, originally intended to aid in capturing foreign spies and saboteurs, was eventually adopted by the other countries of Europe and became a permanent fixture of international life. It is eminently symbolic of the link between war and nationalism that the concept of passports (and the very term *passeport*) originated out of the cauldron of the French Revolutionary and Napoleonic Wars. This document still today gives millions of travelers proof of their nationality and their citizenship in a specific state.[53]

Further reflecting his military officer's penchant for order, Napoleon sought to replace France's four hundred separate legal codes—inherited variously from Roman or medieval practice according to the province of their origin—with a single, uniform, and fully codified body of laws. This had also been the stated ambition of the National Assembly in 1791, but it took a military dictator to achieve the desired outcome, which ran roughshod over particularist traditions. The resulting civil code, the *Code Napoléon*, and five other Codes of Law gave France the most equitable and rational judicial system in Europe. The First Consul was deeply involved in the crafting of the Civil Code, personally presiding at 57 of the 102 sessions of the section of the Council of State that approved the final draft. The resulting product provided for the first time anywhere in Europe a uniform body of laws that applied equally to all male citizens of any class. (Ironically, the Code was promulgated in the same month as Napoleon's most notorious act of international injustice—the kidnapping and summary execution of the Duke of Enghien.) The Napoleonic codes epitomized the Cartesian rationality and centralized rule to which France had aspired since Louis XIV, and they increased public consciousness of France as a unified nation-state. The Civil Code also greatly influenced the development of civil law elsewhere in Europe, both by virtue of its intellectual elegance and because French armies simply imposed it on most of the European countries they occupied. (In the first hundred and fifty years after the Code was promulgated, it was implemented in 35 states and adapted by 35 others.)[54]

Napoleon's domestic reforms were a curious fusion of the spirit of the Enlightenment and the no-nonsense command approach of the military officer. Indeed, *this* was "enlightened absolutism," if there ever was such a thing. The military-ideological fusion can be seen in the Napoleonic approach to education. The man who founded the University of France five months after his victory at Austerlitz and three months after the crushing of Naples well understood that in the modern age an educated society is as much a pillar of military success as a prosperous society. The 45 *lycées* that he established to replace the "central schools" of the Directory (roughly the equivalent of high schools) had a curriculum that encompassed the highest learning of the day: rhetoric, classical languages, mathematics, and science. But the *lycées* simultaneously reflected the martial inspiration of the regime: students wore uniforms to class; strict military discipline was enforced; class began and ended with drum rolls; military instruction was integral to the curriculum. Under Napoleon, the École Polytechnique established by the Convention in 1794 became increasingly devoted to the training of military engineers; after 1805 it fell under the administration of the War Department.[55]

The Abbé Siéyès described Napoleon as the most civilian of all military men, evidently in reference to his visionary domestic achievements. Yet Napoleon's whole regime was irrepressibly, pervasively *military* in character. Simon Schama describes the France of 1793 as a warrior state; after 1799, it became a state governed by warriors as well.[56] A good example is the founding of the Legion of Honor and the "senatoriates" in 1804, which marked the beginning of a new aristocracy of merit in France, theoretically open to all classes. What is most striking, however, is the overwhelming predominance of the military in the new elite. Of the 2,000 members initiated into the Legion in August 1804, *99.5 percent* were military; by 1814, still less than 5 percent of its 32,000 members were civilian. If the Napoleonic nobility as a whole is measured, military officers constituted 59 percent of its ranks, a much higher percentage than in the aristocracy of the Old Regime. The upper crust of this new "militocracy," Napoleon's marshals, acquired fantastic personal fortunes from the new arrangement, becoming without question the richest individuals in France. In 1807 alone, 27 marshals and generals divided among themselves 20,000,000 francs of Polish revenue confiscated from the Grand Duchy of

Warsaw.[57] By any measure, France was the most military of states; its leader, the most military of civilians.

While France was undergoing sweeping changes under its military masters, what of its nemesis, Great Britain? Mobilized to the teeth for war, this unwavering foe of revolution in Europe suppressed political radicalism, trade unionism, and war dissent at home. Yet ironically, the British victory in the denouement at Waterloo served neither to preserve the status quo on the continent—where Napoleon had wrought an irreversible revolution—nor even in Albion itself, where the end of the war uncorked a fountain of reform sentiment. Demands for parliamentary and suffrage reform mounted after 1815, culminating in the Reform Act of 1832. Though many factors contributed to its passage, the Act is another example of how mass military service generates democratizing pressures; as many as one in six adult males had served in the army or navy at the peak periods of the war with France, and their service was evoked in the parliamentary debate over the Act. The political effervescence of Great Britain after 1815 is a reminder that the reformative repercussions of war are not confined solely to the defeated parties (the usual presumption), but may affect the victors as well.

THE NAPOLEONIC TRANSFORMATION OF EUROPE AND THE RISING TIDE OF NATIONALISM

On June 19, 1790, a large delegation of international exiles visited the National Assembly in Paris. Consisting of Arabs, Chaldeans, Dutch, English, Germans, Italians, Prussians, Poles, Swiss, Swedes, Spaniards, Sicilians, Syrians, and others, it came to thank the Assembly for the Declaration of the Rights of Man. The delegation's leader, Anacharsis Cloots, proclaimed exultantly that "the trumpet which sounded the reveille of a great people has reached to the four corners of the globe, and the songs of joy of a choir of 25,000,000 free men have awakened peoples entombed in a long slavery."[58] Even today, the French Revolution is often portrayed in terms akin to those of Cloots—as the trumpet that aroused the nations and spawned the Age of Nationalism, "the springtime of peoples" in which nationalist insurrections sprang up like wildflowers and wars of independence caused a blossoming of new nation-states in Europe.[59]

Given the rhetoric of the nineteenth century—laced with references to popular sovereignty, the will of the people, national identity, and universal rights—it is beyond dispute that the ideological legacy of the Revolution and the *philosophes* had an immense impact on the course of European history after Waterloo. Emphasizing the intellectual influence of the French Revolution, however, risks slighting the critical importance of the French Revolutionary and Napoleonic *Wars* in unleashing nationalism and modernizing influences across Europe.[60] Napoleon in particular is too often interpreted as the culminator of the Revolution, rather than its culmination—as the man who restored order, rather than as the exporter of radical political change. Historical preoccupation with the man's battlefield prowess, rather than with his immense political impact on Europe, is but another example of the tendency to regard wars as primarily outcomes, rather than as vast causal events in their own right.

For Napoleon is pivotal. No figure in European history more perfectly embodied the bond between war and state formation than he. No single factor contributed more to the "awakening of nations" than the march of his armies; no single factor had a greater modernizing impact on tradition-bound dynastic states than the imperium he forged through military conquest and occupation. One prominent German historian, Thomas Nipperdey, argues this brilliantly in his definitive *Deutsche Geschichte 1800–1866*:

> It is true that the fundamental principles of the modern world emerged with the French Revolution. . . . However, for the Germans, the overthrow of the old order first became a practical reality under Napoleon in the form of military imperialism. Only those who have become ideologically blind with respect to the phenomenon of power and concentrate only on the structures and social movements of domestic politics can ignore this basic reality.[61]

So persuaded was Nipperdey of the centrality of Napoleon in the modernization of Germany that he began his massive work of 838 pages with an arresting pronouncement: "In the beginning was Napoleon." By destroying feudal structures and imposing a whole new political order on Europe, this consummate military figure of European history brought about an administrative revolution of continental proportions. Not only did he mold the vessels into which the wine of nationalism was poured, but by provoking bitter opposition to French hegemony, he brewed the wine itself.

The Napoleonic juggernaut elicited two distinct forms of nationalism: a liberal nationalism that responded favorably to the idealism of

the French Revolution and a virulent, martial nationalism that was a
reaction to the dominion of France and the excesses of its armies. The
liberal view was strongest among the proto-Jacobin radicals of Europe
and among the bourgeoisie and artisans who seethed with hatred for
the aristocratic order that Napoleon promised to destroy. In the beginning such groups had welcomed, glamorized, and even worshipped
the French Revolution; and except in the German Rhineland, where
disillusionment was knocking even before Napoleon's advent, they
remained true believers for a time. They saw the Corsican as the sword
of the Revolution, the standard-bearer who would export its principles
to the whole continent and make possible democratic revolution
everywhere. And Napoleon, for his part, actively encouraged such illusions, not as a disciple of Rousseau (though he had studied his works)
but because the shrewd tactician in him wanted to divide and weaken
the multinational empires that opposed him. Wherever his armies
went, like the armies of the Republic before them, they proclaimed the
liberation of peoples and the Rights of Man. And what better adver-
tisement was there for the superiority of such principles than the military successes of the French army?

Yet in sowing a radical nationalism that opposed the Old Order,
Napoleon unwittingly harvested a reactionary nationalism that fought
to defeat the New Order. The harsh realities of French occupation—
the confiscation of state funds, military conscription, punitive actions
against resistance—generated powerful currents of anti-French sentiment, both among disillusioned enthusiasts of the Revolution and
among the aristocratic elites of the Old Guard themselves. Anti-French
defiance ignited a bonfire of nationalism that swept most of occupied
Europe. In Spain, the anti-French gospel unified peasants and magnates as never before, forcing Napoleon to concentrate over 370,000
troops in the peninsula in 1810, the most he ever dispatched against
any one country. In Germany, Freiherr Heinrich vom Stein called for a
crusade against "the obscene, shameless and dissolute French race," to
culminate in the razing of Paris. Goethe wrote of "an inspiring fire"
burning everywhere against French imperialism. In Italy, there were
anti-French uprisings in Parma-Piacenza in 1805 and throughout central Italy and the Vallentina in 1809.[62] As in the eighteenth century,
conflict with a foreign enemy served as an elemental source of nationalism. National identity sprang as much from what a nation hated as
from what it loved.

The experience of Graf Fyodor Vasilevich Rostopchin, Governor of
Moscow in 1812, is a perfect example of this. Like most of Russia's aristocratic elite, the Governor spoke French as his principal language and

imbibed French culture on a daily basis. But as Napoleon's army approached, Rostopchin struggled furiously to rid himself of his French-ness, noting in his diary that he had begun studying the Russian language seriously for the first time in his life. Rostopchin's nationalist epiphany, replicated countless times in dozens of countries, typifies the experience of the European aristocracy during the Napoleonic era. French military hegemony undermined French cultural hegemony and generated the nationalist forces that made the creation of a pan-European empire cen-tered in Paris a complete impossibility. In defeating his enemies, Napoleon created them anew. In seeking to unite Europe under a French imperium, he ensured its permanent division into nation-states.

Soldiers and officers were the segment of European society most affected by contact with Napoleon's armies, and they became a chan-nel for the propagation of nationalist and reform sentiment. Profes-sional officers in particular understood the advantages France had gained by forming a mass citizen army imbued with nationalist fervor, and since such an army was inconceivable under traditional abso-lutism, they often became proponents of political reform.[63] Also of importance was the experience of nearly a million soldiers who were mobilized from outside the borders of France by the Napoleonic con-scription net. Ermolao Federigo, a young Italian officer who served in the *Grande Armée* in 1804, wrote home that it did not matter whom he served, so long as he and his fellow Italians learned to be good soldiers: "The great aim must be to learn to make war, which is the only skill that can free us."[64] This was the sentiment of most of occupied Europe: learn from the French so as to defeat them. Since many of the foreign-ers in the Grande Armée also fought *against* Napoleon in the dénoue-ment, it is fair to assume they were doubly infected: once by fighting with the French army and imbibing its spirit; once more by fighting against it, fired with the anti-French nationalism that Napoleon's con-quests had generated. One consequence of rising nationalism among military officers and soldiers was their frequent involvement in the nationalist uprisings that flared in Europe between 1820 and 1848. Another consequence was the abrupt end of the mercenary army. For-eigners could no longer be trusted to serve in *national* armies; the French segregated them into the Foreign Legion after 1821; other European armies gradually thinned them out of their ranks.[65]

In the rise of the nation-state, the formation of the *state* is as impor-tant as the birth of the *nation*. Napoleon's enduring bequest to France was his forging of a centralized nation-state infused with a secular spirit, substantially divested of traditional impediments to state power, and possessed of a uniform system of administration and laws. His enduring bequest to Europe was the exportation of this Gallic template of government to every corner of the French Empire and to many of the countries subject to his rule. At its peak (1809–12), the French Empire proper was divided into 131 departments encompassing over 750,000 square kilometers and 44 million inhabitants; it encompassed present-day France, Belgium, the Netherlands, the eastern coast of the Adriatic, and much of Italy. Within this empire, a single system of administration prevailed and the Napoleonic legal codes applied. In other areas subject to his control—Spain, the remainder of Italy, the Rhine Confederation, the Helvetic Confederation, the Kingdom of Westphalia, the Grand Duchy of Warsaw—he abolished feudalism, imposed part or all of the French system of administration and law, including the Code Napoléon, and introduced the French system of public finance. In most such areas, the French conqueror also promulgated a new constitution to legitimate the new order and to serve as a model of enlightened statecraft. There is not even a remote parallel in any era of European history to such a continent-wide program of deliberate state formation. Decades after Napoleon's demise, and even in parts of Europe where he and his country were despised, the institutional legacy of the French Empire and occupation lived on.[66] Although the French *philosophes* ultimately may have conquered the mind of Europe, the man whom Hegel called "the secretary of the World-Spirit" was the agent of their conquest.

In this regard, it is fascinating to observe that even prior to the revolutionary wave of 1848, nationalist revolts or conflicts between nationalists and traditionalists had occurred in *every* country that had been occupied by Napoleon's armies or that had even only been allied with him—and many of them were instigated by officers and soldiers who had fought in the Napoleonic wars. Mutinous troops revolted against Ferdinand VII of Spain in 1814. The Spanish revolt triggered uprisings in Portugal, Naples, and Sardinia. The provinces of Belgium (formerly the Austrian Netherlands) revolted against Dutch rule in 1830 and won independence the following year. Russia meanwhile experienced the Decembrist revolt of army officers (1825) and a host of peasant uprisings; Poland rebelled unsuccessfully against Russian rule (1830–31); Montenegro (a French dependency under Napoleon) rebelled against Ottoman rule beginning in 1832; in 1847, the Radicals in Switzerland, who sought to form a more centralized nation-state, won a brief civil war against the Sonderbund league of Catholic cantons; in Germany, an abortive revolution took place in Frankfurt and Baden in 1846; Portugal throughout the 1830s remained in a state of chronic civil war or rebellion. Large portions of the Austro-Hungarian empire also seethed with nationalist ferment: Slovakia, Ruthenia, Galicia, and parts of Italy and Romania.

The presence of so much nationalist strife in virtually every region of Europe that Napoleon touched certainly argues for a causal connection. But not all of this nationalist ferment had an exclusively Napoleonic lineage. Belgium, for example, had experienced revolution as early as 1789, and its rebellion in 1830 was as much (or more) a reaction to its annexation by the Netherlands in 1815 as a result of the earlier French occupation. Nevertheless, when the history and background of the pre-1848 uprisings is examined closely, it is difficult to deny Napoleon's pivotal role as the godfather of nation-state formation and political modernization in nineteenth-century Europe.[67] And if the New World is included, then the wave of Latin American states that won independence, beginning with Argentina in 1816 and ending with Bolivia in 1825, must also be seen as an indirect consequence of Napoleon's occupation of Spain from 1808–1814 and the flight of the king of Portugal to Brazil in 1808. By cutting the umbilical cord between the New World colonies and their imperial centers in Iberia, the Peninsular War encouraged a separate creole identity and the development of autonomous administrations.[68]

In addition to creating new nation-states, the French Revolutionary and Napoleonic Wars also destroyed states—if the political relics of medieval Europe can be regarded as states—with alacrity. The venerable republics of Genoa and Venice disappeared in 1797. The Holy Roman Empire expired in 1806. Ecclesiastical principalities such as Cologne, Mainz, Trèves, and Salzburg perished in the cauldron. The number of German Free Cities shrank to four. By the time the Republic and Napoleon had finished disassembling and reassembling the map of Germany, almost 60 percent of Germany's population had changed rulers at least once; by 1820, the 294 or so Germanic territories that existed in 1789 had been reduced to 39, many of them loosely grouped under the Confederation of the Rhine. The Confederation gave the Germanic states a common identity they had never before experienced, and as such helped prepare the way for the eventual unification of Germany fifty-five years after Waterloo.[69]

Indeed Napoleon, every bit as much as Cavour or Bismarck, must be seen as the architect of modern Italy and Germany, the "late states" of Western Europe whose earlier unification had been impeded by the disintegrative effects of the Italian Wars and the Thirty Years' War. In Italy, the *epoca francese* had far-reaching political ramifications. The absorption of Piedmont into the Grand Empire from 1802 to 1814

extended the administrative system of Napoleon into the Po Valley and
gave a whole generation of Piedmontese administrators valuable formative training in the *Conseils d'État* and prefectures of the Italian
imperial departments. This new managerial elite paved the way for
Cavour and the "Piedmontese miracle" of the 1850s—the rise of a
confident modern state that could act as a core for the unification of
the peninsula. The experience of Cesare Balbo and Massimo d'Azeglio,
the first two constitutional prime ministers of Piedmont, reflects the
influence of Napoleon's rule. Balbo, who worked in the *Conseil* from
1809–1814, recounted that it taught him both to despise the dictatorial
nature of Napoleon's empire and to respect its administrative principles. D'Azeglio, whose childhood was spent under the Empire, became
a virulent critic of Napoleon, but acknowledged that numerous benefits flowed from his rule.[70]

Outside of Piedmont, the excesses of the French imperium triggered a vigorous counterreaction, particularly among the disillusioned
radicals and proto-Jacobins who had initially welcomed the French
Revolution. The most important fruit of this new Italian nationalism
was the Young Italy movement of Giuseppe Mazzini. The nationalism
that Napoleon engendered, like so much nationalism in the Third
World today, had a schizophrenic quality about it, a love–hate syn-
drome. Mazzini and Italy's radical nationalists passionately rejected
the French model as a pattern for Italian state formation and insisted
on Italy's "separateness"—the undeviating claim of nationalism everywhere—yet they, like the liberals of Cavourian Piedmont, accepted the
necessity of a centralized state and in this sense adopted the essential
Napoleonic model. When a unified Italian nation-state finally did
emerge in 1861, its administrative institutions were closely patterned
after those of the Grand Empire.[71]

In Germany, the French Revolution had stirred powerful currents
of nationalist thought among intellectuals—Johann Gottlieb Fichte
being the most prominent—but after Napoleon's devastation of the
Prussian army at Jena and Auerstädt in 1806, German nationalism
took on more xenophobic tones. "I hate all Frenchmen without distinction in the name of God and of my people," was the not atypical
declaration of the poet and historian Ernst Moritz Arndt in 1813.[72] But
along with the nationalist reaction came the reforming impetus of war,
as Prussian officials—Count Neithardt von Gneisenau and the barons
Karl vom Stein and Karl August von Hardenberg—concluded from the
defeat that extensive reforms were essential. Hardenberg justified a
French reform model to Frederick William III as the key to liberating
Prussia from France:

The French Revolution, of which the present wars are an extension, gave the French people through all their turmoil and bloodshed a wholly new vigor. All their latent powers were awakened. . . .

The illusion that we can resist the Revolution most effectively by clinging to the old order has only contributed to strengthening the Revolution and spreading it further. . . . The force of these principles is such . . . that the State which refuses to acknowledge them will be condemned to submit or to perish.[73]

Military defeat thus taught what ideological precepts could not. The resulting "revolution from above" in Prussia abolished serfdom, swept away caste barriers, undertook land reform, and established representative assemblies at the municipal level. The Prussian reformers also restructured the national army by introducing universal military training, creating an effective reserve corps, reforming the system of military justice, and fostering professionalism in the officer corps. Partly because of these reforms, the Prussian army acquitted itself admirably in the final battles against Napoleon.[74]

Outside Prussia, in the states of the Rhine Confederation, even more radical reforms took place under or in response to Napoleonic rule. Their overall effect was to undermine traditional society, strengthen state structures, and pave the way for the rapid progress of industrialization and urbanization.[75] After Napoleon, the traditional, the particularist, the parochial, and the communal in Germany rapidly gave way to the national, the cosmopolitan, the scientific, and the individualistic.[76] Once this turn had been taken, its further evolution was virtually inevitable, despite the fact that after 1815 many of the more liberal Germanic reforms were repealed or allowed to lapse (not, however, in the military arena, where the basic reforms were preserved and built on).

The nationalism engendered by the French conquest and integration of Europe, and the administrative revolution set in motion by Napoleon, required nearly half a century to come to full fruition in Italy and Germany, and then only after and as a result of wars of unification deliberately engineered and manipulated by nationalist-minded Italian and German statesmen. The Italian and German wars of unification offer casebook examples of how war unifies states: in both instances, military conflict reinforced nationalist passions and shifted political loyalties from the regional to the national level; in both instances, modernized states (Prussia and Piedmont) situated on the geographical periphery of their nations became the centers around which national unity coalesced; in both cases, war with Austria and the military involvement of France made possible the very unification that both Vienna and Paris had hoped to avert. Yet the wars of unification are best understood if their French pedigree is kept in mind: a direct lineage of nationalism, military reform, and institutional borrowing that can be traced from Napoleon to Hardenberg and Stein to Bismarck; from Napoleon to Mazzini and Cavour. The owl of Minerva may rise from its nest only at dusk, but the falcon of Mars is ever in flight.

CONCLUSION: TOWARD IMPERIALISM

It was no accident that the High Imperialism of the late nineteenth century arose in full bloom shortly after the Franco-Prussian War and the advent of Germany as a unified state. The proclamation of the German Reich in the Hall of Mirrors at Versailles in January 1871 essentially completed the papering over of Western Europe with centralized nation-states. The coming of age of Napoleon's godchild profoundly upset the European balance, as the General Staff and conscription system of Prussia became the war machine of a much larger state, one that now had full access to the rapidly industrializing heartland of the Ruhr valley. A defeated France roiled with nationalist resentment; a nervous Britannia laid keels for warships. The powerful centralized states of Europe, now closely wedded with their nations and better organized for war than for anything else, could find no ready arena for their rivalry within the confines of the continent without risking catastrophic conflict. The effervescence of nationalism sought escape from geographically too-tight bottles, while the strategic reckoning of statesmen and military officers saw a zero-sum game opening up to them in the non-European world. Three decades of overseas imperialism ensued, ending only when the states made by war again made war.

Even as the continental imperialism of Napoleon had shattered the remnants of feudalism in Europe and set in motion waves of modernizing change, European imperialism shattered the continuity and equilibrium of traditional and tribal societies outside Europe and set in motion a century of violent change. Europe brought the tools and organization of modern war to a world unprepared for it and unable to cope with it. The imperialist powers imported the bureaucracy, the taxation system, the administrative techniques, the legal regime, the conscription system, the military establishment, the concept of fixed borders and sovereign authority—in short, the whole organizational logic and paraphernalia of the modern warfare state—into regions of the world that neither wanted them, asked for them, nor fully accepted them. The resulting legacy of instability and strife has been with us ever since.

There was, however, one non-European country, and one only, that reacted to the encroachments of the imperial powers with such a deter-mined course of military and political modernization that it rapidly won acceptance as their equal: the island kingdom of Japan. The unequal treaties imposed by Western gunships from 1852 to 1864 shook its feudal society to the core and propelled it into torturous orbits of change, impelled by the imperative of attaining military parity with the West. The ancient and feudal Tokugawa Shogunate, unable to rise to the challenge of the West, was overthrown summarily. In a pat-tern highly reminiscent of Prussia after Jena, the new Meiji-era rulers sought frenetically to overcome their military inferiority by learning from the West, to "defeat the barbarian by using the barbarian."

The Japanese modernizers borrowed from French administrative practices, abolishing centuries-old feudal domains and replacing them with prefectures administered directly from the capital. They adopted portions of the *Code Napoléon*. They initially looked to France as a military model also, but after the Prussian victory at Sedan they turned instead to Germany, dispatching military officers to study its General Staff system and Prime Minister Hirobumi Ito himself to study its constitution. A vigorous program of military reform by 1875 gave Japan an officer training school, an arsenal with 2,500 employees, a gunpowder factory, and an artillery range. An 1883 conscription law enlarged the army to 73,000 men, with the potential to expand to 200,000 in war. In 1885, the Meiji government replaced its Executive Council with a cabinet modeled on European lines.[77]

In only seventeen years, Japan transformed itself from a feudal kingdom to a modern nation-state with a Western-style government and military establishment. Its defeat of Russia in 1905 was the first major defeat of a European power by a non-Western state, a signal to the world that the West had no patent on the blueprint for building a modern warfare state. But even before 1905, the European powers had acknowledged the unprecedented political and military achievement of Japan by inviting it to join the 1899 Hague Conference for Peace and Disarmament, the first time in history that the imperialist powers had accepted a non-European power at the conference table as an equal. On that occasion, one Japanese diplomat discerned the rationale behind his country's inclusion: "We show ourselves at least your equals in scientific butchery, and at once we are admitted to your council tables as civilized men."[78] He, at least, had no illusions about what foundation lay beneath the gilded superstructure of the West.

Total War and the Rise of the Collectivist State

Through bitter experience the machine taught that man himself was no longer master of the battlefield. The individual counted for nothing, all that mattered now was the machinery of war.

John Ellis, *The Social History of the Machine Gun*

The machine gun affords the ideal metaphor of industrialized warfare. A product of American ingenuity and technological faith, it originated in the 1860s after the advent of interchangeable parts and machine tooling. From its invention it was not only a machine designed to be a gun, but also a gun made by machines. Even as the essence of the Industrial Revolution was an exponential increase in the productive capacity of the individual laborer, the crux of the machine gun was its multiplication of the killing capacity of the individual soldier. As one French general said of the carnage at Verdun, "Three men and a machine gun can stop a battalion of heroes."[1] By failing to find a tactical solution to this problem until late in the war, the generals of World

War I consigned a generation of European youth to assembly-line obliteration on the plains of France. While machine guns spewed out death at the Somme and at Passchendaele, the armaments factories of the Great War spewed out ten thousand standardized items of war materiel and munitions—all the technological and organizational genius of the industrial age culminating in the mass production of mass destruction.[2]

The industrialized warfare of the twentieth century catalyzed the first great metamorphosis of the modern state since the French Revolutionary and Napoleonic Wars. While modern states had always been instruments of military mobilization, beginning in 1914 they became fulcrums for the waging of *total war*, for marshaling the whole of a nation's capacity—all social strata, all fiscal resources, and all industrial production—for military ends. As Gustav Streseman told the *Bund der Industriellen* in 1916, the goal of the German government during World War I was to turn the whole nation into "a single munitions factory."[3] In actual fact, no state attained the grail of total mobilization during either of the two world wars, but the twice-over effort to do so fundamentally and forever altered the nature of European states.

The political changes wrought by the two world wars went beyond the obvious effects noted in every textbook—the redrawing of the European map, the collapse of monarchy throughout much of the continent, the Bolshevik Revolution, the disintegration of the Austro-Hungarian and Ottoman empires in World War I, the dissolution of the overseas empires of the European imperial powers in the wake of World War II. As the only full-scale wars ever fought among industrialized powers, the First and Second World Wars produced permanent changes in the internal organization and structure of virtually all European states—changes that took place even where catastrophic defeat did not happen, where regime changes did not take place, and where border lines were not redrawn. The extraordinary degree of social and economic mobilization they entailed was a catalyst for the emergence of what might be called the *collectivist state*. This new form of the modern state was really three states intertwined in one: a *regulatory state*, characterized by extensive state intervention in the national economy; a *mass state*, in which political participation and privilege were divorced from class or economic status; and a *welfare state*, assuming direct responsibility for the well-being of its citizens. By the end of World War II, *all* the industrialized states of Europe had assumed these features, though totalitarian states such as Stalinist Russia and Nazi Germany manifested them in an aberrant form.

INDUSTRIALIZATION, WAR AND THE STATE, 1815–1914

In order to demonstrate that rise of the collectivist state was a direct outcome of the world wars, and not simply a result of the process of industrialization alone, it is necessary to go back to the century between 1815 and 1914, when liberalism and laissez-faire capitalism were in their heyday and peace among the powers was the norm. Historians trace the origins of the Industrial Revolution to Great Britain during the period from 1760 to 1830. In France, the process started later and took place more gradually, but was well under way by 1850; in Prussia and the Germanic states, industrialization took place slowly from the late eighteenth century to 1850, then accelerated rapidly. Other countries—Russia, Austria-Hungary, Italy, the Low Countries—lagged behind, but even they were undergoing significant industrialization by the latter half of the century. By World War I, industrialization had already been underway in Great Britain for a hundred and fifty years and in other European states for fifty to a hundred years.

In the beginning, industrialization was a secondary phenomenon, a bubbly froth on the surface of deeply rooted traditional societies. But as industrial technology advanced, it set in motion powerful social and economic forces—population dislocations, class displacements, urbanization, the emergence of the proletariat, growing concentrations of private capital, unionization, and labor unrest—all of which seriously strained the established order in every industrializing country. Yet despite its manifold effects on European societies and economies, industrialization before 1914 had only a limited impact on the structure of European *states*, which proved remarkably resistant to change. Their bureaucratic form bent little under the pressures of industrialization; landed elites and agricultural interests still wielded immense influence in the upper echelons of power, what Schumpeter called "the steel frame" of the state. The inexorable advances of nationalism and *embourgeoisement* notwithstanding, the lip service paid to liberalism aside, the *Zeitgeist* of the Restoration era remained essentially conservative and acted as a brake on political change throughout the nineteenth century.[4]

Why was the political impact of industrialization so muted and delayed by comparison with its social and economic effects? Several reasons come to mind. First, the Industrial Revolution was conceived in its British womb almost entirely independent of central state action. Politically speaking, it was a virgin birth, a nonstate phenomenon driven largely by individual initiative and private capital. Indeed, its success was predicated upon minimal state interference— one reason it took place first in Great Britain and advanced faster than on the continent. France also reduced state economic controls during the nineteenth century, but not nearly to the degree of Great Britain; its high tariffs and still somewhat mercantilist thicket of regulation partly account for the slower pace of industrialization there.[5] In general, the initial tendency of industrialization was to *undermine* state power by creating independent concentrations of private wealth that strengthened the influence and autonomy of bourgeois society. After 1870, certain states—Germany, Russia, and Japan in particular—promoted industrialization as an integral component of their military policy, giving it more of a state-reinforcing character that had previously been the case, and from 1890 to 1914, the naval and armaments race that culminated in World War I spurred industrialization among all the great powers of Europe. But in its initial genesis and evolution in Great Britain, industrialization was not closely linked with state policy.

Likewise, there were initially few links between industrialization and war. Lewis Mumford has argued that war was a central cause of the mechanization of civilization, hastening the pace of standardization and mass production.[6] Although there may be some truth to this after 1870, such definitely was not the case in the first century of the Industrial Revolution. The manufacturing sector that was first industrialized—textiles—had little connection with war, and even as late as 1911, the number of British workers employed in textiles, apparel, and food processing was almost double the number employed in the war-related areas of metals, machinery, vehicles, and chemicals.[7] From Waterloo to Sedan, the prevailing European peace and the traditionalism of military establishments ensured that the industrialization of arms production lagged well behind that of other manufacturing sectors.

Some historians have argued that in Britain government demand for iron during the Napoleonic Wars helped stimulate early industrial development. It is true that iron foundries were heavily involved in the casting of cannon and that government was the single largest purchaser of iron.[8] But increased iron output alone would not have revolutionized the nature of war, nor would it have had any pronounced effects on state development. In fact, the revolutionary character of industrialized warfare is threefold:

1. an exponential increase in the capacity of states to produce weaponry;
2. the application of scientific methods to improvements in the quality of weaponry;
3. the battlefield use of mechanized weaponry, which inherently possesses the essential quality of industrialization: the leveraging of human output (in this case, destructive output).

The industrialization of iron production accomplished none of these; iron was only one input into arms manufacturing, which remained a craft industry in the Napoleonic era. Thus, even if iron output increased exponentially, weapons production could increase only linearly.

Only after Waterloo and only gradually did the technological advances occur that would begin to change the very nature of war. Between 1820 and 1850, the Springfield Armory in Massachusetts and the gun factories of the Connecticut River Valley pioneered the use of interchangeable parts, machine tools, and assembly lines to mass-produce muskets and rifles of increasing precision, range, and speed of firing. This development came too late to make a major impact in the Crimean War, but the American Civil War offered the first inklings of its significance: General Philip Sheridan's 12,000-man cavalry force had more firepower in its repeating carbines than was in the muskets of Napoleon's entire half-million-man army when it marched on Moscow.[9] The massive firepower, extended fronts, complex logistics, and trench warfare of the Civil War portended many features of World War I, but European military officers largely ignored its lessons, distracted by the Crimean War and the wars of Italian and German unification and regarding the Americans as amateurs with little to offer.[10]

At approximately the same time that the Connecticut Valley innovations were going into production, Johann Nikolaus von Dreyse had begun the development of his breech-loading rifle, known as the needle gun, and Claude Minié in France was developing the cylindrical bullet that bore his name. Neither of these breakthroughs in riflery was really a product of the Industrial Revolution *per se*, any more than were earlier technical advances such as the improvements in artillery engineered by Jean Maritz or de Gribeauval of France in the eighteenth century. However, the manufacturing precision required to produce breech-loading weaponry did eventually force Dreyse to turn to machine tools for mass production of his gun. And as the mechanization and resulting improvements in rifle production became more widely known, particularly after the Crimean War, several European countries began importing American metal-milling machines. This marked the start of the long process of converting from craft methods of arms production to true industrialization. Other technical breakthroughs of the mid-nineteenth century included breech-loading artillery, exploding artillery shells, the use of telegraphy in communications, and the use of railroads in warfare. The latter, clearly a product of the Industrial Revolution, first played a role in European conflict in 1859 when France rushed troops by train to Piedmont. Prussia's use of railroads for troop transport likewise proved decisive in all three wars of German unification.[11]

All these advances marked the beginning, but only the beginning, of the industrialization of war, for productive capacity initially expanded very slowly. It took Prussia twenty-six years to equip with Dreyse needle guns the 300,000-man Prussian army that went to war with Austria in 1866. Moreover, none of the above advances infused weaponry with the most revolutionary quality of industrialization—automated, repetitive output. Automated weaponry, such as the machine gun, did not play a significant role in European theaters of war prior to 1914—though it was widely employed in the Russo-Japanese War of 1905. In the scramble for Africa and Asia after 1875, the machine gun did see increasingly common use, but for many military officers this only confirmed their stereotype of it as a specialized weapon for subduing primitive tribes and controlling riots. In general, it is fair to say that the industrialization of armaments production, and especially the development of automated weaponry, continued to lag behind other manufacturing spheres until at least 1870, when the pace of innovation accelerated. Given the primacy of war in the origin and evolution of European states, it was only logical that until war itself became industrialized, industrialization would have only limited effects on state structure.

Another factor inhibiting the impact of industrialization on state development was the long peace that prevailed among the great powers from 1815 to 1914 with only sporadic interruptions. The prolonged peace greatly reduced the incentives for political reform and contributed to the slow pace of innovation in weapons technology, at least prior to 1870. When clashes between the great powers did occur, as in the Crimean War or the wars of German unification, they were simply too brief for national industrial capacity to play a decisive role in their outcome. The social displacements associated with industrialization did foster internal unrest in almost every European country—they were a factor in the revolutionary wave of 1848 and in the Paris Commune, for example—but industrial capacity and mass-produced weaponry *per se* played almost no role at all in the actual fighting that occurred in connection with the endemic popular and nationalist revolts of the century.

Only after 1870 did the industrialization of war occur on a massive scale; only then did it assume the three revolutionary qualities listed earlier. Now, as continental and imperial rivalries heated up, traditionalist regimes collaborated with industrialists and bankers to promote the modernization of war-related industries. The period between 1870 and 1914 witnessed the first systematic and sustained application of scientific methods to weapons development. State-funded laboratories and industrial concerns made stunning advances in military technology: quick-firing artillery, naval fire-control systems, self-propelled torpedoes, steam turbine engines, steel-clad warships of unprecedented speed (cruisers, destroyers, and battleships), fully automatic machine guns, submarines, periscopes, the first reconnaissance aircraft, and military telephone and radio communications. Never before in human history had the technology of war advanced so swiftly. By the turn of the century, the largest industrial concerns in Europe were those involved in armaments manufacture or its raw materials, such as heavy metals. The absence of great-power war, however, concealed the magnitude of what was happening. The cost, complexity, and pace of military advances from 1870–1914 imposed strains on the fiscal and administrative capacities of Germany and Great Britain—particularly after their naval rivalry heated up in 1898—but apart from a few prescient military officers, few imagined how radically the nature of war was changing or how massively that change would affect the organization of the European states.

There was yet another factor, often overlooked, that mitigated the impact of industrialization on state development in the nineteenth century, namely the rise in national wealth generated by the growth of industrial production. Expanding national output enabled governments to sustain and even increase their levels of revenue and expenditure *without* large tax increases or major reforms of their fiscal systems. This was most starkly evident in the case of Great Britain, the earliest and most advanced of the industrial powers. As shown in Table 5–1, the ratio of total state expenditures and of military expenditures to GNP declined more or less steadily for seven decades after the defeat of Napoleon, rising only slightly during the Crimean and Boer Wars. The standard rate of income tax also decreased, with some fluctuations, from 7 pence per pound of earnings in 1842 to 2 pence in 1875, before rising again to 7 pence by 1894.[12] In short, even as Great Britain became the richest country in Europe, the dominant naval power of the world,

Table 5–1.   Total state expenditures and military expenditures as a
             percentage of GNP, Great Britain, 1830–1914.

	1830	1840	1850	[CRIMEAN WAR] 1855	1860	1870	1880	1890	[BOER WAR] 1900	1910
Total state expenditures as % of GNP	12.3	10.6	10.3	14.5	10.4	7.1	5.8	6.0	10.2	7.0
Total military expenditures as % of GNP	3.0	2.7	2.8	4.3	3.6	2.3	2.3	2.4	3.9	3.1

Source: *British Historical Statistics.*

and the master of an overseas empire on which the sun never set, the
fiscal size of the British state *declined* in proportion to the national
economy until near the end of the nineteenth century.

   Without industrialization, the British state would have needed to
be much more aggressive in penetrating and extracting resources from
its national economy in order to sustain the largest blue-water fleet in
the world. But industrialization meant that even a small military slice
of a vigorously expanding economic pie could be formidable. Though
British military expenditures declined relative to national output from
1820 to 1850, and declined again for three decades after the Crimean
War build-up, *in absolute terms* military spending rose steadily to 1890
and more rapidly thereafter. Between 1890 and 1914, the robust
growth of the national economy meant that only a modest increase in
state spending relative to GNP sufficed for Britain to quadruple the
warship tonnage of its navy! As the most industrialized and least statist
of European powers during the nineteenth century, Great Britain
experienced this leverage effect most strongly, but it is a fair assumption that industrialization enabled all the great powers of Europe to
build up impressive arsenals without resorting to the levels of taxation
and state intervention that otherwise would have been required.

   None of this should be taken to suggest that industrialization was
not a powerful force for change in its own right. In addition to its
myriad social and economic effects, the differential pace of industrial
advancement from country to country altered the international power
structure and was a primary cause of the breakdown of the European
state system in 1914. But prior to World War I the accumulated strains
of industrialization were contained and managed by political systems
of fundamentally conservative cast, though often of liberal economic
persuasion, which managed to survive intact precisely because of the

scarcity of war. States that did not experience the inspection effect of war, or the revelatory catharsis of defeat, tended to resist political reform. Their success in doing so contributed to the delusion of stability that prevailed among the ruling elites of the nineteenth century.

In this regard, it is noteworthy how many of the political reforms that did occur in the nineteenth century were linked either to defeat or to poor performance in war: the emancipation of the Russian peasantry in 1861 followed shortly after Russia's defeat in the Crimean War and was directly connected with the war's revelations of Russian backwardness; French losses in the Franco-Prussian War of 1870 precipitated the establishment of the Third Republic; Russia's defeat in the Russo-Japanese War led to the Russian revolution of 1905 and the introduction of parliamentary reforms by Nicholas II; the poor quality of British recruits in the Boer War of 1899–1902 spawned a powerful reform movement bent on restructuring the entire economic, social, and political arrangement of Great Britain. Thus, even in small doses, war forced change on an entrenched political order.

In general, the political elites of the Victorian era attempted to cope with the strains of industrialization largely through remedial measures—regulations on health, safety, and child labor, for example. The Disraeli reforms of 1875–76 in Britain are a prime example of a conservative attempt to reform without affecting the existing structure of power and privilege. France likewise passed a modest law restricting child labor in 1874, but had only the most minimal industrial safety and health regulations until the 1890s. France and Germany further sought to cope with industrialization by means of improvised state controls and subsidies, administered through the archaic regulatory bureaucracies that were still in place from the mercantilist eighteenth century.

As industrialization proceeded apace, the strains it imposed on European liberalism worsened. Throughout industrialized Europe, social reform movements of liberal, socialist, or religious tendency were active in the last quarter of the century; despite divergent ideologies, they united on the need for state intervention in national economies, a broader electoral franchise, and state-sponsored welfare programs. The codification of a progressive reform agenda after 1875 was both a reaction to industrialization and a response to pressures from below. But the successful *advancement* of that agenda at the state level was predicated upon another factor entirely—the intensifying of the imperial rivalry from 1875 to 1914. Imperialism reinforced the impulse toward domestic reform as European leaders came to believe that success in the world arena required the resolution of social and labor problems at home. In retrospect, the reforms of 1870–1914 were largely stopgap measures, intended more to preserve the status quo than to change it fundamentally, but their genesis presaged both in dynamics and in motivation the sweeping political reforms that would occur between 1914 and 1945, when the crucible of total war brought massive change. The sources of the reforms of the Imperial Age are worth examining, for examination reveals that in addition to its social and economic roots, the early welfare state had underlying military origins as well.

SOCIAL-IMPERIALISM AND THE ANTECEDENTS OF THE WELFARE STATE

The industrial magnate Cecil Rhodes rationalized imperialism on the grounds that Great Britain's social problems made it essential to acquire new lands for its surplus population and new markets for the goods produced in its factories: "If you want to avoid civil war, you must become imperialists."[13] Contemporary historians doubt that Britain was actually close to civil war at the turn of the century, but the perception of the ruling elites was in any event more important than the reality. They had not forgotten that over 20,000 had perished during the uprising of the Paris Commune in 1871, and the possibility of class conflict concerned state leaders everywhere. Yet while Rhodes saw imperialism as an outlet for capitalism and a prophylactic for civil war, many of his contemporaries in Europe turned this insight on its head: they saw internal reforms as essential to successful imperialism.

Joseph Schumpeter in 1919 coined the term "social-imperialism," which he and later Franz Neumann used to describe any attempt to encourage mass support for imperialist expansion by granting social concessions or broadening the franchise.[14] Social-imperialism on the European left prior to 1914 was not an anomaly but a highly articulated doctrine, virtually an ideology, subscribed to by such luminaries of socialism as Georges Sorel in France, Enrico Corradini and Antonio Labriola in Italy, Gustav Schmoller and the Katheder-Sozialisten in Germany, George Bernard Shaw and Sidney and Beatrice Webb of the Fabian Society in England.[15] Collectivism and imperialism made natural bedfellows, both being doctrines that advocated the utility of state power; their agendas merged as imperialists recognized that domestic peace would facilitate expansion abroad, and socialists decided that imperialism was a legitimate means of exporting "civilization."

The connection between imperialism and domestic reform was

strongest in Germany. By 1880, industrialization was proceeding at a breakneck pace in the newly unified Reich—a process destined to propel it in less than thirty years from an agrarian state with only 38 percent of Britain's manufacturing output to the exalted status of leading industrial power in Europe. German industrialization was giving rise to a new entrepreneurial class and a rapidly growing working class. In this context, German elites grouped around the social-imperialist *Verein für Sozialpolitik* advocated welfare reforms as a means of ensuring national greatness and thwarting the appeal of radical socialism. Recognizing that the repressive measures of the 1870s had failed to stem social unrest and that support for the banned Social Democrats was rising, Bismarck reluctantly conceded that social concessions were needed. Though personally contemptuous of humanitarian impulses, regarding them as mere "*Humanitätsdusel*" (sentimental rubbish), he was astute enough to realize that repression alone could not contain social unrest and that internal instability posed a greater threat to Germany's world position than any foreign power.

In 1883 the Iron Chancellor secured passage of compulsory sickness insurance for workers; in 1884 and 1885, an accident insurance plan; in 1889, a comprehensive Old Age Insurance Law providing pensions for the aged and disabled. These reforms have been described as a form of "negative integration" insofar as they attempted to integrate the working classes into the existing economic and political system without effecting a real change in the social order. In the Bismarckian conception, imperialism and social reforms were simply two different tools for integrating the masses and undercutting the appeal of socialism. But negative integration of this nature and the social welfare reforms it entailed also served Bismarck's international aims, since domestic accord was essential for successful external expansion. It was no coincidence that the reforms took place at the pinnacle of German imperialism, as epitomized by Bismarck's sensational claims in 1884–85 of German protectorates over Togoland, the Cameroon, portions of Southwest Africa, New Guinea, and Samoa—the single most crucial event in the intensification of imperial rivalry among the powers.[16]

By the turn of the century the militarized, Prussianized German state had the most comprehensive system of labor protection and social welfare insurance of any country in Europe. It is also fascinating to note that much of Bismarck's social legislation was borrowed from the first industrial concern in Germany to enact workers' protection and insurance plans of its own—the Krupp armaments empire.[17] The House of Krupp wanted stable labor conditions, free of strikes and disturbances, so as to crank out the their weaponry more efficiently for the arming of the German Reich and other states. The Reich in turn wanted domestic stability to clear the way for better use of the arms of Krupp; hence the latter's approach became the prototype for industry and government throughout Germany. There is perhaps no better example in European history of how the dictates of national security mesh with the imperatives of domestic peace and social welfare reform.

The example of Imperial Germany had great resonance throughout the continent, its implications magnified by imperial jealousies and the influence of Social Darwinism. In the first decade after the Bismarckian reforms were introduced British leaders spurned the German example, but the shock of the British military setbacks in the Boer War, and of the poor health of the British conscripts, transformed their thinking. How could a mass army expect to succeed in war without a healthy population? The intense national self-criticism that followed spawned the "National Efficiency" movement and public demands for a social organization modeled more closely after Germany.[18] Lloyd George and Winston Churchill—prominent ministers in the reform government of Henry Herbert Asquith, and future wartime leaders of Great Britain—were outspoken advocates of a national insurance program on the German model. Churchill advised Asquith to learn from the German formula for organization in both war and peace, and to "thrust a big slice of Bismarckianism over the whole underside of our industrial system."[19] The German program eventually became the model for the centerpiece social legislation of the Asquith government: pensions for the elderly (1908) and the National Insurance Bill (1911).

In France, the concept of the *état providence* became current during the Second Empire, but its realization was confined largely to the formation of voluntary mutual insurance societies. France's 1870 defeat at Sedan generated powerful internal reform pressures, which naturally if reluctantly came to focus on the German model in military, social, scientific, and educational affairs. This was an ironic counter-point to Prussia having modeled its reforms after France following Napoleon's defeat of Prussia at Jena more than a half-century earlier. The French legislature passed assistance for children in the 1880s, followed by laws on health care assistance (1893), miners' pensions (1894), assistance for the aged and disabled (1905), and old-age pensions (1910). Between 1890 and 1910, national expenditures on public-health assistance increased by a factor of 10. The Chamber of Deputies passed national social-insurance legislation in 1903 by a margin of 552 to 3, but it was blocked in the Senate, which was still dominated by traditionalists. Though the French reforms of the *belle époque* did not go as far as those of Great Britain, much less Germany, they derived in part from the same competitive concerns, above all the fear of falling behind France's highly organized arch-rival to the east.[20]

In summary, the pattern of European state development from 1880 to 1914 entailed the same dual axis of conflict that had driven state development in other historical eras—a conjunction of intense military rivalries abroad and unresolved social tensions at home. But with actual wars limited and rare, and domestic conflict contained at a level well below civil war, the entrenched elites managed to limit the actual degree of change. The tranquility of the Liberal era seemed to justify Immanuel Kant, who in 1795 had argued that the spirit of commerce was incompatible with war. August Comte, Norman Angell, Ivan Bloch, and Guglielmo Ferrero were a choir of intellectuals assuring the world of the absolute incompatibility of the military spirit and industrial society and of the inevitable obsolescence of war. For much of the nineteenth century, rising prosperity and extended periods without war seemed to confirm the optimism of the philosophers, which conformed in any case with the prevailing *Zeitgeist*. But then came 1914, Sarajevo, and the unfolding revelation that industrialization had not made war obsolete but only inconceivably more deadly and more costly than ever before.

INDUSTRIALIZED WAR AND THE RISE OF THE REGULATORY STATE

Having weathered the domestic upheaval of industrialization and the intellectual onslaughts of socialism, European liberalism finally perished on the battlefields of Verdun and the Somme. The magnitude of the slaughter on the plains of France forced the belligerent states of Europe literally to reinvent and redefine themselves in order to compete more effectively with each other. During World War I, they achieved a more radical degree of penetration of their societies and economies than anything contemplated or indeed possible in the mercantilist age. The intensity of total warfare made this imperative, while technical advances in communications, transportation, financial controls, and administration made it feasible. Nor did the end of the war bring a return to the status quo ante at home; despite the dismantling of some wartime controls, European states remained deeply engaged in their national economies, locked into a relationship of penetration and state–society interdependence that has persisted until the present day. In this sense, as in so many other ways, the Great War was a watershed in the relationship between state and society in Europe.

One factor in the collapse of laissez-faire during World War I was the enormous cost of the war, which dwarfed all previous European conflicts in the magnitude of resources required for its waging. The result was an extremely robust fiscal-military cycle of bureaucratic expansion, centralization, and increased taxation. The percentage of national income devoted to military spending in all the major powers rose on the average from slightly over 4 percent to between 25 and 33 percent over the course of the war.[21] Table 5–2 shows the exponential increases that took place in central state expenditures and military expenditures in Great Britain, France, and Germany during the war. The fiscal statistics shown are in absolute terms, but even after inflation is taken into account, overall state spending increased during the war by a factor of at least 5 in the United Kingdom, by 3 in France, and nearly 4 in Germany. The same statistics from the postwar period (Table 5–2 again) indicate that high levels of state spending and employment continued after 1918, despite demobilization and massive reductions in military spending. In real terms, the annual central expenditures of the British and French governments rose to a plateau at least 100 percent higher than before the war; the German figure, more difficult to calculate, also increased substantially.

This same ratchet or "displacement" effect also manifested itself in permanent gains in the size of government bureaucracy at all levels; from 1900 to 1920, the number of administrative personnel in public employment per thousand of the population increased from 8.0 to 16.17 in the United Kingdom; from 7.9 to 12.0 in France; and from 6.3 to 13.9 in Germany. Almost all of these gains took place in the decade from 1910 to 1920, with the war the primary catalyst of bureaucratic growth.[22]

Britain raised its income tax four times during the war, from 6.25 percent to 30 percent; it also levied supplementary duties and an excess profits tax that reached 80 percent. Germany instituted a turnover tax and a war profits tax. France adopted the first general income tax in its history in July 1914, though even then only implemented it in 1916 when fiscal pressures became inexorable. This was a reform that had been impossible to pass in peacetime—200 French income-tax bills had failed to become law between 1871 and 1914! The new income tax was also progressive, as had been advocated unsuccessfully by both Socialists and Radicals since at least 1898.

Table 5–2.   Trends in total central governmental expenditures and
military expenditures in the United Kingdom, France and
Germany, 1913–1918 and 1922

	1913	1914	1915	1916	1917	1918	1922
UNITED KINGDOM (£ million sterling)							
Total State Expenditures	192.3	559.5	1,559.2	2,198.1	2,696.2	2,579.3	1,070.1
Military Expenditures	77.1	437.5	1,399.7	1,973.7	2,402.8	2,198.0	111.0
FRANCE (France, millions)							
Total State Expenditures	5,067	10,065	20,925	28,113	35,320	41,897	45,188
Military Expenditures	1,262	6,048	15,988	21,610	25,686	29,095	4,747
GERMANY (Marks, millions)							
Total State Expenditures	3,521	9,651	26,689	28,780	53,261	45,514	*
Military Expenditures	1,956	7,880	18,942	24,000	33,600	41,250	*

* Published date for Germany for 1922 varies widely, perhaps due to the beginning of
rapid inflation.
Note: The above figures are not adjusted for inflation, because price changes in state
and military expenditures are impossible to calculate precisely. Overall price indices
during the war inflated by a factor of approximately 2.4 in the United Kingdom, 2.6 in
France, and 3.5 in Germany.

Sources: Data from *European Historical Statistics 1750–1975* (Macmillan, 1980); *British
Historical Statistics* (Cambridge University Press, 1988); The Economist, *One Hundred
Years of European Statistics* (London, 1989). German military expenditures were not
published during the war; they are estimated from data in a Carnegie study, *Direct and
Indirect Costs of the War* (Washington, D.C. 1919).

   In all three countries, taxation never came close to paying for the
war, covering only 28 percent of national expenditure in Britain and
about 15 percent in France and Germany. Massive borrowing made up
the gap; this only ensured that tax levels would remain high after the
war.[23] In the British case, for example, just servicing the war debt
required an annual postwar expenditure equivalent to 175 percent of
the entire national budget in 1913.[24] The legacy of wartime debts
weighed heavily on postwar Europe, reinforcing the continuing penetration of national economies by the state.
   Regardless of how much money a state borrows, war-fighting capability depends on currently produced goods and services—on the
capacity to mobilize and deploy specific physical resources, to convert
paper currency and credits into real military equipment in the hands
of flesh-and-blood soldiers. This has always been the case; but in

World War I these administrative and physical challenges loomed larger than the merely fiscal challenge of paying for the war, both because the intensity of total war made normal procurement procedures unacceptably slow, and because the Allied naval blockade and the German U-boat campaign made access to raw materials and home-front productive capacity more critical than in any previous conflict. As the war progressed, the European leaders realized that neither fiscal credits nor the free market alone could possibly sustain the war effort, no matter how much money they spent. Needing immediate access to actual physical assets and resources, they resorted to direct penetration, control, and management of their economies. Central command methods prevailed over free-market mechanisms.

The slide toward "state socialism" in Britain, France, and Germany took place in parallel phases. In the beginning, the leadership of all three countries assumed that the war would last less than a year. The steps taken in the first six months of the war to assert state authority over the economy were relatively limited and were directed primarily at securing the transportation and supply lines of their troops; armaments production remained largely the province of private companies under state contract. The second phase began in the summer of 1915 as each army experienced severe shortages of shells. The resulting "munitions crisis" shattered the mold of "business as usual" and provoked state efforts to control industry directly and to establish state-run munitions factories. Finally, the battlefield stalemate of 1916 and 1917 persuaded political and military leaders on both sides that the war now called for an entirely new order of state control. In every case, this realization was accompanied by pivotal leadership changes and the establishment of governments dedicated to total economic and social mobilization. In Britain and Germany, the Battle of the Somme was the critical turning point, a shock that led to the accession of the Lloyd George government in December 1916 and to formation of the Third Supreme Army Command under Hindenburg and Ludendorff in August 1916—the beginning of military dictatorship in Germany. In France, the debacle of the Somme also led to a change of government, but the decisive leadership shift did not occur until December 1917, when Georges Clemenceau became prime minister.[25]

THE PROGRESSION OF THE WARTIME CONTROLS

The totality of measures introduced by the wartime governments, especially in this third phase, came to touch almost all sectors of industry and all parts of national life.[26]

Nationalization and Control of Industry

The railroad and shipping industries were the first to fall under government control.[27] The armaments industries came next. In June 1915, David Lloyd George became head of a new British Ministry of Munitions that imposed sweeping wage, profit, and labor controls throughout the armaments industry and its subcontractor network. The government also established over 250 state-operated National Factories that eventually produced half the total British output of rifles, shells, ammunition, and explosives. France and Germany had always produced much of their armaments in state-owned factories, but the war brought state control to the entire armaments sector and thereby to much of private industry. In 1916 France, like Britain, formed a new Ministry of Munitions, while in Germany under the Hindenburg Program the administration of weapons production gravitated from the Ordnance Departments of Prussia and other federal states to a centralized Supreme War Bureau set up in August 1916. Control of the arms industry was the wedge by which all three states penetrated the economy. One historian describes the British Ministry of Munitions as "an octopus with its tentacles reaching out into the whole economy."[28] Its controls advanced steadily outward, first encompassing the suppliers and subcontractors of the arms industry, then gradually penetrating virtually every sector of the national economy.

Control of Raw Materials and Commodities

Naval warfare forced all the belligerents to take extraordinary steps to control raw materials and secure supplies of food and consumer commodities. Early in the war, the Asquith government in Britain imposed controls on sugar, dye-stuffs, cotton, and wheat; after 1916, Lloyd George systematized such controls under a new Ministry of Food and a Cotton Control Board. France, having lost much of its coal and iron industry behind German lines or in the battle zone, relied on imports for 40 percent of its raw materials. To cope with the resulting shortages, Minister of Commerce Étienne Clémentel formed a consortium system in which associations of manufacturers allocated raw materials under state supervision. The government also established state monopolies on sugar (1916) and grains (1917) that regulated the supply chain from producer to consumer. At the initiative of industrialist Walter Rathenau, German authorities also formed a consortium system under a War Raw Materials Department set up in August 1914. It requisitioned chemicals, cotton, copper, and synthetic nitrates, allocating them to the arms industry at bargain prices; two years later, coal and steel also fell under central control. In 1916, the German government set up its own central Ministry of Food in response to worsening food shortages in the cities; Austria and Hungary soon followed suit.[29]

Price Controls
Like all large wars, World War I spawned both inflation and shortages. Governments responded with price controls. The German government was the first to act, introducing general price controls on cereals, potatoes, sugar, and feedstuffs in October 1914. Within a year the list was expanded to include butter, fish, milk, pork, fruits and vegetables; by the end of the war, every imaginable food item was under such controls. The British government initially resisted introducing controls, but in the summer of 1915, it froze the rents of lower-income apartments at their 1914 levels, and in September 1917, in response to widespread shortages and queues, it succumbed to the inevitable and introduced retail price control on foods, which it maintained in part by subsidies. In the case of France, poor harvests and the loss of agricultural lands to German troops provoked price controls on wheat in October 1915; these were soon extended to cover all basic foods.

Rationing and Regulation of Consumption
The rationing imposed by the European governments in World War I was unprecedented both in its scope and in the emphasis on curbing consumption—the most intrusive form of economic regulation—rather than on regulating production or trade. Germany acted first, introducing ration cards for flour and bread in January 1915 and expanding this into a system of general food rationing the following year. The British government imposed strict gasoline rationing early in the war, but resisted general rationing until 1918, when unrestricted submarine warfare caused intolerable food shortages. France began rationing at almost the same time, and by June 1918 made ration cards compulsory throughout the country. Everywhere, price controls and rationing required large new bureaucracies, residues of which remained after the war and contributed to the persistence of economic regulation.

Financial and Currency Controls
The war wreaked havoc on European financial markets and led to sweeping state controls on gold, currency, and financial flows. The most significant of these steps involved gold, which the war essentially destroyed as a monetary standard. Germany and France suspended the conversion of bank notes into gold in the first days of the war and never resumed convertibility. Britain maintained nominal adherence

to gold convertibility throughout the war, but in reality the Currency and Bank Notes Act of August 1914 effectively suspended the gold standard and allowed the Bank of England to issue notes not covered by gold; by 1919, the gold standard could no longer be sustained and was dropped.[30] It never recovered from the impact of the war; it was briefly revived in 1925, but Britain abandoned it forever in 1931. Without gold as a peg, currency stability became more dependent than ever on the macroeconomic skills of state officials and central treasuries.

THE PERMANENCE OF THE REGULATORY STATE,
1919–45

After Versailles, the German and Allied governments dismantled the formal machinery of wartime regulation and allowed market mechanisms to operate once again in their national economies. But the Great War had irrevocably damaged the political and intellectual foundations of classical liberalism. The new constituencies, new ways of thinking, and new bureaucracies forged during the war made it politically untenable for states to disengage from their troubled postwar economies. And though laissez-faire policies did make a comeback in the 1920s, the Great Depression reversed the trend and sent the states back to the model of 1914–19. World War II then decisively destroyed the old liberal order forever, converting the political systems that waged it into permanent regulatory states.

"War has always been fatal to Liberalism," wrote Lloyd George in his postwar memoirs. The political trajectory of postwar Britain bore this out. Even traditional journalistic bastions of liberalism such as the *Economist* and the *Manchester Guardian* came to accept the need for state involvement in the postwar economy. A similar trend was reflected in the political arena, where the Labour Party made huge gains at the expense of the Liberals.[31] During the 1920s, the British state was involved in the national economy to a degree unthinkable before the war: it subsidized housing construction; provided extensive aid to agriculture; granted government subsidies to the coal, shipping, and civil aviation industries; and gave guaranteed loans to a large number of private firms. The British government also pursued a policy of forced concentration of the transportation industry (railways and civil aviation), and created public corporations with monopoly control of electrical production and broadcasting.[32]

In France, the experience of the war led Clémentel and other prominent wartime ministers to break with the prewar liberal order and endorse collectivist economic policies. In 1917, well before the war had ended, Clémentel declared, "I have become convinced that a new era is emerging, one in which our old and excessive love of individualism must bow before the necessity of organization and union." After the Armistice, politicians and journalists heaped scorn on the *étatisme* of the war years, but wartime controls remained in place in many industries. The state created numerous mixed companies with joint public and private ownership, it sequestered a share of mining profits, and it formed and assumed partial control of a domestic petroleum cartel. State controls remained in place in the railroad, electrical power, and river transportation industries. The policies of André Tardieu—minister of public works (1926–28) and prime minister (1929–30, 32)—epitomized the new regulatory state. Tardieu and most of his cabinet had been heavily involved in the mobilization effort of World War I; from this experience originated the roots of their economic vision—the "renovation" of the French economy by vigorous government intervention and regulation.[33]

The depression of the 1930s further discredited liberal economic theory and spurred state intervention by Britain and France in their national economies, much of it representing a throwback to the model of World War I. But the impact of the Second World War was far greater than that of the Depression, and essentially completed the conversion of Britain and France into full-fledged regulatory states. When war came again in 1939, the British state assumed direct and almost total control of the national economy, acting much more quickly and thoroughly than in World War I. When the Labour Party came to power in the last months of the war, it was a relatively straightforward matter to nationalize key sectors of the economy, including the Bank of England, the coal mines, the railways, civil aviation, major utilities, and the steel industry. Within a decade of 1945, over 2.1 million British subjects were working in nationalized industries. The warfare state and warfare economy had become prototypes for the postwar reconstruction of Great Britain.

In France, the debacle of 1940 accelerated the decline of liberalism and the advancement of statist policies—both during and after the German occupation, both inside the Vichy regime and within the Resistance. Pétain's government pursued economic policies radically more invasive than those of interwar France, including rationing and strict wage and price controls. Though these did not stem from mobilization efforts, they were a direct by-product of the war and the German occupation and were wholly in keeping with the trend of industrialized wartime Europe. The Resistance decried the "feudal economics" of Vichy but readily adopted much of its basic structure when it retook France. De Gaulle's provisional government (1944–46) nationalized key sectors of the French economy, including the coal mines, the gas and electric power industry, the insurance companies, and the Bank of France. Postwar France introduced a *Commissariat du Plan* under Jean Monnet that set targets and priorities for industrial production; many of the "organization committees" established by Pétain were kept in place as useful conveyor belts for central planning initiatives.[34]

The contrast between the liberal Britain and France of 1914 and the highly regulated, economically engaged states that emerged after 1945 was striking. In little more than three decades, pervasive state regulation and state ownership of key industries had become the dominant trends in Europe's oldest and most preeminent nation-states. Nor was the situation in postwar Germany very different; there the Federal Republic, after repudiating the legacy of Hitler, nonetheless kept in place a vast system of bureaucratic controls, state subsidies, profit supports, protected cartels, tax concessions, and market restrictions.* It is impossible to attribute the rise of the regulatory state in Europe to industrialization alone. During its first century, the Industrial Revolution coincided almost everywhere with the *erosion* of mercantilist strictures, the *elimination* of internal barriers to trade, and the *reduction* of international tariffs. Only in the era of High Imperialism did pressures arise for the reintroduction of state economic regulation and higher tariffs; only after the two world wars did Europe witness the emergence of full-fledged regulatory states in which central command measures were as important as the market in mobilizing large-scale human effort. In short, it was not industrialization per se that brought the state back into the economy—it was the industrialization of war.

---

*The impact of World War I on the Weimar Republic and German development in the 1930s will be examined in the next chapter.

INDUSTRIALIZED WAR AND THE RISE
OF THE MASS STATE

The feverish nationalism that engulfed Europe in August 1914 attested to the status that the nation-state had attained as the supreme claimant on human loyalty. In every country of Europe, internal cleavages—between Liberals and Socialists, factory owners and union organizers, agrarian landowners and urban industrialists, suffragettes and male parliamentarians, the working class and the aristocratic-bourgeois governing class—were subsumed in what Winston Churchill sardonically called "a higher principle of hatred."[35] Rival claimants to the state—such as dynastic bonds, international commercial ties, religious and ideological affiliations, and the international labor movement—were rent in pieces overnight. The nationalism of the war and its consequent unifying effect enabled states to mobilize their human resources on a scale previously unthinkable, including the raising of mass armies totaling over 63 million soldiers and seamen, the recruitment of millions of women into traditionally male occupations, and gains in labor productivity made possible by a new social compact between workers and management.[36]

The mobilization of conscript armies and industrial labor during the two world wars was a primary factor in the emergence of the *mass state* in Europe—of political systems distinguished by universal suffrage, egalitarian values, the relative absence of class privilege in politics, and the pervasive influence of mass opinion on public affairs. The mass state was the logical culmination of the long-term trend toward popular integration into and popular identification with the state that began with the French *levée en masse*. It was a by-product of the intense mobilization of human resources, civilian as much as military, demanded by industrialized war.

Mechanized conflict may be a "war of machines" but it consumes human lives on a colossal scale. The toll in the first two years of World War I alone exceeded the *total* losses of all the major wars since the French Revolution: the Napoleonic Wars, the Crimean War, the Franco-Prussian War, the American Civil War, the Boer War, the Russo-Japanese War, and the Balkan wars. World War II, encompassing large parts of Asia as well as Europe, was yet more devastating, particularly in its toll on civilian lives. Together, the two world wars lasted only a total of ten years, but more persons perished in them (over 60 million) than in all the previous wars of modern history combined.[37] When death is mass produced on mechanized battlefields, states at war must not only manufacture new fighting machines but also find live bodies to operate them; not only procure raw materials but obtain skilled workers to shape them. The experience of the belligerent states of World War I in meeting these challenges sheds light on the origins of the mass state.

CONSCRIPT ARMIES, WAR CASUALTIES, AND THE DEMOCRATIC IMPERATIVE

With respect to manpower consumed, World War I was a whole new order of war. Between 1914 and 1918, the United Kingdom mobilized a grand total of 6.2 million men, Germany 13.25 million, and France, 8.2 million; this represented a military participation ratio of approximately 20 percent of the national populations of France and Germany, about 13 percent for the United Kingdom. By comparison, Napoleon's *Grande Armée* over the much longer period from 1800 to 1815 mobilized at most 1.8 million Frenchmen, about 7 percent of the French population.[38] The mobilization of large armies in the Great War was facilitated by the widespread introduction after 1870 of the Prussian system of short-term conscription and reserve forces; only Great Britain retained a volunteer army, a tradition it maintained in the first eighteen months of the war but was forced to abandon in 1916, when it introduced universal male conscription. It is interesting to note that the originators of the Prussian manpower system had no illusions about its political significance. Germany consistently called up a much smaller percentage of the eligible draft pool than France, in part because the agrarian elites that dominated the government and officer corps well understood that mass military service would mean an enlargement of the officer corps and the recruitment of the lower middle classes, with their Social Democratic leanings, into its aristocratic ranks. This in turn would increase pressures for political reforms.[39]

The sociologist Émile Durkheim saw industrialization as a depersonalizing force, a cause of the profound social anomie that afflicted industrial societies in the late nineteenth century. But the high degree of social discipline and cooperation necessitated by industrialized *war*, beginning in 1914, had a somewhat different effect, undermining both psychologically and socially the individualism upon which laissez-faire capitalism had rested. Even the most mundane industrial task of a worker became part of a higher national purpose in wartime, fulfilling Durkheim's formula for overcoming anomie: the worker must "feel that he is serving something."[40] Stanislav Andreski's hypothesis that the degree of social participation in war determines the subsequent degree of social leveling was also borne out by the experience of the world wars.[41] Military service was an inherently leveling experience, for there were no class divisions in the trenches, and the intensity of the experience—both the camaraderie it created and the searing memories it left—tended to reduce the importance attached to class identity. A similar leveling effect occurred on the home front in both world wars. Rationing, gas masks, bomb shelters, blackouts, identity cards, and other wartime strictures were classless afflictions. World War II in particular elicited an unprecedented spirit of egalitarianism across Great Britain, a spirit so strong that George Orwell believed a social revolution had occurred.[42]

Also of far-reaching political consequence were the enormous casualties sustained in World War I. (Though World War II would be even more murderous, its losses did not cause the same degree of social and political shock as those of World War I, which had no ready precedent and which followed after decades of general peace.) The great philosophers of European Liberalism—John Locke, Adam Smith, Alexis de Tocqueville, Jeremy Bentham, John Stuart Mill—had proclaimed the value of the individual, the sanctity of human freedom, and the pursuit of happiness for all. How then to explain, justify, and fit into this liberal framework the horrors of trench warfare, in which millions of forcibly conscripted soldiers perished in the pursuit of ill-defined goals? How could the carnage possibly be defended, or more to the point, how could the European political systems that permitted such an end possibly be justified?

In his war aims speech of January 5, 1918, Prime Minister David Lloyd George observed that when men by the millions were being called upon to face death, and whole populations were subjected to suffering on an unprecedented scale, the people were entitled to know for what cause they were sacrificing. "Only the clearest, greatest and justest of causes . . . can justify the continuance even for one day of this unspeakable agony. . . ."[43] Though the prime minister had in mind Great Britain's international aims, his words applied to domestic politics as well: having called on the masses in unprecedented numbers to sacrifice their lives for the state, political leaders felt compelled to prove that this sacrifice was not in vain, that a new Britain would arise from the trial of war, a "land fit for heroes." The war made it impossible to sustain the liberal hypocrisy of a political system that proclaimed individual rights while denying political representation to millions. Mass military service and mass carnage had created a democratic imperative. Winston Churchill put this perfectly after World War II in these words about the workers of Britain: "they have saved this country; they have the right to rule it."[44]

The most salient manifestation of this democratic imperative, and the real basis of the mass state, was the suffrage reforms introduced in many European states as a result of the First World War. Near the end of the war, the British Parliament passed the Representation of the People Act, extending the franchise to all adult males and to much of the female population. This raised the number of qualified voters from 8 million to 21 million (three fourths of the adult population), meaning that for the first time in history the House of Commons would be elected by a majority of British citizens.[45] In Germany universal male suffrage had ostensibly existed since 1871, but real political power lay in the Bundesrat, where Prussia had a controlling majority. Prussia's own three-tiered voting system heavily favored property holders, industrial magnates, and East-Elbian Junkers, enabling them to dominate the Bundesrat. The war generated intense pressures for franchise reform. Chancellor von Bethmann-Hollweg told the Prussian cabinet that the long duration of the war made concessions on the voting system essential. In January 1916 and again in his Easter Decree of 1917, the Kaiser promised abolition of the three-tiered system after the war. In May 1918, an attempt to abolish the system failed in the Prussian Landtag by a vote of 235 to 183, but six months later, in the wake of the November revolution, the Weimar Republic proclaimed universal and equal suffrage.[46] Austria, Belgium, and the newly independent states of Central Europe also broadened the franchise within a year or two of the Armistice.

ORGANIZED LABOR DURING WORLD WAR I AND AFTER

The acute labor shortage of World War I gave workers new leverage, enabled trade unions to expand their membership, and boosted female employment in industry. As Arthur Marwick observes, in a "war of machines" it was as necessary to tend to the supply of machine makers in the factories at home as to the supply of machine users at the front. He added, "It is this problem of labour which is the flash-point for many of the major changes in social status, relationship, and environment which are apparent from early 1915 onwards."[47] Britain, France, and Germany all made strenuous efforts to ensure fully staffed factories and labor peace during World War I, but their efforts only accelerated the devolution of state power to a mass basis by revealing the complete dependency of the state on the working classes for the waging of industrialized war.

In August 1914, European trade unions rallied to their respective states with surprising speed as nationalism proved stronger than the attractions of socialism. Governments sought to take advantage of this rallying effect by codifying it in formal agreements or informal understandings with labor leaders. In March 1915, Lloyd George, then Chancellor of the Exchequer, reached an understanding with the British trade unions that they would refrain from strikes for the duration of the war, submit labor disputes to arbitration, and allow a dilution of hiring standards in order to keep the factories operating at capacity. French leaders such as Clémentel promoted an *union sacrée* of government, industry, and labor, while the French government formed commissions of trade unionists and workers to determine which workers at given factories should be exempted from conscription. In Germany, the trade unions had not won official recognition prior to the war, but they nevertheless rallied to the flag, pledging their support of the war effort and renouncing all strikes in the *Burgfrieden* agreement of August 4, 1914.[48]

As the carnage continued and the conscription net widened, labor shortages became an urgent problem. Under the Munitions Act, the British government suspended prewar union–management contracts and clamped tight restrictions on labor mobility, virtually binding workers to their factory. In August 1916, it formed a Man-Power Distribution Board to channel formerly exempted workers into military service and recruit replacements for them. This was followed by the creation of a Department and later a Ministry of National Service, which attempted to mobilize large new numbers of civilian laborers both as a military reserve and to staff the "Great National Factory" of the armaments industry.[49] The French government imposed strict controls on industrial labor, including subjecting skilled workers released from the army to military discipline; beginning in 1915, it also recruited women and unskilled agrarian workers into the arms industry. Germany went even further. The Patriotic Auxiliary Services Law of December 1916 virtually militarized the German population, conscripting all males between 17 and 60 into government service, either in the army or the factories—and placing strict limits on job mobility.

Superficially, such controls represented an expansion of state power vis-à-vis the working classes. In reality, the acute labor shortages of the war gave organized labor enormous bargaining leverage. Governments and industrialists soon learned that neither labor controls nor military recruitment could succeed without union help. Alfred Hugenberg, chief director of Krupps and head of the German Mine-owners Association, early in the war had voiced concern about its social consequences: "One will probably have to count on a very increased sense of power on the part of the workers and labor unions. . . ."[50] This proved prophetic. Social Democratic support for the draconian provisions of the Auxiliary Services Law was obtained only by establishing permanent Workers' Committees in all firms with fifty or more employees. This was a decisive turning point in German social history, the realization of the long-standing union demand for official recognition and legal equality with employers.[51]

In France, the *union sacrée* converted the unions virtually into part of the administrative machinery of the state, but it also gave them new social standing and leverage in collective bargaining. A hallmark of the progress made by British workers was the formation of a Ministry of Labour in 1916 and the inclusion of Labour representatives in the wartime cabinets. Though the new Ministry was small and not highly effectual in its early years, it helped to preserve workers' gains after 1918 and eventually became an important component of British government.[52]

The magnitude of the newfound power of the unions became evident when the no-strikes accords began to break down. In July 1915, faced with a threatened strike by coal miners in South Wales, the British government threatened to invoke the criminal penalties of the Munitions Act. When the strike went ahead anyway, the manifest impossibility of imprisoning 200,000 miners, or forcing them to work either, compelled Lloyd George to concede all their demands within five days. In France, rising strike activity in 1917 strained, but did not break, the *union sacrée*; instead, the unions won numerous concessions, including the establishment of collective employer–union agreements and mixed arbitration committees with full union participation.[53]

In Germany, strike activity mounted inexorably as the war proceeded. In 1915, an average of 1,000 workers a month were on strike; in 1916, 10,000; in 1917, 50,000; in 1918, 100,000—including a January strike of 400,000 workers in Berlin. In 1917, with the strikes mounting, General Wilhelm Groener, Chief of the War Office, appealed for a "social partnership" with the unions and loosened restrictions on their activities.[54] When labor unrest escalated despite the Groener concessions, the Imperial government responded with forcible conscription, court-martials, and the arrest of agitators—a policy that broke the strikes only at a severe cost in social unity. In the autumn of 1918, labor unrest and massive demonstrations erupted again, a relentless crescendo to the November revolution in which massive strikes by workers and soldiers led to the collapse of the government, abdication of the Kaiser, and proclamation of a republic. By then, German industrialists no longer harbored any illusions about the extent of their dependence on the unions. Only *four days* after the Armistice was signed, a national meeting of employers and trade union leaders signed a compact granting German workers wage increases, an eight-hour work day, subsidized social insurance, and collective wage bargaining. The industrialists, with the full support of state authorities, acquiesced in a permanent "social partnership" with the unions as essential to averting a socialist revolution. The accord amounted to the formal incorporation of the trade unions into the German state.[55]

The progress of labor in World War I can be traced in the growth of trade union membership. Between 1913 and 1918, the numbers affiliated with the British Trades Union Congress grew from 2.2 million to 4.5 million, more than doubling in four years. Total union membership in the United Kingdom increased from 4 million to 6.5 million during the war itself, and rose to over 8 million within two years of the Armistice. In France, membership in the Confédération Générale du Travail (CGT) rose from 355,000 in 1913 to 600,000 in 1918; the syndicalist movement grew spectacularly, from 800,000 to over 2 million. In Germany trade union membership declined in the first two years of the war, then increased sharply. By 1919, the total membership of German trade unions was 6,527,000, more than double the 1913 figure of 3,024,000, and though much of the gain took place in the year after the Armistice, it was a continuation of an upward trend that began in 1917. Similar trends were registered in Italy, where the metal and auto workers' union soared from 7,000 to 104,000 between 1914 and 1919, and other unions doubled or tripled their pre-war membership by 1920.[56]

Though the close wartime collaboration between European states and organized labor eroded after 1918—severely so in France, less so in the United Kingdom and Germany—it never entirely broke down. In contrast with the repression or official neglect that the unions had typically encountered prior to the war, they were now an integral thread in the fabric of the state. Even the historian Charles Maier, who argues that the bourgeois political order of Europe largely reconstituted itself after World War I, acknowledges that one enduring change that came out of the war was the integration of organized labor into bargaining systems supervised by the state.[57]

WOMEN IN THE WORK FORCE AND FEMALE SUFFRAGE

Women also made important gains as a result of World War I. Intense demand for labor opened numerous occupations to women that previously had been closed. This effect was especially marked in Great Britain, where the female work force grew by 1,345,000 during the war; female membership in British trade unions tripled from 357,956 in 1914 to 1,086,000 in 1918. In Germany, over 830,000 women joined the work force between 1914 and 1918, and female representation in the Social Democratic trade unions increased from 8 percent to 25 percent. In France, which already had the highest percentage of working women before the war, the number added to the work force was much less, at most 139,000.[58] In all three countries, the growth in female employment was particularly steep in the munitions industry; in Britain, for example, the number of women employed at the Woolwich Arsenal increased from under 100 in November 1916 to 22,000 only six months later. By the end of 1918, 61 percent of the headquarters staff of the Ministry of Munitions were women.[59]

Because much of the growth in female employment dissipated after the war, the result of both dismissals and voluntary resignations, many historians have viewed the wartime gains of women as ephemeral, especially in France.[60] But recently a number of historians have taken a second look. The postwar figures alone do not tell the full story; the war permanently shattered many stereotypes about female abilities, removed at least some barriers to their employment, and bolstered women's confidence as a group. One scholar interviewed numerous British women who had returned to domestic service in 1919 and found that they now felt a far greater capacity to resist exploitation than before the war, and had learned that "I could just move on if I didn't like the place." The British trade unionist Mary Macarthur declared flatly that of all the changes wrought by the war, none was greater than the change in the status of women.[61]

The most dramatic political gain of the war for women was the impetus it gave to female suffrage. During and in the immediate aftermath of the war, women won the franchise in nearly two dozen countries (see Table 5–3). This was not a minor side effect of the conflict, nor the result simply of a wave of imitative behavior; the legislative record almost everywhere makes clear that it was a direct response to the contributions that women had made in the war—in factories, government offices, hospitals, and volunteer service. In Britain, for example, there was overwhelming public sentiment by 1916 to grant

Table 5–3. The extension of the franchise to women during or immediately after World War I (1914–1920)

1915	Denmark, Iceland
1917	Netherlands, Finland, Soviet Russia
1918	Great Britain, Germany, Austria, Sweden, China (6 provinces), Hungary, Poland, Estonia, Latvia, Lithania, Czechoslovakia
1919	Luxembourg, British East Africa, India, Rhodesia
1920	United States (voted by Congress in 1919), Canada, Belgium

Source: Michael Levin, *The Spectre of Democracy* (London, 1992).

women the vote. Converts to the cause included numerous prewar opponents of female suffrage such as Winston Churchill, Lord Derby, Sir Arthur Stanley, Henry Herbert Asquith, Sir Arthur Conan Doyle, and a host of prominent journals. Even in the case of neutral Sweden, the domestic impact of the war was a pivotal factor in the achievement of female suffrage.[62]

France and Italy were among the few belligerent countries not to extend the franchise to women after the war, a failure all the more conspicuous in the case of France, which already had universal male suffrage before the war, unlike Britain or Germany. But the war did elicit strong prosuffrage sentiment there, and in May 1919, only six months after the Armistice, the Chamber of Deputies voted 329 to 95 to enfranchise women. The socialist deputy Bracke told the newspaper *L'Humanité* that the contributions of women in the war refuted the antifeminist case. Jules Siegfried, the oldest deputy in the Chamber, declared that the time had come to give women the vote to thank them for "their admirable attitude during the war."[63] Blocked in the French Senate, female suffrage failed to obtain passage at any time during the 1920s or 1930s. There are many explanations for this—the effect of Catholicism, the absence of a direct linkage with efforts to expand male suffrage (which was already universal), preoccupation with reconstruction—but it may also be significant that France in World War I had registered only a very small percentage of increase in female employment. War yet proved to be a catalyst of enfranchisement, however, when in 1944 the Comité Français de Libération Nationale in Algiers approved De Gaulle's recommendation that women receive the vote in liberated France, in part due to their work in the Resistance. In a strikingly parallel scenario, the advent of female suffrage in Italy also took place while the war was underway (in February 1945), with the role of women in the Resistance obliterating all previous doubts.[64]

In addition to broadening the franchise, the two world wars undermined the traditional class structure of the European states. In Great Britain, the wars briefly resuscitated the fortunes of the aristocracy by virtue of its military leadership, only to seal its permanent decline: draconian tax rates, disproportionate casualties (among peers and their sons, one out of five who fought perished versus one out of eight among other soldiers), and the rising wave of egalitarianism combined to virtually extinguish the institutional power of the nobles in state affairs.

Stanley Hoffman observes that French society in the interwar period was characterized by the dominance of the bourgeoisie, the political ghettoization of the proletariat, and a pervasive individualism that impeded social organization. The crisis of the Third Republic after 1934 began to erode social barriers; World War II destroyed them forever, forging a kind of *société communautaire* in which class privilege was relatively muted.[65] In Germany, the Junker estates were destroyed by World War II; in the cities, class privilege poorly endured the rubble left by the bombing.

Does all this mean that Europe achieved as a result of the world wars the Marxist grail of a classless society? In the sense of formal class privileges in politics having been abolished, almost certainly yes; in the sense of eliminating socioeconomic classes and distinctions, definitely not. The mass state that arose from the wars was a state of equals before the law and in the ballot box, and although there is some evidence that World War II caused a significant reduction in income stratification, it hardly ended economic inequality.[66] But the political effect of economic inequality was at least partially mitigated by another phenomenon that arose in tandem with the mass state and that was reinforced by universal suffrage—the welfare state.

INDUSTRIALIZED WAR AND THE RISE OF THE WELFARE STATE

Scholarly opinion usually sees the rise of the welfare state as an outcome of industrialization and nation-building.[67] The almost universal prevalence of extensive social welfare programs in today's industrial societies lends credence to this point of view. On the other hand, we have already seen how the rudiments of the modern welfare state arose during the era of High Imperialism from 1875 to 1914 and how they were in part shaped by international military rivalry. When the subsequent history of the welfare state is examined, it becomes clear that World Wars I and II also had a profound impact on its evolution. The superstructure was reared during and in the aftermath of World War I, from 1914 to 1923, when the principle of the state's responsibility for the welfare of citizens became widely accepted and welfare programs became an integral component of state administration. The edifice was then essentially finished in its full bureaucratic and fiscal form between 1939 and 1949, the decade dominated by World War II. The Great Depression of course also contributed to the rise of the European welfare state, but largely through the expansion of programs already in place by 1920; it did not play the same pivotal role in Europe as it later would in the United States.

This is not to argue that either imperial rivalry or the world wars were the fundamental or direct *cause* of the welfare state. For one thing, the violence of war does not cause anything other than destruction; and though the cooperative effort entailed by industrialized war gives impetus to collective efforts in other spheres, including social welfare, this impetus stems more from human efforts to transcend the violence of war than from war itself. But the historical linkages between war and the welfare state are too close and too extensive to dismiss as mere coincidences of chronology. The experience of total war on the "home fronts" of Europe greatly facilitated the emergence of welfare states all across the continent; that experience was both an important contributing factor in its own right and a *catalyst* of other underlying causes. This was true even of neutral states such as Sweden and Switzerland, whose internal affairs were greatly affected by both wars and particularly by the Second World War.

The hypothesis of an historical tie between war and the welfare state does not accord comfortably with the ideological premises of either the Right or the Left. Yet many contemporary observers of the world wars were struck, even baffled, by the obvious connections between war and state benevolence. In a time of total war, with its heavy demands on state leaders and administrations, they watched European governments initiate the far-reaching welfare reforms that left-wing activists had advocated without success for decades past. Richard Morris Titmuss, later Professor of Social Administration at the University of London, was such an observer. Commissioned in 1942 to contribute to a social history of the war, he became fascinated by the conflict's enhancing impact on social welfare reforms; after the war he lectured and published on the linkage.[68] He argued that the waging of modern war presupposes a great increase in social discipline, which is tolerable only if social inequities are also addressed.

Further, public concern about the well-being of soldiers and their dependents spreads to encompass the health and well-being of the whole population, and especially of children, "the next generation of recruits."[69] Titmuss was a vigorous advocate of social welfare programs and an adviser to the Labour Party, but he had witnessed the evolution of the welfare state too closely to dismiss its military origins.

The welfare impetus of industrialized warfare stems not only from the implicit bargain of social discipline in exchange for welfare concessions but also from the intense social *cooperation* that this kind of war demands and brings about. This welfare impetus was manifested even in the trenches. Tony Ashworth, in a classic study of trench warfare in World War I, describes the informal associations or "households" of the trenches as "small welfare states" dedicated to providing for the well-being of fellow soldiers. The informal associations that developed in the trenches transcended class boundaries and were the source of the camaraderie that was so much romanticized in memoirs, novels, and even poetry after the war. Similar cooperative bonds were formed across an immense patchwork quilt of human experience from the munitions factories (which had the most advanced social welfare programs then extant), to the bomb shelters, to the private and public organizations that supported the medical, relief, logistical, educational, and social needs of society during wartime. A Carnegie Endowment report written in 1924 proclaimed the Great War to have been the greatest example of human cooperation in world history, which cooperation had generated widespread expectations that after the Armistice economic injustices would be redressed and the social system rebuilt on a new foundation.[70]

The far-reaching impact of the wars on the rise of the welfare state is reflected in the legislative and institutional history of individual European countries; the cases of Great Britain and France are typical of what happened across much of Western Europe.

WAR AND THE BRITISH WELFARE STATE

One way to measure the impact of the world wars on the rise of the welfare state in Great Britain is to look at the trend lines of overall social welfare spending. Alan T. Peacock and Jack Wiseman did a detailed breakdown of British government expenditures from 1890 to 1955 and concluded that the two world wars had exerted a substantial and direct impact on the growth of the British welfare state. Prior to 1914, the British government spent only about 4 percent of total national output (GNP) annually on welfare services. The percentage devoted to welfare spending jumped immediately after 1918, as a result of welfare programs introduced during and shortly after World War I, then remained at an average plateau of around 8 percent throughout the 1920s. The Depression years saw some further growth in the percentage of GNP devoted to social welfare spending, but this was due largely to a declining GNP; actual spending increased only slightly. The next sharp shift upward took place shortly after World War II, as welfare-related spending rose to around 18 percent of GNP by 1950. In a nutshell, the jumps in welfare spending that followed the world wars account for the vast majority of the net growth.[71]

Just as the House of Krupp had provided a model for the social welfare programs of Bismarck in the 1880s, the Ministry of Munitions served as a catalyst for the expansion of welfare measures in Great Britain during World War I. In 1915, Lloyd George set up a special Welfare and Health Section in the Munitions Ministry intended to look after the well-being of its own employees as well as those in the private factories under its purview. As women entered the factories in large numbers, Britain's Chief Inspector of Factories and Workshops predicted that the welfare reforms undertaken during the war would likely be felt long after the war ended, resulting in a permanent improvement in factory life.[72] This proved to be the case, as the welfare program of the Ministry helped to establish the principle of state responsibility for workers' welfare and gave state leaders confidence and a needed precedent for expanding state welfare programs immediately after the war.[73]

The war also stimulated remarkable progress in British infant health care. A widely publicized report in 1915 that nine soldiers died every hour at the front while twelve babies died every hour at home gave rise to the saying that it was safer to serve as a soldier in France than to be born a baby in Britain. As sensitivity to the fragility of human life grew, *The Times* wrote of a "cult of the child" and child welfare services mushroomed. The number of health visitors employed by local authorities more than quadrupled between 1914 and 1918. At the beginning of the war 650 maternity and child-welfare centers were in operation in Britain; at the end of the war nearly 1,300 were open. Expenditures on maternal and infant care nearly tripled from 1916 to 1918, with public programs for the first time overtaking private efforts in scope and reach. The education of children also received a boost, as the Education Act of 1918 extended free public schooling to all children through age fourteen.[74]

In 1917, the War British Cabinet formed a Ministry of Reconstruction, stating that its task was not to rebuild society as it was before the war but to mold a better world out of the social and economic conditions created by the war.[75] The momentum of welfare reform continued strongly in the first two years after the Armistice, largely on the basis of proposals or studies made during the war. In 1917, for example, Lord Rhondda of the Local Government Board had urged the emergency creation of a central Ministry of Health. Though calling it a war measure, Rhondda wanted the new ministry to be permanent and voiced concern that demobilization would make its creation difficult. In 1919, the new Ministry of Health opened its doors. The same year saw passage of the Housing and Town Planning Act ("Addison's Act"), a revolutionary program of public housing that sought to build 600,000 "homes fit for heroes." Finally, in 1920, Parliament passed an act providing for general unemployment insurance, which had existed prior to the war in only a few industries.[76]

By contrast with the welfare activism of 1914–20, no new welfare programs of any significance were instituted in Britain during the interwar period, which left-wing and labor activists came to regard as an era of stagnation, a wholesale retreat from the collectivist consensus of World War I. Even the Great Depression did not result in a British New Deal. The Unemployment Act of 1934 overhauled the Poor Law system, extended unemployment coverage to agricultural workers, and restored some benefits. But in truth neither this Act nor any other welfare legislation of the decade—the 1936 Public Health Act and the 1937 Factories Act—did much more than refine the welfare structure put in place between 1914 and 1920. Instead, the next quantum leap in the development of the welfare state took place as a result of the Second World War. The war witnessed a powerful resurgence of egalitarian and collectivist sentiment, which paved the way for the landslide victory of Labour and a veritable revolution in domestic affairs: the erection of a vastly expanded British welfare state. Kenneth Morgan observed that the war elicited new faith in social planning, that in the wartime mood of unity and equality of sacrifice, "A profound conviction arose . . . that this time the land 'fit for heroes' would not be so wantonly set aside as it was felt to have been in the years after 1918."[77]

In June 1941 the British government announced the formation of an Interdepartmental Committee to make recommendations on postwar reforms in the area of social insurance and workers' compensation. Chaired by Sir William Beveridge, the Committee's report, *Social Insurance and Allied Services*, caused a national sensation upon its publication in 1942. Observing that "the purpose of victory is to live in a better world than the old world; that each individual citizen is more likely to concentrate upon his war effort if he feels that his Government will be ready in time with plans for that better world,"[78] the Report recommended the creation of a full-fledged "cradle-to-grave" welfare state with comprehensive social security provisions, including maternity benefits and child allowances, universal unemployment and health insurance, old age pensions, and death benefits. In a 1944 sequel, *Full Employment in a Free Society*, Beveridge wrote that the war proved that full employment was an attainable goal and should be explicit state policy.[79]

The enthusiastic public response to the Beveridge reports gave rise to widespread expectations that a comprehensive welfare state would be instituted after the war—expectations stoked by explicit government statements in the 1943 budget and a 1944 White Paper. Pressures for change were such that some reform legislation was passed even at the peak of the war, most importantly the Butler Education Act of 1944, which established a Ministry of Education and a comprehensive system of state-funded secondary education. Pressure from workers for swifter progress on the social agenda led the Labour Party in May 1945, just days after the German surrender and before the war with Japan had ended, to withdraw from the government and force new elections. The resulting landslide sent a victorious wartime leader into political exile, a victim of social forces unleashed by the very conflict whose waging had been his central passion. It also laid the way for the passage between 1945 and 1948 of the most sweeping social legislation in British history: the nationalization of 20 percent of the nation's industry, the creation of a National Health Service, and the passage of a comprehensive social insurance program based on the Beveridge recommendations. From 1938 to 1950, British expenditures on social services increased 350 percent in real terms. One could argue that such increases were inevitable once a Labour government came to power unfettered by any coalition partner, but the fact remains that both the Labour victory and public demand for massive welfare expenditures derived directly from the social experience of the Second World War.[80]

WAR AND THE WELFARE STATE IN FRANCE

In World War I France suffered even more than Britain in terms of human casualties, economic damage, and national trauma; the French state consequently suffered more from the purely degenerative effects of warfare. French liberals had always been more ambivalent about social reforms than their British counterparts, and French conservatives more obstructionist than the Tories. With the survival of France continually threatened from 1914 to 1918, there was in any event less possibility for would-be reformers to take advantage of the atmosphere of war to press their agenda. This is perhaps one reason why interwar France lagged significantly behind Britain in the development of the welfare state. The collapse of France in 1940 and the establishment of the Vichy regime also created conditions radically different than those prevailing in wartime Britain in 1940–45. Long-standing traditions of corporatism and industrial paternalism shaped the evolution of the welfare state in France along paths different from those in Great Britain. Despite these differences, the Fourth Republic emerged in 1947 with a markedly advanced welfare system that by 1950 already spent a higher percentage of its gross domestic product (11.5 percent) on social insurance than did Britain (9.6 percent).[81]

During World War I, concern for the families of soldiers and the welfare of workers stimulated emergency welfare measures. Shortly after hostilities began, the French government established a *Fond du Chômage* of 20 million francs for dislocated workers and military dependents. The state also attempted to use its rapidly expanding regulatory powers on behalf of workers—mandating a minimum wage in specific trades and regions, helping to defer rent payments, and intervening on behalf of trade unions in labor disputes. But in the French tradition of industrial paternalism, much of the social welfare implemented during the First World War took place under the aegis of private firms. Employers purchased labor peace with their own expanded benefits such as medical care, maternity benefits, and family allowances, and by building factory-run canteens, libraries, cinemas, and sports clubs.

As in Britain, the influx of women into the armaments factories stimulated French social welfare initiatives. Albert Thomas, the Minister of Munitions, in July 1917 issued a memorandum calling for measures to preserve the health and well-being of female workers. His subsequent initiatives included a tightening of safety and health regulations, but also such benefits as maternity leave, job guarantees, medical care, and housing. Though the motivation for the Thomas reforms was concern over the welfare of women, many of the benefits extended to male workers as well. The French Ministry of Munitions thus became a pioneer of workers' welfare, spearheading reforms that affected not only the arms industry but, through its example, much of the national economy.

As in Great Britain, the interwar period in France was largely marked by drift and stagnation with respect to the development of the welfare state. In the 1920s, France ranked thirteenth out of fourteen

European countries in the percentage of its population covered by national social insurance of one kind or another; even after the passage of national social security legislation in April 1932 it lagged far behind both Germany and the United Kingdom. At its interwar peak in 1937, social insurance represented only a tiny fraction—3.5 percent—of total French public expenditure.[82] One indication of reform stagnation in the interwar years was the fact that even when the Socialists attained power under the *Cartel des Gauches* (1924) or in the Popular Front government of Léon Blum (1936), they failed to achieve most of their reform agenda. The Popular Front's major breakthrough was the institution of paid vacations and the forty-hour week, but other than these, it passed no significant new welfare measures.[83] Nor did the Depression per se generate much momentum for reforms, in part because France was less industrialized than either Britain or Germany and experienced correspondingly lower unemployment.

The one significant exception to this pattern was in the area of family allowances, and here the legacy of World War I was critical. France had already experienced a significant decline in its birth rate prior to 1914, but the loss of 1.4 million lives in the war—the majority of them young men of marriageable age—caused the rate to plunge dramatically after 1920; one consequence of this was an upswelling of fervent pronatalism and profamily sentiment throughout French society.[84] France's low birth rate was a concern of military planners and the target of more than one policy initiative; these included the introduction of family allowances in March 1932 and the Family Code of 1939 that expanded those allowances. The Family Code was proclaimed in July 1939 at a moment of high tension—on the eve of the Second World War and just four months after Hitler's invasion of Czechoslovakia; according to the French sociologist Rémy Lenoir, its enactment was possible only in a political context in which the thought of war was never absent, thus strengthening reform-minded centralizers, both Catholic and secular.[85]

The French collapse in May-June 1940 was a national trauma of almost unparalleled proportions. Just as the French defeat of Prussia at Jena in 1806 had precipitated German soul-searching and an era of dynamic reform, the German defeat of France in 1940 unleashed French soul-searching and powerful reform pressures. The French defeat discredited the political paralysis and perceived decadence of the Third Republic, and created conditions conducive to radical change such as France had not seen since 1870. Determined to redress the conditions that had led to defeat, the French undertook major structural reforms even in the midst of an enemy occupation. Contrary to the postwar myth of a collaborationist regime lacking popular support, the Vichy reforms were indigenous in origin, enjoyed at least some elite and mass support, and in a few cases marked the realization of reform agendas that had been frustrated before the war. They are an example of how defeat in war generates impetus for reform.[86]

The Vichy government sought to capitalize on the pronatalist sentiment that still reigned in France by pursuing a *politique de la famille*, measures intended to support and increase the French birth rate, including an expanded system of family allowances. (Pétain, in his statement justifying the armistice with Germany, had declared that France's problem was "too few children, too few arms, too few allies.") Pétain in March 1941 also issued an old-age pension law modeled on legislation that had failed in the Senate in 1939. Other Vichy reforms included assistance to farmers and artisans, major educational reforms, civil service reforms, and improvements in health care programs, especially for mothers and children. Many of these reforms represented an attempt to reassert traditional values in the face of industrial realities, and as such had a certain antimodernist character. And of course, even their positive aspects must be balanced against the regime's reactionary policies in other areas, including its attempt to abolish trade unions and merge labor into a corporatist system dominated by the state.

In the end, Vichy France offered the paradox of a regime that unblinkingly collaborated in sending tens of thousands of French Jews to their death, while simultaneously seeking to strengthen French society by welfare reform. Given its overall moral record, it is clear that neither altruism nor a sense of Catholic charity motivated the regime, as it sometimes pretended, but rather calculated concerns about national survival, popular support, and postwar social recovery.

The National Council of the Resistance abroad, partly in response to the Vichy reforms, made clear that it also intended to assist French families, and it developed extensive plans for a postwar French welfare state during its years in exile. Both the Vichy collaborators and the Gaullist resistance drew the same conclusion from France's defeat in 1940: that French society was wanting, and that it needed to be revived through state welfare activism. One of the early actions of General de Gaulle shortly after his arrival in France in 1944 as head of the Provisional Government was to increase the family allowances under a system later adopted unanimously in August 1946. De Gaulle also laid down another cornerstone of the postwar French welfare state—a national system of comprehensive social security protection that included unemployment compensation, sickness benefits, and

Table 5–4. French central state expenditures (including social
security) in *constant* 1938 prices: pre-World War I,
interwar period, and post-World War II

	PRE-WAR		INTERWAR			POST-WAR		
	1909	1912	1920	1928	1938	1947	1948	1950
Millions of francs, constant 1978 prices	287	275	745	559	829	1,333	1,464	1,701

Source: DeLorme and Andre, "Long-Run Growth of Public Expenditure in France,"
p. 63 (calculated).

improved safeguards for workers' rights; this program came into effect
in October 1945.

Already by 1947 social security payments constituted over 20 percent of central state expenditures in France, nearly *six times* the interwar level.[87] This increase in the share of spending devoted to social
security is even more impressive given that the two world wars had
resulted in the massive fiscal expansion of the French state *as a whole*.
Table 5–4 conveys a sense of the powerful impact of the wars on the
development of France into a massive, collectivist state; a large and
permanent quantum leap in central state expenditures took place as a
consequence of each war. The Second World War and the period of
reconstruction that followed it also saw a significant centralization of
the French welfare system, as numerous programs that previously had
been administered at the local level were nationalized between 1944
and 1950—a phenomenon that also occurred in the United Kingdom
in the same period.[88]

After 1947, the French welfare state matured in form and grew
rapidly in terms of its fiscal claim on the public treasury. Nonetheless,
the fact remains that the legal and bureaucratic superstructure for this
growth was laid from 1944–47 under the Provisional Government of
Charles de Gaulle and in the first year of the Fourth Republic. The
public statements and larger political actions of those who built that
superstructure make it abundantly clear that one of their primary
motivations was to restore the national glory and international position of France. Once the welfare state was in place, however, it
acquired a logic and momentum of its own, and the large increases in
welfare spending that occurred in France after 1950—like the similar
increases registered in nearly every major country of Europe—derived
largely from domestic political factors and had little if any link to
either war or national security. Whether or not the Cold War in some

indirect sense reinforced the internal cohesion of the West European welfare states between 1948 and 1989 is a difficult question to answer, but surely it was not integral to their development. There appears to be a threshold of development beyond which the social compact implicit in the welfare state becomes self-sustaining, upheld by popular demand and decoupled from its origins in war.

THE WORLD WARS AND THE NEUTRAL STATES: SWEDEN AND SWITZERLAND

If the military origins of the collectivist state are as important as the above analysis suggests, we might logically expect the neutral states of Sweden and Switzerland to have become only minimally welfare states, or at least to have displayed a very different pattern of social-welfare development than occurred in more belligerent states. In fact, Switzerland does have a radically unorthodox system of public assistance, decentralized and lacking in most of the customary accoutrements of the welfare state. Sweden, however, is virtually an archetype of the modern industrial welfare state. But when we examine the historical record closely, we see that the two world wars, and especially World War II, had a profound effect on Sweden's internal politics, including the development of its welfare state. As for Switzerland, the Second World War also shaped the development of its welfare system, but in a distinctive manner that stemmed from the unique Swiss system of governance and defense.

As it did in other parts of Europe, Bismarck's social insurance legislation greatly influenced Swedish thinking and led to the passage in 1884 of the first comprehensive social insurance bill. The next major innovation occurred in 1913–14 with the passage of the Pension Act and the establishment of a National Pension Board. Despite the timing of this reform, it does not appear to have been linked in any significant way with international tensions, and it pre-dated the outbreak of World War I. But much as the income-tax amendment passed by the U.S. Congress in 1912 only became a major source of revenue in World War I, so also the Swedish pension program expanded rapidly during the war, as state leaders sought to maintain labor peace and domestic stability during a European crisis of vast proportions. The economic hardships of the war years aggravated discontent at home, while the Swedish army and navy waxed increasingly restless and even revolutionary. Alarmed by these trends, Sweden's elites resorted to social concessions to buy peace at home—passing universal suffrage and restoring the right to poverty relief in the Poor Law reform of 1918.[89]

Welfare reform stagnated in the 1920s; later, though Sweden suffered relatively lightly from the Depression, the Social Democratic government that came to power in 1932 pushed numerous relief bills through the *Riksdag*. The legislative momentum of the decade, and the intellectual currents in Sweden favoring some form of socialism, give abundant reason to believe that a full-fledged Swedish welfare state would have arisen even without the impetus of international conflict. But the timing of World War II makes a definitive judgment impossible, and a look at the war years reveals some interesting developments. Despite Sweden's neutrality, World War II impelled a high degree of social mobilization and cooperation there because of the ever-present threat from Germany. A coalition government of national unity under Per Albin Hansson drastically boosted taxes in order to support an expanded military force. It introduced extensive regulation of the economy, imposed rationing, and incorporated numerous private interest groups into the wartime state as de facto administrative organs. In language strikingly similar to that of the Beveridge Report, and possibly influenced by it, Hansson articulated the establishment of Sweden as "the People's Home" (*Folkhemmet*). His Minister of Social Affairs, Gustav Möller, put forth proposals for constructing a postwar cradle-to-grave welfare state. The experience of a controlled economy and full employment during the war meanwhile persuaded Sweden's bourgeois parties, the Conservatives and Liberals, to abandon liberalism and accept much of the welfare agenda of the Social Democrats.[90]

When the war ended, a coalition government dominated by the Social Democrats introduced a host of new welfare programs, including a pension reform that abolished means testing and that guaranteed every citizen a pension, sick pay, and child allowances. In 1947, by means of an intensely debated tax reform, the coalition was able to "capture" the tax base of the war years, restructuring the national revenue system but retaining wartime levels of taxation in order to fund the new welfare state. In short, though we will never know what might have occurred in the absence of war, it is clear that World War II spurred the growth of even neutral Sweden's welfare apparatus in ways that were of long-term significance.

The Second World War also had far-reaching consequences for the development of the Swiss welfare state. Immediately after Germany invaded Poland, the Swiss mobilized their entire society and remained in a high state of military readiness throughout the war. They rationed food and fuel, prohibited private automobile use, and imposed controls on industry. By the end of the war, the Swiss national debt had nearly tripled. The consciousness of imminent threat, the solidarity forged by the war, and the fear of postwar recession generated the momentum necessary for the passage of two critical reforms. The first was a constitutional amendment expanding the role of the national government in economic affairs and giving it explicit authority to provide for the people's welfare. The second reform, based on this new authority, was the introduction of an income-compensation plan for all individuals liable for military service. It became the model for the national pension plan instituted in 1947, which remains the cornerstone of the Swiss welfare system today.[91]

Although the Second World War clearly played a crucial role in shaping the Swiss welfare system, that system is unlike any other in Europe. There is no national health service, no centralized programs of income maintenance, poverty relief, or unemployment compensation. The system is highly decentralized, with the national pension and insurance system administered through employer associations and the cantons. It operates as a true insurance system, being self-funded by workers' contributions rather than by central revenues. Public assistance programs are also administered at the local level. With only a tiny central bureaucracy, the Swiss system is both efficient and effective, in large part because it is undergirded by a social milieu that places a high value on self-reliance and hard work.[92]

The Swiss sociologist Walter Rüegg argues that the uniquely decentralized structure of Switzerland's welfare system originated largely from its militia system.[93] Militia service reminds citizens that they have obligations toward the state as well as rights. Officers up to colonel rank remain in private professions, but retain responsibility for the training and well-being of their troops, a responsibility that tends to extend into their private life. The local military units, whose membership embraces the entire male population, thus serve as informal cogs in the social welfare system. A tightly woven network of military associations and clubs further reinforces the social milieu that makes possible the informality and decentralization of the Swiss system. Finally, the centralizing tendencies so characteristic of modern industrial states are limited in the Swiss case by the constitutional delegation of important matters of defense to the cantonal and local level. When defense is decentralized, so also is the welfare state.

The Swedish and Swiss cases demonstrate that the maelstrom of total war affected even the neutral islands of Europe during the world wars and helped shape their political form. Mobilization for war, especially when it is prolonged, may have organizing and formative effects similar to actual war, though perhaps less intense. The success of the Swiss welfare system in providing security to its people without a cumbersome central bureaucracy further suggests that war not only has shaped the modern collectivist state, but may be partly responsible for its characteristic dysfunctions. The excessive bureaucracy and centralization of most European welfare states may derive in part from their origin in war. This suggests that unless and until states organize themselves differently for defense, the welfare state will continue to look much like what it is: a crudely adapted version of the warfare state.

CONCLUSION: WAR AND THE COLLECTIVIST IMPULSE

Industrialized warfare is the most bitterly conflictual of human phenomena but also the most intensely cooperative. While the riveting violence of battle preoccupied human attention during the world wars, over the long run, the cooperative personal effort that they entailed was probably a greater source of permanent social change. The irredeemable tragedy of war lies in what is destroyed, especially in the human lives sacrificed; both lives and property, once destroyed, cannot be brought back. But the legacies that do endure are the experience of collective endeavor—newly forged channels of societal cooperation—and the organizational residues of war, those political institutions forged to make possible its waging. Since full-scale industrialized war cannot possibly be fought by militia forces or in any decentralized manner, it invariably leads to the concentration of immense power in a central government. That power, channeled through the deep grooves of societal cooperation etched by war, is a formidable engine of collective action. The mass state, the regulatory state, the welfare state—in short, the collectivist state that reigns in Europe today—is an offspring of the total warfare of the industrial age.

Ideologues of both the left and the right will resist this conclusion. The rise of the welfare state, as Charles Tilly observes, has both mitigated and obscured the centrality of coercion in our politics.[94] Conservatives cannot believe that war, and the martial life that they so often venerate, can possibly be the source of the collectivism and socialism that they so much abhor. European socialists and social democrats, as

well as American liberals, likewise cannot accept that the welfare institutions which they regard as hallmarks of human progress could possibly have derived in part from anything so horrendous as war. That
flies in the face of their deeply rooted beliefs about the perfectibility of
human nature, the evolutionary direction of history, and the moral
inferiority of all things military in nature. But facts are stubborn
things, and the pervasive influence of imperialism and the world wars
on the politics of the past century is difficult to explain away.

The Great Influenza Epidemic of 1918–20 devoured some 25 million
lives worldwide; it was a toll greater than that of the Great War that
had just ended. The epidemic today is but a footnote to history. The
War, by destroying the old bourgeois order of Europe and burying
classical liberalism in the rubble, transformed our world and continues to transform it yet. The leaders and the masses who fought in the
Great War, and in its turbulent reprise twenty years later, reared a new
Europe, one dominated by the collectivist, paternalistic states that still
reign today. Long before 1914, Auguste Comte observed that the dead
govern the living. This is true also of the Europe that arose from the
ashes of 1945. Nearly fifty years after the surrender of Germany, the
two world wars, and the generation for whom they meant either
tragedy or triumph, still govern the living today.

War and the Totalitarian State

The essential elements of our poetry will be courage, audacity and revolt. . . . We want to exalt movements of aggression, feverish sleeplessness, the quick step, the perilous leap, the slap and the blow with the first. . . . Beauty exists only in struggle. There is no masterpiece that has not an aggressive character. Poetry must be violent assault on the forces of the unknown, to force them to bow before man. . . . We want to glorify war—the only cure for the world—militarism, patriotism . . . we will sing of great crowds agitated by work, pleasure and revolt. . . .

F. T. Marinetti, *The Futurist Manifesto*[1]

Totalitarianism was conceived in war and enamored of conflict. The prophets of the totalitarian movements, both Bolshevik and National Socialist, romanticized the fluidity and dynamism of war, and they conceived of the state as a vast army of the masses, disciplined and all encompassing. Shortly before coming to power, Hitler proclaimed that his political mission was "to transpose a whole nation into a mental state of unconditional military willingness and military readiness."[2] In a similar vein, Lenin, in a lengthy panegyric on the modern army as the ideal organizational model, extolled its flexibility and power "to impart a single will to millions of people."[3] The defining attribute of the totalitarian state was perpetual mobilization for war—war against foreign adversaries, both real and imagined, and war against its own population.

It was no coincidence that the generation that succumbed most easily to totalitarian rule was the "front generation," the millions who had already undergone the leveling, collectivizing experience of mass mobilization in the trenches and armaments factories of World War I. The Great War, as noted earlier, was the pivotal moment in the breakdown of the European classes and their transformation into homogeneous masses. More than any other event or phenomenon, it forged the "mass-man" that José Ortega y Gasset characterized so trenchantly in *The Revolt of the Masses*—the socially atomized "common man," amoral and anchorless, who fell prey to the attractions of Fascism, Nazism, and Bolshevism.[4] The war was the great equalizer, the "mightiest of all mass actions," which fulfilled a widely felt "yearning for anonymity, for being just a number and functioning only as a cog . . ."[5] Just as the architects of the European welfare state sought to tap the collectivist energy generated by industrialized warfare, the leaders of the totalitarian movements sought to recapture the solidarity and classlessness of the trenches—and the order, regimentation, and collective energy of the state-dominated societies of World War I—and in the case of the Bolsheviks, of the Russian Civil War. But instead of pursuing a collectivism that would transcend the violent heritage of the war, they made the organization of violence the very core of their approach to politics. The result was a type of modern state unlike any that had yet appeared on the European stage.

As a historical phenomenon, totalitarianism marked the apotheosis of all that was perverse in the modern linkage between war and the state. All the most negative tendencies of warfare to enhance state power—to centralize, bureaucratize, and foster repression—reached their logical culmination in states organized for the near-total penetration and domination of civil society. Yet the totalitarian states were not simply garrison states, marshalled to the teeth for war, though they sometimes have been portrayed as such. It was not the organizing impetus of war alone that forged them, but its destructive and degenerative effects as well—and the key event was World War I, which devastated the traditional pillars of civil society in both Russia and Germany, and brutalized their cultures, thereby making possible a catastrophic and unchecked assertion of central power.

In this regard, it is surely of significance that every totalitarian or quasi-totalitarian regime of the twentieth century, both in Europe and Asia, came to power only after a devastating civil or international war. What is more, many of the countries that fell prey to totalitarianism were geographically vulnerable states exposed for long periods to the ravages of war. More than one historian has traced the seeds of Germany's tragic history back to the devastation of the Germanic lands during the Thirty Years' War—the consequences of which for Germany's late emergence as a unified state even Hitler expatiated upon more than once. The origins of Tsarist despotism and Russia's susceptibility to totalitarian rule also have been linked with its pervasive sense of territorial and even cultural insecurity, originating as early as the Mongol invasions of the thirteenth century. But more than any other factor, it was the unprecedented destructiveness of World War I that devastated civil society in Russia and Germany (neither of which had a well-rooted consensual tradition to begin with) and spawned states in which wartime levels of mobilization, complete disregard for human rights, and the pervasive dominance of state authority became everyday features of political life in peace as well as war.

In actual practice, of course, no state has ever achieved the total domination of civil society that is implied in the term "totalitarianism." Historians have long recognized that some elements of shared power, elite pluralism, or "polyarchy" endured in Nazi Germany even at the height of Hitler's ascendancy.[6] Certain traditional institutions such as the Catholic Church and the Junker estates of East Prussia retained a measure of autonomy; nor did Hitler ever dare conduct a purge of the Army, at least not prior to the assassination attempt against him in July 1944. Stalin, by contrast, allowed no institutional autonomy of any kind; he collectivized agriculture, turned the Russian Orthodox Church into a servile tool of the state, and brutally purged the Soviet officer corps. Stalinist Russia at the peak of the 1930s purges thus came as close as any state in history to conforming to the theoretical model of totalitarianism. But while Stalin succeeded in obliterating the institutional bases of civil society, even he did not achieve truly total control over human affairs. As for other Communist or Fascist states—such as Mussolini's Italy (where the term *totalitarian state* first entered European discourse) or the Warsaw Pact states of Eastern Europe—they should at most be regarded as "quasi-totalitarian." Like the Soviet Union after the Khrushchev thaw, these states were highly authoritarian, but still allowed room for a small sphere of private activity.

Any attempt to exert total control over society by administrative means only entails a multiplication of watchers and controllers, who in turn must be watched and controlled; and while totalitarian states invariably did multiply control organizations, there were practical limits to how far this could go. No human organization can perfectly embody a single will, if only because it is impossible to purge human beings entirely of their personal interests and affections, not to mention

their weaknesses and incompetencies. The experience of the modern
concentration camp has shown that although physical force can dictate
every detail of an inmate's outward life, even torturing or destroying
the human body, coercive means cannot necessarily reach the inner
sanctum of human will and freedom. The New Soviet Man and the
New Nazi Man were chimeras that never were and never could be.

The nontotality of totalitarianism has led some scholars to question
the usefulness of the term.[7] Perhaps "mass-mobilization states" would
be a better label; whatever the nomenclature, however, the Nazi and
Soviet regimes were radical departures from the absolutist and autocratic states of the past. Nor did the difference lie merely in the degree
of dictatorship; the entire structure, rationale, and functioning of
these new totalitarian states were, historically speaking, sui generis.
Several features distinguished them from traditional nation-states:

- the existence, parallel to the state bureaucracy, of a hierarchi-
  cally organized mass political party led by a charismatic figure
  and imbued with personal commitment to him;
- their adherence to a utopian ideology that claimed an
  absolute monopoly on truth and that provided the *raison
  d'être* of the state;
- the atomization of civil society and the destruction of all
  organized opposition by the calculated use of terror;
- the fostering of ceaseless political activity and deliberate instability, what Trotsky called "permanent revolution";
- the total politicization of all spheres of human life by means
  of mass-mobilization techniques that effectively removed all
  possibility of political neutrality;
- the multiplication of bureaucratic hierarchies so as to achieve
  maximum control over society, coupled with deliberately
  overlapping jurisdictions and a lack of procedural formality
  so as to prevent the coalescence of any subcentral concentration of power.[8]

These six features derived in part from the pervasive sense of struggle, sacrifice, and threat that characterized totalitarianism in all its
forms. Indeed, totalitarian leaders have always conceived of themselves
as more than simply state leaders, their parties as more than mere
political organizations, the states under their control as far more than
ordinary states. The leaders were prophets, warriors, demigods. The
parties were causes, campaigns, world movements. The states were
bastions for waging crusades on ideological infidels and for propagat-

ing the New Utopia abroad. Militant, militaristic, and militarized, the totalitarian states were eternally at war.[9]

THE TOTALITARIAN STATE AS AN ARMY AT WAR

Conventional frames of reference and ordinary political analysis break down when confronted by the totalitarian phenomenon. Any attempt to understand Nazi Germany or Stalinist Russia primarily in terms of the functioning of their governments—by drawing organizational charts or attempting to define a standard hierarchical structure of power—will fail. This is because the totalitarian leaders tendered scant attention to the formalities of government or the structure of bureaucracies, seeing them only as appendages to the main source of their power. This was the larger supranational movement or Party—in the Third Reich, the Nazi Party or NSDAP; in the Soviet Union, the Communist Party or CPSU.* The party controlled the government, as well as the army and the secret police, but even at that its main objective was never to govern in a narrow sense, but rather to pilot the ideological mass crusade that was its very soul. The movement was what mattered, and this meant that the total state and its entire citizenry had to be mobilized for the cause. The totalitarian model of the state was that of an army at war.

Raymond Aron in *The Century of Total War* characterized the impact of all-out war on politics: "the army industrializes itself, industry militarizes itself; the army absorbs the nation; the nation models itself on the army."[10] Sergio Panunzio, a protégé of Mussolini, articulated just such a vision:

> [The Fascist state will be] a great army, an imposing discipline, a living hierarchy. The military organization of the armed forces is no longer sufficient. United to the organization of the armed forces there must be a civilian army that includes functionaries and citizens . . . Not only soldiers are soldiers and combatants; all the citizens from the most lowly to the highest are soldiers and combatants . . ."

---

*The NSDAP is the common acronym for the *Nationalsozialistische Deutsche Arbeiterpartei* (National Socialist German Worker's Party); CPSU stands for Communist Party of the Soviet Union, or in Russian, the *Kommunisticheskaia partiia sovetskovo soyuza* (KPSS).

Yet the model of totalitarianism was not the stodgy, bureaucratic army of peacetime, but rather the fluid, dynamic, revolutionary army of war. The mechanized army, the aggressive, fast-moving army of the *Blitzkrieg*, was the appropriate metaphor for what totalitarianism sought to achieve in the realm of politics. And though every army has a rigid hierarchical structure, hierarchy is not what principally matters in war, but rather personal leadership, boldness, and a capacity for adaptation to the ever-changing needs of the front. Like every effective army, totalitarianism was at once both rigid and supple, dictatorial and fluid.

Every army has a supreme commander, whose authority holds sway over the life and destiny of every soldier and combat unit; the Party leader, the Führer, played this role in the totalitarian state, cultivating around his persona a cult of infallibility and infinite wisdom. Likewise, every army has an officer corps, and in the totalitarian states, the elite functionaries of the Party (in Soviet parlance, the *apparatchiki*) fulfilled this role. The Nazi Party styled itself a *Kampfbund* and consciously modeled its elite formations after the army, while Lenin and Stalin sought to mold the Communist apparatus, as Philip Selznick outlined in exquisite detail over forty years ago, into a "combat party" of highly obedient cadres trained in and dedicated to the art of political war.[12] In a major speech in 1937, Stalin described the structure of the Party as consisting of 3,000 to 4,000 "generals," 30,000 to 40,000 "officers," and 150,000 "NCOs."[13] In this schema, ordinary party members are the voluntary enlistees and mere citizens the conscripts of the totalitarian army-state, their life and labor commandeered by the state, their political rights nonexistent.

In its zeal to subsume all of civil society under the state, to transform it into an instrument of both military and political warfare, the Nazi state declared civil servants to be "administrative soldiers," schoolteachers "soldiers of education," doctors "soldiers of medicine." Soviet propaganda employed similar terms, and the Soviet state under Stalin actually insisted that millions of citizens—even in civilian sectors such as the railway and river transport systems or the coal and iron industries—wear uniforms with army-style rank insignia on their sleeves. (This requirement was abolished only in 1954, after de-Stalinization had occurred.)[14] The shibboleths of totalitarian rhetoric were also largely military in derivation: class conflict, constant struggle, storm troopers, ramparts of socialism, class enemy, shock troops, ideological front. In the CPSU's "war on poor harvests," there were "offensives against the *taiga*" and "sowing campaigns." Even in the most peaceful of human activities, totalitarianism took the language of

struggle and combat, the language of war mobilization, and trans-
posed it into the civil arena.[15]

By keeping the state at war, artificially or otherwise, the totalitarian
leaders ensured that power would always flow toward the center. But
not only were the totalitarian states perpetually at war, they were perpetually at war with two quite different enemies: the enemy abroad
and the enemy at home. This too was an important key to their power,
for as we have seen in earlier chapters, the centralizing impetus of war
is potentially strongest when civil war and international war coincide.
The preoccupation of the totalitarian movements with international
war—the enemy abroad—derived from their ideological zeal; bent on
the propagation of their cause, they could only conceive of its foreign
opponents, as mortal enemies, regardless of how benign or peaceful
the latter might actually be. The totalitarian movements were similarly
obsessed with civil war—the enemy at home—because every failing of
their ideology and state could only be explained by sinister attribution
to "enemies of the people"—Jews, *kulaks*, wreckers, saboteurs, Trot-
skyites, and deviationists of every stripe. This dual sense of enmity
paralleled the experience of the World War I trenches, where soldiers
despised both the unseen enemy that shot at them across the lines and
the faceless enemy in the rear, the staff officers and bureaucrats who
pulled the strings of war and who were blamed for every life-threaten-
ing bungle.[16]

With regard to international war, totalitarianism prospered only
insofar as it was constantly expanding, or at least maintaining an
expansionist thrust in its rhetoric and objectives. The seeds of Nazi
expansionism can be traced in the writings of Hitler and his fellow
National Socialists dating back to the early 1920s. Once in power, the
Nazi movement opted for a classic war of maneuver and attack that
advanced and intensified from the occupation of the Rhineland, to the
Anschluss of Austria, to the seizure of the Sudetenland and Czechoslovakia, to the invasion of Poland, to the conquest of most of Europe
and the Middle East. An orgiastic explosion, economically and
humanly unsustainable, it collapsed under the armed onslaught of the
very enemies its own actions had produced; yet the top Nazi leadership never gave serious thought to abandoning the fight and seeking a
regime-saving peace, even after the war became hopeless.

The seeds of Soviet expansionism were likewise present from the
beginning. The first official decree of the Bolshevik regime, the
Orwellian "Decree on Peace," was a de facto declaration of war on
every power in Europe. But the Soviet Union, unlike Nazi Germany,
opted for a war of attrition rather than one of offensive maneuver; it

conceived of international struggle more as *Sitzkrieg* than *Blitzkrieg*. From November 1917 until July 1988, when the Nineteenth Party Conference signaled an end to the ideological siege of the West, the Soviet state was at least nominally at war with the entire capitalist world. Lenin made aggressive attempts to propagate revolution abroad, spending large sums on foreign Communist movements and creating the Comintern to sustain his efforts. Although his successors spoke of building socialism in one country or, beginning with Khrushchev, of peaceful coexistence, they ever took care to make plain that this was but a truce in a protracted basic conflict between irreconcilable systems. Even during the relatively peaceful years of détente with the West in the 1970s, a study showed that the USSR and its East European allies, as well as other Marxist-Leninist states worldwide, consistently spent a higher percentage of their national income on armaments than did any other type of state.[17] In this sense, the entire Soviet era amounted to a period of ideological siege warfare rivaling in length the Eighty Years' War of the seventeenth century. Once the siege was called off, the USSR only survived for forty-one more months. The Soviet state could not endure without a protracted conflict any more than could Nazi Germany.

The keeping up of perpetual civil war was another key to the power of the totalitarian states. Eric Hoffer described hatred as "a convenient instrument for mobilizing a community for defense." The mobilization of hatred helped to maintain the revolutionary ardor necessary for the totalitarian movements to thrive. Indeed, if tangible domestic enemies could not be readily identified it would have been necessary to invent them, as Hitler said of the Jews. In effect, the totalitarian state acted as an occupying army even in its own country.[18] In Nazi Germany, this obsession with internal enemies actually increased *after* the regime had eliminated its political opponents, a task essentially accomplished by the end of 1934. In 1935, SS General Reinhard Heydrich published an article warning that the threat of the internal enemy (Jewry, Freemasonry, etc.) was *greater than ever*, indeed "all-embracing" in scope:

> We must realize that these enemies will not be dealt with merely by taking over the outward trappings of the machinery of State, since they have spread their tentacles through every branch of our public life and state structure. . . .
>
> We, the fighters, must bring ourselves to realize that we have years of bitter struggle ahead of us if we are finally to drive the enemy to the wall everywhere, destroy him and make Germany racially and spiritually secure against further enemy onslaughts.[19]

The Jewish "threat" about which Heydrich waxed so paranoid was a law-abiding ethnic group constituting less than 1 percent of the population of Germany. No matter the numbers, the enemy was everywhere. Hajo Holborn observes that the vilification, persecution, and ultimate genocide of the Jews enabled Hitler and the Nazi leadership to inculcate in their followers the ruthlessness that they saw as essential to political victory.[20]

Perhaps the ultimate comment on the Soviet Union's war with its own population was the epithet that appeared on the base of the toppled statue of Felix Dzerzhinsky, the first commander of the Soviet Cheka, after the failed coup of August 1991: "Russian Civil War: 1917–1991." From the beginning, the Bolsheviks saw civil war not as an evil forced on them by circumstance but as a central component of the revolutionary struggle. Three months before the October Revolution and again in 1919, Lenin declared that all problems of social life, indeed all serious political questions, are decided by civil war. The same dictum was repeated in his *Letter to American workers*: "In revolutionary epochs the class struggle has always, inevitably, and in every country, assumed the form of *civil war*, and civil war is inconceivable without the severest destruction, terror. . . ."[21] Lenin was referring of course to civil war as an immutable stage in the overthrow of capitalism, but even after the Bolsheviks had solidified their hold on power, their fixation upon internal enemies continued.

The actual Russian Civil War—that fought between the Red and White armies in 1918–21—was among the largest and most brutal wars of modern history, with appalling losses of life, massive population dislocations, interior lines and fronts stretching thousands of miles, and the forced mobilization of peasant armies almost as large as those that fought in World War I. The war constituted the critical formative period of Soviet totalitarianism. But though it is customary to refer to this struggle as *the* Russian Civil War, Soviet Russia underwent two other periods of massive internal bloodletting later, under Joseph Stalin. The first was the agricultural collectivization campaign of 1929–34, entailing hundreds of local uprisings, pitched battles between Soviet forces and the peasantry, and the mass starvation of Ukraine and Kazakhstan in a famine deliberately engineered by the state. This collectivization campaign was a virtual Second Russian Civil War, with participants widely referring to it as a "war" and with regular army troops used on several occasions to quell peasant resistance. As many as 11 million souls perished during the campaign, 7 million of them from famine.

A second orgy of internal bloodletting, the *Yezhovshchina* or Great Purge, took place in 1936–38, during which time another 3 million or more persons perished, one-third by execution, two-thirds in labor camps. While Hitler sought to exterminate a specific racial group, the Stalinist purges of this period were largely random in nature, aimed at no specific ethnic group, nationality, or class—not even for that matter against proven enemies of the Party. Stalin's purges were a unique form of "statistical terror," purely prophylactic in nature, intended to atomize society and destroy or deter any conceivable opposition *even before said opposition existed.* The guilt or innocence of his victims was beside the point; millions died for the sole purpose of keeping hundreds of millions in a state of constant fear. Having murdered the flower of his nation and created potential enemies of hundreds of thousands of bereaved families, is it any wonder that Stalin was paranoid and that his paranoia grew with the passing of time?[22]

Having internal "enemies" to wage war against was so vital to the sustenance of totalitarianism that both Stalin and Hitler willingly sacrificed real military strength in their pursuit of alleged adversaries at home. Stalin's purge of the Soviet officer corps eliminated over 40,000 officers on the very eve of World War II, including 50 out of 57 corps commanders and 154 out of 186 divisional commanders, many of them by execution. It was hardly a logical way to prepare for a possible war with Germany. Hitler's *Rassenpolitik* deprived Nazi Germany of the immense talent of its Jewish population, including some of the nuclear physicists who later were essential to the U.S. atomic weapons program. The physical task of liquidating the Jewish population also consumed important manpower resources that were thus withheld from the collapsing Eastern front. The totalitarian despots saw enemies everywhere; but when push came to shove, they concluded that liquidating presumed enemies at home was more important than defending themselves against the tanks and airplanes of their foreign adversaries. Civil war took precedence over international conflict.

POLITICAL VIOLENCE AND THE PRECURSORS OF TOTALITARIANISM

It stands to reason that states so obsessed with conflict and so immersed in the psychology of war would trace their historical origins to violence and war. The watershed event in the rise of the total-

itarian states was the First World War, with its unprecedented carnage, but many historical tributaries of earlier origin flowed together
to form the flood tide of totalitarianism in our century: the Reign of
Terror in Revolutionary France; late-nineteenth-century Social Darwinism and the application of the concept of "survival of the fittest"
to human affairs; the rise in Central Europe after 1848 of extreme
forms of nationalism culminating in the pan-German and pan-Slav
movements; the experience of late nineteenth-century imperialism,
especially the scramble for Africa; and finally, the militarized character of the imperial Russian and Prussian autocracies. Obviously not
all of these historical lineages apply equally to both Nazism and Soviet Communism, for despite their common totalitarian nature, the
two movements were ideologically far apart. But it is noteworthy
that the antecedents of totalitarianism all shared a common thread: a
belief in the achievement of human progress through violence and
conflict. And even if in some cases this belief was largely theoretical,
or manifested itself more in the form of police terror and low-intensity civil strife than in actual warfare, an affinity with armed force
and with modern military organization and technology was never far
from the surface. The precursors of totalitarianism were all in some
degree either violent or conflict-oriented in their essence.

THE VIOLENT ROOTS OF TOTALITARIANISM

Revolutionary France

The Jacobinist period of the French Revolution and the rule of the
Committee of Public Safety (1793–94) foreshadowed certain features
of modern totalitarianism, including the use of bureaucratically organized terror for political purposes, the mobilization of the peasant
masses for war, and the exaltation of ideology over traditional conceptions of morality and pragmatism. An estimated 40,000 persons
perished in the Terror, while perhaps 200,000 or more died in the
bloody suppression of the revolts in the Vendée and other regions. In
the latter instances, even *after* the military rebellion had been
crushed, republican armies engaged in a brutal civil war of pacifica-
tion and terror against civilians and property that confirmed Saint-
Just's characterization of the revolution as consisting in the
extermination of everything that opposed it. Simon Schama and
other historians have seen in the republican schemes for exterminat-

ing civilians in the Vendée portents of the technological genocide of the twentieth century.[23]

The Jacobins left behind a romantic myth that influenced generations of European revolutionaries. This myth strongly influenced the army officers of the Decembrist movement in Russia, among them Colonel Paul Pestel, whose *Russian Justice* (1824) foretold the use of secret police, censorship, and bureaucracy in the model revolutionary state. "Russian Jacobinism" was also the self-professed philosophy of Peter Zaichnevsky, whose *Young Russia* (1862) proclaimed that the overthrow of Tsarism would require a small conspiratorial party to seize the dictatorial powers of the state, and of Peter Tkachev, publisher of the *The Tocsin*, whose revolutionary doctrine profoundly influenced Lenin. The Bolshevik leader himself was an admirer of the French Jacobins, commending their remorseless use of terror to his own party: "If the revolution gains a decisive victory, then we shall settle accounts with Tsarism in the Jacobin, or, if you like, in the plebeian way . . . ruthlessly destroying the enemies of liberty, crushing their resistance by force. . . ."[24]

In considering this lineage, we should recall that there was a direct link between the internal dictatorship of the Jacobins and the external wars that France was waging against the monarchical powers of Europe in 1792–94.* Whether or not the military threat faced by France actually *caused* the Terror—and Chapter 4 has already presented evidence that there was a close connection, at the least—the war provided the Jacobins with a much trumpeted moral justification for their actions and, by shifting power toward the center, facilitated their creation of a highly centralized bureaucratic state. It is not clear whether Lenin made the connection, but Leon Trotsky certainly did: his *Defense of Terrorism*, written in 1920 as the Russian Civil War was winding down, defended the Bolshevik use of terror in a polemical response to the German Social Democrat Karl Kautsky's condemnatory *Terrorism and Communism*. Trotsky argued that the invasion of revolutionary France by foreign troops had been a compelling justification for the Jacobin terror and that the Bolshevik use of terror was "conditioned by no less difficult circumstances," namely, the war against the White Guards and the Allied Expeditionary Force.[25] In fact, there is abundant evidence that the Civil War was not the only reason the Bolsheviks turned to terror—they had founded the Cheka and decided on a policy of terror even before that war began—but as in

*See Chapter 4, pp. 132–33.

revolutionary France, the new Soviet regime exploited military imperatives (both real and imagined) to justify boundless ruthlessness.[26] Later, Stalin would also justify his purges as a defense against the capitalist enemies of the Soviet state and their alleged bourgeois agents within the USSR.

Social Darwinism

Both Nazism and Marxism-Leninism concurred in one of the fundamental tenets of nineteenth-century Social Darwinism, namely, that struggle and conflict are driving forces of historical progress. The Communists saw the survival of the fittest as applying to classes, and the Nazis as applying to races, but both accepted the inevitability, and even the desirability, of violent conflict in politics. "National Socialism is not a doctrine of inertia but a doctrine of conflict . . . a doctrine of struggle," declared Hitler. Heinrich Himmler spoke of "the selection process of nature" in connection with German plans to conquer Slavic territories, while Reinhard Heydrich cast the extermination of the Jewish people in Darwinist terms. The Bolsheviks also extolled violence as a means of progress, with Lenin insisting that "not a single problem of the class struggle has been solved in history except by violence," and to achieve the final victory of socialism, a violent, cataclysmic revolution must smash and destroy the bourgeois state.[27]

The early Social Darwinists, among whom Herbert Spencer was preeminent, tended to be pacifist apologists for capitalism who defended its social inequalities as the natural evolutionary outcome of the struggle for survival. But Spencer also regarded past wars as having served a positive evolutionary end, and many advocates of Social Darwinism embraced this view uncritically. Nowhere was this more true than in Germany and Austria, where Darwinism profoundly influenced thinkers of every political persuasion from Karl Marx to Max Weber. Adolph Wagner wrote, "The nation must . . . prove its right to existence among other nations by a war of all against all in which only the stronger survive."[28] Friedrich Hellwald denounced peace conferences as contrary to nature. The historian Heinrich von Treitschke was the most influential proponent of war as the testing-ground of nations. Though Treitschke's glorification of war stemmed more from fervent German nationalism than from Social Darwinism, like many German militarists and nationalists he did not hesitate to invoke Darwin as lending scientific credence to his position. And while for our purposes the Social Darwinist sanctification of war was its most significant feature, it is worth noting that certain radical proponents of Social Darwinism in Germany after 1890—August Weismann, Alfred Ploetz, Otto Ammann, Alexander Tille—laid the theoretical foundations for the practice of eugenics and "racial hygiene" in the Third Reich.[29]

Darwinism also influenced the development of Marxist thought by providing a pseudoscientific basis for the dialectical view of history that Marx adapted from Hegel. Though Hegel died well before publication of *On the Origin of Species* and undoubtedly would have rejected the analogy, there were intriguing parallels between Social Darwinism and Hegel's view of the Idea in History manifesting itself through the struggle among states.[30] Marx's followers—Friedrich Engels in particular, and later Lenin—happily appropriated Darwinism as a less philosophical and (blessedly) less abstruse explanation than Hegelianism for the dialectic inherent in history. In effect, Engels plucked a Darwinist kernel from the mystical shell of Hegelianism.[31] If the history of all hitherto existing society had been the history of class struggle, this was only a human extension of the survival of the fittest among the species.

Lenin saw Marx and Darwin as parallel figures and claimed that Marx had achieved for political philosophy what Darwin had done for biology. Lenin and the early Bolsheviks were also influenced by the writings of the French socialist Georges Sorel, whose *Reflections on Violence* (1908) glorified violent struggle as a force for positive change and saw the establishment of socialism in purely apocalyptic terms. In *Imperialism, the Highest Stage of Capitalism*, Lenin propounded a Marxist version of the Social Darwinist view of war, transposing the concept of class struggle into the international arena. And after he attained power, Lenin consistently portrayed the world in dualistic, even Manichaean terms, arguing that "a state of awful war" would reign between capitalism and communism until finally one or the other triumphed—"a funeral dirge will be sung over the Soviet Republic or over world capitalism."[32]

Militant Nationalism

Hans Kohn, Fritz Stern, and other historians have shown how German thought in the nineteenth century diverged from the mainstream of Western thought and became increasingly nationalist, romantic, and reactionary in content. Beginning with and inspired by the great historian Leopold von Ranke, a long and distinguished line of German scholars—Johann Gustav Droysen, Erich Marcks, Rudolf Haym, Otto von Gierke, and Heinrich von Treitschke—substituted for the liberalism and universalism of the Enlightenment a fixation on raison d'état, military power, and the importance of the nation. A common theme of the German intellectuals was the necessity of war (again, the Social Darwinist strain) as the gauntlet of historical progress.[33]

The victory of Prussian forces over Austrian troops at Königgrätz in July 1866 electrified the German nationalists; Bismarck's triumph at Versailles in 1871 further infused German nationalism, now embodied in a unified state, with a thoroughgoing militarism previously characteristic mainly of Prussia. In the decades that followed, even relatively more liberal German thinkers such as Max Weber, Friedrich Naumann, and Theodor Mommsen were caught up in the nationalist euphoria, proclaiming support of Bismarckian *Machtpolitik* despite its avowedly antiliberal, antidemocratic, and anticonstitutional bent. "You must have the will to conquer something, anything in the world, to be something," declared Naumann. But at least Weber and his more liberal colleagues clung, however precariously, to their roots in the rationalism of the Enlightenment. Lesser lights sank deeper into a *völkisch* mysticism and virulently militant nationalism, inspired by the writings of Paul de Lagarde, Guido von List, Alfred Schuler, Julius Langbehn, and other romantic nationalists—the spiritual forebears of fascism in Germany. It is striking how much of the political agenda of the extreme nationalists was later incorporated by the National Socialists: the elimination of the Jews from Germany (almost all the extreme nationalists were anti-Semitic); the conquest of territories in the East for the expansion of the German people; the annexation of Austria and the Germanic lands that lay outside Germany proper.[34]

In the realm of practical politics, the new German nationalism gave rise to the pan-German movement, whose doctrines Hannah Arendt characterized as continental imperialism and which she saw as a forerunner to the Nazi vision of a greater Aryan nation dominating the world. The Pan-German League (*Alldeutscher Verband*) founded in 1894, together with half a dozen other patriotic societies, was the organizational nexus of pan-Germanism, attracting the most virulent nationalists to its ranks and propagating the view that there was a larger German nation, a chosen, inherently superior *Volk*. Its program, though never highly articulated, foresaw the eventual unification of this *Volk* into a single political entity. The psychology of the League's membership was combative in the extreme; as Roger Chickering observes, a cardinal tenet of pan-German ideology was the presence everywhere of enemies.[35] As 1914 approached, the League became increasingly annexationist, militaristic, and anti-Semitic in its views. Its strange mixture of racist, *völkisch*, and romantic philosophy, as well as its *Stufenplan* for a German-dominated Europe to be the center of a world empire, later found an almost exact reincarnation in National Socialism.

The influence of nationalism and the pan movements on the Bolshevik movement is problematic, in part because nationalism in nineteenth-century Russia was never as fully developed or as militant as in Germany. Marxist-Leninist ideology officially repudiated nationalism and professed a sweeping internationalism; the Bolshevik Party was, in fact, one of the few branches of the international socialist movement not swept up or destroyed by the nationalist fervor of 1914. Yet there is little doubt that the mysticism of the pan-Slavs, particularly their vision of Moscow as a Third Rome, in important ways prepared the political soil of Russia for the millennarian and expansionist features of Soviet communism. Adam Ulam argues that a fusion between Marxist internationalism and Russian nationalism occurred during the Russian Civil War, when the Bolsheviks were forced to defend the Russian state against hosts of foreign enemies. (During the war Lenin observed that if you scratched a Russian Bolshevik you would find a Russian nationalist.) The same fusion of nationalism and ideology occurred again in World War II, with even greater potency. Stalin's regime also incorporated many features reflecting pan-Slavist and nationalist influences: the shift to the building of "socialism in one country"; his evocation of Russian national symbols during the war against Hitler; the chronic anti-Semitism that skewed his choice of purge victims; and the determination with which he brought the Slavic nations of Eastern Europe under one political empire after World War II.[36] Though Bolshevism did not originate in nationalism, and though it was always more universalist in its ideological pretensions and aspirations than National Socialism, Russian nationalism reinforced its more militant tendencies.

High Imperialism

Social Darwinism and militant nationalism both contributed to the imperialist frenzy of the late nineteenth century, which was itself an important progenitor of totalitarianism. In distant Africa and Asia—far removed from the traditional moral and legal restraints of the nation-state—those imperial instruments of organized violence, the army and the police, became laws unto themselves and imperial administrators became a class devoted to wielding violence without restraint. Throughout the imperial possessions of the Europeans, but especially in Africa, the international legal restraints on war that had evolved during the eighteenth and nineteenth centuries eroded and then fell apart entirely. Via countless transmission channels—returning officers and soldiers, mercenary adventurers, news reports glorifying European victories, businessmen and investors seizing property and opportunity—Europe suffered a steady erosion of its liberal abhorrence of state-sanctioned violence. For Germany, one consequence was that its imperial experience in Africa planted seeds of racial hatred and love of violence among numerous future adherents of the Nazi movement.[37]

Colonial warfare also saw the introduction on the world stage of that pernicious device, the concentration camp, which would loom so large in the half-century after 1900. Spain first used them in its campaigns against the Cuban insurrection, and the United States against the Philippine insurrection of 1898. But Lord Kitchener in the Boer War perfected the technique and revealed its horrible possibilities. Though the British had no intention of committing genocide, some 20,000 Boer women and children perished in the camps in a little over a year; at least 14,000 Bantus and other blacks also died in segregated South African *laager* under even more miserable conditions.[38] Atrocities against civilians had occurred in previous wars, but the notion of systematically rounding up and incarcerating civilians as a military tactic had no ready historical precedent.

By comparison with some of the other European powers, however, British conduct in Africa was downright humane. Leopold II of Belgium condoned the most brutal measures of repression in the Congo—measures that by some estimates led to the loss of millions of lives. The Germans in South-West Africa and East Africa in 1904–1907 pursued policies of mass extermination that wiped out large portions—sometimes as much as 80 percent—of whole tribes.[39] The descent of the imperialist powers in Africa into an abyss of limitless violence was made easier by the incapacity of white Europeans to regard black Africans as equal human beings. The lamentable reality is that forty years prior to the Jewish holocaust of World War II, smaller and lesser-known African holocausts inured a generation of European soldiers and mercenaries to genocide, and shaped a European mindset that not only accepted but approved the extermination of *Untermenschen* (subhumans); the first to be so labeled were black Africans and white Boers.

Russia and Prussia as Military States

When all the above historical factors are set aside, when Germany's neurosis as a "late state" is ignored or Russia's own peculiar history of despotism is discounted, the military origins of totalitarianism are yet

reflected in the fact that the two totalitarian behemoths of the twentieth century had been for over two centuries prior to 1917 the most
highly militarized—and militaristic—of European states. In both
instances, seventeenth-century encounters with the modernized
Swedish army had galvanized their rulers (the Great Elector and Peter
the Great) into obsessive efforts at military modernization—efforts
that persisted throughout the eighteenth and nineteenth centuries.
Totalitarian rule gave fresh impetus to this obsession. Before coming
to power, Lenin and Hitler both realized that their success would
depend on capturing the pre-existing military-bureaucratic machines
of Russia and Germany. For these, even in 1917 and 1933, and despite
the ravages of World War I, remained (at least in their industrial and
social bases, if not their actual military power) the most solid foundation on which to build a new edifice of state power. Thus, though
totalitarianism was decidedly nontraditional in its nature, it built on
traditional military foundations laid down by the old Russian and
Prussian autocracies.[40]

THE MILITARY ORIGINS OF
TOTALITARIANISM: (I) THE GREAT WAR

The precursors of totalitarianism outlined above show how a diverse
combination of philosophies, movements, and political actors—all of
which either condoned or actually employed large-scale violence—
contributed to the overall ethos in which the totalitarian states arose.
Yet none of the above influences alone, nor even all of them collective-
ly, could possibly have *caused* the sharp break with the traditional
nation-state that Nazi Germany and Soviet Russia represented. Despite
the fatalism of some historians, there was no historically inevitable
path from Luther to Hitler, no predetermined revolutionary course
from the Bastille to the Communist Manifesto to the Winter Palace.
Only an immense historical cataclysm could have forged political
monsters so radically different from any states previously known in
history. Unfortunately for millions of Europeans of every nation,
World War I proved to be just such a cataclysm. Without the extraordinary violence of the Great War, no conceivable historical trends, tendencies, or forces present in 1914 could possibly have given rise to the
totalitarian states only a few years later.

In modern political systems, the main counterweight to centralized power accumulating indefinitely is *civil society*: the vast complex of traditional and private institutions such as universities, churches, professional associations, cultural organizations, trade unions, private clubs, and business firms, all of which wield sufficient social influence to resist encroaching state power. If World War I had merely destroyed the existing autocracies of Russia and Germany, while leaving their civil societies intact and healthy, the result might have been the assumption of state power by the latter—primarily by the bourgeoisie—but also—especially in Germany—by representatives of organized labor. This would have meant the establishment of new political systems based on broader foundations of political consent and popular legitimacy. This was in fact the initial outcome—briefly in Russia with the accession of Kerensky's provisional government; for a longer period in Germany with the establishment of the Weimar Republic. But because World War I also gravely damaged civil society in both countries, the way was left open for the state—its bureaucratic core larger than ever because of the centralizing effect of World War I—to be captured by highly organized, disciplined mass movements able to act decisively and ruthlessly when society was least able to defend itself.

THE TOTALITARIAN PATH OF STATE FORMATION

Totalitarianism resulted when the degenerative effects of war undermined civil society, while war's formative and centralizing effects strengthened the state (not monarchical rule per se, which collapsed, but the central bureaucracies—the permanent state that endured through war and regime change). The process leading to totalitarianism can be divided into five stages, which we will term *the totalitarian path of state formation*:

1. An *all-out industrial war generates powerful centralizing pressures* that enlarge the size and authority of the administrative apparatus of the state;
2. Military defeat causes *the collapse of the traditional regime* (i.e., the entrenched, elite strata that controlled the state and actually led the war effort);
3. *The disintegrative effects of war destroy or substantially weaken civil society*;
4. In the resulting power vacuum, *mass movements capture the*

enlarged bureaucratic center and form a new regime, using an organizational structure and approach to politics modeled on an army at war;

5. After capturing the state, *the new regime centralizes power and atomizes all opposition by mobilizing society for war*—through actual military aggression, or forced-pace economic mobilization and rearmament, or the artificial creation of civil war conditions at home.

The crucial moment in the above path is the fourth stage, the point of totalitarian takeover, which in the case of the Soviet Union took place in 1917, while World War I was still raging; in the case of Nazi Germany, it occurred only after a fifteen-year hiatus—the extended "power vacuum" of the Weimar Republic. In both countries, a fully developed totalitarian state emerged only after all five stages transpired. In the case of Nazi Germany, the final stage took place during World War II; in the case of Soviet Russia, the system became fully totalitarian during the artificial civil war engineered by Stalin during his "Great Leap Forward" campaign of 1929–34.

WORLD WAR I AND THE FAILURE OF CIVIL SOCIETY IN WEIMAR GERMANY

As we have already seen in Chapter 5, the military dictatorship of Ludendorff and Hindenburg during World War I forged a radically centralized state structure that achieved a degree of penetration of society as great as previously achieved by any state in European history. Nevertheless, Germany in World War I was not a totalitarian state, for the underlying structure and legitimizing rationale of the system remained traditional. What is more, the immediate and predictable impact of the war was to *strengthen* democratic sentiment in Germany. This was not dissimilar to what happened in France and the United Kingdom, where the collectivist endeavor of the war unleashed potent democratic and egalitarian sentiments. The first postwar German election of January 1919 resulted in a resounding victory for the democratically-inclined parties: the Social Democrats, the Center, and the Democratic Party together posted over 75 percent of the vote. But only 18 months later, when the next elections were held (June 1920), a sharp reversal had taken place. The democratic parties posted only 47 percent of the vote, considerably lower even than they had managed in the last prewar elections of 1907 and 1912. And they never really regained the lost ground, as shown in Table 6–1.

Table 6–1.   National elections in Germany, 1907–33; democratic
versus authoritarian orientation of the vote

PARTY TENDENCY	PERCENTAGE OF VOTES IN NATIONAL ELECTIONS										
	1907	1912	1919	1920	1924	1924	1928	1930	1932	1932	1933
Democratic	59	63	76	47	46	50	49	43	38	36	33
Authoritarian	33	27	22	50	49	44	37	43	59	59	67

Source: Juan J. Linz and Alfred Stephan, ed., *The Breakdown of Democratic Regimes*, p. 37.

Why did the democratizing impetus of the war prove so short-lived? Because democracy can only take root and flourish where strong private institutions act as countervailing balances against state power. But in postwar Germany all the traditional pillars of social and political stability, the institutions whose influence had set limitations on centralized power in the imperial period—the army, the family, the churches, the main-line political parties, the local and state governments—had all been gravely weakened by the War. Only the trade unions had grown stronger since 1914, but since the era of Bismarck—and especially during the War—these had become closely tied to the state and thus were ill equipped to resist any aggrandizement of central power. Germany emerged from the war badly fragmented, a condition reflected throughout the Weimar era in a plethora of political parties with highly unstable memberships. On top of all this, German society had been badly brutalized by the war and was hence susceptible to the influence of mob violence in its politics; it proved incapable of resisting the rise of National Socialism and the ruthless *Gleichschaltung* (see page 229) that the Nazis imposed on all German institutions after 1933.[41]

The weakness of German civil society after World War I debilitated the Weimar Republic and probably made some form of authoritarian rule close to inevitable. But the humiliation of the Versailles settlement and its adverse economic consequences further reduced whatever chances existed for German democracy. By 1920, Germany's manufacturing output was only 59 percent of its 1913 level—the lowest level of any of the major combatant states except for Soviet Russia. The aftershock of wartime debt and the draconian reparations settlement contributed also to the hyperinflation of 1923, which wiped out the saving of Germany's middle classes and forced manufacturing production back down to 55.4 percent of the 1913 level—at a time when France had nearly recovered its prewar output. Such economic effects of the war and its settlement further stratified German society and fed resentment of the Allied demands, the more so since the inflation coincided with the French army's punitive occupation of the Ruhr.

The war had other, more direct effects on German society that greatly weakened any societal counterweights to violence and centralized power. It inured a generation of soldiers to the violence, brutality, and mass death that would be the trademarks of totalitarianism. Many soldiers had experienced at the front a camaraderie and solidarity, and a sense of purpose, that eluded them when they returned home to devastated economies and war-weary societies. Whereas the epiphany of the trenches gave impetus to the welfare state in Great Britain and France, it magnified the appeal of fascism in Germany and in Italy, where Mussolini and Hitler invoked its memory in rhetoric and ritual. Bernd Hüppauf argues that "Fascist man" was born out of the mythology of the front as it evolved from Langemarck to Verdun—the extreme conditions of the front became a paradigm for life, and the human qualities molded on the front became the model for the new man of the future.[42] Interestingly enough, Robert Ley, leader of the Nazi Labor Front, in 1934 defined the socialism of the Nazi movement as "the relationship of men in the trenches."[43]

The experience of the "front generation" assumed political significance after the war in the formation of a variety of paramilitary organizations, dominated by veterans, that played a crucial role in the rise to power of the Nazi movement. Among the earliest was the *Freikorps*, which attracted veterans of all ranks eager to recapture the spirit of the front and which later became a favorite recruiting pool of Ernst Roehm and the Nazi storm troopers. Eventually four large private armies of divergent political persuasion emerged in the Weimar years: the *Reichsbanner* of the Social Democrats, the Communist Red Front, the nationalist veterans' *Stahlhelm*, and the Nazi *Sturmabteilung* (SA). By permitting such armies to exist (even in part as a way of circumventing the military restrictions imposed at Versailles), the Weimar authorities effectively forfeited the central state's monopoly on armed power. The disastrous consequences of this became apparent after 1930 with the rapid growth of the SA and its use of murder, intimidation, and terror against political opponents. An analogous development occurred in Italy, where the spirit of the trenches (*trincerismo*) forged a new political constituency of veterans imbued with *combattentismo*, who played a key role in supporting Mussolini's bid for power.[44] The Nazi and Fascist takeovers began, in other words, not with a concentration of military power, but with its diffusion to organizations outside the state hierarchy.

The military defeat and humiliation of 1918 greatly magnified the

emotional and psychological impact of the trenches on German politics. The effect on Hitler of his own *Fronterlebnis* was not untypical of
the German veterans who returned home from the war: the enthusiasm with which he greeted the outbreak of war; the solidarity he experienced with his fellow soldiers; his anger with the ineptitude and
passivity of the "authorities" in the rear; and above all his rage on
learning of the German capitulation, as described in the famous passage from *Mein Kampf*:

> And so it had all been in vain. In vain all the sacrifices and privations
> . . . in vain the death of two millions who died. . . . Did all this happen
> only so that a gang of wretched criminals could lay hands on the
> fatherland?
>   Miserable and degenerate criminals!
>   The more I tried to achieve clarity on the monstrous event in this
> hour, the more the shame of indignation and disgrace burned my
> brow. . . .
>   . . . In these nights hatred grew in me, hatred for those responsible
> for this deed.[45]

Hitler's reaction personified the bitterness of the German people over
the signing of the Armistice—a bitterness made worse by the fact that
the Germans had been led until the very end of the war to believe that
victory was imminent. Deep-rooted popular resentment over the outcome of the war was a *leitmotiv* of German politics throughout the
Weimar era—and the foremost lever of Nazi propaganda prior to 1933.

One theory of fascism portrays it as a kind of political palingenesis
(rebirth experience), an ultranationalism whose "mobilizing vision is
that of the national community rising phoenix-like after a period of
encroaching decadence which all but destroyed it."[46] National Socialism sought to summon German glory from the ashes by infusing the
experience of the war with transcendent meaning—by making it, in
Hitler's words, "the highest school of the German nation."[47] General
Horst von Metzsch, a prominent Nazi apologist, made the linkage
between the Great War and the Nazi movement even more explicit:

> The National-Socialist ethos grew entirely logically from the soldier
> ethics of the World War . . . The purification through the National-
> Socialist movement had to come in order to connect us again with the
> rise of 1914 and the powerful achievement of the war . . . Whoever dis-
> regards war (as the inexhaustible source of German resurrection)

abuses blood and soil, folk and space . . . The National-Socialist movement is unthinkable without the war.[48]

Moeller van den Brück, the conservative nationalist whose book, *Das
dritte Reich*, provided the banner for the Nazi movement, likewise
described the war as an educator of the nation and a "necessary
detour" in German history. Nothing in the German past loomed larger. "We, after all, had been, and would remain before history, *the* folk
of the World War."[49]

Had the war ended in an unqualified defeat, perhaps the German
people would have accepted the verdict of history and embarked on a
more permanent reform course, in the usual historical pattern. But the
stillborn nature of the Allied victory, which left Germany's territory
unoccupied and its military machine still intact (if exhausted), led postwar Germany to search for internal scapegoats and to make the war a
springboard not for reform but for the resurrection of the worst ultra-
nationalist and militaristic tendencies of the preceding century. Those
tendencies would eventually be embodied in a state that employed mass
organization to infuse German society with a reinvigorated military
dynamism. And those institutions and strata of civil society that might
have had the power to resist the Nazi takeover in 1933—as well as the
one institution, the Army, that might have overthrown it as late as
Hitler's purge of his general officers in February 1938—instead acquiesced to the Nazi tide, at least partly in the hope that this ultranationalism held the key to erasing the nightmare of 1918.

The economic Depression of 1929–33 was, of course, the immediate catalyst of the Nazis' rise to power, and the NSDAP vote in national
elections correlated closely with rising unemployment in Germany.
But historical interpretations of the Depression as a causal factor in
Hitler's triumph tend to obscure the preeminent role of World War I.
For in fact the NSDAP was growing rapidly in membership *prior* to the
economic downturn, and those who suffered most from the Depression were the working classes; they flocked in greatest numbers to
either the Communist Party or the Social Democrats, not to the
NSDAP. The middle classes, the most important constituency of the
Nazi movement during its climb to power, were much less directly
affected by the Depression. William S. Allen's classic study of
Northeim, an early Nazi stronghold, concludes that the middle classes
were hardly threatened at all by the Depression economically, only
psychologically. Theodor Abel's study of 600 members of the NSDAP
found that 87 percent of them had never changed occupation, 79 percent had never changed residence, 80 percent were never unemployed,

and 80 percent were financially secure when they joined the Party. Party recruits, it seems, were no more or less deprived economically than German society as a whole. The economic factor pales by comparison with the fact that 50 percent of all Nazi recruits were veterans of World War I, a figure far higher than the population as a whole.[50]

Other war-related factors also abetted the rise of the Nazi dictatorship: the precedents set by the Hindenburg-Ludendorff dictatorship, such as the use of deported slave labor from occupied territories; the "psycho-social consequences of generational and sex [i.e., gender] imbalances caused by massive losses of men in their prime of life"; and the economic consequences of the war (or more precisely, per John Maynard Keynes, of the peace).[51] (On the latter point, regardless of the actual degree to which Allied reparations were a cause of the Depression, Nazi propaganda constantly portrayed them as such, seeking to fuse economic grievances and apprehensions with the popular sense of resentment over Versailles.) In the final analysis, it is difficult to imagine that the Depression, either alone or with the other factors often cited in the rise of Nazism—the hypernationalism of the Right, traditional German militarism, or the shock of rapid industrialization—could possibly have created a totalitarian state in Germany absent the overwhelmingly vaster impact of the First World War.

The Degenerative Impact of War on Russian Civil Society, 1914–21

Alain Besançon observes that during World War I the weight of modern warfare effectively destroyed civil society in Russia—the fledgling civil society that had been gaining political ground since the reign of Alexander II—every bit as thoroughly as it destroyed the Romanov dynasty:

> . . . civil society finally disappeared completely. The peasants returned to a natural economy. Inflation destroyed money and the exchanges. Industrial production came to a halt and the workers, abandoning the starving cities, went back to the villages. The deserting soldiers also returned to the villages. This completed the breaking up of the noble estates, and the destruction of the remnants of the nobility. The industrial bourgeoisie and the technical bourgeoisie were ruined and unemployed.[52]

The Orthodox Church, the universities, and the Army were all gravely weakened by the extremities of the war. Only in such circumstances could a fanatical, tightly organized revolutionary party capture the center of government and impose a new dictatorship on a demoralized society. Lenin, even before his arrival at the Finland Station, recognized the opportunity presented by the war; and once in Petrograd he took every advantage of the disillusionment and social disorder that it had generated. In a moment of candor, in one of his last writings, he even referred to the Revolution not in Marxian terms as a workers' uprising, but as "the revolution that broke out in connection with the first imperialist World War."[53]

Little research has been done on the psychological and social impact of trench warfare on Russian soldiers in World War I,[54] but while the Eastern front was less static than the Western, the trauma to soldiers was similar: at Tannenberg, at least 100,000 troops perished in a single battle; in the first six months of the war, close to half a million; in the 1915 "Great Retreat" from Poland, hundreds of thousands more. Logistical and industrial shortcomings exacerbated the military disaster; already by the end of 1914, half of the new troops arriving at the front were issued no rifles and had to rely on those salvaged from their dead compatriots. By the fall of 1915 desertions from the Russian Army had reached massive proportions, and a paralyzing crisis in morale settled over the conscript peasant army for the duration of the war. By 1917, large segments of the Army were in disarray, desertions were endemic, and the mutinies had begun that would culminate first in the February, then the October, Revolution.[55]

By the time World War I ended, Russia had suffered the highest absolute losses of any European state—over 2.7 million fatalities and perhaps 5 million casualties. It also had the highest number of prisoners taken captive—3.9 million or three times those of Britain, France, and Germany combined. Though certain belligerent powers, such as France, would suffer higher relative losses, the social impact of the Russian casualties was immense. In part this was because the peasant masses, the *muzhiki* from which the bulk of the Army were drawn, had little sense of nationalism or patriotic commitment to the war effort and resented deeply the loss of life that it entailed. This, coupled with the refusal of the peasantry at home to sell their crops to the cities despite bumper harvests, caused enormous tensions between town and country. The military disasters on the plains of Poland and the obvious rank incompetence of the government precipitated other tensions between the monarchy and the Duma, the latter representing the politically frustrated civil society of Russia. Military defeat thus dissipated the initial unifying effect of the war, and the Russian polity divided along myriad fault lines.

The war's shattering of the Russian economy further aggravated social tensions. Peasant hoarding of food caused acute shortages in the cities, with Moscow and Petrograd getting only one third of their required supplies by late 1916. A deteriorating transport system and the choking off of Russia's few sea lanes caused acute fuel shortages. Prices reached 400 percent of prewar levels by early 1917. Plummeting economic conditions badly demoralized the urban population, already disillusioned with the government.

Politically, however, the most volatile element in the equation was not the civilian population, but the 2 to 3 million reservists and recruits stationed in or near the major cities, in close proximity with the embittered population; 332,000 of them were in Petrograd and the surrounding environs alone. Their disillusionment and radicalization were the real catalyst of the two revolutions of 1917. The labor disorders of February 1917, for example, only turned into a genuinely revolutionary situation after they had triggered a massive uprising of over 160,000 troops from the Petrograd garrison and the Volynskii Guard Regiment. As Richard Pipes notes, the February Revolution is often depicted as a workers' revolt, but it was first and foremost a mutiny of peasant soldiers.[56]

The politicization of the peasant conscripts that dominated the Army was the downfall not only of the monarchy but of the Provisional Government as well. Mutinous soldiers and officers played leading roles in every important stage of the events leading up to the Bolshevik takeover: the rising wave of "trench Bolshevism" that Kerensky tried so hard to contain in July and August of 1917; the debilitating impact of General Kornilov's revolt on the Provisional government; the critical October defection of the Petrograd garrison to the Military Revolutionary Committee under Trotsky. As is clear from Order No. 1 of the Executive Committee of the Soviets, subordinating the armed forces to the Petrograd Soviet and calling for the formation of soldiers' councils in every military unit, all the revolutionary parties of 1917 saw the Russian Army as the key to destroying the Provisional Government— not only because it possessed armed power, but because the Army contained large masses of disgruntled conscripts radicalized by the war and ripe for political mobilization. By July 1917, the Bolshevik Party was printing 320,000 copies of its newspapers daily; the vast majority of these, special newspapers such as *Soldatskaia Pravda* (Soldier's Truth) and *Okopnaia Pravda* (Trench Truth) were aimed at the soldiers. It is also worth noting that, as in Weimar Germany, the diffusion of armed power to such paramilitary organizations as the Red Guard and the workers' militias set up in Petrograd and other cities contributed to the erosion of the Provisional Government's capacity to defend itself.[57]

When it finally came, the storming of the Winter Palace resembled a military *coup d'état* in almost every aspect except that its ultimate leaders were not military officers. The great tragedy of twentieth-century Russia lies in the failure of the coalition of parties that assumed power after the February Revolution; they represented the best and the brightest that Russian society could then offer, and their control of the state apparatus would have marked a pivotal turning point toward consensual government had it endured. But it was their misfortune to inherit the War and the economic and social catastrophe that it had produced. Divided among themselves, they were unable to maintain the cohesion or demonstrate the leadership necessary to win over the radicalized peasant soldiers who had already overthrown one government. The Bolsheviks, organized along military lines and openly dedicated to waging war against a world of enemies, aimed their appeal specifically at those same peasant soldiers, and with their help succeeded in capturing the state from a war-ravaged civil society.

THE MILITARY ORIGINS OF TOTALITARIANISM: (II) CIVIL WAR

War made the totalitarian states, and the totalitarian states made war. Once the Soviet and Nazi regimes had come to power, they continued to manifest an infatuation with war and "struggle" both at home and abroad. In the Nazi case, the main thrust of its militancy was outward, propelling it rapidly toward external aggression and conquest. This did not prevent it, of course, from waging continuous political warfare at home, with the *Schutzstaffel* (SS) its main agent of repression (and later a military-police force wielding immense power over the occupied territories of Europe). Heinrich Himmler, the head of the SS, called his forces a "modern knighthood"; it was in fact an army outside the regular Army, or (as Himmler termed the SS Death's Head units), "Soldiers; not military, but soldiers." The SS in fact developed its own multinational army independent of the *Reichswehr*, the *Waffen-SS*, which swelled from 23,000 men in 1939 to 39 divisions and over 1 million men by 1944. Bernd Wegner observes that the SS was the catalytic element behind the radicalization of Hitler's regime during the war and that its wartime augmentation of power threatened at times to engulf the whole of German society. It was also Hitler's tool in undertaking the most awful aspect of Nazism's totalitarian war against its presumed enemies, the extermination of the Jews of Europe.[58]

Though Soviet Communism had an expansionist character from the beginning, this manifested itself primarily in support for foreign Communist parties, in Comintern-coordinated acts of subversion, and in clandestine support of revolutions abroad. By contrast, the overtly military thrust of Soviet expansionism was largely muted by caution and expediency, especially after the Russo-Polish War of 1919–20, which Lenin declared to have been a serious policy error.[59] It was a mistake, he said, to use Soviet combat troops in support of revolution abroad. From then until the invasion of Afghanistan in 1979, the USSR largely followed Lenin's advice, supplying arms and assistance to foreign Communist movements, but rarely combat troops, and then only in small numbers. The only full-scale war fought by Soviet Russia was the Second World War—a conflict largely thrust on it by external events, and one that Stalin strove mightily to avoid. But none of this should imply that the Soviet Union was innocent or pacific: the Molotov–Ribbentrop nonaggression pact was a cynical attempt to divide the spoils of battle with Hitler; the Soviet invasion of eastern Poland (1939) and the subsequent Winter War with Finland (1939–40) were brazen acts of aggression. Nor did Stalin hesitate to take advantage of the war with Nazi Germany to occupy Eastern Europe and impose Communist regimes by force; as the later invasions of Hungary (1956) and Czechoslovakia (1968) demonstrated, Communist rule in the Warsaw Pact rested only on the foundation of Soviet military power.

Its various acts of aggression notwithstanding, the fact remains that the Soviet Union was never as boldly expansionist as Nazi Germany, that its leaders were never so imprudent as to set out to conquer the world by direct military force. However when it came to waging civil war against its own population—whether forced on it by armed opposition as in the 1918–21 period, or deliberately incited as a political tactic—the Soviet Union had no peer in the modern world. It offers an excellent example of how unremitting internal conflict can foster extreme centralization.

THE RUSSIAN CIVIL WAR AND THE "CIVIL WAR WITHIN THE CIVIL WAR"

While Germany and the Allied powers received a respite from the carnage after the Armistice of 1918, in Russia's case all the destructive and degenerative effects of World War I were magnified by the onset of the

Civil War (1918–20) and several related conflicts in 1920–21: the
Russo-Polish war, the insurrection of the Green Movement in the
Tambov region, Soviet conquests of the Caucasus and Far Eastern territories, and the suppression of the Kronstadt Revolt.[60] On top of the
losses Russia had suffered in World War I, some 6 to 8 million souls
perished in the combat, famine, and epidemics associated with these
later conflicts. This huge toll—coupled with massive economic damage and the exodus from the country of large segments of the aristocratic and bourgeois elite, including much technical and managerial
talent—ravaged the already decimated remnants of Russia's civil society; the country stood powerless before the combined and organized
juggernaut of the Communist Party, the Red Army, and the Cheka. By
its very nature, Bolshevism was destined to be highly authoritarian—
at least as much so as, say, Revolutionary France under the Committee
of Public Safety. But the Civil War militarized Bolshevism, transforming democratic centralism into rigid conformity, and forging the
"commissarocracy" against which the sailors at Kronstadt would
futilely rebel. In this sense, the Civil War was the true progenitor of
Stalinism.[61]

Some sense of the impact of the Civil War on Russian economy and
society can be gleaned from Table 6–2, which shows selected production indices for the years ending December 1913; December 1916
(shortly before the February Revolution); and December 1921, after
the Civil War had ended. It is apparent that Russian industry survived
fairly well for the first two and a half years of World War I, and even
grew in some sectors as a consequence of economic mobilization. But
a sharp downturn began in 1917 and continued throughout the Civil
War, resulting in the catastrophic disintegration of Russian industry.
By 1921, large-scale industry was producing one fifth of its prewar
output, agricultural production was at less than a third, total exports
had plunged to barely over 1 percent of the 1913 figure. The Civil War
also resulted in the massive deurbanization of Russia's cities; the worst
cases were Moscow, which declined by almost 1 million inhabitants
(50 percent) and Petrograd, which lost 1 million (70 percent). Given
that urban areas tend to be the heart of civil society and hubs of opposition to central authority, the demographics of the war itself became
Russia's destiny.[62]

To raise and supply an army that eventually numbered 5 million,
the Bolsheviks relied on the existing Russian bureaucracy, already
enhanced by the mobilization effort of World War I, as well as on the
services of 48,409 officers and 214,717 NCOs from the defunct Tsarist
army. But they went much further than the wartime monarchy in cen-

Table 6–2.   Russian industrial output, 1913, 1916, and 1921

	1913	1916	1921
Pig iron	4216	3804	117
Steel	4231	4276	220
Oil	9234	9970	3781
Coal	29,117	34,482	9531
Cement	1520	N/A	64
Granulated sugar	1347	1186	51
Railway tonnage	132,400	N/A	39,400
Electrical power	1945	2575	520

Note: All figures are in thousands of tons, except electrical power, which is in millions of kilowatt hours.

tralizing power, imposing a hierarchical system of Party controls on the Army and state bureaucracy and introducing draconian controls throughout the national economy. Under War Communism, the state sought to monopolize all significant production sources and distribution channels, placed labor under a compulsory system of regimentation, introduced strict consumer rationing, and nationalized the banks and all industries considered vital to the war effort. Though at least some of these steps eventually would have been taken by the Bolsheviks for purely ideological reasons, the war accelerated putting in place the structures of totalitarian rule.

The Civil War entailed not only the struggle with the White armies, but also a "war within the civil war" which the Bolsheviks waged against the Russian peasantry and the remnants of bourgeois society that had not fled the country. The Red Guards sent out from the cities to the countryside to requisition grain from the peasantry were the equivalent of the *Armées révolutionnaires* of the French Revolution, whose mission had been similar. But the degree of brutality and coercion the Bolsheviks employed against the rural population far exceeded anything needed to requisition grain. The real objective was to crush all conceivable sources of potential or future resistance, achieve class stratification, and create social schisms that would facilitate the exercise of central power. Among the political tactics employed in this civil war within the Civil War was the deliberate inciting of conflict among different strata of the peasantry. Iakov Sverdlov, a high Bolshevik official, laid out this approach in an announcement of May 1918:

If we say that revolutionary Soviet authority is sufficiently strong in the cities . . . then the same cannot be said in regard to the village. . . .

> *Only if we succeed in splitting the village into two irreconcilably hostile camps, if we are able to inflame there the same civil war that had occurred not so long ago in the cities . . .* only then will be in a position to say that we will do that in relation to the village that we were able to do for the city.[63] (Italics added.)

By artificially inciting civil war, exploiting the resulting social schisms, and unleashing terror in the countryside and cities, the Bolsheviks successfully imposed the most enduring totalitarian regime the world has yet seen.

Until World War II, the Civil War was the heroic era of the Russian Revolution, glorified endlessly in the schools, in the martial rituals of the party, and in every possible propaganda forum. This exaltation reflected not only self-legitimizing efforts by the Communist regime but also the very real social and political impact of a war that loomed nearly as large for Russia as the First World War. The unrestrained violence of the war forged what one prominent Bolshevik called a "military soviet culture," while the intervention of the Western allies in the war infused in the Communist elite their identity as a besieged vanguard in an isolated bastion.[64] The first use of mass terror by the new regime took place during the period of War Communism, and the first forced labor camps were conceived by Trotsky as rear-service battalions in support of the Red Army.[65] The war thus propelled Soviet Russia on the course it would follow for seventy years, and with particular intensity during the Stalinist era, the course proclaimed by the newspaper *Krasnyi Kronstadt* after Tukachevskii's troops had restored orthodoxy on the recalcitrant naval base: "Restrictions on political liberty, terror, military centralism and discipline, and the direction of all means and resources toward the creation of an offensive and defensive state apparatus."[66]

THE GREAT LEAP FORWARD AS A SECOND RUSSIAN CIVIL WAR

Stalin's massive industrialization and collectivization campaign of 1929–34 illustrates how external rivalry and the imperatives of national security can drive internal conflict, with both in turn enhancing state power. The collectivization of Russian agriculture and the force-paced industrialization of the Soviet economy required an expansion of state power unprecedented in modern politics. Not even in World War I had any state attempted to nationalize agriculture, and while

Lenin confiscated food from the peasantry during the Russian Civil War, he had stopped well short of full-scale collectivization. Stalin's struggle with the Right and Left opposition and the revolutionary measures of the First Five-Year Plan are often portrayed as a mere Thermidorean reaction, a return to traditional Russian nationalism and statism. Yet in Stalin's mind, at least, there was a solid military and strategic rationale for the campaign; it derived from the troubled Soviet relationship with the West in the late 1920s and from his conviction that a future military confrontation was inevitable. Hence, the slogan of the campaign—"*dognat i peregnat*"—"overtake and surpass" the Western industrial powers, to which Stalin added, "in the shortest time possible."

Stalin's most famous exposition of this rationale took place in a February 1931 speech. He observed that throughout its history Russia had been beaten by foreign armies—the Tatar Khans, the Turks, the Swedes, the Poles, the Japanese, the Anglo-French capitalists. (He did not, interestingly enough, mention the Germans.) Why was Russia defeated so often?

> She was beaten because of her backwardness, because of her military, cultural, political, industrial, and agricultural backwardness. . . .
>
> . . . Do you want our socialist fatherland to be beaten and to lose its independence? If you do not want that, then you must in the shortest possible time abolish its backwardness and develop a really Bolshevik pace in the establishment of its socialist economy. There is no other way. That is why Lenin said on the eve of October, "Either die or overtake and surpass the advanced capitalist countries." We are fifty or one hundred years behind the advanced countries. We must make good this lag in ten years. Either we do this or we will be crushed.[67]

The dictator's instincts were sound, for only ten years and a few months later Operation Barbarossa began. The military rationale behind the industrialization drive was even starker in the Second Five-Year Plan, in which military spending soared (by official reckoning) from 9.2 percent of state expenditure in 1934 to 32.6 percent in 1940.[68]

But if perceptions of external military threat drove the industrialization program, that program was actually accomplished by the waging of a second merciless civil war against the Russian peasantry, a war in which 25 million peasant households were forcibly conscripted into 200,000 state-managed *kolkhozy* (collective farms). Stalin wanted to capture the agricultural output of the countryside to earn hard currency in the export market, in order to fund the industrialization and rearmament of the USSR. In his own words, this was a "tribute or supertax" imposed on the peasantry for the sake of industry; in fact it amounted to the re-enserfment of the Russian peasantry. In terms of its actual economic results, collectivization was disastrous, with any short-term gains in capital formation more than negated by massive losses in agricultural productivity and output. But economic gains were not the only or even the main reasons for collectivization. Stalin deliberately intensified the campaign in order to ensure the permanent and total triumph of the central state over all facets of Soviet life.

The much maligned *kulaks*, Stalin's designated enemies in this artificially created civil war, were merely scapegoats who were needed to justify the crushing of all vestiges of independence in rural Russia. The historian Moshe Lewin argues that the subordination of the peasantry required that Stalin exaggerate the *kulak* menace and foment the class struggle to a degree of intensity that it would never have reached without official encouragement. By branding all opponents of collectivization as *kulaks* or *podkulachniki* (under-kulaks), regardless of their economic status, the authorities sought to terrify the peasantry into submission.[69] A *kulak* turned out to be little more than a peasant with good weather—no ethnic, nationalist, or even class definition emerged. The Soviet regime literally waged war against its own population, in a manner that had no historical parallel until the Chinese Cultural Revolution. The shock troops of this campaign were some 25,000 industrial laborers, organized in cadres, backed by armed force, and captained in the majority of cases by veterans of the Civil War. Stalin's victory in this Second Russian Civil War, however pyrrhic it may have been in actual economic results, was the key to his unparalleled political power after 1932.

TOTALITARIANISM AS A MALADAPTATION TO MODERN WARFARE

The totalitarian movements despised the institutions of modern life—industry, capital, bureaucracy, science, and even modern art. Nazi anti-modernism reacted with particular venom against the remarkable creative blossoming of arts and science that took place under the despised Weimar Republic. This aversion to modernity revealed itself in the tribal, quasi-mystical rituals of the Nazi Party at Nuremberg, as well as in the anticapitalist bloodletting of the Bolshevik regime, leading some scholars to see totalitarianism as a throwback to premodern forms of politics.[70] But even as Richard Wagner in the *Nibelungen* operas clothed the elemental passions of the *Götterdämmerung* in modern musical forms, totalitarianism clothed its primitive, tribal soul in the most modern of political structures. In its organization and methods, at least, it was a wholly modern phenomenon, deriving its power (as we have seen) from the technological warfare of the modern era.[71]

In revolting against the modern, the totalitarian movements were far from embracing traditional society, which they regarded only as an anachronism, a barrier between the individual and the raw, transforming power of the state. The Nazi term *Gleichschaltung*—coordination, leveling, bringing into line—is an apt description of both Nazi and Soviet efforts to destroy that barrier or at least to capture those traditional institutions that hampered the undiluted exercise of state power. This antitraditional nihilism at the heart of the Nazi movement found grotesque expression in Joseph Goebbels' testament of 1945:

> Under the debris of our shattered cities the last so-called achievements of the middle-class nineteenth century have been finally buried. . . . Now that everything is in ruins, we are forced to rebuild Europe. In the past, private possessions tied us to bourgeois restraints. Now the bombs, instead of killing all Europeans, have only smashed the prison walls which held them captive. . . . In trying to destroy Europe's future, the enemy has only succeeded in smashing its past; and with that, everything old and outworn has gone.[72]

Goebbels may have been veering on mental instability when he wrote this, but his scribblings reveal the essence of the totalitarian mind-set. Traditional society—civil society—must be destroyed to pave the way for a New Modernity, a utopian vision whose realization requires an immense concentration of sheer power. Destruction is the key to creation.

The modern nature of totalitarianism can also be seen in the political transmutations that took place in Germany and Russia between 1917 and 1939, which appear as warped variants of the changes that took place elsewhere in industrialized Europe as a result of World War I. Like the democracies of Western Europe, Germany and the Soviet Union also became collectivist states, but in a perverted form: they were regulatory states, but they carried economic regulation and control to extremes unparalleled elsewhere; they were mass states, but they mobilized mass support only through manipulation, terror, and propaganda; they were welfare states, avowedly socialist in both instances, but their commitment to the welfare of their citizens was linked to the latter's subservience and utility to the state. In short the totalitarian states, though modern, were maladaptations to modernity; above all, they were maladaptations to the demands of modern industrialized warfare, the mastery of which became their ceaseless obsession.

THE HYPERREGULATORY WARFARE STATE

Ludendorff's *Totale Krieg*, published in 1935, argued that the total warfare of the industrial age requires economic mobilization even in advance of hostilities. Fittingly, in the year of its publication Hitler appointed Hjalmar Schacht as Plenipotentiary-General for the War Economy, marking the beginning of the Nazi transition to a highly regulated *Wehrwirtschaft* ("war economy"). Having already put German agriculture under strict production and price controls, the Nazis now imposed pervasive controls on industry as well. Between 1936 and 1939, the regime abolished most small corporations and businesses, driving economic activity under the umbrella of large cartels that could be more easily regulated by central authorities. In 1939 the government introduced rigorous wage and price controls. Walther Funk, the Minister of Economics, estimated that by then official forms and communications with the state constituted half of every German manufacturer's correspondence.[73]

Even as World War I had created the conditions that made Nazism possible, World War II completed the transformation of the Third Reich into a totalitarian state exerting military command over every aspect of its economy. During the first two years of the war, Hitler resisted converting to a full war footing. But when Germany's invasion of Russia slowed in the winter of 1941, he authorized the Ministry of Munitions to reorganize German industry under production "rings" that regulated all manufacturing from raw materials to finished products. The *Führer*-Order of January 10, 1942 subsequently ordered national conversion to a total war footing. The Ministry of Munitions under Speer extended state controls into every conceivable subsector of the German economy, a process that intensified after Germany's terrible defeat at Stalingrad.[74] By the last two years of the war, the Nazi Regulatory State had become a nearly omnipresent force in the German economy.

The Soviet Union in the era of War Communism was the first state in history to undertake the wholesale nationalization of industry as a matter of policy. Socialist ideology motivated the Bolshevik expropriations of "bourgeois" property, but it is noteworthy that the economic model Lenin sought to emulate from 1917 to 1921 was the *Kriegssozialismus* ("War Socialism") of Imperial Germany in World War I, and one of his principal economic advisers, Yurii Larin, was hired because of his expertise in the wartime economic system of Germany. In December 1917, Lenin established a Supreme Council of the National Economy (forerunner of the State Planning Commission or *Gosplan* established in 1921), and six months later announced the nationalization of all enterprises of 1,000,000 rubles' capital or more, a step that stemmed in part from concern about possible German expropriations of property. Trotsky's attempts to militarize Russian labor and impose military command on the entire economy were also linked to the extreme logistical and supply challenges of the Civil War. Though the New Economic Policy would briefly reverse the nationalizing trend, Stalin's Great Leap Forward effectively converted the whole of Soviet Russia into a single integrated state enterprise. It was the first state in history to lay claim to every asset, both physical and human, inside its borders.[75]

Central control of the economy invariably spawns bureaucracy, and both Nazi Germany and the USSR were highly bureaucratized states. Aggregate state employment in Germany at all levels (federal, provincial, local) grew by about 20 percent between 1933 and 1939. This figure, however, belies the high degree of centralization that obtained in the Third Reich, for in January 1934, the Law for the Reconstruction of the Reich formally abolished the federal structure of Germany and transferred the sovereign powers of the individual Länder to the national government. This made all the regional and local governments mere administrative bodies of the Reich, as Minister of the Interior Wilhelm Frick put it. The increase in the aggregate size of the bureaucracy under central control was thus much greater than 20 percent, probably on the order of a 100 or more percent gain over the Weimar years. Yet even this figure is understated, for it does not include the massive bureaucracy that grew up under the NSDAP and its affiliates, which by 1934 incorporated over a million functionaries, both paid and unpaid. And this parallel party bureaucracy—whose functions overlapped with those of the state, and which provided the Nazis with an additional channel of intelligence, control, and manipulation—was further supplemented by the extralegal police agency of the Party, the SS under Heinrich Himmler. Hitler routinely raved against bureaucracy, but the state he created was a Byzantine web of overlapping bureaucracies, larger and more powerful than anything previously seen in Germany.[76]

Lenin, like Hitler, mounted periodic antibureaucracy campaigns, while Trotsky, Bukharin, and Rakovsky warned of the dangers of an entrenched apparatus concentrating power in its hands. None of this had any visible effect on the growth of Soviet administrative and control structures. At the end of the Civil War, the central ministries of the Soviet government employed nearly ten times as many employees as had the Tsarist government. The Supreme Economic Council alone, modeled after the *Kriegsgesellschaften* of Germany, by 1920 had over 1,400 provincial branches and over 25,000 employees.[77] Bureaucratic growth continued apace after 1921; Trotsky observed that much of it represented functions transferred from the Army:

> The demobilization of the Red Army of five million played no small role in the formation of the bureaucracy. The victorious commanders assumed leading posts in the local Soviets, in economy, in education, and they persistently introduced everywhere that regime which had ensured success in the Civil War.[78]

All this was only a prelude, however, to the centralized technocracy that Stalin forged during his struggle with the Opposition and his Great Leap Forward, a system of controls and administrative organs that was, in Moshe Lewin's words, "one of the most powerful and all-pervasive bureaucratic machines of modern times."[79] Between 1929 and 1934, a central planning structure was put in place that made the entire Russian economy a bureaucratized appendage of the state. One consequence of this was that the USSR was the only belligerent state during World War II that required little administrative reorganization in order to convert to a total war economy. It was already there. The organizational innovations that did take place—such as the formation of the State Defense Committee or the Council for Evacuation—were largely top-level coordinating bodies overlaid on the existing bureaucracy.[80]

The bureaucratic ethos of the totalitarian states imbued them with a moral sterility that reinforced their genocidal tendencies.[81] Behind the front-line killers—the SS men and NKVD cadres who did the actual "dirty work" of terror and political murder—stood large impersonal bureaucracies that purchased necessary equipment, acquired land for camps, conducted logistical planning, and in a hundred ways made possible the horror of genocide. Just as it is easier to commit mass murder by pushing buttons in a bomber high above a city than by machine-gunning women and children, the very banality of a bureaucratic machine can disguise the most evil of ends from the consciousness of its human cogs. In this sense, the "central planning" and "political coordination" of High Totalitarianism were political euphemisms whose sanitized vacuousness paved the way for the ultimate euphemism of all, the bureaucratic tasking known to history as the "Final Solution."

"DIRECT DEMOCRACY" IN THE MANIPULATED MASS STATE

The totalitarian states were a peculiar form of the mass state. They endorsed a classless society, celebrated universal suffrage, and sought to inculcate in their populations a uniform mass culture that would uphold and advance their political objectives. Even at the height of Stalin's purges the illusion of freely given popular support had to be maintained, and the 1936 Stalin Constitution, in addition to proclaiming a plethora of hollow rights, promised "universal, equal and direct suffrage by secret ballot."[82] Totalitarian leaders did not elicit mass support on the basis of the traditional War Bargain—military service in exchange for political participation—but rather through the unremitting mobilization of the masses and the manipulated channeling of their energies. By substituting an orchestrated "direct democracy" for genuine political participation, they became the only states in history to wage industrialized warfare without making democratic concessions to civil society.

In the Third Reich, the "nationalization of the masses," as Hitler called it, unabashedly evoked military symbols. Following the electoral triumph of 1933, the regime installed the new parliament with pomp and ceremony at the Potsdam garrison church. Later, the spectacular mass rallies at Nuremberg, Berlin, Potsdam and elsewhere had as their centerpiece a military parade of hundreds of thousands of SS and Reichswehr soldiers marching past and saluting their Supreme Commander. The effect created was one of awe before the crushing power of a mass army; cannon fire, torchlights, and defiant rhetoric raised the enthusiasm of the spectators to a crescendo. The sheer size of these rallies was a tribute to the organizational prowess of the NSDAP: in April 1933 Hitler addressed 600,000 SA and SS men in the Berliner

Sportpalast; in September 1937 in Berlin, three million people participated in a military-political rally in honor of Mussolini's visit.[83]

The propaganda campaigns of Joseph Goebbels's Ministry of People's Enlightenment and Propaganda reflected the regime's preoccupation with war. Popular themes included *Blut und Boden* (blood and
soil), *Volk ohne Raum* (people without space), *Fronterlebnis* (the front
experience), *Blutzeuge* (martyr), *alter Kämpfer* (old warrior).[84] The
propaganda sought to reinforce the self-image of the nation as a
closed, warlike community tightly bound to its supreme commander,
the Führer. It is telling that Hitler himself credited Nazi propaganda
successes to lessons learned from British and French propaganda in
World War I, which had shown "what immense results could be
obtained by a correct application of propaganda."[85]

Education was another means for the nationalization of the masses.
The *Gleichschaltung* of the German public schools turned them into a
system for premilitary training, ideological indoctrination, and social
leveling. A large part of the compulsory reading in those schools was
World War I literature, which made the Great War seem an
omnipresent part of national life. The message of the curriculum, both
subliminal and overt, was that war was normal and force legitimate.[86]
Ewald Banse, a military scientist involved in curriculum development,
wanted the schools to inculcate a "desire for war and victory," to unite
Germans in "a feverish mass of blood and iron," to pour "steel into the
nerves of the German people." In Hesse, an elementary-school primer
contained numerous pictures of uniformed, armed youngsters in formation. High-school mathematics textbooks contained hundreds of
review problems with military themes; students had to calculate
artillery ranges, battlefield coordinates, antiaircraft elevations, and the
geometry of bomb shelters! In the words of one historian, education
in the Third Reich served an apocalyptic function.[87] This was doubly
true of the special schools for the Nazi elite—the Napolas, Order Castles, Adolf Hitler Schools, and the *Hohe Schule* in Frankfurt am
Main—which were organized as quasi-military academies.

The Wilhelmian educational system had already devoted exceptional attention to military-oriented physical education, and the Third
Reich carried this much further, emulating military academies in its
reordering of the classroom and placing enormous emphasis on physical education and training. The development of *Kraft* (physical
strength) was the declared goal of this education, an objective perpetuated beyond the public schools in the sport-and-leisure auxiliary organization of the German Labor Front, "*Kraft durch Freude*" (Strength
through Joy).[88] Paramilitary institutions such as the Hitler Youth and

the Labor Service carried on the task of military training outside the classroom. The Hitler Youth grew from 108,000 members to 3.6 million in 1933–34 alone; by 1939 membership was compulsory. There was no better way of overcoming class conflict, as the leader of the Labor Service, Konstantin Hierl, observed, than dressing "the son of the director and the young worker, the university student and the farmhand, in the same uniform, to set them the same table in common service to *Volk* and *Vaterland*."[89]

The content of Soviet propaganda and education tended to be less overtly militaristic than that of Nazi Germany, but the same basic techniques of mass mobilization and socialization were employed. The Third All-Russia Congress of the Russian Young Communist League, which met in 1920 and was addressed by Lenin, declared physical education to be an essential element in the upbringing of young people, both to prepare them for work and for "the military defense of Soviet power."[90] The Pioneer and Komsomol organizations served purposes similar to the Hitler Youth, including the fostering of premilitary training through combat games and drill. After World War II, Stalin's government consolidated the premilitary and patriotic training of youth and workers under a large paramilitary reserve organization, DOSAAF (Voluntary Organization for Cooperation with the Army, Aviation, and Fleet) which all citizens over the age of fourteen were required to join; it remained a tool of the state for the socialization of Soviet youth throughout the era of the Cold War. Western observers of the Soviet armed forces noted that after Khrushchev's ouster, the military training of Soviet youth intensified dramatically, becoming reminiscent in both content and style of Hitler's education regime in the 1930s.[91]

Through mass mobilization, totalitarianism sought to forge a classless society in which individuals of every social origin would be equal—equally subordinate to the state, as soldiers are to their commanders. In this perverse sense at least, the egalitarian and social-leveling effects of World War I carried over into the totalitarian states as they had in the democracies. In fact, both Soviet Russia and Nazi Germany achieved a degree of social mobility quite uncharacteristic of the traditional states that preceded them. Both states actually succeeded in reducing income stratification—the former drastically, the latter more tentatively. Or, to cite another example, in 1920 66 percent of Reichswehr generals were aristocrats; by 1939 only 27 percent were. During World War II, the number of German officers commissioned from the ranks was more than twice the number so commissioned in all German armies since 1800.[92] In the Soviet Union, the emigration of

Whites and the Stalinist purges likewise created unprecedented social mobility both in the military and in a traditionally rigid Russian civilian society; by the end of the 1930s, so many peasants had entered the ranks of the Party elite that it was possible to speak of a "peasantization" of the Revolution and of the birth of a new Muscovite political culture based on peasant norms of behavior.[93]

All of this amounted to a radically new form of popular sovereignty, a manipulated and stage-managed "direct democracy" that entailed neither true parliaments nor genuine political representation. The General Will of Rousseau was here supreme, embodied in the sovereign Führer or General Secretary whose will could brook no faction of any kind. All were equal in this new state, submerged in the classlessness of the totalitarian trench, citizen-soldiers in a society nominally at peace, but ever organized and braced for war.[94]

THE BARRACKS WELFARE STATE

In their own perverse way, the totalitarian states were also welfare states. This sprang in part from an ideological commitment to various forms of socialism or "social solidarity," which even in the Third Reich was taken more seriously than is usually credited. But it also derived from an acute awareness of the fact that industrialized warfare requires a healthy population, contented workers, and (because of the immense losses it generates) a population that reproduces itself freely. Welfare programs, as the historian Karl Dietrich Bracher noted of Hitler's efforts to forge a *Volksgemeinschaft*, were purposeful tools of control, coordination, and war mobilization.[95] In effect, workers in both Nazi Germany and the USSR fell into a kind of barracks socialism, becoming conscript vassals of the state, mere cogs in its vast military-industrial machinery. Their relationship with the state became that extolled by Dostoyevsky's Grand Inquisitor: bread and security in exchange for total submission.

The Nazi state kept in place the basic social insurance programs of the German welfare state but added several new features, the thrust of which we have already noticed in from our study of Vichy France in the last chapter. These included measures specifically designed to encourage maternity and raise the birth rate: a program of child allowances; special awards for fertility and preferential treatment for pregnant women; and various family support programs, some under the NSDAP, such as "Mother and Child," the *NS-Frauenschaft*, and the *Reichsbund Deutscher Familie*. What is most striking about these programs was their unabashed military purpose: a high birth rate meant a larger, more powerful Army. The fertile German mother was "to occupy the same honoured place in the folk community as the front-line soldier, since the risks to health and life she incurs for *Volk* and Fatherland are the same as those of the soldier in the thunder of battle."[96] Popular awareness of the military purpose behind the fertility campaign spawned a slang term for sexual intercourse: *Recrutenmachen* (making a recruit).

Industrial workers were of course also considered "soldiers of labor" and the campaign against unemployment the "battle of labor." After the *Gleichschaltung* of the trade unions in 1933, the regime established the Labor Front, an organ of the NSDAP, to represent labor and ensure that every individual "perform the maximum possible work." The regime simultaneously abolished the rights to strike and to engage in collective bargaining. The Hereditary Farm Law bound the peasant to the land, while a series of government decrees in 1934–35 restricted industrial job mobility. In 1938, the Four-Year Plan introduced virtual worker conscription. The welfare sugar-coating in the latter provision was a prohibition against any worker being fired without consent of the government—i.e., job security in exchange for virtual serfdom to the state. Programs such as the one-pot meals, the *Winterhilfe* relief fund, and the *Volkswagen* ("people's car") that was promised to every family, further cushioned worker discontent. But the fraudulent nature of the new compact can be seen in the decline of real wages between 1933 and 1939 and the new stringency in the workplace. In his postwar memoirs, Albert Speer claimed that Hitler demanded less of his workers than did the democracies.[97] This was ludicrous, especially after 1942, when during Speer's own tenure as Minister of Munitions, progressively more "total" stages of mobilization reduced German workers to chattels, their hours increased to near their physical limits, their work watched over by Gestapo agents; their theaters, cultural events, and centers of entertainment and sport shut down so as to devote their every resource to the war effort.[98]

Though the Russian Civil War saw the passage of a progressive labor code, it was never implemented in practice. Instead, the regime introduced compulsory labor for all citizens, abolished the right to organize and to strike, and placed large sectors of the civilian economy—railroad workers, medical personnel, technicians, transport employees, coal miners, postal and telegraph workers, wool industry workers, metalworkers, and electricians—under command discipline in the workplace. Industrial occupations thus became progressively "militarized," with the difference between soldiers and workers blurred.[99] Beginning in 1919, the regime stopped demobilizing Red Army units, converting them instead into *Trudarmii* (Labor Armies) assigned to economic tasks at the direction of the state.

At the onset of the New Economic Policy, Lenin's government abolished the Labor Armies, and in 1922 it introduced comprehensive welfare legislation that included a protective labor code, unemployment benefits, and medical assistance. The reprieve from barracks socialism was short-lived, however. In October 1930 Stalin decided that unemployment did not exist in the USSR; by decree, he terminated all unemployment benefits. This was enforced by the simple expedient of branding the unemployed as parasites and carting them off to the labor camps, whose numbers mushroomed dramatically throughout the 1930s. The majority of camp inmates, of course, were gainfully employed, loyal citizens who had the misfortune of falling prey to Stalin's prophylactic terror. The camps provided the state with cheap labor to undertake—in appalling conditions—its most unpleasant and dangerous construction, logging, and mining tasks. Nothing more clearly reflects the contempt of the Total Warfare State for its citizen-conscripts than the rise of the vast Gulag Archipelago of Stalinist Russia.

In the aftermath of World War II, the USSR introduced a system of family allowances and awards for exceptionally fertile mothers (Heroine Mother, Maternity Medal, Order of Maternal Glory) aimed at boosting a declining birth rate and recovering from the human toll of the war. Beginning in 1956 with de-Stalinization, Khrushchev reintroduced some of the progressive social programs that had existed under Lenin and that had become commonplace in the industrial democracies: disability and survivor pensions, old-age pensions, etc.[100] The fact that these and subsequent social-welfare laws were aimed especially at veterans of the war suggests that the social-welfare impulse of World War II was as real in Russia as in the West, but its effects were delayed until after the death of Stalin. However, even after 1956 the Soviet regime continued to insist that all welfare benefits be administered by the state, and it flatly refused to countenance private charity until the last years of the Gorbachev era. The *Great Soviet Encyclopedia* of 1927 defined the Russian word for charity, *blagotvoritel'nost*, as alien to the social system of the USSR, and charity remained officially a bourgeois vice until the 1980s.[101]

Khrushchev after 1956 rapidly dismantled whole provinces of the Soviet *gulag*, and Soviet totalitarianism turned to a less brutal, if still highly authoritarian, politics. The *gulag* did not disappear entirely, however, until Gorbachev dismantled it. For one thing, the Soviet state still needed involuntary labor for undertaking certain crucial tasks, including the dread assignment of work in the uranium mines, where *zek* labor died early and hard to produce the burgeoning nuclear arsenal of the new superpower. Out of similar motivations, the USSR under Khrushchev and Brezhnev regularly promulgated new laws restricting worker and peasant mobility, mandating strict labor discipline, and combating parasitism. A state at war can tolerate no shirkers.

CONCLUSION: THE SELF-DESTRUCTIVENESS OF TOTALITARIANISM

Totalitarianism was the offspring of modern industrial war, and indeed nothing else but war could have spawned so grotesque a monster. Its nasty, brutish, and short life decisively demolished the proposition that history evolves inexorably in the direction of progress; in Germany and Russia, at least, the centuries-long intertwined developments of the modern state and modern war led not to progress, but to a cul-de-sac of unparalleled moral depravity. Nazi Germany survived for twelve years and directly or indirectly caused the death of 30 million persons. The USSR endured for seventy-four years, during which time at least 20 million Soviet citizens suffered violent death at the hands of the Bolshevik regime. States built on the proposition that war was the natural state of man proved to be infernal engines of mass death. In keeping whole societies constantly mobilized for war, the totalitarian regimes contradicted the most basic verities of human life, including the simple truth that the vast majority of people seek only to be left alone and to live in peace. Therefore totalitarianism was an untenable proposition, an inherently unstable form of government that contained the seeds of its own self-destruction.

In embracing the total revolution of total war, the totalitarian states hoped to attain the utopia of total security against all enemies. Yet this entailed a fundamental contradiction, for when one state accumulates massive power in the pursuit of security, it becomes an overwhelming threat to the security of all other states, which will inevitably unite against it. Thus the pursuit of total state power and total security leads only to total insecurity and the collapse of state power. But before we become utterly fatalistic about the evils of industrial warfare and the destructiveness of the bureaucratic state, we should recall that both Nazi Germany and the Soviet Union collapsed in large part because they were met by the overwhelming military power of other industrial states that were also bureaucratically organized to master the technological and operational complexities of modern war. Absent the countervailing power of the democracies, the fate of the world would have been dark indeed.

The Soviet path to self-destruction was less cataclysmic than that of Nazi Germany and took much longer to play out. This is in part because the Soviet leaders sought to minimize the risks of perpetual warfare by engaging in a kind of half-war, half-peace, but this course also proved self-destructive in the end, leading slowly but inexorably to national exhaustion. Throughout the Cold War, Western analysts argued over what percentage of the Soviet GNP was devoted to military spending, with the highest estimates running around 13 percent—two or three times higher than any Western power. After the collapse of the Soviet empire, as more data about the Soviet economy became available, these estimates had to be revised sharply upward. Most analysts now accept that throughout the postwar period, the Soviet Union was spending on the order of 20 percent or more of its GNP on its armed forces. Such a ratio is normally associated only with industrial states at war.

No previous state in modern history sustained such a level of armaments spending in peacetime, and few maintained it even during hot wars. The Western allies during World War I and World War II exceeded this figure by a sizable margin, but only briefly and only because they had access to enormous amounts of borrowed capital. Yet the Soviet Union sustained a wartime level of military spending for over forty years with minimal access to borrowed capital. The result? A collapsed empire, an enervated population, a discredited state, a ruined economy, and an ecological disaster of continental proportions. The Soviet Union may have gone out with a whimper instead of a roar, but its self-destructiveness was only slightly less colossal in its consequences than that of Nazi Germany.

At the highest historical level, once the facade of ideology is stripped away, totalitarianism reveals itself as a desperate attempt by war-ravaged societies to create militarily viable states. For nearly three centuries after their first encounter with the Military Revolution, both Germany and Russia sought to accommodate military modernization within traditional forms of government, reforming only grudgingly when compelled by defeat in battle. Totalitarianism, by contrast, represented a complete rupture with traditional forms. It was an effort to incorporate the mobilizing dynamism of war into the very fabric of the state, to welcome the barbarians as "a kind of solution" to military impotence.[102] The killing fields of the twentieth century bear witness to the pernicious possibilities of the modern state and the brutality latent in human hearts. Yet the military defeat of one totalitarian state and the utter failure of the other still give cause for hope and remind us, in words uttered four score and seven years before the Iron Curtain sundered Europe, of the better angels of our nature.

War and the American Government

The most important occurrence in the life of a nation is the breaking out of a war.

Alexis de Tocqueville, *Democracy in America*

The delegates to the constitutional convention that met in Philadelphia in the summer of 1787 did not think of themselves as creating a new state, at least not in the European sense of the word. For them, the term *state* evoked images of continental despotism, centralized government, standing armies, and monarchical rule—everything they had rebelled against in 1775. Alexander Hamilton, John Jay, and James Madison in the *Federalist Papers* coined sundry names for the political system envisioned by the Constitution—it was a federal government, a union, a national government, an administration, republic, federation, and federal republic—but not once did they refer to it as a *state*. When "Publius" used the term at all, it invariably applied not to the federal system, but to the individual former colonies.

The Constitution undeniably did establish a sovereign state, one capable of controlling and defending territory, but in 1787 its proponents felt compelled to emphasize its federal nature. Talk of a new state or of national sovereignty would have doomed ratification of the document. As a British scholar of American history observed, the early Americans fundamentally rejected any sovereignty vested in any state, including their own.

> Americans may be defined as that part of the English-speaking world which instinctively revolted against the doctrine of the sovereignty of the State and has, not quite successfully, striven to maintain that attitude from the time of the Pilgrim Fathers to the present day. . . . It is this denial of all sovereignty which gives its profound and permanent interest to the American Revolution.[1]

The American revolt against state sovereignty continues today and is even reflected in the title of this chapter. We think nothing of referring to the French state, the German state, the Canadian state, the Chinese state, or even the British state. We rarely, however, say "the American state," falling back instead on the narrower terms *government* or *republic*. As Stephen Skowronek notes, "the absence of a sense of state has been the great hallmark of American political culture."[2] Yet it is not the sovereignty of the state on the international stage that Americans deny, so much as its *internal* sovereignty—the notion that any political power may rightfully stand above the individual. Accordingly, state power in America has made its most significant advances whenever Americans have faced profound threats to the *external* sovereignty of their state, to their national security. This is why the state in America, as in Europe, originated in war and ascended under the impetus of war.

Four main factors have contributed to the internal weakness of the central government in America—to the extraordinary diffusion of power and authority that characterizes the American system. The first and perhaps foremost factor was geographical isolation, which has meant the absence of powerful, proximate foreign enemies throughout most of American history. As Alexis de Tocqueville observed in 1835, America is the ultimate island power.[3] The Atlantic Ocean offers a protective buffer against attack a hundred times as wide as the English Channel. Moreover, with the short-lived exception of the Confederacy, no organized state in the Western hemisphere has been capable of mounting a serious military challenge to the United States. Hegel, that supreme apostle of the modern state, cited this absence of enemies as one reason why "a real State" did not exist in America. Without a standing army, he thought, it was doomed to weakness and obscurity.[4]

Hegelian strictures aside, it is true that American exceptionalism has always been linked to geographical isolation. It is also the case that the central state in America has only been powerful when the country was at war or under threat of war. Between 1815 and 1914, the only all-out war that Americans fought was among themselves; the absence of protracted external war enabled the American state to retain a minimalist national administration. During the Civil War, the northern half of America transformed itself into a highly centralized, militarily powerful, administratively strong state with a clear sense of national mission. Then, in a quintessential act of American exceptionalism, the whole structure was dismantled after the war—just the opposite of what happened to the Prussian state five years later after it too achieved national unity in war. The Spanish-American War marked the debut of the United States as a world power, but did little to fundamentally alter the structure of American government. It took two world wars and a protracted Cold War to shatter a deep-rooted sense of insular security and forge for the first time an enduring public consciousness of America as a sovereign, unitary state in a world of hostility and threat. The post-Sputnik marriage of nuclear weapons with ICBMs further diminished the security advantage of insular geography and reinforced the rise of a postwar American state that is as preoccupied with security as any of the traditional states of Europe.

A second factor contributing to the dilution of state sovereignty in America was the Tudor origins of its political institutions. America inherited from England a rich legacy of legal and judicial institutions that were essentially medieval in character and that had survived in England only because of the latter's isolation from the winds of continental warfare. And these institutions endured in America even after modernizing and centralizing tendencies had diluted or destroyed them in England. The American colonists adopted the Tudor tradition of representative government tied to local interests; a sharing of power among legislative, executive, and judicial bodies; the concept of a bicameral legislature; a tradition of reliance upon militia forces for defense; and even a republican version of constitutional monarchy, complete with royal court, as seen in the American presidency.[5] The American state—a child of the New World, a consummate product of the Enlightenment, and seemingly the sui generis creation of thirty-nine American patricians—owed its freedom in part to the representative and antiauthoritarian spirit of premodern institutions inherited from England. It was thus of profound importance not only that

America was an insular power, but that the European country that first settled it had itself been an island state, isolated from the shock waves of the Military Revolution.

But though the Tudor legacy was immensely important in the shaping of American institutions, the American system departed fundamentally from its English predecessor in one critical respect: its federal structure. Like the Swiss Confederation and the Dutch Republic before it, the United States initially followed the coalitional path of state formation, originating as a confederation of provinces revolting against a common sovereign. From the War of Independence to the ratification of the Constitution, the Continental Congress was the only central authority of the nation. Although such an arrangement might have sufficed for countries of diminutive size, it proved unsuitable for a large state like America. Montesquieu in *The Spirit of the Laws* observed that small republics risk destruction by outside forces, large republics by internal corruption; he held that only federal republics could be simultaneously large, powerful, and free.[6] The American founders accepted his logic, creating a federalist system that acted as a structural barrier against the abuses of a powerful center, while simultaneously ensuring that the American state retained the capacity to field strong military forces when necessary. The result was a radical departure both from the large absolutist states of continental Europe and from the small Swiss and Dutch confederations with their extreme decentralization and intrinsic executive frailty.

Yet another factor contributing to the weak sense of state in America was the lack of a sense of nation. The thirteen colonies had separate origins and individual histories that long predated the Revolution; until at least 1754 their vertical links with England, both political and commercial, were far more important to each of them than their horizontal ties with each other. Inter-colonial military cooperation, beginning with the French and Indian Wars (1754–1763), changed this, creating for the first time a distinct sense of American identity and community. That war also boosted the stature of the provincial assemblies in Virginia, Massachusetts, and elsewhere, because without their cooperation the colonies' royal governors could not raise arms and troops, thus making possible the pivotal role the assemblies would later play in the Revolution.[7] Similarly, rising opposition to British taxation focused the collective identity of the colonies in the decade leading up to 1775, and the Revolutionary War crystallized that identity into the first real sense of American nationalism.

Neither in the Revolution nor in the ensuing two centuries did American nationalism ever focus on the state as the embodiment of the nation, in part because geographic isolation made America a sanctuary for generations of the most independent-minded, antistatist Europeans and Asians, many of whom were fleeing the depredations of war and despotism in their homelands. Their deep-rooted hostility to centralized power fueled the ceaseless American revolt against sovereignty, while ethnic and cultural diversity made it ever less feasible to base American nationalism on nationality. The diversity and antistatism of the American population made the collective efforts entailed in waging war one of the most important factors in shaping America's consciousness of itself as a unified nation. Geoffrey Perret argues that war for America was "a factor as important as geography, immigration, the growth of business, the separation of powers, the inventiveness of its people, or anything else that contributed strongly to its unique identity among the nations of the Earth."[8] War served as an engine of nationalism, a socializing and integrating force that united Americans of diverse origins in common efforts both on the battlefield and the home front. Every constitutional extension of the suffrage in American history—the 15th, 19th, and 26th Amendments—was enacted during or in the immediate aftermath of war.

If America's wars helped form its national identity, they also had an enormous impact on development of its political system, shaping the institutions of American government and stimulating its growth. The mirror image of war is deeply imprinted on the face of the American state, primarily as the result of its five largest wars: the War of Independence, the Civil War, World War I, World War II, and the Cold War (of which the conflicts in Korea and Vietnam can be regarded as subsets). Lesser wars—the War of 1812, the War with Mexico, the Spanish-American War, and the Persian Gulf War—had lesser, but not insignificant, effects on the institutions and form of American government. The remainder of this chapter will trace the impact of war and related military factors on five dimensions of the American state: its institutional formation and development; its bureaucratic and fiscal expansion; the development of American nationalism; the power of the executive branch; and the rise of the welfare state in America.

THE REVOLUTIONARY WAR AND THE
FORMATION OF THE AMERICAN STATE

The tendency among historians in recent decades has been to view the American Revolution as primarily a process of intellectual and social change, and to minimize the importance of the War of Independence in the transformation that occurred. This tendency reached its apotheosis in the work of Gordon S. Wood, perhaps the most prominent American historian of the Revolution. His classic work, *The Creation of the American Republic 1776–1787*, analyzes the Revolution entirely in terms of intellectual thought and makes not a single substantive reference to the war. An alien reading the book might not realize that a war had taken place at all; the Revolution appears in these pages to have been nothing but an extended intellectual argument. Even Wood's analysis of its intellectual roots slights the fact that many of the legal and political issues of the day—popular sovereignty, representative government, separation of powers—revolved around practical problems of war, national security, and military service.[9] Though Wood's work is profound intellectual history, his overall approach does suggest that the distinction between the Revolution and the war, between military history and other forms of history, can be taken too far. The war was not a mere epiphenomenon of the larger Revolution; it was its central event and a significant cause of its far-reaching social and political repercussions.

It is true, as Bernard Bailyn has shown, that the ideas behind the Revolution pervaded the rhetoric of American pamphleteers for decades prior to the war.[10] But ideas alone could not give birth to an independent state, nor cause an unalterable breach in sentiment between the colonists and their fellow Britons. It was the coming of war that radicalized the propertied elites who led the Revolution, the war that infused the ideals of pamphleteers and philosophers into the hearts and minds of yeoman farmers, militiamen, and Continentals. Like the Dutch who rebelled against Philip II, the colonists hesitated to break with their sovereign even after hostilities began. But bloodshed transformed their thinking: "Men died at Bunker Hill, and each time an American died so did some part of moderation. . . . The news of the fighting spread, and soldiers from the middle and southern colonies began to march toward Boston. As they left home so also did the spirit of compromise."[11] War, not ideas alone, wrought the radical change in American opinion that Wood, Bailyn, and other historians have documented.

Contrary to a popular conception of the War of Independence as a civilized and rather tidy affair, it was in fact marked by extraordinary violence and upheaval. The number of soldiers killed in set battles is officially set at 4,435, but a more detailed estimate of the total number who perished from wounds, disease, or in prison puts the figure at 25,324, nearly one percent of the American population in 1780, and more than one in ten of all soldiers who served. Proportionately, as a percentage of national population the losses were three times greater than World War II and were surpassed only by those of the Civil War.[12] Nor should the impact of the post-1776 "civil war within the war" be overlooked: anti-Tory reprisals were a factor in the emigration of between 50,000 and 100,000 British loyalists from America during the war and of tens of thousands more after the war; this was a ratio of exiles to population at least *five times* as high as the émigré wave that fled France during the French Revolution. When we examine these statistics together with the brutality that came to characterize the war on the Indian frontiers and in the South, we have a picture of an upheaval far more violent than the popular images of the war. The War of Independence was an event of immense proportions, a major cause in its own right of the larger American revolution.[13]

It is also worth recalling that the proximate causes of the American revolt were military in substance, stemming from Britain's attempt to maintain a permanent military force in the western territories of the colonies. The whole purpose of the Sugar Act of 1764, the Stamp Act of 1765, and the Townshend Revenue Act of 1767 was to raise revenue for maintaining British frontier garrisons whose presence was deemed essential to maintain security in western America after the French and Indian Wars. The Quartering Act of 1765 simply sought to shift a portion of the burden of maintaining those troops onto the colonies. The taxes were needed to support the troops—but before long the troops were needed to enforce collection of the taxes. Following stiff colonial resistance to the revenue acts, the British government began shifting redcoats from their western forts to eastern cities, where they could better enforce the will of Parliament. The American Revolution, like so many rebellions and insurrections throughout modern history, originated as a revolt against taxes levied to support an army.[14]

The unifying potential of the war became evident at an early date in the selection of George Washington, a Southerner, to head American forces initially dominated by militia from the North. But reliance on the poorly trained and ill-disciplined militias of the several colonies proved politically divisive and militarily disastrous. As late as December 1776, Washington felt that Americans were wavering in their loyalties "as much owing to the want of an Army to look the Enemy in the

Face, as to any other cause."[15] Fed up with the poor discipline of the militia and its "unwillingness . . . to submit to that regularity and order essential in every Army," Washington pleaded for creation of a truly professional army, a body of well-drilled regulars who would remain in service for the duration of the war.[16] He rejected the strategy proposed by Charles Lee and Horatio Gates, both of whom advocated using militia forces to fight a guerrilla war against the British; Washington not only felt such a strategy would fail, but correctly sensed that it would lay no foundation for postwar unity.[17]

The Virginian's vision of a professional army after the continental pattern ran up against the deeply ingrained American aversion to the very concept of a "standing army." The mere phrase was anathema, conjuring up images of continental despotism, of British redcoats quartered in civilian homes. Jonathan Trenchard's *History of Standing Armies* was standard fare among literate Americans, the equivalent in its day of a *New York Times* best-seller. The vast majority of America's landowning aristocracy had an almost congenital distrust of standing armies, which their ancestors for generations had identified with despotism, both royal and Cromwellian. They glorified instead the yeoman militiaman, linked to the land and closely tied to local interests.[18] Yet the war posed a dilemma: if the Americans wanted freedom from the depredations of a standing army, they would have to create one of their own.

The Congress had actually voted in June 1775 to form a Continental Army to fight alongside the militia, but a corrupt recruiting system and perilously short terms of enlistment made the measure ineffective. Enlistments were initially for one year, but some recruiters offered 10-dollar bounties in exchange for six weeks of service—if this was a standing army, it did not stand for long! Military necessity eventually persuaded Congress to build up an institution it fundamentally distrusted. In June 1776, it voted three-year enlistments, and in September began offering 20 dollars and 100 acres of land to any men who enlisted for the duration. By 1777, a regular system of recruiting was in place, with quotas assigned to each state.[19] The Baron von Steuben and a coterie of European (mostly French) military advisers proved vital to Washington in his project of belatedly bringing the Military Revolution to American shores.

The formation of a regular army under a single command had crucial integrative and unifying effects for the new republic. At the Battle of Brandywine in 1777, Nathaniel Greene from Rhode Island led a Virginia division, while Anthony Wayne of Pennsylvania commanded troops from New Jersey. This arrangement, unthinkable at the onset of the war, epitomized the unifying effect of military service. Likewise, soldiers from the different regions of the country initially viewed one another with suspicion or even animosity, but this changed as they camped, served, and fought together. The war thus forged the first sense of a distinctive American nationality.[20]

Even as the army helped to make the nation, the war helped to forge the state: the first central administrative organs of American government came into being during the conflict. With the exception of the Post Office, established in 1775, they were almost exclusively military or fiscal in their function. The formation of central structures accelerated after the mutiny of the Philadelphia Line in January 1781, which persuaded Congress that financing and directing the war effort could not be left to the individual states. Within two months it opened a Department of Foreign Affairs, created the office of Secretary of War, and established a Department of Finance whose first Superintendent, Robert Morris, became the virtual financial dictator of the United States. Other national institutions created during the war included departments of military supply and organization, the Springfield Armory in Massachusetts, and the Bank of North America, which was first formed in Philadelphia in June 1780 by citizens wanting to assist the army.[21]

When state militias are included as many as 200,000 Americans, one in twelve of the population, took up arms at some time in the war, a very high military-participation ratio, especially given that the colonies were not well organized for mobilization and did not employ mass conscription.[22] Such a high level of participation inevitably had a profound impact on the development of national consciousness across almost all strata of American society: the landed aristocratic elite who led the revolt; the rural militiamen who fought in it; and the lower-class recruits who filled the ranks of the regular army. In a striking example of Andreski's "leveling effect" of conflict, the war also stimulated demands for wider political participation: "As Cromwell's men had demanded the right to vote if they were deemed fit to fight . . . colonials of military age demanded the same right for the same reason."[23] Over half the states broadened the franchise during or shortly after the war; class barriers eroded; egalitarian sentiments waxed strong; the service of free black soldiers gave impetus to the anti-slavery movement in the North.[24] The mass emigration of Tories also altered the class structure and shifted the internal balance of power in America, leaving only vestiges of support for monarchical government.

THE MILITARY AND SECURITY ORIGINS OF THE CONSTITUTION

Historians have written extensively of the political, intellectual, economic, and social origins of the American constitution. Without minimizing the rich and complex descent of the document, it is important to examine the military factors that entered into its framing as well, for a host of widely felt concerns about security, both internal and external, led to the convening of the Constitutional Convention in Philadelphia and preoccupied its attention.

The Treaty of Paris led to the rapid decline of nationalist sentiments in the former colonies, as the centralizing impetus of the conflict ebbed. Nationalist-minded leaders hoped to exploit a near revolt of army officers early in 1783 to encourage formation of a stronger central government, but the Newburgh Affair only hastened demobilization of the army.[25] By 1784 it had shrunk to 700 men under Major General Henry Knox. Still distrustful of standing armies, Congress disbanded even this force, leaving only two garrisons of 25 and 55 men each. The administrative departments established by Congress also atrophied, and several states began conducting their affairs almost as if the Articles of Confederation did not exist. The American mistrust of sovereignty thus manifested itself in two habits that would resurface after nearly every war: rapid, nearly total demobilization of the army and partial dismantling of the federal administration as well.

That the American Confederation did not fall apart entirely after 1783 can be attributed to the twin security imperatives of internal order and external defense. Nationalist leaders such as James Madison, Alexander Hamilton, Samuel Chase, Robert Morris, and Gouverneur Morris pressed the case for a central government largely on military grounds, arguing that individual states could not wield adequate forces for either defense or the maintenance of order. The course of events vindicated their argument. Rising internal anarchy in several states exposed the inadequacy of local militias to maintain order. The most serious incident, Shays' Rebellion, boosted pronationalist feeling in several states. Similar uprisings threatened New Hampshire and Connecticut, while mobs in western Virginia burned courthouses and prisons. Meanwhile the Northern states, especially those bordering on English or French possessions, increasingly worried about the vulnerability of their trade. England was no longer an enemy, but nor was its navy a protector—how could overseas commerce be conducted safely without a strong navy, which no one state could afford? In the South, Georgia's burgeoning population was alarmed by the presence of sometimes hostile Indian tribes on its borders; its state militia was inadequate to the task of providing frontier security alone.[26]

Revolutionary War veterans also played a crucial role in the movement for a strong central government between 1783 and 1789. The victory over England had enhanced their political standing, while the experience of the war had made them the most nationalist-minded interest group in America. Congress had ended the war with large domestic debts, including nearly $10 million owed to veterans whose pay was in arrears or who had been promised pensions of half pay for life. Veterans lobbied hard for either the Congress or the states to meet this obligation. Some fiscally healthy states did assume the debt, but other states could not; veterans in these states regarded the formation of a strong national government as their best hope for redress. Nationalist leaders such as Hamilton pressed for Congress to assume the full debts, believing this would turn the debts into a potential "cement" of the Union.[27] Thus, in the American case, as in the Dutch case before it, war debts helped consolidate a fractious polity by binding creditors across the nation to the fate of the central state.[28]

The mounting concerns over national security, civil order, and war debts culminated in the gathering at Philadelphia in 1787. Edmund Randolph made the first formal speech to the convention, an indictment of the existing Confederation that "produced no security against foreign invasion" and "could not check the quarrels between states, nor a rebellion in any."[29] This same preoccupation with national security permeates the final document itself, from the "insure domestic tranquility, provide for the common defense" of the Preamble to the guarantee (Article IV, Section 4) of the United States to protect the states against invasion and domestic violence. Of the eighteen clauses defining the powers of Congress, nine directly concern military affairs. The *Federalist Papers* similarly reflect this pervasive concern with security. The first nine letters, as well as Numbers 22–29 and 41–43, concentrate entirely on security issues: defense against external enemies; internal order; the risks of civil war; the roles of the militia, army, and navy.[30]

The new Constitution stripped the states of the right to maintain standing forces in peacetime, conduct foreign policy, or engage in war unless invaded. It gave the national government sole responsibility for defending the country, made the President commander in chief of the armed forces, and gave him authority over the state militias if and when they were called into national service. But having created a central executive capable of waxing strong in war, the convention sought to check and balance the exercise of its *internal* power at every point.

The Constitution reserved to Congress the right to declare war, to make appropriations to the military, and to actually call the militia into national service (a clause that Lincoln would deftly sidestep). Fears of the despotic proclivity of standing armies continued: the Constitution recognized the role of the militia—but not of the national army—in suppressing internal insurrections. Repressive power, though a necessary evil, was to be kept as close as possible to the local level.

The invention of federalism was a stroke of genius, which simultaneously gave the American system the decentralized form of the Swiss and Dutch systems, the constitutional safeguards of Great Britain, *and* the powerful executive of the continental states. The immense potential power of the Presidency, however, would flow to it only in times of war or grave national crisis—which is why the accretion of central power in America has occurred most easily during wars. Such an enormous grant of power to one individual, even with all the safeguards that accompanied it, was acceptable only because everyone took for granted that the first holder of the office would be the former commander in chief of the Continental Army. The first new republic in over a century, the jewel of the Enlightenment, would be headed by a military officer, an aristocrat who epitomized the martial virtues of his class. Not surprisingly, he was known throughout his tenure in office simply as General Washington.

THE ANTE-BELLUM INTERREGNUM, 1789–1860

The new republic's first decade unfolded in a volatile international context, marked by Britain's retention of military posts in the Northwest, friction with Spain over the Mississippi and the southwestern border, the Nootka Sound crisis, and the rising tensions associated with the French Revolutionary and Napoleonic wars. It was precisely this context that made it feasible for Federalist leaders such as Hamilton to pursue an agenda of centralization—an agenda that ran contrary to the American distrust of state power. Throughout the 1790s, they sought to build up a regular army, form a permanent defense establishment, and enhance federal authority. The Whiskey Rebellion and battles with Indian tribes in the Northwest gave them further opportunity: "bureaucratization accelerated dramatically in 1794, [with] a succession of new programs—for coast forts, corps of engineer and artillerists, new arsenals, ships for a navy. . . ."[31] By 1794, 40 percent of the new republic's spending was military. Yet "bureaucratization" is too lavish a term, for by comparison with any European state the Federalist agenda was modest indeed. In 1796, a French visitor to Washington was stunned to find the War Office staffed by only two clerks.[32]

The military activism of the Federalists peaked in 1798 with the quadrupling of the regular army after the XYZ Affair. During the ensuing Quasi-War with France (1798–1800), several events—passage of the Alien and Sedition Acts, the struggle between Adams and Hamilton over command of the New Army, and rising opposition to defense spending—culminated in a split in the Federalist party, the election of Jefferson, and the demise of Hamilton's vision of strengthening the state by waging war with France. The triumph of the Jeffersonian vision of a limited state, based on republican ideals rather than on military and bureaucratic power, meant the rapid demise of the Federalist Party. Jefferson's one concession to Federalism was the founding of the military academy at West Point in 1802. Otherwise the U.S. military establishment remained much as Adams had left it: an officer corps of fewer than five hundred men, a civilian bureaucracy of under a hundred, a few widely scattered forts and armories, and a small navy—this in a country that in 1803 would nearly double its territorial expanse.[33] The United States had emerged as the least bureaucratic, least militarist, least centralized—in short, the least *statist*—large state in the world.

In the six decades preceding the Civil War, the United States remained wedded to a Jeffersonian vision that at its core was both antimilitary and antistate. During this period, there were only two major wars, lasting a total of 49 months. The War of 1812 and the War with Mexico exposed similar systemic weaknesses of the American state: sectional cleavages, an ill-prepared military force, a weak national administration unequal to the task of mobilizing resources or governing its vast territory when violence threatened. British fixation on Napoleon cut short the first war, giving Americans an illusory victory and convincing them they required no urgent reforms; in the Mexican War of 1846–47, territorial expansion compensated for mediocre military performance and similarly anesthetized American reform sentiment. Victory in war in both cases had the effect of curtailing domestic reform; for this a high price would later be paid. Invaded by a foreign army for the last time in its history in 1814, the United States a year later faced no serious threats to its security from abroad. By any measure of internal power, the federal government remained diminutive and weak. In 1816, it employed only 535 employees in Washington, D.C., of which 190 were in the War and Navy departments. The Army turned to fighting Indian tribes; by 1821, it had been slashed to only 6,183 men.

The War of 1812 did have a democratizing effect, stimulating efforts in almost every state to eliminate property requirements for male suffrage. Connecticut reformers in 1816 argued that the state militia had been ineffective in the war "because young men were not very concerned about protecting a state in whose government they had no share."[34] Even in states that did not immediately extend the suffrage, the war spurred reform efforts. In Harrisonburg, Virginia, in June 1815,

> . . . a most remarkable meeting was held, composed almost wholly of non-freeholders. A committee was appointed at this meeting to prepare a petition for suffrage reform. . . . It referred pointedly to the fact that militia men had fought because they had sincerely believed they had a permanent interest in the community, although Virginia suffrage legislation rested upon contrary assumptions. If militia men had acted on these assumptions, they would not have fought and the state would have been defeated.[35]

Between 1815 and 1830, several states abolished property requirements for male suffrage; the Eastern states, whose militia were most heavily engaged in the war, led the way. The wave of democratic populism that resulted helped sweep Andrew Jackson into office—the beneficiary rather than the author of democratizing reforms, contrary to what historians once assumed.[36]

Jackson's presidency was the apex of the long peace that prevailed from 1815 to 1846. Though a war hero elected by men who won the franchise in part through military service, Jackson disdained professional soldiers, and the Army suffered from neglect or open hostility throughout the era that bears his name. Jacksonian Democrats in Congress even tried to close West Point in 1837.[37] The militias degenerated into social clubs of marginal military utility. The forcefulness of Jackson's leadership was shown in his threat to use force against South Carolina and in his determined rationalization of the federal bureaucracy. Nevertheless, he remained fully in the Jeffersonian tradition, embodying the American aversion to central power even as he wielded it—a paradox revealed in his attack on the Bank of the United States.

The Jacksonian reforms had little long-term centralizing effect. Between 1831 and 1841 (two years for which data are readily available), federal employment in Washington, D.C. increased from 666 to 1,014 persons. This represented only 5.6 percent of total federal employment, a figure lower than at the beginning of the decade. The same index crept up only marginally over the next two decades, reaching 6 percent on the eve of the Civil War. The geographical dispersion of federal officialdom was not the result of central power being extended outward into the states; rather, the bureaucracy was overwhelmingly dedicated to one objective: delivering the mail. From 1816 to 1861, civilian employment in the executive branch increased eightfold (from 4,479 to 36,106), but over 85 percent of that growth was in the postal service.[38] Thousands of post offices across the country provided patronage for the spoils system, but constituted neither a centralized state apparatus nor a source of effective federal power. A state so weak in internal sovereignty was a free state, but also an inherently fragile state.

We have seen in earlier chapters how civil wars are often provoked in part by external wars. There are several reasons for this: war exposes the internal defects of a state; the increased power of central government during war provokes resentment; the end of an external war causes national unity to decline. These same patterns ensued in the War with Mexico, which aggravated sectionalism and helped to provoke the Civil War. The effect was more delayed than in other civil wars we have examined, but the causal chain was real and direct. Support for the war was sectionally divided; highly popular in the South, it was deplored in much of the North, where a vigorous antiwar movement existed (Lincoln was among its ranks.) The settlement with Mexico intensified Northern concerns over the future of slavery, but Northern attempts to limit slavery in the new territories, such as the Wilmot Proviso, spurred deep resentment in the South; for the first time Whigs and Democrats divided along sectional rather than party lines. Finally, the fact that the majority of troops sent to Mexico were from the South also aggravated sectional cleavages, while solidifying Southern identity and military confidence.[39] Yet given that by 1850 American territory was three times the size it had been in 1800, the real historical question is not why the Civil War took place ten years later, but how such a vast state, decentralized and demilitarized, held itself together at all in the decades prior to the war.

CIVIL WAR AND RECONSTRUCTION

Prior to leaving Springfield for Washington, Lincoln told an army officer, "I must run the machine as I find it."[40] In truth, there was not much of a machine to run. There were approximately 16,000 men in the U.S. army in 1860; the federal government's budget was $63 million; and a mere 2,199 persons worked in its central offices in Washington. Of these, fewer than 1,000 were in the War and Navy Departments.[41] The notion that such a diminutive state could hang on to a territory larger than France, England, and Germany combined, whose entire population was in mass rebellion, appeared ludicrous to outside observers. Yet four years after the attack on Fort Sumter, a fiscal-military revolution had transpired: the federal budget had soared to over $1.2 billion, and the Union fielded an army of over one million men—the largest, best equipped, best fed, and most powerful war machine ever assembled in the history of the world to that date. In proportion to the base from which it began, it was the largest mobilization in American history.[42] As for the federal bureaucracy, despite shedding thousands of employees in the South, it had mushroomed into a centralized apparatus of over 53,000 persons. Behind both Army and bureaucracy stood a radically transformed Presidency wielding authoritarian power over almost every aspect of Union life. The Confederacy, too, had undergone a fiscal-military process of state formation that had gone much further in creating a strong central administration than is generally realized.[43]

The rebellion of the South was by far the greatest revolt against sovereignty in American history. The Union defeat of that revolt consequently sustained and permanently enhanced the sovereign power that had been challenged. Chapter 1 observed that civil wars sometimes strengthen a state in the long run by resolving the issues that rent it in the first place. In the American case, the Civil War decisively settled the question of whether or not the Union was dissoluble. The possible secession of individual states or the break-up of the entire Union had bedeviled the American republic numerous times before 1860; it has never been even a minor issue since. By confirming the permanence and supremacy of federal power, the war shifted the basis of national legitimacy at least partly back toward its Hamiltonian and Federalist roots.

THE CIVIL WAR AND STATE PENETRATION OF THE NATIONAL ECONOMY

The Civil War prefigured not only the massive firepower, extended fronts, and complex logistics of World War I, but also the economic mobilization integral to that war.[44] In connection with the war the Lincoln administration attempted to intervene in areas of the national life and economy that the federal government had never touched before. At the onset of the war, the weakness of the federal government made this effort ineffectual and haphazard—Lincoln was shocked to find the Washington Armory totally unguarded months into the war—but over time the effects of economic mobilization on the battlefield were immense. By penetrating the American economy at numerous points and in a variety of previously untried ways, the federal government significantly altered the relationship between state and economy in America. Some of those ways are discussed below.

Purchasing Power
Prior to 1861, the national government had been a minor purchaser in the American economy. During the war, it became the largest single purchaser in the country, a catalyst of rapid growth in key industries such as iron, textiles, shoe manufacturing, and meat packing. In Philadelphia, industrialists built 58 new factories in 1862, 57 in 1863, and 65 more in 1864. Iron mills proliferated in New York, Pennsylvania, and New Jersey, with six mills erected in Pittsburgh in one year. Pig-iron production increased 30 percent; shoe production doubled; woolen mills increased their output in the cotton-starved north by 62 percent. The massive federal procurement effort influenced prices, investment patterns, and financial practices throughout the economy, and also stimulated Congressional efforts to impose stricter regulation.[45]

Direct Production
The urgent pressure to procure war-related items led the federal government to establish and operate its own manufacturing facilities, something it had never previously attempted outside the armaments industry. There were federal clothing factories in Cincinnati and Philadelphia; pharmaceutical laboratories in New York, Philadelphia, and St. Louis; meat-packing facilities in Knoxville and Louisville. Federal arms factories also expanded, the most prominent of which was the Springfield Armory in Massachusetts. At the peak of the conflict, it had 3,000 employees and produced 350,000 rifles annually, one third of the national output.

Taxation Reform

The Civil War spawned a revolution in taxation that permanently altered the structure of American federalism and the relationship of the central government to the national economy. Prior to the war, over 80 percent of federal revenue had come from customs duties, but despite numerous upward revisions of the tariffs during the war, those could provide only a fraction of what was needed to sustain the Union armies. On August 5, 1861, the first income tax in U.S. history came into effect, followed by the Internal Revenue Act of 1862, which levied a whole series of new taxes: stamp taxes, excise taxes, luxury taxes, gross receipts taxes, an inheritance tax, and value-added taxes on manufactured goods. The latter Act also created the Bureau of Internal Revenue, perhaps the single most effective vehicle of federal power ever created:

> Reaching into almost every hamlet and town through a network of 185 collection districts, [it] rapidly became the most coercive civilian agency of the national government. Aside from the military itself, no other bureaucratic expansion in the nineteenth century brought so many citizens into direct contact with central state authority.[46]

By 1864, 41 percent of federal revenue came from internal sources; by 1865, 63 percent. This shift proved to be permanent: prior to the war, the ratio of internal revenues to total receipts had averaged barely over 1 percent; after 1865, it never once dropped below 32 percent, notwithstanding the abolition of the income tax in the 1870s. Numerous other taxes—sin taxes, excise taxes, inheritance taxes, etc.—remained permanently in place after the war.[47]

Fiscal and Monetary Reform

The formation of an internal revenue system was part of a larger Civil War revolution in the nation's financial structure. In February 1862, Congress enacted the Legal Tender Act, authorizing the Treasury to issue $150 million in notes, "greenback dollars" not covered by hard specie. The creation of a national currency forever altered the monetary structure of the United States. "It asserted national sovereignty to help win a war to preserve that sovereignty."[48] By 1865, Congress had authorized issuance of $450 million worth of greenbacks, and federally-issued paper money remained has the national currency ever since.

Neither taxes nor paper dollars, however, came close to covering the enormous costs of the war. Dire fiscal straits forced the federal government to borrow over 80 percent of its cost, or more than $2.6

billion. Here, too, a dual metamorphosis occurred, with important
long-term implications. First, the Lincoln administration created a
captive source of credit by granting a monopoly on issuance of the
new national currency to banks that agreed to purchase large quantities of federal bonds. The National Banking Acts of 1863 and 1864 also
imposed a 10 percent tax on certificates issued by state-chartered
banks, thus virtually compelling the large Eastern banks to purchase
federal bonds in order to obtain the new greenback currency. But to
qualify to purchase the federal bonds, the banks had to agree to accept
federal regulation and federal charters. Thus, almost overnight, a
national banking system came into being. It was dominated by large
banks in urban and industrial centers that could meet the minimum
capital requirement for federal incorporation of $50,000 in bond pur-
chases.

The second component of the government's deficit financing was
the sale to the public of $1.2 billion of war bonds in denominations as
low as 50 dollars, payable in monthly installments. This greatly broadened the base of the national debt and gave tens of thousands of ordinary citizens a stake in their government. If the Banking Act was elitist
and procapitalist in nature, the bond sales were democratic and egalitarian. They tied the financial fortunes of diverse socioeconomic classes to the fortunes of the federal government in a manner analogous to
the role that Revolutionary War debt had played in 1787. Historians
still dispute whether or not the financial revolution of the Civil War
was a factor in accelerating postwar industrialization, but its effects on
political development are less debatable. Eric Foner writes that the fiscal measures represented in their "unprecedented expansion of federal
power . . . what might be called the birth of the modern American
state."[49]

Institutional Formation

Another component of state-building during the Civil War that facilitated societal penetration by the federal government was the creation
of new administrative institutions. In addition to the Bureau of Internal Revenue, the war saw the founding of the Department of Agriculture, the Bureau of Immigration, and the National Academy of
Sciences, founded in 1863 in the hope of harnessing science for the
war effort. An activist Congress passed the Homestead Act of 1862, the
Morrill Agricultural College Act of 1862, and the Immigration Act of
1864; it also established the Union Pacific and Central Pacific Railroad
companies as federally chartered corporations. All these measures had
some link to the war effort—it was vital to retain Western support

against the South, to protect industry from competition, and to obtain cheap labor from abroad—but their long-term thrust was to favor industrial growth, westward expansion, and the interests of Eastern urban capital over those of agriculture. Appomattox thus represented not just the defeat of the South, but the defeat of the whole Southern economic and political system, and the triumph of a state-fostered industrial and financial complex in the North.

THE CIVIL WAR AND STATE REPRESSION

In addition to thrusting the central state more deeply into the American economy, the Civil War brought about an increase in the repressive power of the federal government, an effect perhaps more psychological in its long-term effects than legal or Constitutional. Federal authority intruded into the lives and violated the rights of American citizens to a extent that had never been seen before. Less than two weeks after Fort Sumter fell, Lincoln suspended the writ of habeas corpus in Maryland; he eventually suspended it in other states as well, resulting in thousands of arrests without judicial process. And in August 1862 the War Department authorized U.S. and local officials to arrest and detain persons engaged in any "disloyal practice." The same orders permitted civilians to be tried before military commissions. In the view of one historian, Mark Neely, the subsequent arrests constituted "the lowest point for civil liberties in U.S. history to that time, and one of the lowest for civil liberties in all of American history."[50]

Another manifestation of the expanded repressive power of the federal government was the introduction of national conscription for the first time under the authority of the Enrollment Act of March 3, 1863. The main effect of conscription was to dramatically boost the number of volunteer enrollees; large numbers of draftees also furnished substitutes or paid a commutation fee of $300 to avoid service. As a result, less than 8 percent of the 2,100,000 men who served in the Union Army were conscripts; all the rest were at least nominally volunteers. But despite the small numbers actually drafted, the expansion of federal power inherent in the conscription law stirred deep resentment. The draft ignited the largest civil insurrections in American history outside the rebellion of the Confederacy itself. In the cities and towns of the Eastern seaboard and Midwest, scores perished in the rioting, including 38 federal draft officials. Union troops fresh from the victory at Gettysburg were required to restore order to New York City, where the worst violence occurred. Nor was this the only occasion during the war in which the national armed forces served as the final bulwark of state power in the North: the army also intervened to quell strikes at arms factories in New York and Missouri and in the minefields of Pennsylvania.[51]

Another example of repressive power during the war was the widespread seizure of private property by national authorities, in the North as well as the South. The most significant action involved the railroads. In January 1862, Congress authorized Lincoln to seize any railroad line that public safety required. In the North, he used the authority sparingly, but the threat of federal intervention ensured that military traffic received priority and that the rail companies made needed repairs promptly. In the South, federal authorities seized a total of 2,100 miles of track that fell behind Union lines. U.S. Military Railroads, a military-civilian organization of 25,000 employees, operated the system. Though the railroads were the only industry over which the federal government asserted its sovereignty during the war, the action extended the perimeter of acceptable state power and set a precedent that would be evoked in World Wars I and II.

Repression of dissent did not create a dictatorship as some had feared. Neely points out that Lincoln used his power judiciously, and rarely against opponents of the war or of his administration as long as they did not collaborate with the South; most military arrests of civilians occurred in the Southern states. Though the administration forcibly closed a handful of opposition newspapers, it imposed no general press censorship. A loyal opposition functioned throughout the war; the press never stopped criticizing Lincoln; and Congress established a Committee on the Conduct of the War to oversee the executive branch. But wartime conscription and repression left a deep and enduring impression on the public in the Northern states as to the potential power and reach of the federal government, with which most citizens had never had dealings beyond the Post Office. The war thus altered the attitudes and perceptions of Americans regarding their government in ways that were profound, pervasive, and permanent.

THE CIVIL WAR AND THE NEW AMERICAN NATIONALISM

Woodrow Wilson in 1915 described the main achievement of the Civil War as "the creation in this country of what had never existed before—a national consciousness."[52] It was a logical conclusion coming from the Southern-born scholar whose doctrine of the self-determination of nations would do as much to stimulate nationalism in Central Europe as Lincoln did in America. But in fact the unique contribution of the Civil War was not national consciousness but the irrevocable commitment of that consciousness to the constitutional structure established in 1787. The population in the North was initially ambivalent about fighting to preserve the Union, but the fact of war itself generated a surge of nationalism that both won the war and redefined the nation. Prior to 1860, America had been a sovereign state, if a loosely structured one; only after 1865 did it become a nation-state as well.

The Civil War imparted a new social mobility to American society that diminished regional and local loyalties and encouraged the transference of public allegiance to the central state. The integrative effect of military service also broadened the basis of American nationalism. Some 200,000 black soldiers served in the war, nearly 37,000 of whom perished by combat or disease.[53] Their service was evoked in the debate over passage of the Civil Rights Act of 1866 and the 14th and 15th Amendments; the latter provided the minimal constitutional basis for integrating the former slave population into the American nation— long delayed and troubled though that integration would be.

The war had other integrative and socializing effects as well. It revived the American labor movement and gave impetus to the budding women's movement, as hundreds of thousands of female workers replaced men on factory lines and farms, dispelling myths of female inadequacy and stimulating social activism. The campaign for female suffrage began in earnest after the war, though it took another major conflict, World War I, to bring it to success.[54]

THE AFTERMATH OF THE WAR: RECONSTRUCTION AND INDUSTRIALIZATION

The precipitous demobilization that followed the war was a striking act of exceptionalism, reflecting both the absence of foreign enemies and a uniquely American ambivalence about military and political power. Within less than a year after Appomattox, the Army had shrunk to only 57,000 men; by the end of Reconstruction in 1877, to barely over 24,000. The federal bureaucracy also contracted, though not so drastically; in 1871, there were still 6,222 civilian employees in Washington, far fewer than during the war but still double the prewar figure. Yet of these, only 237 had permanent slots in the War and Navy Departments. The Presidency retained little of the prestige or authority that had prevailed under Lincoln. Andrew Johnson, his immediate successor, was impeached and lost virtually all power to a radical Congress; the next President, General Ulysses S. Grant of wartime fame, ran an ineffectual administration mired in corruption. No European state had ever demobilized so quickly or totally after a major war, for in Europe, it is assumed that the adversary will live to fight another day. In America, insular geography and federal structure reasserted themselves strongly after 1865.

The rapidity of postwar demobilization did not portend, however, a return to a Jeffersonian state. Beneath the chaos and corruption of the Reconstruction period, the effects of the war continued to influence the content and direction of American politics. By starkly demonstrating the power of government to bring about radical change, the war stimulated public awareness of the positive utility of political power. One effect was a marked increase after 1865 in governmental activism throughout American society. This was true not only at the national level but at state and local levels as well. "Between 1860 and 1870, taxes tripled in five Northern states, quintupled in Michigan, and rose by six times in New Jersey. . . ."[55] After the war, city budgets increased in both the Northern and Southern states, while state and local governments made large new investments in public works and public health facilities. As Allan Nevins has cogently argued, one of the most important effects of the war was to transform an unorganized nation into an organized one, with an impetus toward every higher degrees of organization.[56]

At the national level, the war advanced social welfare reform via the classic Titmussian linkages discussed in Chapter 5. The first national welfare programs in U.S. history stemmed from the disability pensions provided to injured veterans and their survivors. Civil War veterans, organized in the encompassing "Grand Army of the Republic," constituted a large and activist segment of the postwar electorate. Competition for their votes led Congress (in the Arrears Act of 1879 and the Dependent Pension Act of 1890) to expand the original 1862 pension act into a de facto old-age and disability-pension program for all veterans over age 62, both Union and Confederate, including those who had served only briefly or had suffered no injury. Given the large numbers this entailed, the veterans' program was the closest thing the United States had to a comprehensive social welfare program prior to the New Deal.[57]

Veterans' pensions are also one reason why federal spending remained so high after 1865; the federal budget was 4.6 percent of national income in 1869 versus 1.5 percent in 1859.[58] But even when

Table 7–1.   Federal proportion of total domestic governmental
              expenditures, 1840–1913.

PREWAR		POSTWAR	
Year	Federal proportion	Year	Federal proportion
1840	.16	1870	.33
1852	.22	1880	.28
1860	.13	1890	.31

Source: William Paul Alexander, Jr., "The Measurement of American Federalism," in
William H. G. Riker, *The Development of American Federalism* (Boston: Kluwer
Academic Publishers, 1987), p. 103.

interest payments and veterans' compensation are factored out, as
being essentially sunk costs of the war effort, the ratio of civil expenditures to total civil plus military expenditures still indicated a dramatic
shift: from an average of 35 percent in the prewar period to an average
of 65 percent in the postwar period from 1870 to the Spanish-American War.[59] The American state was simply larger and more activist
after the Civil War than before. This new state activism was clearly a
long-term effect of the war itself and not simply a secondary consequence of Reconstruction, for the shift in federal spending priorities
continued after 1877.[60] Another long-term index of how the Civil War
contributed to the centralization of the American state is the ratio of
federal domestic spending to total governmental domestic spending
(federal, state, and local). Since the capacity to spend flows from the
capacity to tax, this is a rough measure of the balance between local
and central political power in the American system. Table 7–1 shows
the index for the three decades before the Civil War and the three
decades after it. The marked increase from the prewar to the postwar
period demonstrates the manifest centralizing effect of the war.

   None of this should be taken to suggest that the American state had
now become a "strong" state on the European model. By European
standards, the American state remained weak and decentralized. The
postwar state was certainly stronger than the antebellum one, but it
remained structurally and politically limited in the degree of its internal authority. This can be seen both in the rapid decline of federal
power in the South after 1865, leading to the failure of Reconstruction,
and in the exceptionally stormy course of American industrialization
in the post-Reconstruction era.

   The Radical Republican vision of remaking the South in the image
of the North reached its apex from 1867 to 1869, when Congress

imposed military rule on the South and mandated the rewriting of its state constitutions. The historiography of Reconstruction, dominated prior to 1960 by Southern academics, for too long gave the era an image of sweeping radicalism and punitive harshness. Yet in retrospect what is most striking about Reconstruction is not the loftiness of its aims nor the strength of its execution, but the magnitude of its failure. The reality was that, militarily and bureaucratically, the North either never had or quickly relinquished the means necessary to impose a new social order on the South. Reconstruction did not fail because it applied too much coercive power, but because it had too little.

The Federal government's main agents for effecting change in Southern society were the federal army and the Freedmen's Bureau. At peak strength, the Bureau had only 900 agents in the South, with only twelve in Mississippi in 1866, and never more than twenty in Alabama. There were a few thousand other federal officials in the South, but these were mostly postal and customs workers. The Freedmen's Bureau was impotent without military backing, yet by 1867 the *entire* U.S. army consisted of only 57,000 troops, of which only slightly more than 15,000 were deployed in the South, not counting those engaged in border defense or in fighting Indians in Texas. This represented one solider per 725 inhabitants, hardly a ratio conducive to wielding federal power effectively. By 1870, the number had declined to 6,600; by 1876, to 3,000.[61] The U.S. military presence sufficed—barely—to police large cities, appoint and remove governors and other officials, censor the press, and supervise elections; it was woefully inadequate to protect the rights of former slaves, much less remake the fabric of Southern society, which resented and resisted it at every step, often violently. That greater armed force might have made a difference—in protecting black citizens, if not in remaking Southern society—is shown in the partial successes obtained by federal troops against the Ku Klux Klan during the wave of Klan terrorism that swept the South from 1868 to 1871.[62]

The main hope for Reconstruction's long-term success was the survival of a viable Republican Party in the South. Where it could, the army acted to bolster Republican prospects by disenfranchising former Confederate officials, encouraging loyalist sentiment, and preventing the intimidation of black voters. But its shrinking garrisons were spread too thin to prevent a Republican collapse. Richard Bensel has shown a correlation between the presence of federal troops in Southern counties and the support for the Republican party in the 1868 and 1876 presidential elections. He argues that a more forceful approach to Reconstruction, employing more troops and a larger administrative presence, might have prevented the collapse of the party and enabled it to acquire enduring roots.[63]

A further indication of the weakness of the American state in the last decades of the nineteenth century was its inadequacy in coping with industrial growth. The period from 1870 to 1900 witnessed the most violent clashes between labor and capital ever to occur in any industrializing country. In an attempt to cope, American leaders engaged in what Stephan Skowronek has called "patching," the ad hoc improvisation of administrative solutions for the problems of industrial development.[64] Absent a military threat, the American system had difficulty making structural changes. Unable to cope with widespread labor unrest through effective reform measures, American leaders at both the state and national level resorted to the last bastion of public order: military force. Between 1870 and 1900, the National Guard was mobilized some 150 times to cope with industrial disputes (though, significantly, not once did it serve under federal authority, as the Constitution allows). Only when the militia proved ineffectual did Federal troops intervene—in eight states during the Great Strike of 1877, in eleven states during the labor disturbances of 1894, and in the Coeur d'Alene mining region of Idaho on three occasions in the 1890s.[65] Hampered by its own structural impotence as the Industrial Age unfolded, the American state could only resort to repressive power and political improvisation.

The patchwork nature of American reform began to change with the electoral successes of the Progressive movement after 1900, but not decisively so until World War I. Even the Spanish-American War, which exposed critical problems in the army, was too brief a conflict and too easy a victory to generate significant pressure for reform. It is nevertheless interesting that the ascendancy of the Progressive movement coincided both with the period of High Imperialism in Europe and with the brief imperialist phase of the American state. The same belief in the utility of state power that motivated the Social-Imperialists in Europe motivated the Progressives in America, and in both cases international activism coincided with—and partly motivated— internal reform. In America, the partisan poles of this tendency were Theodore Roosevelt and Woodrow Wilson. The former spoke of national greatness and military might while presiding over peace; the latter glorified peace and progress while leading the nation into war and repression.

WORLD WAR I AND THE WILSONIAN REVOLUTION IN GOVERNMENT

America's participation in the First World War was even shorter than the War of 1812, but far more intense. In the nineteen months that passed from the declaration of war to the Armistice of November 1918, the United States drafted 2.8 million men, transported two million of them to Europe, and lost over 100,000 soldiers in combat. Federal spending increased nearly 1,000 percent, and the size of the federal bureaucracy more than doubled. "Patching" came to a decisive end as the federal government asserted its authority vigorously throughout the American economy—regulating industry, imposing price controls, and intervening in labor disputes. World War I was more industrialized than any previous conflict, with armor-plated fleets, submarines, airplanes, machine guns, mechanized artillery, and tanks transforming the face of battle. The cost per soldier was immense, rising by 1918 to nearly seven times that of the Civil War in constant dollars.[66] The cost and complexity of mechanized warfare drove a vigorous fiscal-military process of government centralization and growth.

A complex of federal agencies—the War Industries Board, the Shipping Board, the Fuel Administration, the War Finance Corporation, the Railroad Administration, the War Trade Board, the Bureau of Aircraft Production, and a host of other boards, bureaus, and commissions—sought to mobilize American manpower and industry in support of what was then the largest overseas military intervention ever undertaken by any state. The war saw the first significant use of the corporate form of organization by Washington, the dissolution of former restraints on the establishment of government agencies independent of the cabinet departments, and the first direct federal aid to state and local governments. The war thus wrenched the American state into the industrial age and brought the structure of the federal government more into line with the requirements of an increasingly complex American society and economy.

Despite its brevity, World War I generated intense fiscal and bureaucratic expansion. Adjusted for inflation, annual per capita spending during the war was nearly twice as high as in either the Civil War or World War II—in purely fiscal terms, it was the most intense conflict the nation ever fought. Federal outlays soared from $713 million in 1916 to $1.95 billion in 1917, $12.7 billion in 1918, and $18.5

billion in 1919—a 2,500 percent increase in less than three years.[67] A significant ratchet effect followed as postwar spending failed to drop below $2.85 billion (1927), still four times the 1916 level. The challenge of financing the war had a profound effect on the fiscal mechanisms of the federal government, including the Federal Reserve System, established in 1913; in the course of the war, it became a more centralized and subservient arm of the Treasury, acquiring much of the importance and function that it holds today in the American banking system.[68]

In virtually all cases of state-building since the Renaissance, war-induced taxation was the wedge by which state power advanced. The United States in World War I conformed to the historical pattern, despite the fact that over three fourths of the cost of the war was funded by borrowing. The Income Tax Amendment ratified in 1913 had been a minor source of federal revenue until Congress passed the Wartime Revenue Act of October 1917. The Act lowered the exemptions on all taxpayers, while drastically elevating taxes on the upper income brackets—from a maximum of 13 percent in 1916 to a maximum of 67 percent during the war. This elevation of the top brackets was in accord with a long held Progressive position, but it was probably of lesser long-term significance than the *doubling* (from 2 to 4 percent) of the lowest or "normal" tax bracket. The number of tax returns filed jumped from 437,036 in 1916 to 3,472,890 in 1917, then doubled again by 1920. Never before had federal taxation affected so many Americans so directly.[69] The Revenue Act of 1918 went further, increasing the total income-tax load on American citizens by nearly 250 percent over the 1917 Act. The top bracket reached 77 percent, while the "normal" tax bracket rose to 6 percent. The burgeoning tax burden also included corporate income taxes, a war estate tax, excise and import taxes, and an excess-profits tax.

The tax legislation of World War I permanently altered the structure of American taxation. Not only did this legislation greatly elevate the importance of the income tax, but it made the principle of progression a permanent fixture of the nation's tax system. On the eve of entry into the war, personal and corporate income taxes constituted only 24 percent of internal revenue. This figure rose sharply during the war and remained high afterward, averaging 75 percent throughout the 1920s. Federal tax receipts never again dropped lower than five times the prewar level. World War I thus catalyzed the transformation of the income tax—the most direct and intrusive of all forms of revenue extraction—into becoming the mainstay of American federal financing.[70]

Revenue from war bonds and the income tax not only fed and supplied the American Expeditionary Force, but also funded a burgeoning
army of civilians who manned the machinery of state at home. In
1916, civilian employment in the Executive Branch numbered
391,133. During the war, the federal government hired over 453,000
civil servants, more than doubling the size of the bureaucracy in only
two years. By 1923, postwar layoffs had eliminated some two thirds of
these jobs, resulting in a permanent net gain of 141,000 employees—a
30 percent "ratchet effect." This growth did not take place only or primarily in the war-related components of the government, but across
almost all agencies. By mid–1920, when demobilization had ended,
the only federal agencies that had *not* experienced net growth were the
Interstate Commerce Commission, the Smithsonian Institution, and
the Panama Canal Company (which had finished building the Canal
in 1914). Treasury had gained nearly 40,000 employees, Commerce
8,000; and State, Justice, Interior, Agriculture, Labor, and the Post
Office had all grown in size despite the acute labor shortage, which
hampered industrial support of the military.[71]

The bureaucratic growth that resulted from World War I was of
obvious long-term import for the structure of the U.S. government.
But the enhancement of the power of the Presidency that accompanied
the expansion was even more significant. A series of legislative measures passed in 1916 and 1917 gave the Wilson administration
unprecedented authority to intervene in the national economy. The
National Defense Act compelled factories to sell their products to the
government on a priority basis at prices determined by the Secretary
of War.[72] The Army Appropriations Act authorized the seizure of
transportation. (Taking a page from Lincoln, Wilson used this to take
control of all U.S. railroads in December 1917.) The Lever Act
imposed presidential authority on food and fuel production. Together,
these acts effectively subjected the entire industrial, agricultural and
transportation base of the United States to direct federal control.
"Never before had such sweeping powers of economic control been
granted by Congress to the President."[73]

The Lever Act also established the U.S. Food Administration, but
otherwise the above statutes left the president without an effective
bureaucratic structure through which to exercise his enlarged powers.
The Overman Act of May 1918 remedied this, giving Wilson vast
authority to restructure the Executive Branch. The Act was a milestone
in the advance of presidential power in the United States.[74] It resulted
in the creation of numerous new federal agencies, the most powerful
of which was the War Industries Board (WIB) under Bernard Baruch.

As the primary instrument for mobilizing U.S. industrial capacity, the WIB placed the U.S. industry under a system of production schedules tied to Army requirements, and set prices for raw materials.[75] Though the WIB tried to cooperate with companies and avoid confrontational tactics it had the power to cut off fuel supplies, redirect shipments to other plants, and seize factories if necessary.

Given that one fourth of total U.S. GNP was going to the Army, the magnitude of the WIB's task was immense. With only 750 employees, it worked largely through joint government-industry committees, an arrangement that strengthened ties between the state and the private sector. The WIB's wartime activities thus permanently altered the relationship between business and government in the United States.[76] Symptomatic of the new relationship was the large number of industrial trade associations formed to enable business to deal with federal regulation in a coordinated fashion. In 1914, there were 800 trade associations in the United States; by 1919, their ranks had swelled to 4,000! When the war ended, it was industry and not government that clamored for the WIB to continue regulating prices and markets. Only Baruch's insistence that the Board dissolve itself prevented its continuation as a postwar recovery agency. But though government regulation greatly diminished in the 1920s, World War I left the line between public and private interests blurred. The war that was a watershed in Europe was a watershed in the development of the American state as well.

WORLD WAR I AND STATE REPRESSION

The high degree of national unity attained during World War I was enforced in part by repression and was not simply the result of a wartime "rallying effect." Prior to the war, Wilson reportedly had stated that if Americans entered the war, "they'll forget there ever was such a thing as tolerance. To fight you must be brutal and ruthless, and the spirit of ruthless brutality will enter into the very fibre of our national life. . . ."[77] Perhaps Wilson had his own self in mind, for his subsequent crusading zeal bore partial responsibility for a sharp increase in government repression during World War I: the forceful quelling of dissent, the persecution of minorities and aliens, the attacks on Socialist and labor organizations, the coercive marketing of war bonds, arbitrary arrests and imprisonment, censorship of the media and of personal speech. These civil rights violations occurred at all levels of government and were exacerbated by a climate of public hostility toward dissent that promoted widespread mob violence and vigilantism. Among the more egregious abuses were the hundreds of prosecutions brought under the Espionage Act of June 1917 and the Sedition Act of May 1918, which made even verbal opposition to the war illegal. A Wisconsin official received a thirty-month sentence for criticizing a Red Cross fund-raising drive; a Hollywood producer, a ten-year sentence for a film that portrayed atrocities committed by British troops during the Revolutionary War.[78] All told, as many as 8,000 to 10,000 Americans faced imprisonment, official suppression, deportation, or mob violence during the war.[79]

Most dissent during World War I was prosecuted at state and local levels, with the Justice Department and federal courts rendering critical backing to local efforts. The Wilson administration also created two new agencies—the Censorship Board and the Committee on Public Information—that exercised broad discretion over what could be published by the press. Another tool of repression was the Post Office, previously a font of political patronage and indirect power, but never of direct state power. This changed when the Espionage Act instructed the Postmaster General to withhold mailing privileges from publications deemed injurious to the war effort; at least 75 publications were banned under this authority. In addition to conducting censorship, the Committee on Public Information also undertook a massive propaganda effort aimed at promoting patriotic feeling and boosting popular support for the war; it distributed millions of propaganda pamphlets, published a bulletin to help public school teachers inculcate nationalism in their pupils, and sponsored a small army of public speakers. All of this went beyond censorship into that quintessentially modern form of state power, the manipulation of public opinion.[80]

Wartime repression reached its apex in the formation of numerous private or quasi-official organizations to supplement official control, among them the American Defense Society, the National Security League, the Knights of Liberty, the Home Defense League, and the All-Allied Anti-German League. Nativist and anti-intellectual, these groups espoused a chauvinistic brand of nationalism and sought to enforce public support of the war. The largest of such organizations, the American Protective League or APL, was sponsored in part by the Justice Department. It had hundreds of units and over 250,000 members who conducted private but federally sanctioned investigations into the loyalty of their fellow citizens—proceedings of dubious legality that often veered into vigilantism. Americans briefly experienced what it was like to have a pervasive network of informers reporting on their private speech and activities. "That an organization such as the APL was allowed to exist at all testifies to the unusual state of American society in World War I."[81] Though much of the apparatus of wartime repression was dismantled after 1918, World War I left an altered balance of power between state and society that made future assertions of state sovereignty more feasible—beginning with the New Deal.

WORLD WAR I AND THE BROADENING OF
AMERICAN NATIONALISM

The Great War was a period of intensified social and economic mobility that, by a variety of indices, moved the American system nearer to the status of a true mass state, one in which formal barriers to mass political participation were abolished and class distinctions became less important. As in Great Britain and Germany, endemic labor disturbances from 1915 to 1919 only strengthened the hand of American unions vis-à-vis national and local authorities, who were quick to compromise for the sake of wartime production. The demand for labor bolstered the trade union movement, whose ranks grew from 3.1 million members in 1917 to 5.1 million by 1920. Though the aggregate size of the female labor force did not increase nearly as much as it later would in World War II, an important shift in female employment did take place: women moved in large numbers from household work and traditionally female occupations to employment in businesses and factories. From 1910 to 1920, the number of women employed as laborers or semiskilled operatives in manufacturing increased by over 400,000, and numerous inroads were made into other skilled occupations and professions traditionally dominated by men.[82] Wartime labor shortages also opened new employment opportunities for Southern blacks, greatly accelerating their migration from the South to northern cities.

Such social effects had political side effects. As in the Civil War, World War I broadened the basis of American nationalism, as new social groups received citizenship and suffrage. For American women, the integrative effects of the war culminated less than six months after the Armistice in the passage by Congress of the 19th Amendment, granting female suffrage. Congress also granted all Native Americans U.S. citizenship in 1924, largely in response to the contributions of 10,000 Indian volunteers in the war. The one segment of American society that gained little from the integrative impetus of the conflict was African-Americans, who in many states were still denied genuine rights of suffrage and legal redress. Having fought in record numbers in the war, blacks had expected that their service would finally be rewarded with recognition of their civil rights; they returned instead to the "Bloody Summer" of 1919 and the worst racial violence since Reconstruction.[83]

WAR COLLECTIVISM AND THE COMING OF THE NEW DEAL

Prior to World War I, Wilson had expressed concern that the conflict would mean the end of progressive reform, and other Progressive leaders such as Jane Addams and Senator Bob La Follette had been similarly apprehensive.[84] The decline of the Progressive movement after 1918 amply bore out their misgivings. Given that the end of American wars usually sees a decline in the power of the Presidency, it is also no surprise that the decade of the 1920s was one of relatively ineffectual presidents. The surface froth of the 1920s, however, obscured the very real impact of the war in stimulating collectivist thinking and boosting public support for collectivist solutions. In this way, the experience of World War I helped pave the way for public support of the New Deal with its statist approach to economic recovery.

There were, after all, in 1917, other Progressives, both Democratic and Republican, who had welcomed the coming of the war, seeing it as a potential catalyst of social change. Much like the Social-Imperialists of Europe, they hoped that by magnifying state power the war would foster the implementation of reform. Walter Lippmann, John Dewey, Herbert Croly and other thinkers linked with *The New Republic* were among them, as well as Progressive Republicans such as Theodore Roosevelt and William Allen White. They wanted a strong central state and a socialized economy, efficiently administered by strong, progressive leaders. And to a lesser degree than in Western Europe, World War I did stimulate social welfare reforms: the Women's Bureau was launched in 1918 as a wartime agency; the Children's Bureau (formed in 1912) enjoyed rapid growth; and the Sheppard-Towner Bill providing federal aid to local health programs gained great impetus (though it was not actually passed until 1921).[85] Lippmann wrote effusively in 1917 of "national collectivism . . . so deadly in war, so full of benign possibilities for peace, so capable of being used for a war after the war."[86]

The repression of the war years caused some Progressives to doubt that progressive ends could really justify coercive means. But enthusiasm for state power overcame qualms about its possible abuse. After the Armistice was signed, *The New Republic* carried a remarkable paean to the collectivist order of the war:

> The whole issue hinges on social control. For forty years we have been widening the sphere of this control, subordinating the individual to the group and the group to society. Without such control, vastly magnified, we should not have been able to carry on the war. . . . We conscripted lives, property and services; we took over railroads, telegraphs and other economic instruments. We fixed wages, prices, the quantity of coal, power, labor or transportation a man might command, and the quantity of food he might consume. . . . All this we did on the narrowest of legal bases, for no one dared question our power.

Portraying American society as "fluid as molten iron" and capable of being directed into any mold, *The New Republic* called for the continuation of wartime controls as tools for remaking American society.[87] Such sentiments were shared by many of Wilson's war managers, and the early debate on postwar reconstruction revolved around how much of the wartime federal structure to preserve.

Ideological proponents and bureaucratic defenders of the wartime agencies fought to convert them into permanent agencies during 1919 and 1920. Wilsonian activists formed an Industrial Board in the Commerce Department and a High Cost of Living Division in the Justice Department. The Fuel Administration was revived briefly, and a series of federally sponsored Industrial Conferences sought to revitalize the labor-management détente of the war period. But by 1921, the only surviving bureaucratic vestiges of war mobilization were those involved in the regulation of public transportation.[88] But though the traditional American aversion to central power asserted itself strongly in the decade after 1918, the collectivism of World War I nonetheless made a lasting impression on the political appointees and dollar-a-year industrialists who had spearheaded it, as well as on the Progressives and socialists of the Left who celebrated it. Even Herbert Hoover's experience as head of the Food Administration during the war probably contributed to his later interest in revitalizing antitrust and regulatory agencies such as the Federal Trade and Interstate Commerce Commissions.

The lessons of World War I for social reform were magnified in 1930–31, after the magnitude of the economic crisis facing America became apparent. In the ensuing national debate, the war years were often evoked as a possible model for recovery. Bernard Baruch and

William Gibbs McAdoo called for the formation of a Peace Industries Board patterned after the WIB. A movement of former war administrators and industrialists, with the support of the American Legion, called for "economic government" and the establishment of a revamped Council of National Defense. Even Hoover, while rejecting central planning, proposed a new federal lending corporation based on the War Finance Corporation. Faced with an unprecedented national crisis, Americans looked to their most recent war, the high point of cooperative and collectivist endeavor in their history, in search of a solution.[89]

Franklin Roosevelt's own views of government had been profoundly shaped by his service as Assistant Secretary of the Navy under Wilson, and he evoked the analogy of World War I extensively. In the 1932 primary campaign, he proclaimed, "we are in a crisis in our national life comparable to war." As the Democratic nominee, he expanded on the theme:

> Fifteen years ago my public duty called me to an active part in a great national emergency—the World War. . . .
>
> The generalship of that moment conceived of the whole Nation mobilized for war, economic, industrial, social, and military resources gathered into a vast unit. . . .
>
> In my judgement, the nation faces today a more grave emergency than in 1917. . . .
>
> It is high time to admit with courage that we are in the midst of an emergency at least equal to that of war.[90]

If the New Deal was an exception to the rule that the Presidency tends to be weak in peacetime, this was partly because Roosevelt succeeded in imparting a warlike urgency to the economic crisis.

In its formative years, the New Deal derived considerable inspiration from Woodrow Wilson's wartime administration. The National Industrial Recovery Act of 1933, one of the legislative milestones of the "Hundred Days," established the National Recovery Administration, consciously modeled after the War Industries Board of 1918–20. Fittingly, the agency was headed by a military officer, General Hugh Johnson, a West Point graduate who had served on the WIB under Bernard Baruch. Other New Deal agencies were also patterned after World War I predecessors: the Securities Exchange Commission after the Capital Issues Committee of the Federal Reserve Board; the Reconstruction Finance Corporation after the War Finance Corporation.

And at a time when Roosevelt was scrambling to put in place new central structures, it made sense to put the Civilian Conservation Corps under the Army, which, budget cuts aside, still remained one of the most effective mobilization instruments of the federal government. Over 2.5 million young men passed through the CCC camps, administered by such future luminaries of the Army as one Colonel George Catlett Marshall.[91]

In addition to Baruch and Johnson, numerous other prominent New Dealers had served in Wilson's wartime administration: the list includes George Nelson Peek, Louis Howe, Jesse H. Jones, Robert Fechner, Marvin McIntyre, Morris Llewellyn Cook, and Daniel C. Roper. This list does not reflect mere serendipity or proximity to Roosevelt, for only one of these individuals served in the Navy Department in World War I; most were associated primarily with the War Industries Board. There was a direct lineage of learning and experience between the Wilsonian activism of World War I and the Rooseveltian activism of the New Deal.

None of this is to argue that the New Deal was a war-driven phenomenon, for it obviously was not. Its World War I lineage was secondary to other of its economic and social origins. But, driven by a severe domestic crisis, its dynamics resembled those of a war, and it was the only time in U.S. history when the power of the central state grew substantially in the absence of war. Since World War II followed immediately on the heels of the Great Depression, it is difficult to separate the long-term impacts of the war and the New Deal on state–society relations in America. But in general, liberal and conservative mythologies alike have tended to overstate the importance of the New Deal—and undervalue the role of the two world wars—in the massive expansion of the American state that occurred from 1916 to 1945. The heady political transformations of 1933 to 1938, while of great import for the nation's future, did not affect the size and structure of the American state to nearly the same extent as the world wars. World War II in particular transformed the federal government into an immense bureaucracy capable of assuming the kind of predominant role in American society that New Dealers could only dream of in the 1930s.

THE SECOND WORLD WAR AND THE TRANSFORMATION OF AMERICA

The extraordinary impact of World War II on the federal government is best displayed graphically. Figure 7–1 shows the growth of the government (in terms of civilian employment in the executive branch) from 1900 to 1990. The graph shows that every war in the twentieth century, as well as the New Deal, resulted in net growth in the federal bureaucracy. But it also underscores the central, even dominant, role of World War II in that growth. In 1939, when massive rearmament began, the executive branch employed roughly 936,000 civil servants. By 1945 a nearly *fourfold* increase in federal employment had taken place, with the number of civilian employees surpassing 3.8 million, the highest number before or since. By 1950, after four years of post-war demobilization, this number had declined to a postwar low of 1.93 million, which still represented a net gain of 1.0 million civil servants over the 1939 payroll, or a permanent increase of over 100 percent from a much higher base than in any previous conflict. In absolute terms, the net increase was three times that from 1933 to 1939, when the New Deal was the primary source of federal growth. This amounted to a veritable revolution in the size of the federal government.

Beginning in 1939, when the War Resources Board opened its door, New Deal programs became a decidedly secondary source of government expansion. In 1940 alone, Roosevelt created the National Defense Advisory Commission, the Office of Emergency Management, the Office of Price Administration, and the Supply Priorities and Allocations Board, all aimed at facilitating war mobilization. In the fall of 1940, the first peacetime draft in American history went into effect, raising the size of the armed forces to 1.8 million persons by June 1941. The War and Navy Departments also more than doubled in size from 1939 to 1941. All of this, however, was only a prelude to the explosive growth that took place after U.S. entry into the war. Six months after Pearl Harbor, the War and Navy Departments registered total civilian employment of 1,291,000, more than double that of the previous year; for the first time in history, they were larger than all other departments and agencies combined. By 1945, they had more than doubled in size yet again to over 2.6 million persons, a *1,600 percent* increase in seven years.

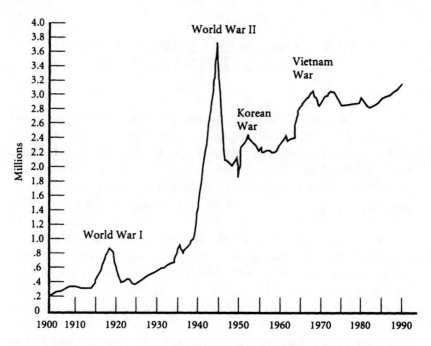

Figure 7–1.   The growth of federal civilian employment, 1900–90

A logical presumption would be that the growth of the federal bureaucracy during World War II occurred mainly in the War and Navy Departments, while government growth during the New Deal primarily affected civilian agencies. This was not the case, however. Detailed examination of the pattern of bureaucratic expansion from 1933 to 1950 (using the annual Civil Service reports) reveals a startling statistic: the *nonmilitary* sectors of the federal government actually grew at a faster rate in World War II than under the impetus of the New Deal! From 1933 to 1938, they experienced 7.5 percent average annual growth; this figure rose to 7.7 percent from 1939 to 1945. Most independent agencies and all but two cabinet departments—Agriculture and Interior—achieved net growth during the war. This is particularly remarkable in light of the acute national labor shortage caused by the conscription of nearly 12 million men. The United States by 1945 was as near to being a totally mobilized state as a democracy possibly could be.

The growth of the nonmilitary sectors of the bureaucracy was integrally linked to the war effort. With federal revenues rising by 842 percent from 1939 to 1945, it is obvious why Treasury added 40,000 employees to its ranks (a 67 percent increase). But even where the linkage was tenuous, the war afforded openings for federal agencies to enlarge their staffs. A case in point was Mr. S. A. Rohwer's testimony before a House Subcommittee on behalf of the Bureau of Entomology and Plant Quarantine regarding an appropriation for "Control of Incipient and Emergency Outbreaks of Insect Pests and Plant Diseases":

The Chairman: This is another front in the War?

Mr. Rohwer: That is right.

The Chairman: We have the Japanese on one side and the Germans on the other side, and these pests in between?

Mr. Rohwer: That is correct; and these pests have a very definite bearing on food production.[92]

Similarly, armed with Executive Order No. 9165, "providing for the protection of essential facilities from sabotage," the Bureau of Reclamation sought a sizeable appropriation for hiring 150 supplementary forest-fire fighters. "The normal fire hazard is ordinarily severe enough," the Bureau argued, "but a planned campaign of incendiarism by enemy forces or agents which may develop could conceivably cause untold destruction and havoc."[93] In 1944, the Interior Department sought an added $90,000 for the Reindeer Service in Alaska, arguing that reindeer "are a valued asset in military planning."[94] That Congress would grant serious consideration to such dubious requests reveals much about why bureaucracy grows in wartime.

Bureaucratic expansion must be managed bureaucratically: during the war, the Civil Service Commission expanded its own ranks vigorously and undertook a massive recruiting drive. Civil service testing was largely abandoned and the legal restrictions on hiring greatly relaxed.[95] In 1941 and 1942, an estimated 5,000 new federal workers moved to Washington every month, transforming the nation's capital into the thriving metropolis and power center it has remained ever since. Over a million additional workers joined the vast regulatory and defense bureaucracy being erected throughout the rest of the country. To manage the explosive growth of the War and Navy Departments, the government built what still remains the largest office building in the world; 13,000 laborers working in nonstop shifts raised the Pentagon in less than a year. By 1945, the Federal government had built, leased, bought, or seized an additional 358 buildings in Washington. The federal government also created more records during the war than in its entire previous history.[96] If the modern state is regarded as a set of institutions—positions, personnel, files, procedures—then World War II produced state-building run amok.

After 1945, the civilian component of the defense bureaucracy experienced a net ratchet effect, rising from under 200,000 before the war to over 870,000 in 1948 (about one third the wartime peak). By contrast, most nonmilitary departments and agencies actually *increased* their personnel levels after 1945, despite their extraordinary wartime growth. A Congressional committee concluded that the growth resulted largely from "the transfer of functions from scattered war agencies which had been . . . liquidated."[97] The Agriculture and Interior departments were at the forefront of these postwar increases, with the result that from 1939 to 1949, the "war decade," every cabinet department and all but a few minor agencies experienced substantial net growth.

World War II far surpassed the fecundity of the New Deal with respect to institutional creation. The War Powers Act of December 1941 gave Roosevelt the same authority that Wilson acquired in the Overman Act—the right to redistribute functions and personnel among existing agencies—but Roosevelt received this authority earlier and held it much longer than Wilson. Before the war had ended, over 150 new agencies, bureaus, commissions, and boards had been established to prosecute the war effort.[98] This was made possible in part by the abolition of New Deal agencies, many of whose functions and personnel were transferred to wartime agencies. Malcolm Cowley proclaimed in *The New Republic* in 1943 that "the New Deal is being abandoned."[99] But what neither Cowley nor other proponents of the New Deal reforms appreciated at the time (and what remains largely unappreciated in American political discourse today) was that the administrative behemoth reared during the war would prove to be a far more potent instrument of social welfare and economic regulation than anything created before 1939. World War II did not dismantle the welfare state in America; indeed, it bequeathed it a permanent bureaucratic base.

The federal impact on the national economy during World War II went far beyond anything implied in the term "economic regulation" and came closer to what Robert Higgs termed "wartime socialism."[100] As in World War I, a single superagency—the War Production Board until May 1943 and thereafter the Office of War Mobilization under James Byrnes—coordinated the efforts of numerous regulatory agencies. Among the most important were the Office of Price Administration and the Office of Economic Stabilization, which together administered comprehensive controls on prices, rents, profits, and wages, as well as a nationwide program of rationing. Wage controls, unheard of in World War I, exacerbated labor relations, impelling establishment of a new permanent agency, the National War Labor Board. Under the authority of the First War Powers Act, the Reconstruction Finance Corporation also formed numerous subsidiary corporations—the Defense Plant Corporation, the Petroleum Reserves Corporation, War Emergency Pipelines, Inc., etc.—that made the federal government a major industrial manufacturer in its own right. The Second War Powers Act broke new precedents, giving the executive branch almost unlimited power over the American economy, including the right to purchase or seize any personal property needed for the war effort and to allocate any and all resources necessary to the public defense.

By 1943, the federal government had become the consumer of nearly half the national output of goods and services and of a much higher percentage of the total industrial output. The federal budget grew from $6.8 billion in 1938 to an unthinkable $98.3 billion in 1945. This meant that the federal government was spending eleven times as much, in real terms, at the height of World War II as in the peak spending year of the Great Depression. The total cost of the war exceeded $288 billion, over 80 percent of which was borrowed, raising the national debt by 1945 to $259 billion; World War II debts remained a component of the total U.S. debt structure as late as 1993. Nor did V-J Day mark the end of massive federal spending. In 1948, the nadir of postwar federal expenditures, the federal budget stood at $32.9 billion, a net ratchet effect of almost three times the 1938 figure after adjusting for inflation.[101]

As in earlier American wars, wartime expenditures were an important impetus of fiscal reform. The most important innovation was the introduction in 1943 of income-tax withholding on a "temporary" basis. Needless to say, it remained a permanent fixture after the war. By making income taxation largely invisible and hence less painful, withholding not only helped finance the war effort but greatly facilitated postwar revenue extraction and the permanent maintenance of a large federal bureaucracy. Armed with tax withholding and other new authorities, the Internal Revenue Service became more assertive. The number of tax returns filed went from 7.5 million in 1939 to 50 million in 1945. With the lowest tax bracket raised from 5.5 percent to 23 percent, income tax receipts increased 1,800 percent during the war. Before 1941, less than half of internal revenues had come from individual and corporate income taxes; by 1945, the figure was 80 percent, and it never dropped below 70 percent again.[102]

AMERICAN STATE–SOCIETY RELATIONS DURING WORLD WAR II

The structure of state repressive power in World War II differed from that of 1917–18, when most prosecutions had taken place locally; from 1941–45, the repression of dissent was essentially federalized. This fact alone indicated the changing locus of power in the American system. In large part owing to Supreme Court rulings, there were relatively few prosecutions of persons expressing verbal opposition to the war, but active dissent was another matter. Federal authorities suppressed numerous dissident groups and closed at least a hundred publications. Over 6,000 draft resisters went to jail, a rate four times higher than in World War I. The First World War had seen numerous cases of mob violence against Germans and other aliens, but nothing compared to the forced internment from 1942 to 1945 of 120,000 Americans of Japanese and Issei descent. Geoffrey Perret estimates that for every person facing official or spontaneous persecution in World War I, there were ten in World War II.[103] One measure of the massive increase in federal repressive power was the growth of the Federal Bureau of Investigation: in 1939, it had 785 special agents; by 1945, 4,370.[104]

Whether coercively enforced or derived from genuine nationalism, the unifying effect of the war was strong from 1941 to its conclusion. But as in World War I, the conflict exposed critical fault lines in American society. Arthur A. Stein has argued that American society was not nearly as unified during World War II as is generally supposed—racial violence proliferated; the crime rate was substantially higher than before the war; numerous labor strikes took place, even in war industries; and incidents of domestic violence increased.[105] Lack of social cohesion is not necessarily a measure of public opposition to the war, but Stein's work does suggest that the unifying effects of conflict are complex and uneven in their actual manifestation. A mobilization effort may unify large segments of the polity, but at the same time alienate and provoke resentment among other segments. Another possible explanation for societal turmoil in World War II was the extraordinary physical dislocation of the war years: over 15.3 million civilians relocated across county lines between 1941 and 1945.[106]

The tumult of mobilization notwithstanding, the social transformation of the war included many positive, integrative effects. The acute labor shortage forced government and industry to hire millions of women and minorities, often in positions where traditionally they were underrepresented; blacks may have fought in segregated military units, but at home their share of federal civilian employment rose from 8 to 18 percent, with a marked increase for them in white-collar employment.[107] The war likewise shattered barriers to female employment; by mid-1945, 16.5 million women were employed—36 percent of the civilian labor force. The archetype of the female worker in World War II was "Rosie the Riveter," but even the New York Stock Exchange hired its first female clerk in 1943. The large-scale entry of women into occupations from which they had been largely excluded permanently altered the composition of the American labor force.[108] As Merlo Pusey observed in 1943, "the whole pattern of our economic and social life is undergoing kaleidoscopic changes without so much as a bomb being dropped on our shores."[109]

Another example of the integrative impetus of World War II was its impact on Native Americans. Alison Bernstein writes that the war "had a more profound and lasting effect on the course of Indian affairs in this century than any other single event or period."[110] Some 25,000 Native Americans fought in the war, one third of all able-bodied Native men aged 18 to 50; unlike blacks, they served in integrated military units. It was their first large-scale exodus from the reservations since their defeat by the U.S. Army.[111] Despite being moved to Chicago and relegated to lowest priority among federal agencies, the Bureau of Indian Affairs actually grew in size from 1939 to 1945, a growth justified by the contribution of Native Americans to the war effort and a striking example of bureaucratic expansion during wartime.

As in World War I, some of the social advances made possible by the war proved temporary and fragile. Once again, 920,000 African-American soldiers found that the rights they had fought for did not apply to themselves. The difference this time was that the war experience helped place the issue of racial discrimination firmly on the national agenda, where it has remained ever since. During the war, the Urban League tripled in size, while the National Association for the Advancement of Colored People grew from 50,000 to nearly 500,000 members. The Fair Employment Practices Commission, established in 1941 as an emergency war agency, scored its first important victories during the war and managed, despite heated opposition in Congress, to endure beyond the war. For blacks, the war was "the watershed of the post-Emancipation struggle for equality."[112] By breaking down racial, ethnic, and gender barriers, the war initiated a long process of broadening the basis and inclusiveness of American nationalism. It was in fact the beginning of the modern civil rights movement.

THE COLD WAR AND THE PERMANENCE
OF THE BUREAUCRATIC STATE

In contrast to the pattern of previous wars, the United States never fully demobilized after the Second World War. By 1946, the armed forces had shrunk from 12.5 million to 3 million troops; by 1948, to under 1.5 million; by American standards this was a still massive force, nearly five times its 1939 size. The downward trend abruptly ceased that year with the coming of the Berlin airlift and the onset of the Cold War. Notwithstanding brief periods of partial détente, the U.S.-Soviet rivalry continued for forty-two years, until the reunification of Germany in 1990. During that time, the United States spent over six trillion dollars on defense, maintained standing military forces numbering 2.4 million persons on the average, supported a civilian defense bureaucracy of over one million employees, and funded a vast military-industrial complex against whose influence even the 34th president, the most famous general of World War II, felt compelled to warn.[113] The coming of the Cold War thus gave a permanent cast to the transmutations of World War II.

World War II had already bequeathed the nation with a massive bureaucratic state; the Cold War kept it intact. Truman only partially dismantled the wartime regulatory agencies, and though the United States avoided the large-scale nationalization of industries that took place in Europe after 1945, it became in every other way a mature regulatory state, with heavy penetration of the economy by the central government. The American state also emerged from the war more centralized than ever: in 1938, at the peak of the New Deal, the federal share of all governmental spending in the United States had been 46 percent; by 1950, it was 58 percent.[114] The National Security Act of 1947 ensured that the large defense establishment formed in World War II would also endure more or less permanently. It established the triumvirate that shaped U.S. security policy throughout the Cold War: the National Security Council, the Central Intelligence Agency, and a unified "National Military Establishment" under a Secretary of Defense (in 1949, this became the Department of Defense). So large a peacetime security establishment would have been unthinkable before 1939. Everywhere, Hamilton's vision of government was triumphant, Jefferson's in full retreat.

Harold Lasswell in 1950 warned that the Cold War might turn the United States into "a garrison-police state" dominated by specialists on violence.[115] The litany of Cold War repression by the federal government during the Truman and Eisenhower administrations—the Taft-Hartley Act, the McCarran Internal Security and Immigration Acts, the McCarthy allegations, the purging of China experts in the State Department, the blacklisting of American writers and film producers—at least partly vindicated his viewpoint. The worst abuses ceased after the censure of Senator Joseph McCarthy in 1954, but federal repressive activities continued throughout the Cold War. One example of increased state power was the proliferation of background investigations for federal employees, uniformed service personnel, and industrial and transport concerns linked with national security. During World War II, an estimated 100 federal employees were dismissed and 30 resigned as a result of background investigations. By comparison, from 1947 to 1956, there were 2,700 dismissals and 12,000 security-related resignations. By 1958, some 9.8 million Americans had been subject to background investigations, loyalty oaths, or security clearance procedures. There was nothing even remotely comparable in American history prior to 1945.[116]

The security apparatus and procedures put in place between 1948 and 1956 persisted throughout the Cold War and beyond, with obvious consequences for the relationship between state and civil society in America. Yet the fact remains that the United States during the Cold War never did become anything approaching a true garrison state. Aaron Friedberg has argued that this is because there remained numerous domestic sources of resistance to central authority, both popular and elite, after World War II. Moreover, the U.S. choice of a national strategy—reliance on the relatively cheap alternative of nuclear deterrence, rather than massive conventional force—also mitigated pressures for further "garrisonization" of the state after 1948.[117]

The federal bureaucracy grew by nearly one million personnel from 1948 to its peak in 1969. Part of the impetus for this came from the growth in entitlement programs, but not nearly as much as is often supposed. Most of the growth in fact coincided with the wars in Korea and Vietnam. Each war spurred large increases in federal civilian employment, and in both cases a significant ratchet effect occurred: after Korea, the net gain was 437,000 (22 percent); after Vietnam, 269,000 (11 percent). During the Vietnam War, federal employment climbed to its highest level since 1945, with 3,000,000 employees at the peak of the war in 1968—an increase of 540,000 over 1964. The Defense Department accounted for half the increase, but by 1973 it had laid off almost as many employees as it had hired during the war. The executive branch was left with a net postwar employment increase of 250,000. Since the Postal Service and the Veterans Administration accounted for nearly half of this net growth, the contribution of Great Society programs to bureaucratic expansion between 1964 to 1973 was *at most* some 131,000 employees, less than 5 percent of total federal employment. What is more, within five years of the end of the Vietnam War, the number of federal employees in welfare-related departments and agencies began a slow but steady decline that continued until 1990.[118] Thus, contrary to a widely held perception, the Great Society and the growth of welfare programs in the United States after 1966 did not spawn a massive new bureaucracy, and certainly were not responsible for the rise of Big Government—in the sense of massive bureaucracy—in America.

The contribution of welfare programs to the exponential increase in federal *spending* after 1950 was much more substantial, of course. From 1950 to 1980, welfare expenditures as a percentage of total federal spending grew from 26.2 percent to 54.2 percent, then declined under Ronald Reagan to slightly under 50.0 percent.[119] A large percentage of the increase, however, was in transfer payments, which require only a small bureaucracy to manage. In 1988, for example, the 69,000 employees of the Social Security Administration (2 percent of executive branch employment) distributed over $300 billion in social security payments (28 percent of federal spending.) The bureaucratic size and the fiscal size of the federal government do not necessarily correlate.

The expansion of the postwar welfare state in America would have been inconceivable without the bureaucratic, regulatory, and taxation structures built up during World War II. But the question remains as to why the two world wars did not lead more directly to the establishment of a full-fledged welfare state in America, as they did in the large industrial states of Europe. Several factors explain this. For one thing, the degree of human losses and suffering experienced by the American population was far less than that experienced in Europe; the cathartic effect of the wars was correspondingly less, the sense of urgency that drives reform missing. Pent-up consumer demand, coupled with a physically undamaged industrial base, also resulted in a decade of prosperity and high labor demand after each war—and reform sentiment is always weaker in periods of economic well-being. Finally, the rise of a federally funded welfare state was inhibited by the ever vigorous American resistance to central power: conservative and libertarian-minded Congressmen fought hard after both wars to dismantle wartime agencies and prevent the emergence of a bureaucratic state at the national level. This inevitably inhibited social welfare legislation.[120]

There was at least one factor of a military nature that did contribute to the postwar development of the welfare state in America. That was the passage of the GI Bills of 1944 and 1948, which habituated a whole generation of Americans to the notion that governmental assistance was for the middle classes, not just the poor. It is also fascinating to observe that the largest jump in postwar federal welfare spending, as measured in five-year increments, occurred from 1965–70 and coincided with the peak of the Vietnam War. Is it possible that the war in some manner gave impetus to the welfare reforms of the Great Society, just as the earlier world wars had done in Europe?

The short answer is that it did not. This, after all, was a limited war that did not entail the high degree of national mobilization usually associated with Titmussian (i.e., war-related) welfare effects. Indeed, most observers of the period would argue that, if anything, the war undermined the reform agenda of Lyndon Johnson, irrevocably damaging his prestige and nearly destroying his presidency. Certainly the long-term political effects of the war, especially after the fall of Saigon in 1975, were almost entirely degenerative in thrust: executive power was weakened, the American polity divided, and national self-confidence badly debilitated. The latter years of the war witnessed the worst domestic upheaval the United States had experienced since the Civil War. Acutely aware of the potential of Vietnam to undermine their reform agenda, Johnson and his advisers bent over backward to escalate slowly, keep the war limited, and hide its true costs from the public.[121]

The War and the Great Society were not entirely diametrical events, however. The architects of each—Johnson, his Cabinet, and his top advisers—were imbued with a supreme statism, the spirit of American invincibility that had reigned since 1945 and was coupled with a "can-do" confidence in the capacity of government to accomplish anything, whether it be ending poverty at home, creating safe hamlets in Vietnam, or conducting limited warfare by "search and destroy" missions, bombing raids, and infiltration detection devices. In the early years of the war, particularly from 1965 to 1966, public and congressional support for the war remained fairly high; the Imperial Presidency that then served as a catalyst of the most far-reaching welfare reforms in the nation's history was certainly not weakened by the war, and in some respects may have been strengthened as a result of the power that tends to flow to the presidency during wartime. The vote by which the Tonkin Gulf resolution was passed (416 to 0 in the House; 98 to 2 in the Senate) and Johnson's phenomenal legislative record in the 89th Congress that followed (181 measures passed out of 200 requested) both reflect a presidency at the apex of its power in domestic and foreign affairs. Doris Kearns observes that Johnson's determi-

nation not to let the war derail his reform agenda motivated the fre-
netic pace at which he pushed Great Society initiatives.[122] It was only
after the Tet Offensive of January–February, 1968, when popular support for the Vietnam War plummeted, that its degenerative effects
seriously undercut both executive power and social reform in America.
Over seven years of national agony followed.

A final note on the Cold War. The era is closely linked in the public
mind with nuclear weapons. Their existence contributed in several
ways to the increase in the repressive power of the federal government
that occurred after Stalin detonated his own bomb in 1949. The existence of an adversary that could attack and destroy American cities at
will created a sense of direct and pervasive threat unlike anything the
American consciousness had ever faced. This sense of territorial vulnerability reinforced the conflictual atmosphere of the Cold War and
justified in the minds of many the extraordinary security measures
taken from 1949 to 1990. The possession and handling of nuclear
weapons also imposed unique and extraordinary security requirements; these included supersecret facilities, special and higher levels of
security clearance, and the concealment of budgetary and defense
information from the American public. And finally, the possession of
nuclear weapons gives an almost mythic quality to any state, a mys-
tique which all by itself may subtly alter a state's relationship with its
civil society.

Nuclear weapons did not, however, radically alter or expand the
bureaucratic structure of the American state; one reason for this is that
their overall cost within the larger national defense budget was relatively small. Despite their immense firepower, nuclear warheads are
almost absurdly cheap by comparison with large conventional programs, and even if the cost of delivery systems (bombers, ICBMs, and
ballistic missile submarines) is included, strategic-weapons spending
has averaged only about 11 percent of the U.S. defense budget, or less
than one-half percent of U.S. GNP, throughout the Cold War period.
This is too low a figure to have required massive organizational reform
or bureaucratic expansion. In this sense, at least, the weapon that revolutionized international relations was only a ripple in the ocean of
American domestic political development.

In the first four years after the Cold War ended, the United States
fought only one major conflict overseas, the Persian Gulf War. The
campaign to liberate Kuwait and destroy the military machine of Sad-
dam Hussein was too brief and too easily victorious to cause any significant change in the structure of the American state. The war

elevated the power and prestige of the national executive, but only very briefly, as George Bush learned to his dismay less than two years later. The war did, however, offer a potent reminder of the integrative effects of military service and conflict. For the first time in the nation's history, the senior military officer of the U.S. Armed Forces was a black American, and 33 percent of all enlisted personnel and officers were minorities. The number of women in uniform had also climbed to over 10 percent, many of whom served in the Persian Gulf, some of whom perished in combat support operations.[123] What is most impressive about these statistics, perhaps, is that they were achieved in a highly meritocratic institution with few formal programs of affirmative action. As was the case since 1776, war and military service continued to stir the melting pot of American society even in the post-Cold War era.

CONCLUSION: WAR, PEACE AND THE FUTURE OF THE AMERICAN REPUBLIC

Throughout the history of the United States, war has been the primary impetus behind the growth and development of the central state. It has been the lever by which presidents and other national officials have bolstered the power of the state in the face of tenacious popular resistance. It has been a wellspring of American nationalism and a spur to political and social change. Table 7–2 gives a sense of the impact of warfare on the evolution of the federal government. It lists every current U.S. cabinet department and agency established during wartime, in the immediate aftermath of a major war, or whose establishment was clearly linked with military requirements. To ensure a close correlation in time, only the largest wars—the War of Independence, the Civil War and the two World Wars—are assumed to have a causally significant postwar period, and this is restricted to five years; for all other wars, only the actual period of hostilities is considered. To further ensure no bias, we will restrict consideration of the Vietnam War to the period from 1964 to 1967; agencies created after 1968 probably had no significant link to the war effort, which by then had become extremely unpopular and was serving to weaken rather than strengthen executive power.

Table 7-2.   U.S. Cabinet Departments, Sub-Departments, and Major
Agencies created during wartime or in the first five years
after major wars, 1787–1990

CABINET DEPARTMENT OR AGENCY	DATE OF ESTABLISHMENT
Department of Agriculture	1862
Department of Defense	1949; originally War and Navy Departments, established 1781 during War of Independence
Department of Housing and Urban Development	1965, outgrowth of Housing and Home Finance Agency (1947)
Department of the Interior	1849, linked with War with Mexico
Department of Justice	1870 (Attorney General in 1789)
Department of State	Predecessor established in 1781
Department of Transportation	1966
Department of the Treasury	Department of Finance formed 1781
Department of Veterans Affairs	1921
Food and Drug Administration	(Food Administration) in World War I
Bureau of Indian Affairs	Created under War Department, 1824
Coast Guard	1915 (concern for coastal defense during World War I)
Federal Highway Administration	1967 (linked to earlier Eisenhower initiative on Defense highway system)
Federal Railroad Administration	1966
Maritime Administration	1950
Comptroller of Currency	1863
Customs Service	1789
Internal Revenue Service	1862
Bureau of Engraving and Printing	1862
Central Intelligence Agency	1947
Equal Employment Opportunity Commission	1965
General Services Administration	1949
National Science Foundation	1950
Nuclear Regulatory Commission	Originally Atomic Energy Commission, 1946
Small Business Administration	1953; linked to Korean war; outgrowth of Small Defense Plants Administration (1950)
United States Information Agency	Original authority 1948
United States Postal Service	Originally Post Office, 1775

The total number of years that fall in war-related eras thus encompasses some forty-eight or barely over one-fifth of American history.
Yet during this time, all but five cabinet departments were created and
the majority of smaller federal agencies came into being. Even if one

does not accept the conclusion that war made the American state, it is difficult to deny that its government was reared during war.

Admittedly, a correlation in time does not necessarily prove causality; particularly in the case of the Vietnam War there were surely some agencies created during those years that had no close connection to the war. On the other hand, linkages often exist that are not readily apparent. The Federal Highway Administration is an example. Formed in 1967, it was an outgrowth of the Highway Trust Fund established during the Eisenhower administration. Eisenhower had argued for a "National System of Defense and Interstate Highways" on the grounds that a well-maintained road system was critical to the movement of troops and the evacuation of cities in the event of nuclear war. Though Eisenhower obviously wanted the highway system for more than military reasons, the former general understood that in the American system any enhancement of federal authority is most easily justified by appealing to national security.[124]

Throughout American history, two visions of the state have competed: the Hamiltonian vision of a strong, centralized state, and the Jeffersonian vision of a limited state, where human liberty was the highest ideal. In considering the expansion of the federal government and the enormous accretion in state power that has occurred since the Civil War, it is tempting to conclude that the Hamiltonian vision has triumphed unconditionally. As Robert Tucker and David Hendrickson observe:

> The institutions that characterize American public life today—the standing military establishments, the ballooning debt and high taxes, the subordinate position of state governments in relation to national power. . . . all this he [Jefferson] would have beheld with a kind of sacred horror, as constituting the victory of Alexander Hamilton's vision of American life.[125]

Yet the premise of a total Hamiltonian victory is faulty and itself derives from excessive fixation on the state. As Tucker and Hendrickson observe, "the ideals of American life remain Jeffersonian, even in the midst of all these powerful and corrupting institutions."[126]

At the end of the Cold War, despite nearly fifty years of full or partial national mobilization, civil society in America remains stronger, more independent-minded and more antistatist than in virtually any country of Europe or Asia. The rapid decline of the U.S. defense budget following the collapse of the Soviet empire, the absence of influential voices calling for maintenance of a large U.S. presence overseas, the growing intensity of anti-incumbent and anti-Washington sentiment all point to the survival of that whiff of rebellion that Jefferson deemed vital to democracy. The genius of the Constitution was that it created a structure that would allow civil society to continue to flourish in freedom even as the nation-state that was its political manifestation became a global military power. In this sense, at least, America still remains the great exception. The very weakness of the American state as an apparatus of power is the source of its greatest strength: a vibrant, free, and democratic civil society.

But if the United States has fought shy of becoming a modern-day Sparta, can it also avoid the fate of Lebanon? If war built the American state, is it possible that the absence of war will unleash forces that could threaten to unravel it? The end of the Cold War, after all, places the United States in the same position it faced after the War of 1812, the War with Mexico, the Civil War, and World War I. Suddenly, it has no serious enemies and faces no military threat from abroad. In similar situations in the past, American unity has deteriorated and the power of the state has waned. Will the same happen again? Will the end of a half century of superpower rivalry and proxy wars abroad mark the beginning of a new turbulence within America itself?

The perennial revolt against state sovereignty that reasserts itself after every American war can actually take two forms. In its simplest manifestation, Americans after every large war have substantially dismantled the defense establishment and whittled down the structure of state that supported it. The one exception was World War II, but in that case the swift coming of the Cold War altered the equation drastically. If historical patterns prevail, since the Cold War is over the United States would now drastically cut back the massive state structure that grew up during the world wars and that has persisted ever since. No gambler, however, should take odds on this proposition. In the sense of real reductions in the size of the federal bureaucracy and level of federal spending, a shrinkage of the American state appears about as remote as a drying up of the oceans. At some point in the last fifty years, the United States crossed the welfare threshold discussed in Chapter 5—the point at which the state transcends its military origins and acquires a new *raison d'état* as the pilot of the economy and provider of social welfare. Military basis or not, the American state will not go gentle into that good night.

Ronald Reagan entered office boldly proclaiming his intent to dismantle large sectors of the federal government; in the end, he left it virtually unscathed. Federal employment from 1981 to the end of his term actually grew by nearly 1 percent; most of this was in the ever-resilient

Post Office, but even if it is excluded, net growth occurred.[127] At best, the Great Communicator transferred marginal bureaucratic resources from the social agencies to the defense and foreign affairs establishment. What Reagan was trying to do—to trim the sails of Big Government, while simultaneously engaging in a massive defense build-up—was in fact a contradiction in terms. No state in history has ever managed to shrink bureaucratically and expand militarily at the same time.

But if the end of the Cold War is unlikely to reduce the *size* of the American state, will it reduce public *confidence* in the political system? Will freedom from military threat give new vigor to the American revolt against state sovereignty? In this light, the political troubles of George Bush and the stunningly rapid decline of President Clinton's prestige in his first months in office may have stemmed not only from personal factors, but from the deep-rooted will of Americans to resist central authority in the absence of urgent crises. Taken further, if the end of the Cold War does not mean the dismantling of the state, it may nevertheless mean both the contraction of the Presidency and a prolonged era of gridlock, ungovernability, and intractable domestic discord in Congress and among the public. Given the growing diversity of American culture and values today, our society, no longer united by foreign threats, might find that its own internal cleavages are greater than anyone realized.

With ethnic and national identities reasserting themselves, with traditional values and anchors of social stability under siege, with the problems of a complex postindustrial economy proliferating, *and in the absence of foreign threats to unify a diverse American polity*, the post-Cold War era is likely to be not an era of good feeling, peace dividends, and economic boom (à la the post-1945 era), but an era of political turmoil and divisiveness rivaling the 1850s. This time around, however, the cleavages will not be along sectional lines, but along multiple axes of social, racial, religious, and class tensions. We can expect growing public disdain for the political process, rising unrest in the inner cities, proposals for radical constitutional change, third-party movements, one-term presidents, and a serious national identity crisis over what it means to be an American. We may even see a variety of attempts to solve all these problems through foreign diversion: finding or inventing enemies (Japan is a likely candidate) against which united efforts can be directed. But unless an actual military foe arises, or the United States becomes embroiled in a serious war, the problem of keeping America unified in the face of profound centrifugal tensions is likely to be *the* political problem of the 1990s and beyond.

This is not a promising vision of the future, but nor is it an inevitable fate. The philosopher William James observed that the challenge of politics in peacetime is to find a moral equivalent of war. Franklin Roosevelt demonstrated that this can be done, that it is possible even in peacetime to rally the American people and infuse some of the dynamism of war into peaceful efforts at social cooperation—and he did it in a way that preserved civil liberties and shunned the extremes of socialism and fascism. If an American crisis lies in the near future, it is likely to be more chronic than acute, but dynamic leadership and vision may still perform Rooseveltian miracles.

Throughout this work, we have seen that states whose leaders were unwilling or unable to rally their societies in the common defense perished in war or suffered long-term and serious damage. Perhaps the same is true of confronting the challenge of peace. All that America will require to prosper in the future is presidents with the dynamism of a Roosevelt, the compassion of a Lincoln, and the strength in adversity of a Washington. This may seem an impossibly tall order, but great times tend to summon forth great leaders, and the more so from a society as free and diverse as this one. Certainly the American republic has surmounted greater obstacles in the past. There is every reason to believe it will yet again verify the truth of the folk adage that God takes care of fools, drunkards, and the United States of America.

Epilogue

THE PARADOX OF THE STATE

In 1904, G. K. Chesterton published *The Napoleon of Notting Hill*, a whimsical fantasy about London in the then-future year of 1984.[1] Chesterton conjures up a sophisticated and modernizing London in which but one antique pocket of tradition remained intact: the quaint neighborhood of Notting Hill in North Kensington. Hidden behind high walls, Notting Hill stood as an island of vitality and color amidst the sterile, leveling modernity of London. Here, and here only, faith, pageantry, personality, and community still endured. Believing himself commissioned by the King to defend this last bastion of traditional society, a fanatical young man named Adam Wayne wages a holy war to defend Notting Hill against the encroaching world. Eventually, after very un-modern battles of swords and battle-axes, Wayne employs stratagem and shrewdness to seize a stunning victory. It is a triumph of character over anonymity; of community over impersonal mass; of value over ethical desolation; of personal vibrancy over anomie.

The parable of Notting Hill presents an almost precise counterpoint to the actual trend of modern history. Chesterton portrays traditional society as briefly saved by war; in fact, it has almost everywhere been destroyed by war. Modern warfare, by upsetting the equilibrium of traditional society with its emphasis on local autonomy and privilege, paved the way for a steady increase in state power and military might. This in turn meant the trampling of local privileges by central governments, the destruction of medieval constitutionalism and representative estates, and the rearing of ever more highly organized killing machines. The End of History—for millions, the literal end—was Verdun and the Somme, Auschwitz and Buchenwald. In the five centuries since Charles VIII crossed the Alps into Italy and ushered in the era of modern warfare, over 150 million souls have perished violently. Modernity exacted a high price indeed.

The entire process of modernization since the fifteenth century can be seen in broadest historical perspective as an attempt to transcend the medieval. But we should recall that the medieval order placed severe restraints on centralized power and prevented any large-scale concentration of the means of violence, whether for war or repression. Otto Hintze and Barrington Moore, as well as more recently Brian Downing and Robert Putnam, have given us classic studies demonstrating that the roots of political liberty and democracy are medieval, not modern, in origin; local, not cosmopolitan or national.[2] Democracy is not simply a fruit of modernity, but in fact has arisen in opposition to certain modernizing trends, above all in opposition to the centralizing juggernaut of the bureaucratic warfare state. Democracy thrives when local communities, private associations, visionary leaders, and diverse social strata resist the aggrandizements of the state, the power of which invariably flows from its organization of and for violence.

It is too simplistic, however, to portray war as the sole parent of autocracy or the centralized state as immutably a foe of democracy. The consensual features of the medieval order did not constitute liberal democracy as we know it today, nor is it conceivable that true democracy could ever have developed in a world of such rigid class structure and random violence. By breaking down class, ethnic, gender, and ideological barriers, the wars of the modern era—some of them, at least—contributed to the emergence of such positive fruits of modernity as egalitarianism and a more meritocratic and mobile social structure. Modern warfare centralized power in the short term but helped democratize political life *over the long run*. This seeming paradox derives from war being not only a destructive phenomenon but also a cooperative one as well. The intense social cooperation mandated by war, especially by industrialized war, fostered social equality and collectivist politics. This occurred, however, only when civil society was strong enough to force political leaders into a bargaining position—trading political concessions for the sinews of war. Whenever the violence and degenerative effects of war overwhelmed civil society, there was left no counterweight to the raw power of the central state; despotism or totalitarianism invariably resulted.

* * *

The paradoxes of war are replicated in the paradox of the modern state. Though the state is a creature of war and the source of virtually all of the truly large-scale violence in the past half-millennium, it is simultaneously a bulwark against foreign aggression. Though it may serve as an instrument of internal repression, it is also a guardian of internal peace, preventing civil anarchy through its monopoly of coercive power. Insofar as the rise of centralized states brought forth oases of civil calm from the turbulence of the Middle Ages, they fostered the spread of capitalism, commerce, science, technology, education, and eventually industrialization—all of which contributed to the later rise of liberal democracy. In the narrow strait between the Scylla of the Omnipotent State and the Charybdis of social anarchy is found the Haven of democracy, the only form of government that has managed to strike an enduring balance between the dictates of defense and the imperatives of freedom and order.

The most hopeful sign that mankind may yet escape from the Sisyphean cycle of war and state formation in which it has labored since at least 1494 is the advancement in recent decades of democracy as the favored organizing form of states.[3] Michael Doyle, in the tradition of Immanuel Kant, has argued that while liberal democracies may wage wars of remarkable ferocity against autocratic and totalitarian states, they are singularly disinclined to wage war against one another. Because of this, the world's democracies form a community of pacific states, a veritable zone of peace.[4] Thus, if democracy spreads, so presumably will the prospects for a more peaceful world. But this leads to the much larger question of what the future holds in store for the modern state.

WHITHER THE STATE?

The Yugoslav Civil War that began in 1991 epitomized the paradox of the modern state and simultaneously raised sharp questions about its future. An artificial state conceived in the cauldron of World War I, this hybrid of former Austrian territories, joined with formerly independent Serbia and Montenegro, was held together only by the force of a highly centralized dictatorship from 1918 to 1941. Even then, tensions between Serbs and Croats constantly threatened to sunder it.

United in the partisan battles against the Nazi occupation, and later in the shadow of an aggressive Soviet Union, the Yugoslav Federal Republic held together under the strong hand of Tito and his successors until 1991. But the end of the Cold War and the waning of the Soviet threat loosed the critical unifying threads that bound it together, and mounting ethnic and sectional tensions erupted into civil war. Otherwise welcome tidings of international peace were blemished by the explosion of artillery shells in—of all places—Sarajevo.

The end of the Cold War also played a role in eroding internal unity and encouraging challenges to the status quo throughout the industrialized democracies. The troubles of Presidents Bush and Clinton, as well as those of President Mitterand of France, the crisis of the Liberal Democratic Party in Japan, the near collapse of the Christian Democratic party in Italy, and the mounting sense of internal crisis in both Germany and the United Kingdom all derive in part from the international peace that has reigned in the wake of the Cold War. And the troubles of the Western democracies pale, of course, by comparison with the proliferation of ethnic and national strife across the entire former empire of the Soviet Union since 1989. In accordance with an historical pattern that has occurred throughout the modern era, the end of an era of international rivalry and conflict has marked the beginning of internal conflict and disarray almost everywhere.

Are we doomed to be united only in war? Do collective endeavors flow best from the passions of conflict, so much so that when conflict abroad ceases, cooperation at home ends? Perhaps the most remarkable finding of this study concerned the critical role of civil wars in the formation of states and rise of their sovereignty. But the process may be a one-way street; further internal strife may only unravel established states. If the end of the Cold War is sharpening domestic cleavages, this may portend a post-modern era of waning state sovereignty. Is the state, the Great Middle Polity that arose between the empires and the fragmented principalities of the medieval world, on its last legs?

The end of the Cold War has seen a resurgence of the nineteenth-century pattern of nationalism in which each ethnic or national group seeks to form its own independent polity. After Bosnia-Herzegovina won recognition as an independent state in 1992, it promptly sank into a civil war, aggravated by outside intervention, first from Serbia, then from Croatia. Many participants in the war proclaimed that the only possible solution was the creation of three independent states *within* Bosnia—a Croatian, a Serbian, and a Muslim state—each of which, of course, would only be another Yugoslavia, with minorities inside its borders. The confederative solution advocated by the Western powers envisioned no less than ten autonomous cantons—a Swiss-like solution unfortunately not graced by such Swiss-like qualities as commitment to representative government and respect for different linguistic and ethnic communities. We should reflect seriously on the implications of such solutions. Given that there are perhaps 1,000 or more possible political communities in Europe—what might loosely be termed "communal affinity groups"—if every claimant to the right to autonomy won out, we would effectively witness the devolution of state structures in Europe to a much reduced geographical level. The Middle would splinter into oblivion as tiny self-centered polities replaced centralized states. Structurally, at least, this would amount to the remedievalization of Europe. Post-modernity would loom as a return to the past.

Martin van Creveld offers a yet darker vision of the future of the state, based upon his assessment of the future of military conflict. He argues that the tools of war are gradually slipping out of the control of central states, as the international arms market enables almost any militia force, terrorist group, or would-be potentate to obtain technically advanced weaponry. He sees state-centered, large-scale warfare as having played out its last cards; he suggests that terrorism, low-intensity conflict, and the pervasiveness of personal, street-level violence will replace it. With the end of bureaucratized warfare, the state will become increasingly irrelevant and impotent.[6] The Middle would descend into a muddle from whence it would not return. The future is Lebanon.

An entirely different view of the future sees the preeminence of the sovereign state as threatened by a return of empire. In a complex world of economic interdependence and mass communications, large-scale organizations that transcend national borders are growing in importance: transnational corporations, regional associations, international institutions, trading blocs and cartels.[5] The recent marked increase in the importance of the United Nations Security Council and the burgeoning of U.N. peacekeeping missions is a case in point. The signing of the Maastricht Treaty and implementation of a tighter European Union is another. By the year 2000 or 2010, it is conceivable that Western Europe will again be a unified empire, its former states having surrendered a significant share of their sovereignty to the transnational bureaucracy in Brussels. Thus, in a few years the Middle may be transcended by the Higher.

All these visions are compelling in their own way, and evidence can be adduced for all of them. But they are also mutually contradictory and so cannot all come to pass. The fact remains that the tools of war are still organized and wielded today only by sovereign states. Neither corporations nor international institutions nor mini-states nor terrorists can undertake anything beyond limited and sporadic activity on a world scale. Terrorists can wreak small-scale havoc, but only states possess the capability of organizing military power on a large scale. The United Nations and the European Community can spearhead cooperative endeavors, but only if their constituent self-organized states freely subordinate themselves to their authority and implement those endeavors on the state level. Unlike old soldiers, the state will not simply fade away.

Is it possible that instead of declining, the modern state will experience yet another iteration of massive change, that the collectivist state that reigns in Europe and the United States today will give way to a new form? If past patterns hold true, this would happen only if another round of large-scale war erupts, employing weapons of an entirely new order of technology. Until recently, full-scale warfare between major powers seemed unthinkable because of the existence of nuclear weapons; some scholars even referred to such warfare as obsolete.[7] New technological developments, however, may make this conclusion premature. A Military-Technical Revolution may be in the offing, a new class of nonnuclear, conventional warfare predicted by Soviet Marshal Nikolai Ogarkov in 1982.[8]

Imagine a world in which precision guidance, cruise missiles, smart weapons, satellite surveillance, real-time data fusion, supercomputing, "stealthy" weapons platforms, and high-technology sensors have rendered the weaponry of World War II utterly obsolete. Fixed and even moving platforms as we now conceive of them—tanks, aircraft carriers, armored fighting vehicles, surface warships, artillery positions, etc.—if not hidden or disguised, would be vulnerable to swift and certain destruction from the air in the first hours of such a war. The Persian Gulf War offered a preliminary glimpse into this new breed of warfare, which still remains largely beyond the horizon. Given the enormous expense of the new weaponry, a Military-Technical Revolution will only occur if great powers with high technical capabilities— the United States, Japan, and Germany are the most likely candidates—should again become rivals. We might then see the rise of the Scientific Warfare State—a new kind of political system in which society would be intensely organized toward the aggressive exploitation of high technology for military purposes.

In such a system, fiscal wealth and sound management would remain crucial, for the new warfare would be enormously expensive, but the Scientific Warfare State would also place a high premium on scientific education, the mobilization of engineering talent and skill, the efficient management of research-and-development laboratories, and sophisticated and highly secure communications networks linking the scientific community. Even without the use of nuclear weapons, the Military-Technical Revolution could take conventional warfare to new and unparalleled heights of destructiveness, the modern state to yet higher levels of organization. Since the wars fought by such states would be highly capital-intensive and would not require large conscript armies, and since military power would become the province of a technical-scientific elite, the interesting question arises whether the Scientific Warfare State would remain either liberal or democratic. With mass participation in war rendered obsolete, would a new scientific aristocracy arise, having both a monopoly on the tools of war and a lockhold on political power, much like the aristocracy of old? The prospect is frightening; the possibility distant, but not remote.

"The decisive means for politics is violence," wrote Max Weber, "Anyone who fails to see this is . . . a political infant."[9] But if a randomly selected group of educated Americans or Europeans were asked to list the five words that best characterize Western civilization, it is a fair bet that only a handful would include "violence." We resist acknowledging, much less squarely confronting, the pervasive role of war in our history and politics, conditioned as we are by three centuries of Enlightenment vanity to think of the history of the West as a tapestry of progress, a steady ascent from medieval darkness to the light of reason. When faced with the nonetheless undeniable prevalence of violent conflict in the modern era, we shrink, ostrichlike, from the implications of our own history. The tendency of scholarship has been to marginalize the study of war into compartmentalized niches of military history and international security, to treat war as an aberration, an anomaly, an interruption in the development of the West. Should we not rather discard evolutionary and progressive models of change and humbly acknowledge this tragic—and fundamental—thread in Western civilization?

Perhaps in this regard our inquiry has been too aseptic. By concentrating on such neglected aspects of war as bureaucracy, taxation, socialization, internal bargaining, ratchet effects, and the home front we have averted our gaze from its more horrific aspects. No study of war, however academic or clinical, should ever overlook the gruesome visage of battle. Instead of introducing each chapter with a pithy quotation from a political philosopher or observer, perhaps each chapter should have opened with excerpts such as this:

> We see men living with their skulls blown open; we see soldiers run with their two feet cut off, they stagger on their splintered stumps into the next shell-hole; a lance corporal crawls a mile and half on his hands dragging his smashed knee after him; another goes to the dressing station and over his clasped hands bulge his intestines; we see men without mouths, without jaws, without faces; we find one man who has held the artery of his arm in his teeth for two hours in order not to bleed to death.[10]

War is indubitably Hell, and it remains such even in those instances when it is wholly just, justified, and defensive in intent. If war has been an engine, a catalyst, an accelerant of modernization, then perhaps we need to revaluate the linkage between progress and modernization; we likely would be better today if the modern world had emerged more gradually and less convulsively.

In the final analysis, any contemplation of war must return to the neglected First Image, the nature of humanity, which yet stands as the root cause of war and the wellspring of History's inestimable tragedy. Throughout time, governments, like wars, have both flowed from and reflected human nature in both its positive and negative manifestations. If we are to overcome the massive violence that has typified modern civilization for five centuries, our ultimate challenge is nothing more or less than transforming the image we see in the mirror. That, however, is a task that lends itself to no purely political solution. As the poet Marianne Moore* reminds us:

> There never was a war that was
> not inward; I must
> fight till I have conquered in myself what
> causes war, but I would not believe it.
> I inwardly did nothing.
> O Iscariot-like crime!
> Beauty is everlasting
> and dust is for a time.

Notes

Prologue: The Paradox of War

1. James M. McPherson, *Battle Cry of Freedom: The Civil War Era* (New York and Oxford: Oxford University Press, 1988), pp. viii and ix, cites several examples of how "time and consciousness took on new dimensions" during the American Civil War, with sweeping personal, social, political, and economic changes compressed into very short time periods.

2. On this point, see Anthony Giddens, *The Nation-State and Violence*, Vol. 2 of *A Contemporary Critique of Historical Materialism* (Berkeley: University of California Press, 1987), pp. 232–36.

3. Quoted in Henry Jacoby, *The Bureaucratization of the World*, trans. by E. L. Kanes (Berkeley: University of California Press, 1973), p. 213.

4. Harold Lasswell, *National Security and Individual Freedom* (New York: McGraw-Hill, 1950), pp. 23–49.

5. Heinrich von Treitschke, *Politics*, Vol. 1, trans. by Blanche Dugdale and Torben de Bille (New York: Macmillan, 1916), pp. 29 and 66–67.

6. V. I. Lenin, *Collected Works*, Vol. 21, p. 40.

7. Max Weber, *General Economic History*, trans. by Frank H. Knight (Glencoe, IL.: The Free Press, 1950), pp. 325–26.

8. Ramsay MacDonald, cited in Kenneth O. Morgan, ed., *The Oxford Illustrated History of Britain* (Oxford: Oxford University Press, 1984), p. 528; Léon Abensour, cited in James F. McMillan, "World War I and Women in France," in Arthur Marwick, ed., *Total War and Social Change* (London: Macmillan, 1988), p. 5; Deborah Dwork, *War is Good for Babies and Other Young Children: A History of the Infant and Child Welfare Movement in England 1898–1918* (London: Tavistock Publications, 1987). J. M. Winter, *The Great War and the British People* (Cambridge, MA: Harvard University Press, 1986) discusses the social reforms of World War I at length in Part II of his book, aptly titled "The Paradox of the Great War."

9. Mitchell Goodman, *The End of It* (New York: Farrar, Straus & Giroux, 1989), p. 28. The phrase "immaculate contraption" appears on p. 20.

10. H. G. Wells, *Italy, France and Britain at War* (New York: The Macmillan Company, 1917), p. 144.

11. Charles Tilly, "Reflections on the History of European State-Making," in Tilly, ed., *The Formation of National States in Western Europe* (Princeton: Princeton University Press, 1975), p. 42.

12. Ernest Renan, "What is a Nation?" trans. by Alfred Zimmern, excerpted in

William Ebenstein, *Modern Political Thought* (New York: Rinehart, 1954), p. 650. For a very different perspective on the paradoxical nature of war, particularly as it pertains to the causes of war and its military outcomes, see Zeev Maoz, *Paradoxes of War: On the Art of National Self-Entrapment* (Boston: Unwin Hyman, 1990).

13. William Shakespeare, *The Tragedy of King Lear*, Act V, sc. ii, l. 9; Herbert J. Muller, *The Uses of the Past* (Oxford: Oxford University Press, 1952), p. 394.

Chapter 1: The Mirror Image of War

1. To be precise, Machiavelli said that the "the principle foundations which all states have . . . are good laws and powerful armies." But he went on to say that "since there can be no good laws where there are not strong armies . . . I shall set aside any discussion of laws and proceed to speak of armies." Niccolò Machiavelli, *The Prince*, trans. by A. Robert Caponigri (Chicago: Henry Regnery, 1963), p. 70.

2. An excellent look at that subject is David B. Ralston, *Importing the European Army: The Introduction of European Military Techniques and Institutions into the Extra-European World, 1600–1914* (Chicago: University of Chicago Press, 1990).

3. Kenneth N. Waltz, *Man, the State and War: A Theoretical Analysis* (New York: Columbia University Press, 1954).

4. The seminal work was Charles Tilly, ed., *The Formation of National States in Western Europe* (Princeton: Princeton University Press, 1975), with Tilly's "Reflections on the History of European State Making," pp. 3–83, of particular importance. Tilly has continued to write on the subject, culminating recently in a more fully developed theory of state formation, *Coercion, Capital, and European States, A.D. 990–1990* (Oxford and Cambridge: Basil Blackwell, 1990). An important book-length work devoted entirely to the subject is Karen A. Rasler and William R. Thompson, *War and State Making* (Boston: Unwin Hyman, 1989). Several other scholars—Richard Bean, James E. Cronin, Brian Downing, Anthony Giddens, Keith Jaggers, Arthur Marwick, William H. McNeill, Theda Skocpol, and others—have also written articles or books illuminating various aspects of the link between war and state formation. Their works will be cited at appropriate points later in the text.

5. Otto Hintze, "The Formation of States and Constitutional Development: A Study in History and Politics," *Historische Zeitschrift*, Vol. 88, (1902), reprinted in Felix Gilbert, ed., *The Historical Essays of Otto Hintze* (New York: Oxford University Press, 1975), p. 159; and Hintze, "Military Organization and the Organization of the State," in Gilbert, ed., *The Historical Essays of Otto Hintze*, pp. 181 and 215.

6. On this point, see Arthur A. Stein and Bruce M. Russett, "Evaluating War: Outcomes and Consequences," in Ted Gurr, ed., *The Handbook of Political Conflict* (New York: Free Press, 1980), pp. 399–402. On a similar neglect in sociology and anthropology, see Anthony Giddens, *The Nation-State and Violence*, pp. 22–31; Morris Janowitz, *Military Conflict* (Beverly Hills: Sage Publications, 1975), p. 70; and Keith F. Otterbein, "Warfare: A Hitherto Unrecognized Critical Variable," *American Behavioral Scientist* 20 (May/June 1977):693–710.

7. Peter Gourevitch, "The Second image Reversed: the International Sources of Domestic Politics," *International Organization* 32 (Autumn 1978):881–911, broadens the concept of "the second image reversed" to cover all possible sources of international influence on domestic politics: international commerce, eco-

nomic interdependence, transnational institutions, and the world capitalist system. Such factors clearly also influence the internal politics of states, but in keeping with Waltz's original concern, this study will concentrate on the impact of war and military rivalry.

8. There is a vigorous debate in political science and sociology between the "Return to the State" school and its critics on the validity of the state as a focus of research and analysis. See Gabriel A. Almond, "The Return to the State," *American Political Science Review* 82 (September 1988):853–74, and the responses to him in the same volume by Eric Nordlinger, Theodore J. Lowi, and Sergio Fabbrini, "The Return to the State: Critiques," pp. 875–901. See also Eric A. Nordlinger, *On the Autonomy of the Democratic State* (Cambridge, MA: Harvard University Press, 1981).

9. Anthony D. Smith, "State-making and Nation-Building," in John A. Hall, ed., *States in History* (Oxford: Basil Blackwell, 1986), p. 228. Smith's article is an excellent discussion of the distinction (and the connections) between states and nations.

10. Fred Halliday, "State and Society in International Relations: A Second Agenda," *Millennium: Journal of International Studies* 16 (Summer 1987):217. See also Alan James, *Sovereign Statehood* (London: Allen and Unwin, 1986), p. 13: "A state may therefore be said to be made up of territory, people and a government."

11. From the "Return to the State" literature, see Peter B. Evans, Dietrich Rueschemeyer, and Theda Skocpol, *Bringing the State Back In* (Cambridge: Cambridge University Press, 1985); John A. Hall and G. John Ikenberry, *The State* (Stony Stratford: Open University Press, 1989); John A. Hall, ed., *States in History*; Edward W. Lehman, "The Theory of the State Versus the State of the Theory," *American Sociological Review* 53 (December 1988):818–21; and Karen Barkey and Sunita Parikh, "Comparative Perspective on the State," *Annual Review of Sociology* 17 (1991):523–49. Other important theoretical studies on the state include Bill Jordan, *The State: Authority and Autonomy* (Oxford: Basil Blackwell, 1985); James A. Caporaso, ed., *The Elusive State: International and Comparative Perspectives* (Newbury Park, CA: Sage Publications, 1989); Gianfranco Poggi, *The Development of the Modern State: A Sociological Introduction* (Stanford: Stanford University Press, 1978), and Gianfranco Poggi, *The State: Its Nature, Development and Prospects* (Stanford: Stanford University Press, 1990). A review of Marxist perspectives is Bob Jessop, *State Theory: Putting the Capitalist State in its Place* (University Park, PA: Pennsylvania State University Press, 1990).

12. Max Weber, "Politics as a Vocation," in H. H. Gerth and C. Wright Mills, eds., *From Max Weber: Essays in Sociology* (New York: Oxford University Press, 1946), pp. 77–82. This article was originally a speech given by Weber at the University of Munich, 1918.

13. John Gerard Ruggie, "Continuity and Transformation in the World Polity: Toward a Neorealist Synthesis," *World Politics* 35 (January 1983):273.

14. The concept of the Military Revolution will be discussed in detail in Chapter 2. The term was first used by the historian Michael Roberts in a lecture at Queens University in Belfast in 1955. See Michael Roberts, "The Military Revolution," in his *Essays in Social History* (Minneapolis: University of Minnesota Press, 1967). An early article by a contemporary scholar that postulated a direct link between war and early modern state formation was Richard Bean, "War and the Birth of the Nation State," *Journal of Economic History* 33 (1973):203–21.

15. Charles Tilly, *Coercion, Capital, and European States*, p. 5.
16. Perry Anderson, *Lineages of the Absolutist State* (London: Verso Press, 1979); Samuel P. Huntington, *Political Order in Changing Societies* (New Haven: Yale University Press, 1968); Immanuel Wallerstein, *The Modern World System*, 3 vols. (New York: Academic Press, 1974–1988; Mancur Olson, *The Rise and Decline of Nations: Economic Growth, Stagflation, and Social Rigidities* (New Haven: Yale University Press, 1982); Bruce Bueno de Mesquita, *The War Trap* (New Haven: Yale University Press, 1981); Stein Rokkan, "Dimensions of State Formation and Nation-Building," in Charles Tilly, ed., *The Formation of National States in Western Europe*, pp. 562–600. Tilly in *Coercion, Capital, and European States*, pp. 5–14, discusses these and other theories and divides them into four general categories: modes of production, statist, world system, and geopolitical.
17. Stanislav Andreski (also spelled Andrzejewski) *Military Organization and Society* (London: Routledge & Kegan Paul, 1954); Samuel Finer, "State- and Nation-Building in Europe: The Role of the Military," in Charles Tilly, ed., *The Formation of National States in Western Europe*, pp. 84–163; David C. Rapoport, "A Comparative Theory of Military and Political Types," in Samuel P. Huntington, ed., *Changing Patterns of Military Politics* (New York: The Free Press of Glencoe, 1962), pp. 71–100; Friedrich Engels, "The Armies of Europe," *Putnam's Monthly*, 6 (1855):193–206 and 306–317, cited in David Rapoport, op. cit., p. 71. Another study that emphasizes the close connections between military organization and state structure, albeit in less theoretical terms, is André Corvisier, *Armies and Societies in Europe, 1494–1789*, trans. by Abigail T. Siddall (Bloomington: Indiana University Press, 1979).
18. David C. Rapoport, "A Comparative Theory of Military and Political Types," p. 97.
19. These three basic incarnations of the modern state are neither comprehensive nor necessarily exclusive. Republics and confederations were anomalies that did not fit the general pattern. Some nation-states retained dynastic monarchies, and most industrial states were also nation-states. But the characteristic features associated with each period are sufficiently stark to justify the demarcation.
20. Michael Mann, "The Autonomous Power of the State," in John A. Hall, ed., *States in History* (Oxford: Basil Blackwell, 1986) draws a similar distinction between "despotic power" and "infrastructural power" (p. 114). I have chosen to use Anthony Giddens's term, "administrative power," a concept he discusses at length in *The Nation-State and Violence*, pp. 41–48 and 172–91.
21. James Madison, "Political Observations," *Letters and Other Writings of James Madison*, Vol. IV (Philadelphia: J. B. Lippincott & Co., 1865) pp. 491–92.
22. Alexis de Tocqueville, *Democracy in America*, Henry Reeve text, Vol. 2 (New York: Vintage, 1990), p. 269.
23. This thesis is brilliantly argued by Brian Downing in his book, *The Military Revolution and Political Change: Origins of Democracy and Autocracy in Early Modern Europe* (Princeton: Princeton University Press, 1992); Downing's book will be examined at several points in this study. Ted Robert Gurr makes a somewhat similar argument in "War, Revolution, and the Growth of the Coercive State," in James A. Caporaso, *The Elusive State*, pp. 49–68.
24. On the tendency of war to strengthen the power and capacity of states, see Ted Robert Gurr, Keith Jaggers, and Will H. Moore, "The Transformation of the Western State: The Growth of Democracy, Autocracy, and State Power Since 1800," *Studies in Comparative International Development* 25 (Spring 1990):73–108.

25. Mark Greengrass, ed., *Conquest and Coalescence: The Shaping of the State in Early Modern Europe* (London: Edward Arnold, 1991), pp. 1–2. I have borrowed the phrase "conquest and coalescence" from the title of this book.

26. Ernest Renan, "What is a Nation?" trans. by Alfred Zimmern, excerpted in William Ebenstein, *Modern Political Thought* (New York: Rinehart, 1954), p. 650.

27. Jean Bodin, in *Six Books of the Commonwealth*, trans. by M. J. Tooley (Oxford: Basil Blackwell, undated), Book V, Ch. v., p. 168, observes that "the best way of preserving a state, and guaranteeing it against sedition, rebellion, and civil war is to keep the subjects in amity one with another, and to this end, to find an enemy against whom they can make common cause." G. F. W. Hegel, *Philosophy of Right*, trans. by T. M. Knox (Oxford: Oxford University Press, 1952), p. 210 (para. 324) makes a similar point; Hegel's views on the impact of war on state unity are summarized in Pierre Hassner, "Georg W. F. Hegel," in Leo Strauss and Joseph Cropsey, eds., *History of Political Philosophy*, 3rd ed. (Chicago: University of Chicago Press, 1987), p. 752, which rephrases Hegel's argument in these words: "only a great danger or a great external undertaking permits the achievement of the sacred union of state by silencing divisions and particular interests." The Scottish philosopher Adam Ferguson also argued that a sense of national union derived in large part from the existence of adversaries. See Adam Ferguson, *Essay on the History of Civil Society*, 7th ed. (Boston: Hastings, Etheridge, and Bliss, 1809), p. 41.

28. The most dramatic example perhaps was World War I, which caused an almost immediate healing of deep social rifts in most European countries. The Franco-Prussian War also offers a powerful example. M. Jules Favre, the French Minister of Foreign Affairs under the brief-lived Government of National Defense, describes the spirit of Paris during the period of Germany's siege: ". . . during these first days it would have been difficult to discover the germ of any serious division. All party spirit seemed forgotten by those who had lost the supreme power, as well as those who had taken possession of it. The deputies of the Opposition and Centre showed themselves in large numbers at the Hôtel de Ville, and offered their concurrence with entire disinterestedness." M. Jules, Favre, *The Government of the National Defence*, trans. by H. Clark (London: Henry S. King, 1873), pp. 144–45.

29. William Shakespeare, *Henry IV, Part II*, Act IV, sc. 5, ll. 213–15; Sully, cited in David Buisseret, *Sully and the Growth of Centralized Government in France 1598–1610* (London: Eyre & Spottiswoode, 1968), p. 177. A superb study of whether or not diversion is a major cause of war is Jack Levy, "The Diversionary Theory of War: A Critique," in Manus I. Midlarsky, ed., *Handbook of War Studies* (Boston: Unwin Hyman, 1989), pp. 259–88. See also Leo A. Hazelwood, "Diversion mechanisms and encapsulation processes: the domestic conflict-foreign conflict hypothesis reconsidered," in P. J. McGowan, ed., *Sage International Yearbook of Foreign Policy Studies* 3 (Beverly Hills: Sage, 1975), pp. 213–44.

30. Youssef Cohen, Brian R. Brown, and A. F. K. Organski, "The Paradoxical Nature of State Making: The Violent Creation of Order," *American Political Science Review* 75 (December 1981):902.

31. Various scholarly theories on the growth of bureaucracy are reviewed in Robert Higgs, *Crisis and Leviathan: Critical Episodes in the Growth of American Government* (New York: Oxford University Press, 1987), pp. 3–19, and in Bruce D. Porter, "Parkinson's Law Revisited: War and the Growth of the American Government," *The Public Interest*, No. 60 (Summer 1980):50–68. The latter article

discusses why these theories are inadequate as explanations of bureaucratic growth.

32. *New York Times*, June 19, 1978. The first account of Parkinson's law appeared as an anonymous essay in *The Economist*, 177 (November 19, 1955):635–37. This was subsequently published as the first chapter of C. Northcote Parkinson, *Parkinson's Law and Other Studies in Administration* (Boston: Houghton Mifflin Company, 1957).

33. Thomas Paine, *Prospects on the Rubicon*, 1787.

34. Gabriel Ardant, "Financial policy and economic infrastructure of modern states and nations," in Charles Tilly, ed., *The Formation of National States in Western Europe*, pp. 164–242; Edward Ames and Richard T. Rapp, "The Birth and Death of Taxes: A Hypothesis," *Journal of Economic History* 37 (1977):161–78. Michael Mann, "State and Society, 1130–1815: An Analysis of English State Finances," *Political Power and Social Theory* 1 (1980):165–208, studies the finances of the English state for nearly seven centuries and concludes that "somewhere between 75 percent and 90 percent of its financial resources were almost continuously deployed on the acquisition and use of military force (p. 197)." If this is the case with an island state relatively isolated from the winds of war, what would a careful analysis such as Mann's indicate for the continental states?

35. Rasler and Thompson, *War and State Making*, p. 153; see the entire analysis, pp. 119–54.

36. This is the explanation proposed by Alan Peacock and Jack Wiseman, *The Growth of Public Expenditures in the United Kingdom* (Princeton: Princeton University Press, 1961), pp. 24–30. Robert Higgs, *Crisis and Leviathan*, pp. 30–33, 57–74, discusses at length the concept of the "ratchet effect" as it applies to government growth.

37. Arthur Marwick, *War and Social Change in the Twentieth Century: A Comparative Study of Britain, France, Germany, Russia and the United States* (London: Collier-Macmillan, 1974), p. 12. Marwick offers a model of war's social effects, involving four "tiers" of which the test of war is one. The others are the destructive and disruptive effects of war, the element of social participation in war, and the psychological experience of war. See pp. 11–14. An earlier iteration of these points is in Marwick, *Britain in the Century of Total War* (London: Bodley Head, 1968).

38. As Walter Laqueur observes, "War appears to have been the decisive factor in the emergence of revolutionary situations in modern times; most modern revolutions, both successful and abortive, have followed in the wake of war." See Walter Laqueur, "Revolution," *International Encyclopedia of the Social Sciences*, XIII, p. 501. Laqueur offers several possible explanations: the dislocation caused by war; the material and human losses that create a climate conducive to radical change; the wartime distribution of arms among large segments of the population; defeated regimes are discredited, making them vulnerable to revolution; wounded national pride enhances the appeal of radical proposals for change.

39. Bruce Bueno de Mesquita, Randolph M. Siverson, and Gary Woller, "War and the Fate of Regimes: A Comparative Analysis," *American Political Science Review* 86 (September 1992):638–46.

40. Keith Jaggers, "War and the Three Faces of Power: War Making and State Making in Europe and the Americas," *Comparative Political Studies* 25 (April 1992):26–62, argues that the dislocation and societal trauma associated with large wars greatly weakens the capacity of states to govern effectively at home. Jaggers conjectures that in wars involving high levels of human suffering and dislocation,

regimes lose public support and legitimacy, causing an overall decline of state capacity.

41. This is of course the central thesis of Paul Kennedy, *The Rise and Fall of the Great Powers: Economic Change and Military Conflict from 1500 to 2000* (New York: Random House, 1987).

42. The term "audit of war" comes from Correlli Barnett: "total war submits nations to a ruthless audit of resources, talents and failings: human, social, cultural, political and technological no less than military." See Correlli Barnett, *The Audit of War: The Illusion & Reality of Britain as a Great Nation* London: Macmillan, 1986), p. xi. The inspection effect is discussed in Peacock and Wiseman, *The Growth of Public Expenditure in the United Kingdom*, p. xxiv; see also pp. 67–68.

43. See the discussion in Peter Riesenberg, *Citizenship in the Western Tradition: Plato to Rousseau* (Chapel Hill: University of North Carolina Press, 1992), pp. 6–15 and 22–27.

44. A similar process later occurred in the developing world, as military forces were modernized along European lines and officers were recruited from outside the traditional sources of military manpower: "Because the new, European-style armed forces could thus bring people from what were the less eminent, less prestigious strata of society into positions of potential power . . . they functioned as agents of social mobility within a fundamentally ascriptive order." David B. Ralston, *Importing the European Army*, pp. 175–76.

45. David Ben-Gurion speech, August 19, 1952, *Divrei Haknesset* (Parliamentary Debates), Vol. 12, p. 3022. Translated by Alon Peled.

46. Stanislaw Andreski [Andrzejewski], *Military Organization and Society*, pp. 20–74.

47. An excellent discussion of the military bases of nationalism is found in Endre B. Gastony, *The Ordeal of Nationalism in Modern Europe 1789–1945* (Lewiston, NY: The Edwin Mellen Press, 1992), pp. 101–135. See also Barnaby C. Keeney, "Military Service and the Development of Nationalism in England, 1272–1327," *Speculum: A Journal of Medieval Studies* 22 (October 1947):534–49, which discusses the first manifestations of modern nationalism as arising from military service. On the earlier point that nationalism can divide nations, unify them, or promote reform, see John Breuilly, *Nationalism and the State* (Chicago: University of Chicago Press, 1985), which sets forth a typology of nationalisms including separatist nationalism, unification nationalism, and reform nationalism, and discusses examples of each.

48. For a detailed discussion of Adam Smith's views on this point, see Peter Minowitz, "Invisible Hand, Invisible Death: Adam Smith on War and Socio-Economic Development," *Journal of Political and Military Sociology* 17 (Winter 1989):305–15.

49. William H. McNeill, *The Pursuit of Power: Technology, Armed Force, and Society since A.D. 1000* (Chicago: University of Chicago Press, 1982), p. 117.

50. Max Weber, "The Meaning of Discipline," in *From Max Weber: Essays in Sociology*, p. 261.

51. Mussolini, cited in William Ebenstein, ed., *Man and the State: Modern Political Ideas* (New York: Rinehart & Co., 1947), p. 296. See also Benito Mussolini, *Fascism: Doctrine and Institutions* (New York: Howard Fertig, 1968), pp. 27–31, and the discussion of Fascist doctrine on the state in A. James Gregor, *the Ideology of Fascism: The Rationale of Totalitarianism* (New York: The Free Press, 1969), pp. 154–66 and 183–97.

52. F. E. Manning, *The Middle Parts of Fortune: Somme & Ancre, 1916* (London: Peter Davies, 1977), p. 182.

Chapter 2: War and the Passing of the Medieval Age

1. Hugh R. Trevor-Roper, "The General Crisis of the Seventeenth Century," in Trevor Ashton, ed., *Crisis in Europe 1560–1660* (London: Routledge & Kegan Paul, 1965), p. 70.

2. Numerous historians have pointed to the extensive influence of warfare on historical development during this era. See, for example, Bernard Guenée, *States and Rulers in Later Medieval Europe*, trans. by Juliet Vale (Oxford: Basil Blackwell, 1985), pp. 137–44; Christopher Allmand, *The Hundred Years' War: England and France at War c. 1300–c. 1450* (Cambridge: Cambridge University Press, 1988), pp. 91–115 and 136–150; Eugene F. Rice, Jr., *The Foundations of Early Modern Europe, 1460–1559* (New York: W. W. Norton, 1970), pp. 10–18 and 92–106; J. H. Shennan, *The Origins of the Modern European State 1450–1725* (London: Hutchinson & Co., Ltd. 1974), pp. 33–40. Joseph R. Strayer, *On the Medieval Origins of the Modern State* (Princeton: Princeton University Press, 1970), dissents somewhat from this point of view, arguing that major wars such as the Hundred Years' War actually "discouraged the normal development of the apparatus of the state. There was a tendency to postpone structural reforms . . ." (p. 60). But even he admits earlier: "But in a sense the wars were necessary to complete the development of a system of sovereign states" (p. 58).

3. Joseph R. Strayer, *On the Medieval Origins of the Modern State*, p. 3. On the nature of feudalism as a system of government, see also the essays by Strayer and Coulborn in Rushton Coulborn, ed., *Feudalism in History* (Hamden, CT: Archon Books, 1965), pp. 3–25.

4. Heinrich Mitteis, for example, uses the term "state" in his discussion of medieval constitutional history, *The State in the Middle Ages: A Comparative Constitutional History of Feudal Europe*, trans. by H. F. Orton (Amsterdam: North-Holland, 1975), but he acknowledges, "the word 'state,' as used in this context, still lacked the full significance of modern terminology" (p. 4). See also the discussion by Sidney Z. Ehler, "On Applying the Modern Term 'State' to the Middle Ages," in J. A. Watt, et al., *Medieval Studies* (Dublin: Colm O. Lochlainn, 1961), pp. 493–501.

5. An excellent short discussion of the salient features of medieval versus modern politics is John Gerard Ruggie, "Continuity and Transformation in the World Polity: Toward a Neorealist Synthesis," *World Politics* 43 (1983), pp. 261–85 and especially pp. 273–81.

6. On the central importance of military service in the life of the medieval aristocracy, see Marc Bloch, *Feudal Society*, trans. by L. A. Manyon (London: Routledge & Kegan Paul, 1961), pp. 289–82; John H. Kautsky, *The Politics of Aristocratic Empires* (Chapel Hill: University of North Carolina Press, 1982), pp. 144–150; and K. B. McFarlane, *The Nobility of Later Medieval England* (Oxford: Clarendon Press, 1973), pp. 41–60.

7. On the nature of medieval warfare, see Philippe Contamine, *War in the Middle Ages*, trans. by Michael Jones (Oxford: Basil Blackwell, 1986); Hans Delbrück, *History of the Art of War Within the Framework of Political History*, Vol. 3: *The Middle Ages* (Westport: Greenwood Press, 1982); John Beeler, *Warfare in Feudal Europe, 730–1200* (Ithaca: Cornell University Press, 1984). See also the discussion of violence in medieval Europe in Bloch, *Feudal Society*, pp. 410–12.

8. "It is . . . misleading and lacking in historical perspective to classify the patrimonial bureaucrats of the feudal age and their immediate successors as 'public ser-

vants' and embryonic 'civil servants' in the modern sense." Hans Rosenberg, *Bureaucracy, Aristocracy and Autocracy: The Prussian Experience 1600–1815* (Cambridge, MA: Harvard University Press, 1966), p. 6.

9. On the importance and role of the Estates, see Bernard Guenée, *States and Rulers in Later Medieval Europe*, pp. 157–70; A. R. Myers, *Parliaments and Estates in Europe to 1789* (London: Thames and Hudson, 1975), pp. 9–33; C. H. McIlwain, "Medieval Estates," *Cambridge Medieval History* (Cambridge: Cambridge University Press, 1968), Vol. VII, pp. 664–713; Gianfranco Poggi, *The Development of the Modern State: A Sociological Introduction* (Stanford: Stanford University Press, 1978), pp. 36–59.

10. Brian M. Downing discusses the importance of medieval constitutionalism to democratic development, and the deleterious impact of warfare, in *The Military Revolution and Political Change: Origins of Democracy and Autocracy in Early Modern Europe* (Princeton: Princeton University Press, 1992). The concept of the dualism of the *Ständestaat* was first developed at length by the nineteenth century German jurist Otto von Gierke in his multivolume work *Das Deutsche Genossenschaftsrecht*; see also the discussion in Gianfranco Poggi, *The Development of the Modern State*, pp. 46–51. W. P. Blockmans, "A Typology of Representative Institutions in Late Medieval Europe," *Journal of Medieval History* 4 (1978):189–215, challenges the notion of a dualistic *Ständestaat* and offers a more complex schema of late medieval constitutionalism.

11. On this point, see J. H. Elliott, *Imperial Spain 1469–1716* (London: Penguin Books, 1990), p. 86.

12. A. W. Lovett, *Early Habsburg Spain 1517–1598* (Oxford: Oxford University Press, 1986), p. 15. The Cortes of Madrigal (1476) initially approved this move; a few months later (perhaps as the implications dawned on the nobility) a meeting of deputies in Dueñas voiced "stormy opposition" to its existence. See also John Lynch, *Spain under the Habsburgs*, 2 vols. (Oxford: Basil Blackwell), 1:5.

13. Charles Ross, *The Wars of the Roses: A Concise History* (New York: Thames and Hudson, 1976), p. 152. Many early histories assert that the decline of aristocratic power was due to the physical casualties of the nobility in battle. Recent research discounts this. More important than the loss of life was the havoc that the civil war wreaked upon the economic life of the large landed estates, disrupting production and breaking the will to war of the magnates. See Ross, pp. 151–58, and Anthony Goodman, *The Wars of the Roses: Military Activity and English Society, 1452–97* (London: Routledge & Kegan Paul, 1981), pp. 208–10.

14. "The revolution of 1485 was a revolution of the middle class in alliance with Henry Tudor." Frederick C. Dietz, *English Government Finance 1485–1558* (Urbana: University of Illinois Press, 1921), p. 19.

15. B. Guenée, *States and Rulers in Later Medieval Europe*, p. 144. For more detail on the development of artillery in France and other European countries in the High Middle Ages and early Renaissance, see Contamine, *War in the Middle Ages*, pp. 138–150 and 193–200.

16. Philippe Contamine, *War in the Middle Ages*, p. 148; J. R. Hale, *War and Society in Renaissance Europe*, p. 234; William H. McNeill, *The Pursuit of Power*, pp. 87–89.

17. Goodman, *The Wars of the Roses*, p. 160–61; Norman Skentelbery, *Arrows to Atom Bombs: A History of the Ordnance Board* (London: Her Majesty's Stationery Office, 1975), p. 12.

18. P. Contamine, *War in the Middle Ages*, p. 132. Many military historians describe cavalry as the predominant fighting force in the Middle Ages, with infantry constituting the largest force in armies only in the Renaissance. Contamine makes clear that the primacy of cavalry was only a relatively brief chapter in medieval warfare. See also John Gillingham, "Richard I and the Science of War in the Middle Ages," in John Gillingham and J. C. Holt, eds., *War And Government In The Middle Ages* (New York: The Boydell Press, 1984), pp. 78–91. "The infantry arm [in the Middle Ages] was vitally important . . . it would be difficult to think of generalisations more misleading than such statements as in the Middle Ages 'the principal arm in any military force was the heavy cavalry' . . ." (p. 91).

19. Eugene F. Rice, Jr., *The Foundations of Early Modern Europe, 1460–1559*, p. 16; see also pp. 10–18 and Rice's discussion of the rise of the modern state, pp. 92–121. John U. Nef, *War and Human Progress: An Essay on the Rise of Industrial Civilization* (Cambridge, MA: Harvard University Press, 1952), pp. 23–41, and William McNeill, *The Pursuit of Power*, pp. 65–95, also discuss the implications of the new military technology for this period. A vigorous dissent on the political importance of artillery and firearms is in J. R. Hale, *War and Society in Renaissance Europe 1450–1620* (Leicester: Leicester University Press, 1985), pp. 248–51. Hale argues that Renaissance monarchs never successfully maintained a monopoly on artillery, and that walled cities and certain powerful magnates also possessed it. Although this is true, the fact remains that the majority of cannon were in the hands of the monarchs by 1500.

20. Malcolm Vale, in *War and Chivalry: Warfare and Aristocratic Culture in England, France and Burgundy at the End of the Middle Ages* (London: Duckworth, 1981), pp. 147–74, discusses at length the effect of changing military technology on chivalric warfare, concluding, "In the sixteenth century the cumulative effects of rapid changes in firearms effectively ruined the battle as a chivalric exercise . . . chivalry entered a period of decay from which it never recovered" (pp. 173–74).

21. In 1448, a third *Ordonnance* added companies of archers, the *Francs-Archers*, with every community in France expected to contribute at least one man to the new formations; but the new companies never became an important military force. On the significance of the *Ordonnances* and the role of the Hundred Years' War in strengthening monarchical control in France, see *The Cambridge Medieval History* (Cambridge: Cambridge University Press, 1969), Vol. 8, pp. 253–62.

22. Lovett, *Early Habsburg Spain*, p. 19.

23. On this point see Gianfranco Poggi, *The Development of the Modern State*, pp. 66–67.

24. John Guy, *Tudor England* (Oxford: Oxford University Press, 1988), pp. 60–61.

25. This basic argument was laid out seventy-five years ago by Joseph Schumpeter and reprinted in "The Crisis of the Tax State," *International Economic Papers*, No. 4 (1954):5–38. On the origins of modern taxation in Renaissance France and England, see also Margaret Levi, *Of Rule and Revenue* (Berkeley: University of California Press, 1988), pp. 10–40 and 95–121.

26. Richard Bean, "War and the Birth of the Nation State," *Journal of Economic History* 33 (1973):213. Even if this estimate is high and understates the effects of inflation, the general upward trend was unmistakable.

27. Christopher Allmand, *The Hundred Years War*, p. 104 and pp. 169–171. See also *Cambridge Medieval History*, Vol. VII, pp. 361–62.

28. Martin Wolfe, *The Fiscal System of Renaissance France* (New Haven: Yale University Press, 1972), pp. 29–30.
29. Martin Wolfe, *The Fiscal System of Renaissance France*, p. 25. Excellent information on taxation under Charles VII is found in Wolfe's account, pp. 25–52. Among other things, Wolfe thoroughly demolishes the revisionist thesis that the taxation reforms of Charles VII amounted to only a modest evolution from medieval practices. See also *The Cambridge Medieval History* (Cambridge: Cambridge University Press, 1969), Vol. VIII, p. 254 and pp. 260–62, and Allmand, *The Hundred Years War*, pp. 102–111 and 166–67. On the decline of the Estates General, see J. Russell Major, "The Loss of Royal Initiative and the Decay of the Estates General in France, 1421–1615," in J. Russell Major, *The Monarch, the Estates and the Aristocracy in Renaissance France* (London: Variorum Reprints, 1988), Chapter VIII, pp. 247–259. J. H. Shennan, *Government and Society in France 1461–1661* (London: George Allen and Unwin, 1969), p. 34, suggests that after the war was over Charles VII was able to reduce the burden of taxation in central France and that *this* is what led many of the provincial assemblies to cede their right to approve taxation.
30. On the draconian taxation measures of Louis XI, see Martin Wolfe, *The Fiscal System of Renaissance France*, pp. 52–59.
31. Hale, *War and Society in Renaissance Europe*, p. 233. The *maravedí* was the standard currency of account in Castilian Spain; it was not an actually currency or coin, but only a unit of account, worth a varying amount of silver coin, the standard of which was the *real*. See John Lynch, *Spain 1516–1598*, Appendix I and Angus MacKay, *Money, Prices and Politics in Fifteenth-Century Castile* (London: Royal Historical Society, 1981), pp. 12–13.
32. That is, from under 900,000 *reales* to 26,000,000 *reales*; Elliott, *Imperial Spain*, p. 92. See also Lynch, *Spain under the Habsburgs*, 1:11; Lovett, *Early Habsburg Spain*, p. 16.
33. See the *Oxford Illustrated History of Britain*, pp. 148–49 and 208; Heinrich Mitteis, *The State in the Middle Ages: A Comparative Constitutional History of Feudal Europe*, trans. by H. F. Orton (Amsterdam: North-Holland Publishing Co., 1975), pp. 357–63.
34. R. S. Schofield, Ph. D. dissertation, cited in Levi, *Of Rule and Revenue*, p. 105.
35. John Guy, *Tudor England*, pp. 65–66. See also *Oxford Illustrated History of Great Britain*, pp. 234–37; Michael Van Cleave Alexander, *The First of the Tudors: A Study of Henry VII and His Reign* (Ottawa: Rowman and Littlefield, 1980), pp. 70–82; Kenneth Pickthorn, *Early Tudor Government; Henry VII* (Cambridge: Cambridge University Press, 1949), pp. 117–21.
36. The classic account of this reform is Richardson, *Tudor Chamber Administration 1485–1547*, pp. 58–78.
37. Michael Van Cleave Alexander, *The First of the Tudors*, pp. 69–70.
38. Max Weber, *Wirtschaft und Gesellschaft*, Part II, Ch. 6, quoted in H. H. Gerth and C. Wright Mills, *From Max Weber: Essays in Sociology* (New York: Oxford University Press, 1946), p. 211.
39. Hans Rosenberg, *Bureaucracy, Aristocracy and Autocracy*, p. 14.
40. Bernard Guenée, "The History of the State in France at the End of the Middle Ages, as Seen by French Historians in the Last Hundred Years," in P. S. Lewis, ed., *The Recovery of France in the Fifteenth Century* (London: Macmillan, 1971), p. 350. Guenée does not elaborate on this point, but he does observe that the "era

of bureaucracy" in French diplomacy began at the end of the fifteenth century. Also of interest is his observation that "war and diplomacy were pretty concrete facts which the history of the state cannot afford to ignore." He notes that many French historians, especially early in the twentieth century, ignored or slighted the importance of war and other external events in analyzing the development of French administration (pp. 336–37). The entire essay is an excellent reference on the historiography of the origins of the French state.

41. "This exclusion of the great magnates from voting on matters of state meant that the traditional offices of some of the proudest families of Castile were transformed into empty dignities." Elliott, *Imperial Spain*, p. 90.

42. On educational reform in Spain and its link to the new bureaucracy, see Richard L. Kagan, *Students and Society in Early Modern Spain* (Baltimore: Johns Hopkins University Press, 1974), pp. 70–71; Elliott, *Imperial Spain*, p. 90.

43. Michael Van Cleave Alexander, *The First of the Tudors*, p. 69; Roger Lockyear, *Tudor and Stuart Britain 1471–1714*, 2nd ed. (London: Longmans, 1985), pp. 9–15. A detailed study of Henry VII's administration is W. C. Richardson, *Tudor Chamber Administration: 1485–1547* (Baton Rouge: Louisiana State University Press, 1952). See also John Guy, *Tudor England*, pp. 54–79, and *The Oxford Illustrated History of Britain*, pp. 230–37.

44. Joseph A. Schumpeter, "The Sociology of Imperialisms," in *Imperialism and Social Classes: Two Essays*, trans. by Heinz Norden (New York: Meridian Books, 1955), p. 25.

45. On nationalism in early modern Spain, see Helmut G. Koenigsberger, "Spain," in Orest Ranum, ed., *National Consciousness, History and Political Culture in Early Modern Europe* (Baltimore: John Hopkins University Press, 1975), pp. 144–72. See also J. H. Elliott, *Imperial Spain*, p. 109.

46. J. de M. Carriazo, in R. Menéndez Pidal, ed., *Historia de España (Madrid)*, xvii, I, p. 387, cited in J. N. Hillgarth, *The Spanish Kingdoms 1250–1516*, 3 vols. (Oxford: Clarendon Press, 1978) II:367.

47. J. N. Hillgarth, *The Spanish Kingdoms 1250–1516*, Vol. II: p. 393.

48. See, for example, G. R. Elton, in *The New Cambridge Modern History*, vol. 2, p. 8, and the series of articles reprinted in Arthur J. Slavin, ed., *The "New Monarchies" and Representative Assemblies: Medieval Constitutionalism or Modern Absolutism?* (Lexington: D.C. Heath, 1964).

49. Christopher Duffy, *Siege Warfare: The Fortress in the Early Modern World 1494–1660* (London: Routledge & Kegan Paul, 1979), p. 9.

50. Robert L. O'Connell, *Of Arms and Men: A History of War, Weapons, and Aggression* (Oxford: Oxford University Press, 1989), p. 114.

51. Donald R. Begot, introduction to Claude de Seyssel, *The Monarchy of France*, trans. by J. H. Hexter (New Haven: Yale University Press, 1981), p. 1.

52. On the watershed year of 1494, and how it was viewed by contemporaries, see J. R. Hale, "War and Public Opinion in Renaissance Italy," in J. R. Hale, *Renaissance War Studies* (London: The Hambledon Press, 1983), pp. 359–388. On the impact of the French invasion on Machiavelli, see Friedrich Meinecke, *Machiavellism: The Doctrine of Raison d'Etat and Its Place in Modern History*, trans. by Douglas Scott (London: Routledge and Kegan Paul, 1957), pp. 29–30.

53. On this point, see Wolfe, *The Fiscal System of Renaissance France*, p. 86.

54. James Collins, *The Fiscal Limits of the Absolutist State: Direct Taxation in Early Seventeenth Century France* (Berkeley: University of California Press, 1988), p. 32.

For more on the reforms of this period, see J. H. M. Salmon, *Society in Crisis: France in the Sixteenth Century* (London: Ernest Benn, 1975), pp. 73–76; Shennan, *Government and Society in France, 1461–1661*, pp. 49–51.

55. The long-term obligations of the Valois monarchy reached over 12 million *livres* by 1559, more than an entire year's income. Wolfe, *The Fiscal System of Renaissance France*, p. 99 and pp. 104–113; James Collins, *The Fiscal Limits of the Absolutist State*, p. 50–52; Frederic J. Baumgartner, *Henry II: King of France 1547–1559* (Durham, NC Duke University Press, 1988), pp. 134–40; R. J. Knecht, *French Renaissance Monarchy: Francis I and Henry II* (London: Longman, 1984), pp. 47–53.

56. Geoffrey Parker, *The Military Revolution: Military Innovation and the Rise of the West, 1500–1800* (Cambridge: Cambridge University Press, 1988), p. 24; J. R. Hale, *War and Society in Renaissance Europe*, p. 239; R. J. Knecht, *French Renaissance Monarchy: Francis I and Henry II*, p. 15; Wolfe, *The Fiscal System of Renaissance France*, pp. 11 and 99.

57. Pierre Achard, "History and the Politics of Language in France: A Review Essay," *History Workshop Journal* 10 (Autumn 1980): 175–83.

58. Geoffrey Parker, *The Military Revolution*, p. 45.

59. H. Koenigsberger, "The Empire of Charles V in Europe" in *The New Cambridge Modern History*, Vol. 2 (Cambridge: Cambridge University Press, 1958), p. 315.

60. On this point, see J. H. Shennan, *The Origins of the Modern European State 1450–1725*, pp. 54–55.

61. "Over a period of thirty-seven years, Charles V, whose normal annual revenue as King of Spain was about 1,000,000 ducats a year, rising to 1,500,000 after 1542, was able to borrow 39,000,000 ducats on the strength of the credit of Castile." Elliott, *Imperial Spain*, p. 206.

62. Henry Kamen, *Spain 1469–1714: A Society of Conflict* (London: Longman, 1983), pp. 86 and 90. See also Elliott, *Imperial Spain*, pp. 199–202; Douglass C. North, *Structure and Change in Economic History* (New York: Norton, 1981), p. 151.

63. Charles Tilly, *Coercion, Capital, and European States, A.D. 990–1992*, rev. ed. (Oxford: Basil Blackwell, 1992), pp. 16–20, 87–91.

64. Frederick Dietz, *English Government Finance 1485–1558* (Urbana: University of Illinois Press, 1921), pp. 90–91.

65. G. R. Elton, *The Tudor Revolution in Government: Administrative Changes in the Reign of Henry VIII* (Cambridge: Cambridge University Press, 1953). See also Penry Williams, *The Tudor Regime* (Oxford: Clarendon Press, 1979), pp. 59–62. Another factor driving financial reform was the imperative of obtaining revenue to improve English defenses in response to the increased international tensions that followed the King's divorce of Queen Catherine and consequent break with the Church of Rome. On the financial impact of the break with Rome and consequent English defense expenditures, see Frederick Dietz, *English Government Finance 1485–1558*, pp. 105–107.

66. G. R. Elton, *The Tudor Revolution in Government*, p. 415.

67. Williams, *The Tudor Regime*, pp. 115–119. Hales, *War and Society in Renaissance Europe*, p. 234.

68. When Henry died, he left behind "a debt of £100,000 Fl. in Flanders; an empty treasury, a debased currency, depleted estates and charges vastly increased by the necessity of maintaining a post war establishment in France and against Scotland." Frederick Dietz, *English Government Finance 1485–1558*, p. 158.

69. O. F. G. Hogg, *Artillery: Its Origin, Heyday and Decline* (London: C. Hurst and Company, 1970), pp. 50–56; O. F. G. Hogg, *English Artillery 1326–1716* (London: Royal Artillery Institution, 1963), pp. 18–19 and 102–108.

70. The figure on the number of ships is from Geoffrey Parker, *The Military Revolution*, pp. 90–91.

71. Otto Hintze, "Military Organization and the Organization of the State," in Felix Gilbert, ed., *The Historical Essays of Otto Hintze* (New York: Oxford University Press, 1975), p. 214.

72. Helen Miller, *Henry VIII and the English Nobility* (Oxford: Basil Blackwell, 1986), pp. 157–61. On the organization of the Tudor army, see Gilbert John Millar, *Tudor Mercenaries and Auxiliaries 1485–1547* (Charlottesville: University Press of Virginia, 1980), pp. 5–7, 12–14, and 20–21.

73. Lawrence Stone, *The Crisis of the Aristocracy 1558–1641* (Oxford: Oxford University Press, 1965), p. 200.

74. Wilhelm Oechsli, *History of Switzerland 1499–1914*, trans. by Eden and Cedar Paul (Cambridge: Cambridge University Press, 1922), p. 2. In addition to items specifically cited, other sources used for this section include Ernst Bohnenblust, *Geschichte der Schweiz* (Zurich: Eugen Rentsch Verlag, 1974); John Martin Vincent, *State and Federal Government in Switzerland* (Baltimore: John Hopkins Press, 1891); Bernard Moses, *The Federal Government of Switzerland: An Essay on the Constitution* (Oakland: Pacific Press, 1889); Horst Zimmerman, *Die Schweiz und Grossdeutschland* (Munich: Wilhelm Fink Verlag, 1980), pp. 25–49; Hanno Helbling, *Geschichte der Schweiz* (Frankfurt: Societäts-Verlag, 1982); Julian Grande, *A Citizen's Army: The Swiss System* (London: Chatto & Windus, 1916); Henry Demarest Lloyd, *The Swiss Democracy: The Study of a Sovereign People* (London: T. Fisher Unwin, 1908).

75. Hans Nabholz and Paul Klaui, *Quellenbuch zur Verfassungsgeschichte der Schweizerischen Eidgenossenschaft und der Kantone von den Anfängen bis zur Gegenwart* (Aarau: Verlag Sauerländer, 1940), p. 3. This source contains the original document in Latin, and a German translation from which this is taken.

76. Archer Jones, *The Art of War in the Western World* (New York and Oxford: Oxford University Press, 1989), p. 177.

77. On these battles and the significance of the Swiss defeats, see Archer Jones, *The Art of War in the Western World*, pp. 188–90; *New Cambridge Modern History*, Vol. 2, pp. 497–98.

78. Montesquieu, *The Spirit of the Laws*, trans. and ed. by Anne M. Cohler et al. (Cambridge: Cambridge University Press, 1989), p. 132.

79. The best account is Garrett Mattingly, *Renaissance Diplomacy* (Boston: Houghton Mifflin Company, 1955).

80. Michael Mullett, *Popular Culture and Popular Protest in Late Medieval and Early Modern Europe* (London: Croom Helm, 1987), p. 133.

81. Lauro Martines, *Power and Imagination: City-States in Renaissance Italy* (Baltimore: Johns Hopkins University Press, 1988), p. 296.

82. J. N. Stephens, *The Fall of the Florentine Republic, 1512–1530* (Oxford: Clarendon Press, 1983), p. 183. See also R. Burr Litchfield, *Emergence of a Bureaucracy: The Florentine Patricians 1530–1790* (Princeton: Princeton University Press, 1986), pp. 1–23.

83. J. R. Hale, "The End of Florentine Liberty: The Fortezza Da Basso," in J. R. Hale, *Renaissance War Studies*, p. 31.

84. Niccolò Machiavelli, *The Prince*, p. 124.
85. William McNeill, *The Pursuit of Power*, p. 80; see his entire discussion, pp. 79–98.
86. On the historical development of these fortresses, and the Italian contribution, see J. R. Hale, "The Early Development of the Bastion," in J. R. Hale, *Renaissance War Studies*, pp. 1–30.
87. John Julius Norwich, *A History of Venice* (New York: Alfred A. Knopf, 1982), p. 379.
88. Bernard Guenée, *States and Rulers in Medieval Europe*, p. 144.
89. Douglass C. North, *Structure and Change in Economic History* (New York: W. W. Norton, 1981), p. 138.
90. Max Weber, *Wirtschaft und Gesellschaft*, Part II, Chap. 6, quoted in Gerth and Mills, *From Max Weber*, p. 211.
91. All quotations are from J. R. Hale, *War and Society in Renaissance Europe 1450–1620* (Leicester University Press, 1985). The case against war as a political factor covers pp. 232–52; the point about artillery is in an earlier essay, p. 228. Hale also argues that major wars did not have a great impact internally, because their costs were usually met by loans, but admits, "Eventually war was paid for by taxes, and every expedient to spread their incidence increased the final bill." He also notes that war costs made up the bulk of the budget of Renaissance states, that the taxes required to pay for wars affected aspects of national life, and that there were "surges in tax demands clearly attributable to war that did have an identifiable and lasting effect on constitutional procedures."
92. J. H. Shennan, *The Origins of the Modern European State: 1450–1725*.
93. Gianfranco Poggi, *The Development of the Modern State: A Sociological Introduction*, p. 61; see also pp. 60–65.
94. Immanuel Wallerstein, *The Capitalist World-Economy* (Cambridge: Cambridge University Press, 1979); see, for example, Chapter 2, pp. 37–48. See also Perry Anderson, *Lineages of the Absolutist State*.
95. See Chapter 3, "The Reality of Power," of Shennan, *The Origins of the Modern European State*, pp. 44–68, especially pp. 50–51. Gianfranco Poggi, in *The Development of the Modern State*, pp. 66–7, identifies "momentous developments in the material and social technology of warfare" as causing the decline of the nobility's role in warfare and the rise of absolutist states with standing armies. Wallerstein, *The Capitalist World-Economy*, p. 46, acknowledges that the most important factor in the rise of a strong Tudor state was the weakening of the nobility in the Wars of the Roses. Charles Tilly's main premise, of course, is that "war made the state, and the state made war." His most recent exposition of the thesis is *Coercion, Capital and Nation-States*.

Chapter 3: The Military Revolution and the Early Modern State

1. Michael Roberts first proposed the term "Military Revolution" in 1955 in his Inaugural Lecture at Queens University in Belfast. While subsequent historians have differed over the nature and significance of the Military Revolution, a general consensus has developed that the period in question was a watershed in the military and political history of the continent. Roberts's lecture is reprinted, with some revisions, as "The Military Revolution, 1560–1660," in Michael Roberts, *Essays in Swedish History* (London: Weidenfeld and Nicolson, 1967), pp. 195–225. The discussion in this section is also based on Geoffrey Parker, *The Military Revolution: Military Innovation and the Rise of the West, 1500–1660*

(Cambridge: Cambridge University Press, 1988) and Russell F. Weigley, *The Age of Battles: The Quest for Decisive Warfare from Breitenfeld to Waterloo* (Bloomington: Indiana University Press, 1991), pp. 3–44. Other studies that look at the political and social impact of the Military Revolution include: Jeremy Black, *A Military Revolution? Military Change and European Society 1550–1800* (Atlantic Highlands, NJ: Humanities Press International, 1991; Michael Duffy, *The Military Revolution and the State, 1500–1800* (Exeter: University of Exeter, 1980); J. R. Hale, "The Military Reformation," Ch. 2 of *War and Society in Renaissance Europe 1450–1620*.

2. Christopher Duffy, *Siege Warfare*, p. 89. On Maurice of Nassau's use of engineers, see pp. 81–82. Duffy's entire discussion of the role of fortifications in the Eighty Years' War (pp. 58–105) is invaluable.

3. The figures in this table fluctuate according to whether or not the given state is at war; the largest numbers represent the maximum size of armies in the field. The figures for 1700 show that the growth continued after 1660 almost everywhere but in Spain, which was by then in decline. During peacetime, the size of armies would decline, but where standing armies existed, their average peacetime numbers also increased. Further discussion of the significance of the growth of European armies can be found in Michael Roberts, "The Military Revolution," in Roberts, *Essays in Swedish History*; J. R. Hale, *War and Society in Renaissance Europe 1450–1620*, pp. 61–66; John A. Lynn, "The Pattern of Army Growth, 1445–1945," in John A. Lynn, ed. *Tools of War: Instruments, Ideas, and Institutions of Warfare, 1445–1871* (Chicago: University of Illinois, 1990), pp. 1–27.

4. Theodore K. Rabb, *The Struggle for Stability in Early Modern Europe* (New York: Oxford University Press, 1975), p. 61; Geoffrey Parker, *The Military Revolution*, pp. 61–64.

5. Michael Roberts, "The Military Revolution, 1560–1660," p. 218. On the development of administrative structures to manage standing armies, see André Corvisier, *Armies and Societies in Europe 1494–1789*, trans. by Abigail T. Siddall (Bloomington: Indiana University Press, 1979), ch. 4.

6. Inexplicably, many leading historians of the Military Revolution only briefly mention its relationship to the Protestant Reformation. For example, neither Geoffrey Parker, *The Military Revolution* nor Jeremy Black, *A Military Revolution?* make any substantial reference to the Reformation, though it arguably contributed greatly to the historical conditions that fueled both conflict and military change.

7. David Held, *Political Theory and the Modern State: Essays on State, Power, and Democracy* (Stanford: Stanford University Press, 1989), p. 218.

8. Background information on the Thirty Years' War in this chapter is taken from Geoffrey Parker, *The Thirty Years' War* (London and New York: Routledge & Kegan Paul, 1984); Richard S. Dunn, *The Age of Religious Wars, 1559–1715*, 2nd ed. (New York: W. W. Norton, 1979), pp. 82–91; Hajo Holborn, *A History of Modern Germany*, Vol. 2, *The Reformation* (Princeton: Princeton University Press, 1982), pp. 305–374; Charles S. Wilson, *The Transformation of Europe 1558–1648* (Berkeley and Los Angeles: University of California Press, 1976), pp. 242–64.

9. Michael Roberts, *Gustavus Adolphus and the Rise of Sweden* (London: English Universities Press, 1973), p. 9.

10. David Kaiser, *Politics and War: European Conflict from Philip II to Hitler* (Cambridge, MA: Harvard University Press, 1990), p. 90.

11. On the significance of the Thirty Years' War and the agreement at Westphalia, see Theodore K. Rabb, *The Struggle for Stability in Early Modern Europe*, (New York: Oxford University Press, 1975), pp. 60–82; Geoffrey Parker, *The Thirty Years' War*, Ch. 5. Geoffrey Parker, in his *Europe in Crisis 1598–1648* (Ithaca: Cornell University Press, 1979), pp. 281–92 has an interesting discussion of the Peace, and the entire book is a good overview of the era under examination. On the impact of war on the state specifically, see pp. 66–75.

12. Innocent X, cited in Charles Wilson, *The Transformation of Europe 1558–1648*, p. 262.

13. "The all-pervasive issue was the increase in central governmental power, exemplified by the growth of bureaucracies. The infiltration of these multiplying public servants into regions and activities that never before had tasted their presence was met by stiffening resistance, primarily from nobles who quickly recognized the threat to their power base in the localities. And the chief instrument, both of the weakening of local lords, and of the proliferation of bureaucrats, was warfare." Theodore Rabb, *The Struggle for Stability in Early Modern Europe*, p. 60.

14. On the wars of religions, see Julien Coudy, ed., *The Huguenot Wars*, trans. by Jule Kernan (Philadelphia: Chilton Book Co., 1969), and J. H. M. Salmon, *Society in Crisis: France in the Sixteenth Century* (London: Ernest Benn, 1975). Other useful background information is found in David Buisseret, *Henry IV* (London: George Allen & Unwin, 1984), pp. 15–86; Robin Briggs, *Early Modern France: 1560–1715* (Oxford: Oxford University Press, 1977), pp. 11–34; and Richard S. Dunn, *The Age of Religious Wars*, pp. 30–40.

15. Robin Briggs, *Early Modern France*, p. 32, refers to the declaration of war as a "shrewdly judged move to unite France behind a monarch who knew how to exploit his own prowess on the battlefield."

16. On peasant revolts during the wars of religion, see J. H. M. Salmon, *Society in Crisis*, Ch. 11 and his article, "Peasant Revolt in Vivarais," in Salmon, *Renaissance and Revolt: Essays in the Intellectual and Social History of Early Modern France* (Cambridge: Cambridge University Press, 1987), pp. 211–234. On the increase in the *taille*, see graphs 2, 3, 4, and 5 in Robin Briggs, *Early Modern France: 1560–1715*, pp. 215–19.

17. On the disintegration and reconstitution of the central taxation system during the Wars of Religion, see Martin Wolfe, *The Fiscal System of Renaissance France*, pp. 137–214.

18. Edmund H. Dickerman, *Bellièvre and Villeroy: Power in France under Henry III and Henry IV* (Providence: Brown University Press, 1971), pp. 5–6 and 153–55. On the French secretaries of state during the religious wars, see N. M. Sutherland, *The French Secretaries of State in the Age of Catherine de Médicis* (London: The Athlone Press, 1962).

19. The following discussion of France under Sully, Richelieu, and Mazarin is based on Robin Briggs, *Early Modern France 1560–1715*; David Buisseret, *Sully and the Growth of Centralized Government in France 1598–1610* (London: Eyre & Spottiswoode, 1968); Buisseret, *Henry IV*; G. R. R. Treasure, *Seventeenth-Century France*, 2nd ed. (London: John Murray, 1981); Victor-L. Tapié, *France in the Age of Louis XIII and Richelieu* trans. by D. McN. Lockie (Cambridge: Cambridge University Press, 1984); Richard Bonney, *Political Change in France under Richelieu and Mazarin 1624–1661* (Oxford: Oxford University Press, 1978); Bonney, *Society and Government in France under Richelieu and Mazarin, 1624–61* (London: Collier-Macmillan Ltd., 1988).

20. The suppression of the tax revolts and the Fronde are discussed later in this chapter. Space does not permit a review of the continuing struggle against the Huguenots under Louis XIII, but two works offer considerable insight into how this civil war contributed to the consolidation of absolutist monarchy in France: A. D. Lublinskaya, *French Absolutism: The Crucial Phase, 1620–1629*, trans. by Brian Pearce (Cambridge: Cambridge University Press, 1968) Ch. 2; and David Parker, *La Rochelle and the French Monarchy: Conflict and Order in Seventeenth-Century France* (London: Royal Historical Society, 1980).

21. The quotation is from L. Jablonski, *L'Armée Française à Travers les Ages*, Vol. 1 (Paris: Librairie et Papéterie, 1890), p. 367. Financial data are taken from David Buisseret, *Henry IV*, Table 11.1, p. 152.

22. John A. Lynn, "The Pattern of Army Growth, 1445–1945," in John A. Lynn, ed., *Tools of War: Instruments, Ideas, and Institutions of Warfare 1445–1871* (Urbana: University of Illinois Press, 1990), p. 3. For a thorough description of the development of the French army in this period, see Bonney, *Political Change in France under Richelieu and Mazarin*, pp. 259–83.

23. On the tax increases and their significance, see Richard Bonney, *Political Change in France under Richelieu and Mazarin*, pp. 171–77; on the revolts, the overall crisis of the French state during this period and their relationship to the wars it was fighting, see Robert Knecht, *Richelieu* (London: Longman, 1991), Chs. 7 and 8; and Michael S. Kimmel, *Absolutism and Its Discontents: State and Society in Seventeenth Century France and England* (New Brunswick, NJ: Transaction Books, 1988), Chs. 2–4.

24. On the system of tax farming, see A. D. Lublinskaya, *French Absolutism: The Crucial Phase*, pp. 236–41, which makes clear that the tax farmers had the full backing and support of the central government and were perceived as representing it.

25. On the tax revolts in France, see Hickey, *The Coming of French Absolutism: The Struggle for Tax Reform in the Province of Dauphiné 1540–1640* (Toronto: University of Toronto Press, 1986); Robin Briggs, *Early Modern France 1560–1715*; p. 115; P. J. Coveny, *France in Crisis 1620–1675* (Totowa, N. J.: Rowman and Littlefield, 1977). From the Marxist school, two key works are Perry Anderson, *Lineages of the Absolutist State*, and Boris Porchnev, *Narodnie vosstaniia vo Frantsii pered Frondoi, 1623–1648* (Moscow: Akademicheskii Nauk SSSR, 1948). On the process of revolt and revolution in early modern Europe and its significance for politics, see Roland Mousnier, *Peasant Uprisings in Seventeenth Century France, Russia, and China* (New York: Harper and Row, 1970) and Yves-Marie Bercé, *Revolt and Revolution in Early Modern Europe: An Essay on the History of Political Violence*, trans. by Joseph Bergin (Manchester: Manchester University Press, 1987).

26. The British scholar Richard Bonney, after extensive research on the evolution of the *intendant* system, concluded that war, and especially the fiscal demands of war, was the decisive factor in its establishment. See Richard Bonney, *Political Change in France*, p. 36.

27. The military functions of the provincial *intendants* should not be confused with those of the army *intendants*, royal inspectors whose only responsibilities were with the field army. It is possible that the provincial *intendants* in some provinces evolved from the office of army *intendant*. On the origins and functions of each, see Douglas Clark Baxter, *Servants of the Sword: French Intendants of the Army 1630–70* (Urbana and Chicago: University of Illinois Press, 1976), pp. 3–19. On

the *fusiliers pour les tailles,* see Knecht, *Richelieu,* p. 123. Karen Barkey, "Rebellious Alliances: The State and Peasant Unrest in Early Seventeenth Century France and the Ottoman Empire," *American Sociological Review* 56 (December 1991): 699–715, emphasizes that the crucial determinant of the peasant rebellions was the capacity of the peasants to form alliances with disgruntled nobles; if correct, this would call into question the Marxist characterization of the rebellions as class-based and lend support to their having been primarily a revolt against waxing state power.

28. David Kaiser, *Politics and War,* pp. 20–21, argues against the proposition that significant centralization occurred in the early seventeenth century. He argues that the real revenue of the monarchs was not rising in that century, due to price inflation. While records of tax revenue do not prove a real rise in royal income during the century in question, there is little doubt that the total *share* of national revenues going to the Crown increased; tax records also usually did not show the large number of fines and levies imposed on local cities and populations by army garrisons stationed in the provinces.

29. A. Lloyd Moote, *The Revolt of the Judges: The Parlement of Paris and the Fronde, 1643–1652* (Princeton: Princeton University Press, 1971), cited in D. C. Baxter, *Servants of the Sword,* p. 114. There remains as yet no good military history of the Fronde. One early study that gives some military details is Paul Rice Doolin, *The Fronde* (Cambridge, MA: Harvard University Press, 1935). Richard Bonney, "The French Civil War, 1649–53," *European Studies Review* 8 (1978):71–100, emphasizes the importance of the government's victory over the Fronde in consolidating absolutist rule in France; he also observes (p. 92) that the war-weariness of France undercut the appeal of the rebellious nobles.

30. David Buisseret, *Henry IV,* p. 127. See also Buisseret, *Sully,* pp. 153–54.

31. The text of his communication is found in a collection of documents published by Richard Bonney, *Society and Government in France under Richelieu and Mazarin, 1624–61,* pp. 9–11. This quotation is from p. 9. See also Cardinal Richelieu, *Political Testament,* trans. by Henry Bertram Hill (Madison: University of Wisconsin Press, 1961), p. 120.

32. Geoffrey Parker, *The Military Revolution,* pp. 42–43.

33. On Vauban's accomplishments, see Henry Guerlac, "Vauban: The Impact of Science on War," in Peter Paret, ed., *Makers of Modern Strategy: from Machiavelli to the Nuclear Age* (Princeton: Princeton University Press, 1986), pp. 64–90; Pierre Gaxotte, *The Age of Louis XIV,* trans. by Michael Shaw (New York: The Macmillan Company, 1970), pp. 103–120; Russell F. Weigley, *The Age of Battles,* pp. 53–58.

34. The rivalry between Crown and aristocracy is discussed at length in Lawrence Stone, *The Crisis of the Aristocracy, 1558–1641* (Oxford: Clarendon Press, 1965), pp. 199–270, on which much of the following discussion relies.

35. T. Birch, *The Works of Sir Walter Raleigh,* 1751, Vol. I, p. 206, cited in Stone, *The Crisis of the Aristocracy,* p. 223.

36. The information in this paragraph comes largely from M. Oppenheim, *A History of the Administration of the Royal Navy and of Merchant Shipping in Relation to the Navy—From MDIX to MDCLX with an Introduction Treating of the Preceding Period* (London: Bodley Head, 1896), pp. 115–63. The figures on per annum expenditures were calculated from the table on p. 161. Due to attrition, the English navy actually only possessed seven more ships of 100 tons or more at the end

of Elizabeth's reign than at the beginning. These numbers are deceptive, however, for the new ships were larger and better built than the old, and boasted far more cannon and ordnance, purchased at great expense. See also Julian S. Corbett, *Drake and the Tudor Navy*, Vol. I (London: Longmans Green and Co., 1898), p. 370.

37. John Morrill, "The Stuarts (1603–1688)" in *The Oxford Illustrated History of Britain*, pp. 298–99.

38. G. E. Aylmer, *The King's Servants: The Civil Service of Charles I: 1625–1642*, rev. ed. (London: Routledge & Kegan Paul, 1974), pp. 27, 253–55, and 439–44. Aylmer's book is an exceptionally detailed account of English administration under Charles I, with lengthy lists of every paid position in the government.

39. Conrad S. R. Russell, "Monarchies, Wars, and Estates in England, France, and Spain, c. 1580–1640," *Legislative Studies Quarterly* 7 (May 1982): 205–220, argues that the troubles of the French and English monarchies arose from similar factors, above all the expense of war; the difference in the outcome had to do with England's insularity and greater strength both of parliament and of local government in England. Richard Lachmann, "Elite Conflict and State Formation in 16th- and 17th-Century England and France," *American Sociological Review* 54 (April 1989): 141–62, offers a very different explanation of why one monarch succeeded in civil war, while the other perished.

40. Information on the civil wars and the Interregnum is taken from many sources, including J. P. Kenyon, *The Civil Wars of England* (New York: Alfred A. Knopf, 1988); Robert Ashton, *The English Civil War: Conservatism and Revolution 1603–1649* (London: Weidenfeld and Nicolson, 1978); Roger Lockyear, *Tudor and Stuart Britain 1471–1714*, 2nd ed. (New York: Longman, 1985); C. H. Firth, *Cromwell's Army: A History of the English Soldier during the Civil Wars, the Commonwealth and the Protectorate*, 4th ed. (London: Methuen, 1962); John Morrill, *Oliver Cromwell and the English Revolution* (London and New York: Longman, 1990); Charles Harding Firth, *The House of Lords During the Civil War* (Totowa, NJ: Rowman and Littlefield, 1974 [1910]).

41. On the organization of the New Model Army and its role in politics, see C. H. Firth, *Cromwell's Army: A History of the English Soldier during the Civil Wars, the Commonwealth and the Protectorate*, 4th ed., and Correlli Barnett, *Britain and Her Army 1509–1970* (New York: William Morrow and Company, 1970), pp. 90–98.

42. An excellent discussion of this point, on which the following is partly based, is Brian Downing, *The Military Revolution and Political Change*, pp. 171–75.

43. On the impact of the Civil Wars on the development of English nationalism, see Liah Greenfeld, *Nationalism: Five Roads to Modernity* (Cambridge, MA: Harvard University Press, 1992), pp. 73–78. All of Chapter 1, "God's Firstborn: England" is recommended as a discussion of the rise of English nationalism and a reminder that nationalism was a phenomenon that antedated the French Revolution. In addition to the rise of a standing army, the post-Restoration era saw an increase in the size and importance of the Ordnance Office—the bureaucratic core of the new Army; see H. C. Tomlinson, *Guns and Government: The Ordnance Office under the Later Stuarts* (London: Royal Historical Society, 1979).

44. J. H. Elliott, *Imperial Spain, 1469–1716* (London: Penguin Books, 1990), p. 246. In addition to the sources referenced, this book and two other works by Elliott, *The Count Duke of Olivares: The Statesman in an Age of Decline* (New Haven: Yale

University Press, 1986) and *Spain and its World 1500–1700: Selected Essays* (New Haven: Yale University Press, 1989), provided valuable background information for this section.

45. *History of the Reign of Philip III* (1783), p. 309, cited by J. H. Elliott, "The Decline of Spain," in Trevor Aston, ed., *Crisis in Europe 1560–1660: Essays from Past and Present* (London: Routledge & Kegan Paul, 1965), p. 193.

46. Henry Kamen, in *Spain 1469–1714: A Society of Conflict* (London and New York, Longman, 1983), p. 90, points out that this event was not strictly speaking a bankruptcy, but a consolidation of short-term debt into the long-term *juros*. He notes that the Crown retained credit with many lenders and continued to remit cash payments to the Fuggers. But most historians describe it as a bankruptcy, which was its practical effect on Spain's credit standing and the way it was perceived at the time.

47. Jonathan Israel, *The Dutch Republic and the Hispanic World 1606–1661* (Oxford: Clarendon Press, 1982), p. 149. According to another source, "The ending of the Twelve Years' Truce . . . caused an immediate escalation of costs." Henry Kamen, *Spain 176–1914*, p. 216. See also I. A. A. Thompson, *War and Government in Habsburg Spain* (London: University of London, The Athlone Press, 1976), p. 37 and tables on pp. 288–307.

48. I. A. A. Thompson, *War and Government in Habsburg Spain 1560–1620*, p. 289.

49. By far the best account is Geoffrey Parker, *The Army of Flanders and the Spanish Road 1567–1659: The Logistics of Spanish Victory and Defeat in the Low Countries' Wars* (Cambridge: Cambridge University Press, 1972). See especially pp. 185–206 and Appendix J, pp. 290–92, for a list of the mutinies. See also Geoffrey Parker, "Mutiny and Discontent in the Spanish Army of Flanders, 1572–1607," in Parker, ed., *Spain and the Netherlands, 1559–1659: Ten Studies* (London: William Collins, 1979), pp. 106–21.

50. John Lynch, *Spain 1516–1598: From Nation State to World Empire* (Oxford: Basil Blackwell, 1991), pp. 267–84; I. A. A. Thompson, *War and Government in Habsburg Spain*, pp. 38–42. On the reforms attempted by Olivares, see J. H. Elliott, *The Count-Duke of Olivares*, pp. 169–202, 295–308. Immanuel Wallerstein, *The Modern World System: Capitalist Agriculture and the Origins of the European World Economy in the Sixteenth Century* (New York: Academic Press, 1976), observes that the large bureaucracy needed to administer a multi-national empire such as Spain's "tended to absorb too much of the profit, especially as repression and exploitation bred revolts which increased military expenditures" (p. 15).

51. France also had its autonomous provinces, the *pays d'état*, but its central government drew revenues from a larger segment of the overall kingdom, and its wars were fought for France alone, not for a larger imperium.

52. Alamos de Barrientos, cited in J. H. Elliott, "The Spanish Peninsula 1569–1648" in *The New Cambridge Modern History*, Vol. 4, p. 461. A detailed account of Olivares's attempt to forge a Union of Arms is found in J. H. Elliott, *The Count-Duke of Olivares*, ch. 7.

53. I. A. A. Thompson, *War and Government in Habsburg Spain*, pp. 103–59; John Lynch, *Spain 1516–1598*, p. 485; on the impact of war on Spain's decline in the late sixteenth century, see pp. 429–85. On the deleterious impact of the war with the United Provinces following the Twelve-Year Truce, the Thirty Years' War, and other conflicts of the early seventeeth century, see J. H. Elliott, *The Count-Duke of Olivares*, pp. 409–98.

54. Henry Kamen, *Spain 1469–1714*, pp. 268–71.
55. The use of the term is explained and defended in Jan Lindegren "The Swedish 'Military State,' 1560–1720," *Scandinavian Journal of History* 10 (1985):305–336, which also discusses the costs the war imposed on the Swedish society and economy.
56. Like most Western students of Swedish history I have relied heavily on the work of Michael Roberts. See, in particular, *The Swedish Imperial Experience, 1560–1718* (Cambridge: Cambridge University Press, 1979); *Gustavus Adolphus and the Rise of Sweden* (London: English Universities Press, 1973); "Sweden and the Baltic," *The New Cambridge Modern History*, Vol. 4, pp. 385–410; and *Essays in Swedish History* (London: Weidenfeld and Nicolson, 1967). Other sources include Jan Lindegren, "The Swedish 'Military State', 1560–1720"; Jerker Rosén, "Scandinavia and the Baltic," *New Cambridge Modern History*, Vol. 5, pp. 519–22; Gunnar Artéus, Ulf Olsson, Kerstin Strömberg-Back, "The Influence of the Armed Forces on the Transformation of Society in Sweden, 1600–1945," *Militärhistorsk Tikskrift 1981* 185 (1981):133–38.
57. The figure of 183,000 Swedish troops comes from Geoffrey Parker, *The Military Revolution*, p. 40. Roberts gives a more conservative figure of 149,000.
58. Sweden's copper and iron industries, and their relationship with war during this period, are discussed at length in Eli F. Heckscher, *An Economic History of Sweden* (Cambridge, MA: Harvard University Press, 1954), pp. 84–100. See also Lindegren, "The Swedish 'Military State,'" pp. 310–14.
59. Geoffrey Parker, *The Military Revolution*, p. 24.
60. Brian Downing, *The Military Revolution and Political Change*, pp. 187–211.
61. The population of Sweden in 1630 is from Ingvar Andersson, *A History of Sweden* (London: Weidenfeld and Nicolson, 1957), p. 246. Geoffrey Parker, *The Military Revolution*, p. 46, erroneously claims that in 1696, under Louis XIV, one in four adult Frenchmen were in the ranks. The figure was nowhere near to that, even if mercenaries are included.
62. Casualty figures are from Lindegren, "The Swedish 'Military State,'" p. 317. Other information is from Michael Roberts, *The Swedish Imperial Experience, 1560–1718*, pp. 43–63. On Sweden's success in averting civil conflict and maintaining unity at home, see also pp. 64–69.
63. Sun Tzu, *The Art of War*, Chapter 2, paragraph 7.
64. The following account of the rise of the Dutch Republic is based, except as noted, on Simon Schama, *The Embarrassment of Riches: An Interpretation of Dutch Culture in the Golden Age* (New York: Alfred A. Knopf, 1987); Pieter Geyl, *The Netherlands in the Seventeenth Century*, Part One, *1609–1648* (New York: Barnes & Noble, 1961); K. H. D. Haley, *The Dutch in the Seventeenth Century* (London: Thames and Hudson, 1972); Pieter Geyl, *The Revolt of the Netherlands (1555–1609)* (New York: Barnes & Noble, 1958); Geoffrey Parker, *The Dutch Revolt* (Ithaca: Cornell University Press, 1977); G. N. Clark, "The Birth of the Dutch Republic," in Lucy S. Sutherland, ed., *Studies in History: British Academy Lectures* (London: Oxford University Press, 1966); Bernard H. M. Vlekke, *The Evolution of the Dutch Nation* (New York: Roy Publishers, 1945); E. H. Kossman, "The Low Countries," *New Cambridge Modern History*, Vol. 4 (New York: Cambridge University Press, 1970), pp. 361–65; Horst Lademacher, *Geschichte der Niederlande: Politik—Verfassung—Wirtschaft* (Darmstadt: Wissenschaftliche Buchgesellschaft, 1983).
65. See Herbert H. Rowen, "The Dutch Revolt: What Kind of Revolution?" in

Renaissance Quarterly 43 (Autumn 1990):588. Rowen's article is a good summary of recent historical interpretation of the Dutch Revolt.

66. Charles Tilly, *Coercion, Capital, and European States*, pp. 89–90; Brian Downing, *The Military Revolution and Political Change*, pp. 225–27.

67. Geoffrey Parker, *The Dutch Revolt*, p. 237; Jonathan Israel, *The Dutch Republic and the Hispanic World*, p. 149; Duffy, *Siege Warfare*, pp. 81–82; Simon Schama, *The Embarrassment of Riches*, pp. 252–53.

68. Simon Schama observes, "the Dutch revolt was directed . . . against most of the tendencies—fiscal centralization, professional bureaucracy, executive justice, dynastic absolutism, the erosion of urban and seignorial privileges—that characterized the High Renaissance state. To *be* Dutch was to be local, parochial, traditional and customary." *The Embarrassment of Riches*, p. 62; see also pp. 63–65. Other sources include Walter Morgan, *The Expedition in Holland 1572–1574*, Duncan Caldecott-Baird, ed. (London: Seeley Service, 1976), p. 37; Jonathan Israel, *The Dutch Republic and the Hispanic World*, pp. 150–52; *New Cambridge Modern History*, Vol. 4, p. 362.

69. On the role of the gentry in the war and the place they assumed in the States-General and governments of the provinces, see Sherrin Marshall, *The Dutch Gentry, 1500–1650: Family, Faith, and Fortune* (New York: Greenwood Press, 1987), pp. 117–57.

70. Simon Schama, in *The Embarrassment of Riches*, p. 224, observes that while other states of the era had experienced the upheaval of civil war, "the Dutch polity had proved remarkably resilient under stress, effective in administration and ingenious at sustaining the minimal consensus needed to contain discord within the bounds of civil war." See also Brian Downing, *The Military Revolution and Political Change*, p. 234, where he suggests that successful estate rule requires "the absence of deep social and regional divisions at the elite level." Elite-level divisions existed in the Provinces, of course, but they were sublimated in the larger cause of the war effort, which was the real key to Dutch unity.

71. C. R. Boxer, *The Dutch Seaborne Empire 1600–1800*, pp. 1–33; William H. McNeill, *The Pursuit of Power*, pp. 117 and 139.

72. Simon Schama, *The Embarrassment of Riches: An Interpretation of Dutch Culture in the Golden Age* (New York: Alfred A. Knopf, 1987), p. 226. Schama's discussion of the military culture of the Dutch and the significance of their wars with Spain and England (pp. 221–56) is highly recommended.

73. Herfried Münkler, *Im Namen des Staates: Die Begründung der Staatsraison in der frühen Neuzeit* (Frankfurt: Fischer Verlag, 1987), p. 171.

74. Information on the physical destruction of the war is taken from Geoffrey Parker, *The Thirty Years' War*, pp. 208–215; Richard S. Dunn, *The Age of Religious Wars*, pp. 89–90.

75. On the attempt to create a third force, see Geoffrey Parker, *The Thirty Years' War*, pp. 111–120 and 126–27.

76. Geoffrey Parker, *The Thirty Years' War*, p. 224. Parker's last chapter, pp. 190–226, is a superb summary of the impact of the war on German society and politics.

77. On the early rise of Prussia, see F. L. Carsten, "The Rise of Brandenburg," in *The New Cambridge Modern History*, Vol. 5, pp. 543–58; Sidney B. Fay, *The Rise of Brandenburg-Prussia to 1786*, rev. by Klaus Epstein (New York: Holt, Rinehart and Winston, 1964).

78. David Kaiser, *Politics and War: European Conflict from Philip II to Hitler*, pp. 14–25, citing the continuing influence of the nobility and their frequent struggles with monarchs, argues that while the *aim* of European governments may have been to centralize power, attempts to do so prior to Louis XIV only provoked chaos and violent conflict. The fact remains that the monarchs won almost all of the conflicts that ensued. The court of Louis XIV with its slavish courtiers did not emerge suddenly out of nowhere; it was the product of over two centuries of royal aggrandizement at the expense of seignorial autonomy.

79. The revolts and insurrections of this period stemmed both from the passions unleashed by the Reformation and from the growing power of central states. At several points we have noted that their challenge, and the success of states in subduing them, were critical factors in the emergence of internal state sovereignty. Useful general works on the phenomenon include Michael Mullett, *Popular Culture and Popular Protest in Late Medieval and Early Modern Europe* (London: Croom Helm, 1987); Yves-Marie Bercé, *Revolt and Revolution in Early Modern Europe: An Essay on the History of Political Violence*, trans. by Joseph Bergin (Manchester: Manchester University Press, 1987). In the latter work, see especially pp. 127–130 on the role of soldiers (whose numbers were increasing as the Military Revolution proceeded) in instigating and leading these revolts.

Chapter 4: War and the Rise of the Nation-State

1. R. R. Palmer, "Frederick the Great, Guibert, Bülow: From Dynastic to National War" in Peter Paret, ed., *Makers of Modern Strategy from Machiavelli to the Nuclear Age* (Princeton: Princeton University Press, 1986), pp. 91–105; Christopher Duffy, *The Army of Frederick the Great* (London: David & Charles, 1974), especially pp. 13–23, 208–212; Russell F. Weigley, *The Age of Battles: The Quest for Decisive Warfare from Breitenfeld to Waterloo*, pp. 167–68; David Kaiser, *Politics and War: European Conflict from Philip II to Hitler*, pp. 139–41 and 152–56.

2. Colbert, cited in Maurice Ashley, *The Golden Century: Europe 1598–1715* (New York: Praeger, 1969), p. 195. Betty Behrens refers to the absolutist monarchies as "military-bureaucratic monarchies." See her discussion in *The Cambridge Economic History of Europe*, Vol. 5, *The Economic Organization of Early Modern Europe* (Cambridge: Cambridge University Press, 1977), Ch. 8. The military logic that undergirded mercantilism did not mean, however, that states did not take nonmilitary goals such as economic prosperity seriously, even in the pursuit of international objectives. See Jacob Viner, "Power Versus Plenty as Objectives of Foreign Policy in The Seventeenth and Eighteen Centuries," *World Politics* 1, pp. 1–29, reprinted in Mark Blaug, *The Later Mercantilists* (Aldershot: Edward Elgar Publishing Co., 1991), pp. 77–105.

3. On the linkage between the Seven Years' War and the reforms of enlightened absolutism (another example of the "inspection effect" of war), see James C. Riley, *The Seven Years' War and the Old Regime in France: The Economic and Financial Toll* (Princeton: Princeton University Press, 1986), pp. 192–222; W. O. Henderson, "Enlightened Mercantilism in Prussia," in Stuart Andrews, *Enlightened Despotism* (New York: Barnes & Noble, 1967), pp. 20–26; David Kaiser, *Politics and War*, pp. 205–206. A good general source on the reforms of the era is John Gagliardo, *Enlightened Despotism* (Arlington Heights, IL: Harlan Davidson, 1986 [1967]).

4. On the army reforms undertaken during the reign of Louis XIV, see Russell Wei-

gley, *The Age of Battles*, pp. 45–72; Geoffrey R. Treasure, *Seventeenth-Century France*, 2nd ed. (London: John Murray, 1981), pp. 257–72; W. H. Lewis, *The Splendid Century* (New York: William Sloane Associates, 1954), pp. 126–44; Orest and Patricia Ranum, eds., *The Century of Louis XIV* (New York: Walker and Co., 1972), pp. 319–24; F. J. Hebbert, *Soldier of France: Sebastien Le Prestre de Vauban 1633–1707* (New York: P. Lang, 1990).

5. On the impact of France on the smaller German states, see David Kaiser, *Politics and War*, pp. 178–96.

6. Sidney B. Fay, *The Rise of Brandenburg Prussia to 1786*, ed. rev. by Klaus Epstein (New York: Holt, Rinehart and Winston, 1964) p. 51.

7. Robert A. Kann, *A History of the Habsburg Empire 1526–1918* (Berkeley: University of California Press, 1974), pp. 174–78; Christopher Duffy, *The Army of Maria Theresa: The Armed Forces of Imperial Austria, 1740–1780* (London: David & Charles, 1977), pp. 149–67 and 206–209; Max Beloff, *The Age of Absolutism 1660–1815* (London, Hutchinson & Co., Ltd., 1954), pp. 123–26.

8. This account of Peter the Great's reforms draws primarily on three sources: the masterful classic by Vasili Klyuchevsky, *Peter the Great* (New York: Random House, 1958); Evgennii V. Anisimov, *The Reforms of Peter the Great: Progress through Coercion in Russia*, trans. by John T. Alexander (Armonk, New York: M. E. Sharpe, 1993); and Richard Pipes, *Russia Under the Old Regime* (New York: Charles Scribner's Sons, 1974), pp. 115–32.

9. Vasili Klyuchevsky, *Peter the Great*, p. 77; Evgennii V. Anisimov, *The Reforms of Peter the Great: Progress through Coercion in Russia*, pp. 57–69. Marc Raeff, *Understanding Imperial Russia: State and Society in the Old Regime* (New York: Columbia University Press, 1984), p. 36, expresses doubts about Klyuchevsky's thesis, arguing that "it seems highly unlikely that the needs of war, narrowly interpreted, would have required such energetic reforms and such radical innovations." In fact, nothing *but* the needs of war would have impelled such radical reforms, and Raeff does not offer an alternative explanation.

10. See the interesting discussion in Christopher Duffy, *Russia's Military Way to the West: Origins and Nature of Russian Military Power 1700–1800* (London: Routledge & Kegan Paul, 1981), pp. 233–41.

11. Charles Tilly, "War Making and State Making as Organized Crime," in Peter Evans, Dietrich Rueschemeyer and Theda Skocpol, eds., *Bringing the State Back In* (Cambridge: Cambridge University Press, 1985), pp. 169–91. C. B. A. Behrens, in *The Ancien Regime* (New York: W. W. Norton, 1967), p. 88, observes, "The standing armies concentrated in the hands of the government a degree of force which it had never possessed before, and thereby made successful rebellion impossible . . ." On the nature of absolutism, see the essays by E. H. Kossman and Georges Durand in Ragnhild Hatton, ed., *Louis XIV and Absolutism* (Columbus: Ohio State University Press, 1976), pp. 3–36, as well as Max Beloff, *The Age of Absolutism 1660–1815*.

12. The War of the Grand Alliance was also known as the War of the League of Augsburg.

13. Sebastian Haffner, *The Rise and Fall of Prussia*, trans. by Ewald Osers (London: Weidenfeld and Nicolson, 1980), p. 33.

14. Christopher Duffy, *The Army of Maria Theresa*, pp. 123–24; Christopher Duffy, *Russia's Military Way to the West*, pp. 32–41, paints a vivid picture of the military machine assembled by Peter the Great.

15. The Prussian state "demanded total avowal, absolute submission and readiness for service." Arno Lubos, *Germans and Slavs* (1974), cited in Sebastian Haffner, *The Rise and Fall of Prussia*, p. 33.

16. Geoffrey Treasure, *The Making of Modern Europe 1648–1715* (London: Methuen, 1985), p. 211. Austrian revenue figures are from Christopher Duffy, *The Army of Maria Theresa*, pp. 123–24.

17. French revenue figures are from Georges Durand, "What is Absolutism?" in Ragnhild Hatton, ed., *Louis XIV and Absolutism*, pp. 35–36, see also C. B. A. Behrens, *The Ancien Regime*, p. 140.

18. Niccolò Machiavelli, *The Discourses*, trans. by Leslie Walker, ed. by Bernard Crick (Harmondsworth: Penguin Books, 1974), p. 302.

19. Joel 3:10, King James Bible. On the taxation systems of France and Prussia under the Old Regime, see C. B. A. Behrens, *Society, Government, and the Enlightenment: The Experiences of Eighteenth-Century France and Prussia* (New York: Harper & Row, 1985), pp. 68–88, and Geoffrey Treasure, *Seventeenth-Century France*, pp. 465–70.

20. The phrase "cult of bureaucratic institutions" is from Evgenii Anisimov, *The Reforms of Peter the Great*, p. 145; see also pp. 143–63. On the post-Soviet revival of the Table of Ranks concept, see Victor Yasmann, "The Russian Civil Service: Corruption and Reform," *RFE/RL Research Report* 2 (April 16, 1993):19.

21. John Brewer, *The Sinews of Power: War, Money and the English State 1688–1783* (Cambridge, MA: Harvard University Press, 1990), p. 67. The review of British state development in the eighteenth century that follows relies heavily on this work.

22. John Brewer, *The Sinews of Power*, p. 30 and pp. 114–119.

23. Brewer discusses this at length in Chapter V, "The Paradoxes of State Power," *The Sinews of Power*, pp. 137–61.

24. Edmund Burke, Second Speech on Conciliation with America. The Thirteen Resolutions. March 22, 1775. Text found in Albert S. Cook, ed., *Edmund Burke's Speech on Conciliation with America* (New York: Longmans, Green and Co., 1896).

25. The destructiveness and political consequences of the Great Northern War are treated in Norman Davies, *God's Playground: A History of Poland*, Vol. I, *The Origins to 1795* (New York: Columbia University Press, 1982), pp. 496–504. Russell Weigley, *The Age of Battles*, pp. 109–11, points to the Great Northern War as an example of how the restraints on violence that had developed in Western Europe still did not apply in Eastern Europe. Wieslaw Majewski, "The Polish Art of War in the Sixteenth and Seventeenth Centuries," in J. K. Fedorowicz, ed., *A Republic of Nobles: Studies in Polish History to 1864* (Cambridge: Cambridge University Press, 1982), pp. 179–97, makes clear that one source of Poland's military weakness, despite numerous tactical innovations, was its continuing heavy reliance on cavalry and relative weakness in artillery and infantry; the latter, of course, were products of the Military Revolution best wielded by more centralized states.

26. An excellent overview of how Polish political weakness led to the partitions is Robert Howard Lord, *The Second Partition of Poland: A Study in Diplomatic History* (Cambridge: Harvard University Press, 1915), pp. 3–55; on the role of war in the first partition, see Herbert H. Kaplan, *The First Partition of Poland* (New York: Columbia University Press, 1962), Ch. 11.

27. "Nationalism is primarily a political principle which holds that the political and

the national unit should be congruent." Ernest Gellner, *Nations and Nationalism* (Ithaca: Cornell University Press, 1983), p. 1. This definition applies only to the narrow doctrine of nationalism as it arose in the nineteenth century; it does not encompass the much larger political phenomenon of nationalism that is the main object of our discussion here. Important recent scholarship on nationalism (in both senses of the word) includes Benedict Anderson, *Imagined Communities: Reflections on the Origin and Spread of Nationalism*, rev. ed. (London and New York: Verso Press, 1991); John Breuilly, *Nationalism and the State* (Chicago: University of Chicago Press, 1985); E. J. Hobsbawm, *Nations and Nationalism since 1780: Programme, Myth, Reality* (Cambridge: Cambridge University Press, 1990). Three earlier works that remain important are Carlton J. H. Hayes, *The Historical Evolution of Modern Nationalism* (New York: Russell & Russell Ltd., 1968 [1931]); Elie Kedourie, *Nationalism* (London: Hutchinson & Co., Ltd. 1960); and Hans Kohn, *Nationalism: Its Meaning and History*, rev. ed. (Princeton: D. Van Nostrand Co., 1965).

28. On pre-eighteenth-century nationalism in France, see Liah Greenfeld, *Nationalism: Five Roads to Modernity* (Cambridge, MA: Harvard University Press, 1992), pp. 91–133; and Conor Cruise O'Brien, "Nationalism and the French Revolution," in Geoffrey Best, ed., *The Permanent Revolution: The French Revolution and Its Legacy 1789–1989* (Chicago: University of Chicago Press, 1988), p. 19. On other manifestations of nationalism in Europe prior to 1789, see The Royal Institute of International Affairs, *Nationalism* (New York: Frank Cass, 1963 [1939], pp. 8–21; Otto Dann, ed., *Nationalismus in vorindustrieller Zeit* (Munich: R. Oldenbourg Verlag, 1986), and Barnaby C. Keeney, "Military Service and the Development of Nationalism in England, 1272–1327," *Speculum: A Journal of Medieval Studies* 22 (October 1947):534–49.

29. Niccolò Machiavelli, *The Prince*, Ch. 26. On Machiavelli as a forerunner of modern nationalism, see Hans Kohn, *Nationalism: Its Meaning and History*, pp. 13–14.

30. Hans Kohn, *Nationalism*, pp. 16–18. This does not mean that England did not experience nationalism. Liah Greenfeld, *Nationalism: Five Roads to Modernity*, pp. 29–87, argues that England was the first country to experience modern nationalism, which arose in connection with Henry VIII's break with the Church of Rome and was consolidated in the English Civil Wars.

31. Quotations are from Liah Greenfeld, *Nationalism: Five Roads to Modernity*, pp. 158–59; Leibniz, *Political Writings*, p. 135; Conor Cruise O'Brien, "Nationalism and the French Revolution," in Geoffrey Best, ed., *The Permanent Revolution: The French Revolution and Its Legacy 1789–1989* (Chicago: University of Chicago Press, 1988), pp. 21, 44. On the historical development of eighteenth-century nationalism, see Jacques Godechot, "The New Concept of the Nation and its Diffusion in Europe," in Otto Dann and John Dinwiddy, *Nationalism in the Age of the French Revolution* (London: The Hambledon Press, 1988); Carlton J. H. Hayes, *The Historical Evolution of Modern Nationalism*, Chs. 1, 2, and 3; and Greenfeld, *Nationalism*, pp. 153–54.

32. Cited in Christopher Duffy, *The Army of Maria Theresa*, p. 210.

33. On Frederician patriotism and the "spirit of the army," see Pentti Airas, *Die Geschichtlichen Wertungen "Krieg und Friede" von Friederich dem Grossen bis Engels* (Rovaniemi: Societas Historica Finlandiae Septentrionalis, 1978), pp. 74–83 and 95–99. Simon Schama, *The Embarrassment of Riches: An Interpretation*

of Dutch Culture in the Golden Age, also interprets the emergence of a strongly felt sense of sense of Dutch nationality as "the result, not the cause, of the revolt against Spain" (p. 54). He describes the development of this early Dutch national feeling, and its connection with the war against Spain, at length in Chapter 2, "Patriotic Scripture"; see especially pp. 69–92.

34. A good discussion is found in Benedict Anderson, *Imagined Communities,* pp. 37–46.
35. Michelet, cited in Conor Cruise O'Brien, "Nationalism and the French Revolution," p. 19; Hans Kohn, *Nationalism,* p. 64.
36. Simon Schama, *Citizens: A Chronicle of the French Revolution* (New York: Alfred A. Knopf, 1989), p. 591.
37. On the impact of the American War on French nationalism and the coming of the French Revolution, see Liah Greenfeld, *Nationalism,* pp. 180–84, and Louis Gottschalk, "The Place of the American Revolution in the Causal Pattern of the French Revolution," *Publications of the American Friends of Lafayette* 2 (1948):495–510, reprinted in Peter Amann, *The Eighteenth-Century Revolution: French or Western?* (Boston: D. C. Heath, 1963), pp. 56–65.
38. James C. Riley, *The Seven Years' War and the Old Regime in France: The Economic and Financial Toll,* pp. 183–84.
39. Simon Schama, *Citizens,* pp. 61–62; see also pp. 63–71.
40. On this point, see Albert Soboul, *The French Revolution 1787–1799: From the Storming of the Bastille to Napoleon,* trans. by Alan Forrest and Colin Jones (London: Unwin Hyman, 1989 [1982]), pp. 97–100; Simon Schama, *Citizens,* pp. 62–63.
41. Samuel F. Scott, *The Response of the Royal Army to the French Revolution: The Role and Development of the Line Army* (Oxford: Clarendon Press, 1978), pp. 29–36 and 45–50; Simon Schama, *Citizens,* pp. 272–77. Another factor fanning military discontent was the Ségur decree of 1781, which restricted direct commissioning into the officer corps to individuals with four generations of nobility. This had exacerbated class cleavages in the army and demoralized NCOs, officers of fortune, and enlisted commoners.
42. Camille Desmoulins, *La France Libre,* in M. Jules Claretie, ed., *Oeuvres de Camille Desmoulins* (Paris: Charpentier, 1874) p. 127.
43. T. C. W. Blanning, *The Origins of the French Revolutionary Wars* (London and New York: Longman, 1986), pp. 69–70, 86–89, 96, 206–207; Albert Soboul, *The French Revolution 1787–1799,* pp. 235–41; Simon Schama, *Citizens,* p. 587.
44. Samuel Scott, *The Response of the Royal Army,* p. 163; Russell Weigley, *The Age of Battles,* pp. 284–86.
45. Peter Paret, "Conscription and the End of the Ancien Régime in France and Prussia," in Paret, ed., *Understanding War,* pp. 59–62; Samuel Scott, *The Response of the Royal Army,* pp. 70–80, 96–97, 112–14, 147–168, and 177; John A. Lynn, *The Bayonets of the Republic: Motivation and Tactics in the Army of Revolutionary France, 1791–94* (Urbana: University of Illinois Press, 1984), pp. 46 and 71.
46. *Chronique de la Révolution 1788–1799* (Paris: Larousse, 1988), p. 361.
47. In practice, many managed to evade conscription, and more easily so after the Directory passed exemptions and restored the practice of buying a substitute; the fusion of nation and army never did reach the ideal that its proponents envisioned. On the disconnect between nationalism and actual military service, see

Peter Paret, "Nationalism and the Sense of Military Obligation," in Paret, ed., *Understanding War: Essays on Clausewitz and the History of Military Power* (Princeton: Princeton University Press, 1992), pp. 39–52. On the social composition of the levy, see John Lynn, *The Bayonets of the Republic*, p. 57.

48. John Lynn, *The Bayonets of the Republic*, pp. 119–41; Simon Schama, *Citizens*, pp. 764–66; William McNeill, *The Pursuit of Power*, pp. 192–96.

49. Donald Greer, *The Incidence of the Terror During the French Revolution: A Statistical Interpretation* (Cambridge, MA: Harvard University Press, 1935), pp. 38–70.

50. Richard Cobb, *The People's Armies: The Armées Révolutionnaires: Instrument of Terror in the Departments April 1793 to Floréal Year II* (New Haven: Yale University Press, 1987), pp. 2, 150–61, 253–88, 300–303. On the central importance of the civil war in causing the Terror, see also the analysis in Rosemary H. T. O'Kane, *The Revolutionary Reign of Terror: The Role of Violence in Political Change* (Aldershot: Edward Elgar Publishing Co., 1991), pp. 57–85.

51. Theda Skocpol, *States and Social Revolutions: A Comparative Analysis of France, Russia, and China* (Cambridge: Cambridge University Press, 1979), pp. 188–89, 200–205.

52. Gabriel Hanotaux, cited in Simon Schama, *Citizens*, p. 760.

53. Louis Bergeron, *France under Napoleon*, trans. by R. R. Palmer (Princeton: Princeton University Press, 1981), pp. 23–24; Peter Paret, "Nationalism and the Sense of Military Obligation," p. 44; Philip John Stead, *The Police of France* (New York: Macmillan Publishing Company 1983), pp. 43–53; Eric A. Arnold, Jr., *Fouché, Napoleon, and the General Police* (Washington, DC: University Press of America, 1979), pp. 33–51. The rise of modern police forces in Europe is itself an important dimension in the development of the modern state, but one which will not be treated in this book. Good treatments include Hsi-Huey Lian, *The Rise of Modern Police and the European State System From Metternich to the Second World War* (Cambridge: Cambridge University Press, 1992); Richard Vogler, *Reading the Riot Act: The Magistracy, the Police and the Army in Civil Disorder* (Philadelphia: Open University Press, 1991).

54. Robert B. Holtman, *The Napoleonic Revolution* (Baton Rouge: Louisiana State University Press, 1967), pp. 96–98.

55. Bergeron, *France under Napoleon*, pp. 32–36; Charles Breunig, *The Age of Revolution and Reaction, 1789–1850*, 2nd ed. (New York: W. W. Norton, 1977), pp. 72–73.

56. Simon Schama, *Citizens*, p. 755.

57. Bergeron, *France under Napoleon*, pp. 65–70 and 122–25; Stuart Woolf, *Napoleon's Integration of Europe* (London and New York: Routledge, 1991), pp. 174–84.

58. Anacharsis Cloots, cited in Blanning, *The Origins of the French Revolutionary Wars*, p. 74.

59. See, for example, R. R. Palmer, *The Age of the Democratic Revolution: A Political History of Europe and America, 1760–1800*, (Princeton: Princeton University Press, 1964); E. J. Hobsbawn, *The Age of Revolution 1789–1848* (New York: Mentor, 1962), pp. 137–42. Two thoughtful essays that deal with the ideological dimension of the Revolution's legacy are Eugene Kamenka, "Revolutionary Ideology and 'The Great French Revolution of 1789–?'" and Geoffrey Best, "The French Revolution and Human Rights," in Best, ed., *The Permanent Revolution*, pp. 75–100 and 101–128.

60. As T. C. W. Blanning, *The Origins of the French Revolutionary Wars*, p. 211, observes: "It was not the French Revolution which created the modern world, it was the French revolutionary wars."

61. Thomas Nipperdey, *Deutsche Geschichte, 1800–1866: Bürgerwelt und starker Staat* (Munich: C. H. Beck, 1983), p. 11. Another important work that similarly emphasizes the importance of Napoleon's impact on Germany is James J. Sheehan, *German History 1770–1866* (Oxford: Clarendon Press, 1989).

62. Geoffrey Bruun, *Europe and the French Imperium 1799–1814* (Westport, CT: Greenwood Press, 1983 [1938]), p. 166; Goethe, cited in Endry B. Gastony, *The Ordeal of Nationalism in Modern Europe* (Lewiston, NY: The Edwin Mellen Press, 1992), p. 41; T. C. W. Blanning, "The French Revolution and the Modernization of Germany," *Central European History* 22 (June 1989):124. For a general analysis of Napoleon as a catalyst of nationalism, see Robert B. Holtman, *The Napoleonic Revolution*, Ch. 9.

63. On the impact of the Napoleonic wars on nationalism in European armies, see Charles Breunig, *The Age of Revolution and Reaction*, p. 187; Geoffrey Best, *War and Society in Revolutionary Europe* (Leicester: Leicester University Press, 1982), Chs. 21 and 22.

64. Cited in Stuart Woolf, *Napoleon's Integration of Europe*, p. 230.

65. Geoffrey Best, *War and Society in Revolutionary Europe*, pp. 254–56.

66. On the politics and administration of Napoleonic Europe, two excellent works are Owen Connelly, *Napoleon's Satellite Kingdoms* (New York: The Free Press, 1965) and Stuart Woolf, *Napoleon's Integration of Europe*.

67. The Greek revolt against Ottoman rule, which began in 1821, and a flurry of abortive revolts in other parts of the Ottoman Empire—Bosnia-Herzegovina (1830–32 and 1834), Albania (1832–35), Serbia (1833 and 1841), and Bulgaria (1835 and 1847)—prove that nationalism was rapidly spreading beyond the borders of the former Napoleonic imperium. The success of the Spanish revolt and the example of other uprisings in Western Europe, however, had a great impact in Greece and was a major reason for the revolt there. The success of the Greek Revolt in turn instigated similar bids for independence in other parts of the Ottoman empire; see Breunig, *The Age of Revolution and Reaction*, pp. 138–50.

68. An interesting perspective on the emergence of nationalism in the New World is Benedict Anderson's chapter "Creole Pioneers" in Anderson, *Imagined Communities*, pp. 47–65. Anderson notes the importance of Napoleon, but also emphasizes the important role that local pilgrims of nationalism, both political leaders and writers, played in the process of defining new nation-states.

69. The figure of 60 percent is from James J. Sheehan, *German History 1770–1866* (Oxford: Clarendon Press, 1989), p. 251.

70. Michael Broers, "Italy and the Modern State: The Experience of Napoleonic Rule," in François Furet and Mona Ozouf, *The Transformation of Political Culture 1789–1848*, Vol. 3 of *The French Revolution and the Creation of Modern Political Culture* (Oxford: Pergamon Press, 1989), pp. 492–95; Stuart Woolf, *Napoleon's Integration of Europe*, p. 229.

71. Michael Broers, "Italy and the Modern State: The Experience of Napoleonic Rule," in François Furet and Mona Ozouf, eds., *The Transformation of Political Culture 1789–1848*, pp. 489–503; Jacques Godechot, "The New Concept of the Nation and its Diffusion in Europe," in Otto Dann and John Dinwiddy, eds. *Nationalism in the Age of the French Revolution*, pp. 21–26.

72. Ernst Moritz Arndt, cited in John L. Snell, *The Democratic Movement in Germany, 1789–1914* (Chapel Hill: The University of North Carolina Press, 1976), p. 19.

73. Leopold von Ranke, ed., *Denkwürdigkeiten des Staatskanzlers Fürsten von Hardenberg*, 5 vols. (Leipzig: Duncker & Humbolt, 1877), Vol. IV, Appendix pp. 7–8.

74. A classic account of the reforms and the liberation of Prussia from Napoleon, written from the perspective of a German nationalist, is Friedrich Meinecke, *The Age of German Liberation, 1795–1815* (Berkeley: University of California Press, 1977).

75. On the Prussian and Rhineland reforms, their link to the war with France, and their long-term significance, see Thomas Nipperdey, *Deutsche Geschichte*, pp. 31–79; James J. Sheehan, *German History 1770–1866*, pp. 207–323; Marion W. Gray, *Prussia in Transition: Society and Politics under the Stein Reform Ministry of 1808*, Vol. 76 of *Transactions of the American Philosophical Society* (Philadelphia: American Philosophical Society, 1986); Geoffrey Bruun, *Europe and the French Imperium*, pp. 171–76; Geoffrey Best, *War and Society in Revolutionary Europe, 1770–1870*, pp. 150–67.

76. A good summary of Nipperdey's view of modernization is T. C. W. Blanning, "The French Revolution and the Modernization of Germany," *Central European History* 22 (June 1989):109–129. On the longer-term impact of the Revolutionary and Napoleonic era on the Rhineland states, see Jonathan Sperber, "Echoes of the French Revolution in the Rhineland, 1830–1849," *Central European History* 22 (June 1989):200–217.

77. W. G. Beasley, *The Rise of Modern Japan* (New York: St. Martin's Press, 1990), pp. 54–69. See also E. H. Norman, *Origins of the Modern Japanese State*, ed. by John W. Dower (New York: Pantheon Books, 1975), pp. 142–55 and 435–64.

78. Cited in Geoffrey Best, "Restraints on War by Land Before 1945," in Michael Howard, ed., *Restraints on War: Studies in the Limitation of Armed Conflict* (Oxford: Oxford University Press, 1979), p. 23.

Chapter 5: Total War and the Rise of the Collectivist State

1. Georges Blond, *Verdun* (Paris: Presses del la Cité, 1980), p. 24.

2. An excellent short study of the historical significance of the machine gun is John Ellis, *The Social History of the Machine Gun* (Baltimore: Johns Hopkins University Press, 1975).

3. Speech by Gustav Streseman entitled "War and Industry," cited in Robert B. Armeson, *Total Warfare and Compulsory Labor: A Study of the Military-Industrial Complex in Germany during World War I* (The Hague: Martinus Nijhoff, 1964), p. vi. The concept of "total war" was first articulated by the eminent General Erich Ludendorff in his book, *Der totale Krieg* (Munich: Ludendorff, 1939), which first appeared in 1935.

4. Arno J. Mayer, *The Persistence of the Old Regime* (New York: Pantheon Books, 1981), argues that much of the structure and spirit of the Old Regimes remained intact in the nineteenth century. Though his main thesis is highly controversial, the statistical evidence he presents underscores the point that industrialization had failed to transform politics fundamentally prior to 1914.

5. It is interesting to note that the European states that successfully industrialized all obtained less than 25 percent of their income from direct taxation. See the discussion and table on pp. 154–55 of W. R. Lee, "Tax Structure and Economic

Growth in Germany (1750–1850)," *The Journal of European Economic History* 4 (Spring 1975):153–77. On the role of the state in the industrialization of France, see Roger Price, *The Economic Modernisation of France* (New York: John Wiley & Sons, 1975), pp. 158–67; on England, see Eric J. Evans, *The Forging of the Modern State: Early Industrial Britain 1783–1870* (London: Longman, 1983), Chs. 4, 11, and 12.

6. Lewis Mumford, *The Pentagon of Power* (New York: Harcourt Brace Jovanovich, Inc., 1970), pp. 148–49.

7. Mayer, *The Persistence of the Old Regime*, p. 37.

8. E. J. Hobsbawm, *The Age of Revolution 1789–1848* (New York: Penguin, 1962), p. 123; McNeill, *The Pursuit of Power*, pp. 210–212.

9. Geoffrey Perret, *A Country Made By War* (New York: Random House, 1989), p. 241.

10. On the essential modernity of the Civil War, see Edward Hagerman, *The American Civil War and the Origins of Modern Warfare: Ideas, Organization, and Field Command* (Bloomington: Indiana University Press, 1988). On the belated European recognition of the military significance of the Civil War, see Jay Luvaas, *The Military Legacy of the Civil War: The European Inheritance* (University Press of Kansas, 1988); see especially pp. 203–32.

11. On the advances in rifles, artillery, and railroads, and their application in war in the nineteenth century, see Dennis E. Showalter, *Railroads and Rifles: Soldiers, Technology, and the Unification of Germany* (Hamden, Connecticut: Archon Books, 1976); Hew Strachan, *European Armies and the Conduct of War* (London: George Allen & Unwin, 1983), ch. 8. Strachan makes the important point that the nature of warfare after 1870 was affected not only by industrialization but by the growth in population it entailed, which coupled with the short-service conscript system enabled the major European states (France, Germany, Italy, Russia, and Austria-Hungary) to double the collective size of their armies between 1870 and 1914. The task of deploying and commanding such large armies of amateurs became the ultimate technical and tactical challenge of World War I.

12. "Standard Rate of Income Tax—United Kingdom 1799–1980," in B. R. Mitchell, *British Historical Statistics* (Cambridge: Cambridge University Press, 1988), p. 645.

13. Cecil Rhodes, cited in Lenin, *Imperialism: The Highest Stage of Capitalism*, in Stephen T. Possony, ed., *The Lenin Reader* (Chicago: Henry Regnery, 1966), p. 290.

14. Both are cited in Bernard Semmel, *Imperialism and Social Reform: English Social-Imperial Thought, 1895–1914* (Cambridge, MA: Harvard University Press, 1960), p. 13.

15. Semmel, *Imperialism and Social Reform*, pp. 18–24.

16. The most extensive discussion of "negative integration" is Dieter Groh, *Negative Integration und Revolutionäre Attentismus: die Deutsche Sozialdemokratie am Vorabend des Ersten Weltkrieges* (Frankfurt am Main: Propyläen Verlag, 1973); see also Hans-Ulrich Wehler, *The German Empire 1871–1918* (Leamington Spa/Dover: Berg Publishers, 1985), pp. 90–94, 131–36, 173–79. Other sources on Bismarck's social welfare reforms, which emphasize their links both with his foreign policy and his efforts to achieve political unity at home, include Gordon Craig, *Germany 1866–1945* (Oxford: Clarendon Press, 1978), pp. 150–64 (and on Bismarck's imperialist policies, see pp. 101–123); Gerhard A. Ritter, *Sozialver-*

sicherung in Deutschland und England (Munich: Verlag C. H. Beck, 1983), pp. 18–52, *passim*; see especially p. 37; Lothar Gall, *Bismarck: The White Revolution-ary*, Vol. 2, 1871–1898, trans. by J. A. Underwood (London: Allen & Unwin, 1986), Chs. 13 and 15; Volker Hetschel, *Geschichte der deutschen Sozialpolitik 1880–1980* (Frankfurt am Main: Suhrkamp Verlag, 1983), pp. 9–11. The phrase "Humanitätsdusel" is cited in Erich Eyck, *Bismarck and the German Empire*, 3rd ed. (London: Allen & Unwin, 1968), p. 312; Eyck, pp. 310–315, takes a dim view of Bismarck's motivations for social reform.

17. William Manchester, *The Arms of Krupp 1587–1968* (New York: Bantam, 1970), pp. 168–72.

18. On the impact of the Boer War on social welfare in the United Kingdom, see Deborah Dwork, *War is Good for Babies and Other Young Children: A History of the Infant and Child Welfare Movement in England 1898–1918* (London and New York: Tavistock Publications, 1987), pp. 11–12, 15–21, 167–200, 221–22; G. R. Searle, *The Quest for National Efficiency: A Study in British Politics and Political Thought, 1899–1914* (London: The Ashfield Press, 1990), pp. 34–60. See also Bernard Semmel, *Imperialism and Social Reform*, p. 23. On the role of Social-Darwinism in the crisis of the liberal state, see H. W. Koch, "Social Darwinism as a Factor in the 'New Imperialism,'" in H. W. Koch, *The Origins of the First World War: Great Power Rivalry and German War Aims*, 2nd ed. (London: Collier-Macmillan, 1984), pp. 319–42.

19. E. P. Hennock, *British Social Reform and German Precedents: The Case of Social Insurance 1880–1914* (Oxford: Clarendon Press, 1987), p. 169. Hennock reviews the effect of the Bismarckian program on social insurance legislation in Britain in detail.

20. Allan Mitchell, *The Divided Path: The German Influence on Social Reform in France after 1870* (Chapel Hill: University of North Carolina Press, 1991); Jean-Marie Mayeur and Madeleine Rebérioux, *The Third Republic from its Origins to the Great War, 1871–1914*, trans. by J. R. Foster (Cambridge: Cambridge University Press, 1984), pp. 54–55.

21. Paul Kennedy, *The Rise and Fall of the Great Powers*, p. 262.

22. Inflation figures were calculated using the tables on central-government expenditures and cost-of-living ratios in Brian R. Mitchell, *European Historical Statistics* (London: Collier-Macmillan, 1980), pp. 779–80, and the Sauerbeck-*Statist* price indices in Mitchell, *British Historical Statistics* (Cambridge: Cambridge University Press, 1988), p. 726. (Cost-of-living ratios if anything exaggerate the degree of inflation in military spending, because armaments manufacturing achieved enormous productivity gains in contrast to other sectors of the society.) The figures on the growth of administrative employment are from Richard C. Eichenberg, "Problems in Using Public Employment Data," in Charles Lewis Taylor, ed., *Why Governments Grow: Measuring Public Sector Size* (Beverly Hills: Sage Publications, 1983), pp. 142–48.

23. The borrowing totals were as follows: Great Britain, 6,860 million pounds sterling; Germany, 137.2 billion marks; France, 144.5 billion francs; Russia, 25.8 billion rubles. Gerd Hardach, *The First World War 1914–1918* (Berkeley, University of California Press, 1977), p. 155.

24. Keith Hutchison, *The Decline & Fall of British Capitalism* (Hamden, CT: Archon books, 1966), p. 161. Wartime inflation accounts, of course, for part of this increase.

25. On the connection with the Battle of the Somme in Great Britain, see Robert J. Scally, *The Origins of the Lloyd George Coalition: The Politics of Social-Imperialism, 1900–1918* (Princeton: Princeton University Press, 1975), p. 318. On the evolution of British cabinet government during the war, see John Turner, "Cabinets, Committees and Secretariats: the Higher Direction of War," in Kathleen Burk, ed., *War and the State: The Transformation of British Government, 1914–1919* (London: George Allen & Unwin, 1982), pp. 57–83, and Hans Daalder, *Cabinet Reform in Britain* (Stanford: Stanford University Press, 1963). On the evolution of French government during the war, see Pierre Renouvin, *Les Formes du Gouvernement de Guerre* (Paris: Les Presses Universitaires de France, 1925), especially pp. 143–48.

26. There are numerous excellent studies that review government mobilization and control measures during World War I: Arthur Marwick, *The Deluge: British Society and the First World War* (New York: W. W. Norton, 1965), pp. 29–44 and 151–88; Gerd Hardach, *The First World War 1914–1918*; Kathleen Burk, *War and the State: The Transformation of British Government, 1914–1919*; Gerald D. Feldman, *Army, Industry and Labor in Germany 1914–1918* (Princeton: Princeton University Press, 1966); John F. Godfrey, *Capitalism at War: Industrial Policy and Bureaucracy in France 1914–1918* (Leamington Spa, Hamburg: Berg Publishers, 1987); J. M. Winter, *The Great War and the British People* (Cambridge, MA: Harvard University Press, 1986); and Trevor Wilson, *the Myriad Faces of War: Britain and the Great War, 1914–1918* (Cambridge: Polity Press, 1986), pp. 149–238, 507–540, and 641–70.

27. The British, particularly sensitive to maritime factors, immediately requisitioned all shipping in waters adjacent to the United Kingdom, and by December 1916, effectively nationalized all shipping under a new Ministry of Shipping.

28. Chris Wrigley, "The Ministry of Munitions: an Innovatory Department," in Burk, ed., *War and the State*, pp. 46–47.

29. Pierre Renouvin, *Le Formes du Gouvernement de Guerre*, pp. 59–60; John F. Godfrey, *Capitalism at War*, pp. 106–143 and pp. 150–57; Gerald D. Feldman *Army, Industry and Labor in Germany 1914–1918*, p. 49.

30. See Kathleen Burk, "The Mobilization of Anglo-American Finance During World War I" in N. F. Dreisziger, ed., *Mobilization for Total War: The Canadian, American and British Experience 1914–1918, 1939–1945* (Waterloo, Ontario: Wilfrid Laurier University Press, 1981), pp. 23–42, as well as her article, "The Treasury: from Impotence to Power," in Burk, ed., *War and the State*, pp. 84–107.

31. David Lloyd George, *War Memoirs of David Lloyd George*, Vol. 2, *1915–1916* (Boston: Little, Brown and Co., 1937), p. 189. On the emergence of an intellectual and political climate favoring collectivism in the U.K., see Arthur Marwick, *The Deluge*, pp. 166–79.

32. Derek H. Aldcroft, *The Inter-War Economy: Britain, 1919–1939* (New York: Columbia University Press, 1970), pp. 345–49.

33. Richard F. Kuisel, *Capitalism and the State in Modern France* (Cambridge: Cambridge University Press, 1981), pp. 31–92. Clementel is quoted on p. 40. Further on the permanent impact of the war on French industry, see the summary of its legacy in Arthur Fontaine, *French Industry During the War* (New Haven: Yale University Press, 1926), Ch. 5.

34. Dough McEachern, *The Expanding State: Class and Economy in Europe since 1945* (New York: Harvester Wheatsheaf, 1990), pp. 74–82; G. D. H. Cole, *The Post-war*

Condition of Britain (London: Routledge & Kegan Paul, 1956); Richard Kuisel, *Capitalism and the State in Modern France*, pp. 202–11; John Hackett and Anne-Marie Hackett, *Economic Planning in France* (Cambridge, MA: Harvard University Press, 1963), pp. 37–43.

35. Winston Churchill, cited in Keith Hutchison, *The Decline and Fall of British Capitalism*, p. 158.

36. The figure of 63 million reflects the total number who served during the four years of the war.

37. John Keegan, *World War II* (New York, Viking, 1990), p. 590, estimated World War II losses at 50 million; Ernest L. Bogart, *Direct and Indirect Costs of the Great World War* (New York: Oxford University Press, 1919), p. 274, puts World War I losses at 12.9 million. These figures contain civilian casualties, including those who died in bombings, concentration camps, and as a result of forced labor.

38. Paul Kennedy, *The Rise and Fall of the Great Powers*, p. 274, cites these figures, but offers a total figure only for the British Empire of 9.5 million. J. M. Winter, *The Great War and the British People*, p. 72, gives a more precise total for the U.K. alone of 6,146,574, from which the figure used here is taken. The figure for the Napoleonic armed forces is from E. J. Hobsbawm, *The Age of Revolution 1789–1848* (New York: Mentor Books, 1962), p. 119.

39. Gerhard Ritter, *Die Hauptmächte Europas und das Wilhelminische Reich (1890–1914)*, Vol. II of *Staatskunst und Kriegshandwerk: Das Problem des "Militarismus" in Deutschland* (Munich: Verlag Oldenbourg, 1960), pp. 262–63; Karl Demeter, *Das Deutsche Offizierkorps in Gesellschaft und Staat 1650–1945* (Frankfurt am Main: Bernard & Graefe Verlag, 1962), pp. 18–23. Other factors, including budgetary considerations, also entered into the German decision to keep the active army relatively small.

40. Emile Durkheim, *The Division of Labor in Society*, trans. by George Simpson (Glencoe, IL: The Free Press, 1947), pp. 353–73; the quotation is from p. 372.

41. Stanislav Andreski [Andrzejewski], *Military Organization and Society*, 2nd ed., (London: Routledge & Kegan Paul, 1967), pp. 20–39.

42. Kenneth O. Morgan, "The Twentieth Century (1914–1984)" in *The Oxford Illustrated History of Britain*, pp. 562–63.

43. David Lloyd George, *War Memoirs*, Vol. 5 (London: Ivor Nicholson & Watson, 1936), Appendix II, p. 2515.

44. Cited in David Cannadine, *The Decline and Fall of the British Aristocracy* (New Haven: Yale University Press, 1990), p. 636.

45. On the debate over the Representation of the People Act and its link to military service, see Arthur Marwick, *The Deluge*, pp. 95–105.

46. Gerald D. Feldman, *Army, Industry and Labor in Germany 1914–1918*, p. 121–23.

47. On the suffrage reform issue in Germany during the war, see Gerald D. Feldman, *Army, Industry and Labor in Germany 1914–1918*, pp. 9–10, 121–22, 334–38, 364–69, 444–45, 490–92.

48. Arthur Marwick, *The Deluge*, p. 56.

49. A detailed and useful study of British manpower policy in World War I is Keith Grieves, *The Politics of Manpower, 1914–1918* (Manchester: Manchester University Press, 1988). On the establishment and evolution of the Ministry of National Service, see also Trevor Wilson, *The Myriad Faces of War*, pp. 533–36.

50. Cited in Gerald Feldman, *Army, Industry, and Labor in Germany 1914–1918*, p. 136. For more on the impact of the war on German trade unions, see pp. 127–38

as well, and Gordon Craig, *The Politics of the Prussian Army 1640–1945* (New York: Oxford University Press, 1964), pp. 307–13.

51. Gerald Feldman, *Army, Industry and Labor in Germany*, pp. 197–249.

52. Rodney Lowe, "The Ministry of Labour, 1916–1919: a Still, Small Voice?" in Kathleen Burk, ed., *War and the State*, pp. 108–34.

53. Tom Kemp, *The French Economy 1919–39: The History of a Decline* (New York: St. Martin's Press, 1972), p. 43. On the strikes in Great Britain and their consequences, see Trevor Wilson, *The Myriad Faces of War*, pp. 224–31.

54. Feldman, *Army, Industry and Labor in Germany*, p. 321.

55. On the events leading up to this agreement and its significance, see Feldman, pp. 519–33. Feldman argues that the workers probably gained less than was possible, and that the deal was better than the employers had hoped for.

56. Alistair Reid, "World War I and the Working Class in Britain," in Arthur Marwick, ed., *Total War and Social Change* (London: Collier-Macmillan, 1988), p. 22; Alistair Reid, "The Impact of the First World War on British Workers," in Richard Wall and Jay Winter, eds., *The Upheaval of War: Family, Work and Welfare in Europe, 1914–1918* (Cambridge: Cambridge University Press, 1988), p. 227. Figures on French trade-union membership are from Patrick Fridenson, "The Impact of the War on French Workers," in *The Upheaval of War*, p. 243. German trade union figures are from Juergen Kocka, *Facing Total War: German Society 1914–1918*, trans. by Barbara Weinberger, (Cambridge, MA: Harvard University Press, 1984), p. 66. On the growth of Italian trade unions, see Donald Meyer, *Sex and Power: The Rise of Women in America, Russia, Sweden, and Italy* (Middletown, CT: Wesleyan University Press, 1987), pp. 19–20.

57. Charles S. Maier, *Recasting Bourgeois Europe: Stabilization in France, Germany, and Italy in the Decade after World War I* (Princeton: Princeton University Press, 1975), p. 11. On the general strike and its consequences, see pp. 154–58.

58. Statistics on female employment are from Norbert C. Soldon, *Women in British Trade Unions 1874–1976* (Dublin: Gill and Macmillan, 1978), pp. 80–81. Deborah Thom, "Women and Work in Wartime Britain," in Wall and Winter, eds., *The Upheaval of War*, pp. 312 and 320, gives somewhat larger figures of 1,663,000 workers added and wartime trade-union membership growing from 437,000 in 1914 to 1,209,000 in 1918. The French figures are from Jean-Louis Robert, "Women and Work in France during the First World War," and the German figures are calculated from tables in Ute Daniel, "Women's Work in Industry and Family: Germany, 1914–18," both in Wall and Winter, eds., *The Upheaval of War*, pp. 252 and 268–71 respectively. On the increase in female representation in German unions, see Juergen Kocka, *Facing Total War: German Society 1914–1918*, p. 66. Most of the increase in France occurred in the war industries; for a more detailed breakdown, see Arthur Fontaine, *French Industry During the War*, pp. 42–46.

59. Chris Wrigley, "The Ministry of Munitions: an Innovatory Department," in Kathleen Burk, ed., *War and the State*, pp. 42–43; see also Samuel J. Hurwitz, *State Intervention in Great Britain*, pp. 131–46.

60. See, for example, Steven C. Hause, "More Minerva than Mars: The French Women's Rights Campaign and the First World War," in Margaret Randolph Higonnet, Jane Jensen et al., eds., *Behind the Lines: Gender and the Two World Wars* (New Haven: Yale University Press, 1987), pp. 99–113; James F. McMillan, "World War I and Women in France," in Arthur Marwick, ed., *Total War and Social Change* (London: Collier-Macmillan, 1968), pp. 1–15.

61. Deborah Thom, "Women and Work in Wartime Britain," in Wall and Winter,

eds., *The Upheaval of War*, pp. 297 and 317. See also Penny Summerfield, "Women, War and Social Change: Women in Britain in World War II," in Arthur Marwick, ed., *Total War and Social Change*, pp. 95–118.

62. See Alexander Davidson, *Two Models of Welfare: The Origins and Development of the Welfare State in Sweden and New Zealand, 1888–1988*, No. 108 of *Skrifter utgivna av Statsvetenskapliga föreningen i Uppsala* (Stockholm: Almqvist & Wiksell, 1989), pp. 77–78; Arthur Marwick, *The Deluge*, pp. 95–105.
63. James F. McMillan, "World War I and Women in France," in Arthur Marwick, ed., *Total War and Social Change*, p. 7.
64. Paula Schwartz, "Redefining Resistance: Women's Activism in Wartime France," and Jane Jenson, "The Liberation and New Rights for French Women," in Margaret Higonnet et al., *Behind the Lines*, pp. 141–53, 272–83; François Bédarida, "World War II and Social Change in France," in Arthur Marwick, ed., *Total War and Social Change*, pp. 89–91. On the passage of female suffrage in Italy, see Donald Meyer, *Sex and Power: The Rise of Women in America, Russia, Sweden, and Italy*, p. 34.
65. Stanley Hoffmann, "The Effects of World War II on French Society and Politics," in Clive Emsley, Arthur Marwick, and Wendy Simpson, eds., *War, Peace and Social Change in Twentieth-Century Europe* (Milton Keynes [U.K.]: Open University Press, 1989), pp. 233–54.
66. David Cannadine, *The Decline and Fall of the British Aristocracy*, pp. 71–87 and 617–36. On the effects of World War II on income stratification, see Penny Summerfield, "The 'Levelling of Class,'" in Emsley, Marwick, and Simpson, eds., *War, Peace and Social Change*, pp. 255–80.
67. See, for example, John S. Ambler, "Ideas, Interest, and the French Welfare State, in Ambler, ed., *The French Welfare State: Surviving Social and Ideological Change* (New York: New York University Press, 1991), pp. 2–23; Derek Fraser, *The Evolution of the British Welfare State: A History of Social Policy since the Industrial Revolution* (London: Collier-Macmillan, 1973); Douglas E. Ashford, *The Emergence of the Welfare States* (Oxford and New York: Basil Blackwell, 1987); and Peter Flora, "On the History and Current Problems of the Welfare State," in S. N. Eisenstadt and Ora Ahimeir, eds., *The Welfare State and its Aftermath* (London and Sydney: Croom Helm, 1985), pp. 11–30.
68. The key work setting forth the thesis of Richard Morris Titmuss on war and the welfare state was Titmuss, *Problems of Social Policy*, rev. ed. (London: Her Majesty's Stationery Office, 1976). See also his essay, "War and Social Policy," in Titmuss, *Essays on 'The Welfare State'* (New Haven: Yale University Press, 1959).
69. Richard Morris Titmuss, "War and Social Policy," ibid., p. 80.
70. Tony Ashworth, *Trench Warfare 1914–1918: The Live and Let Live System* (New York: Holmes & Meier, 1980), pp. 153–57; E. M. H. Lloyd, *Experiments in State Control at the War Office and the Ministry of Food*, in the British series of the Carnegie Endowment for International Peace, *Economic and Social History of the World War* (Oxford: At the Clarendon Press, 1924), pp. 1–2.
71. Peacock and Wiseman, *The Growth of Public Expenditures in the United Kingdom*, p. 74 and pp. 80–95.
72. On the welfare measure of the Ministry of Munitions and the linkage between the war and welfare advances, see Samuel J. Hurwitz, *State Intervention in Great Britain: A Study of Economic Control and Social Response, 1914–1919* (New York: Columbia University Press, 1949), pp. 109–119; cited in Arthur Marwick, *The Deluge*, pp. 113–15.

73. Chris Wrigley, "The Ministry of Munitions: an Innovatory Department," in Kathleen Burk, *War and the State*, pp. 32–56; J. M. Winter, *The Great War and the British People*, pp. 205–208. Chapters 4, 5, 6, and 7 of Winter's book all deal with the paradox of the Great War advancing social welfare in Great Britain.

74. Deborah Dwork, *War is Good for Babies and Other Young Children*, pp. 211–16. See also J. M. Winter, *The Great War and the British People*, pp. 141–53 and 189–203.

75. Derek Fraser, *The Evolution of the British Welfare State*, p. 165.

76. Idem, pp. 166–72.

77. Kenneth O. Morgan, "The Twentieth Century," pp. 563–64.

78. Sir William Beveridge, *Social Insurance and Allied Services* (New York: The Macmillan Company, 1942), p. 171.

79. William H. Beveridge, *Full Employment in a Free Society* (London: George Allen & Unwin, Ltd., 1944), p. 29.

80. A detailed account of wartime reconstruction planning in Great Britain and the introduction of the welfare state after the war is found in James E. Cronin, *The Politics of State Expansion: War, State and Society in Twentieth-Century Britain* (London and New York: Routledge, 1991), pp. 131–87.

81. Statistic is from Peter Flora, "On the History and Current Problems of the Welfare State," in S. N. Eisenstadt and Ora Ahimeir, eds., *The Welfare State and its Aftermath*, p. 18.

82. Calculated from table in Christine Andre and Robert Delorme, "The Long-Run Growth of Public Expenditure in France," *Public Finance/Finance Publiques* 33 (1978):63.

83. J. Carpentier and F. Lebrun, eds., *Histoire de France* (Paris: Éditions du Seuil, 1987), p. 331.

84. Rémi Lenoir, "Family Policy in France since 1938," in John S. Ambler, ed., *The French Welfare State: Surviving Social and Ideological Change* (New York: New York University Press, 1991), p. 150; William L. Shirer, *The Collapse of the Third Republic: An Inquiry into the Fall of France in 1940* (New York: Simon and Schuster, 1969), pp. 142–43.

85. On the reform impulse generated by the French defeat, see Robert O. Paxton, *Vichy France: Old Guard and New Order 1940–1944* (New York: Columbia University Press, 1972), pp. 136–48.

86. The Pétain quotation is from Rémi Lenoir, "Family Policy in France since 1938," p. 150. On the Vichy reforms, see Robert Paxton, *Vichy France*, pp. 136–67, 352–57. This analysis has focused primarily on the impact of the internal reforms undertaken by Pétain's government. The direct impact of German policies on France in the occupied territory was also enormous; on this, see Alan S. Milward, *The New Order and the French Economy* (Oxford: Oxford at the Clarendon Press, 1970).

87. Christine Andre and Robert Delorme, "The Long-Run growth of Public Expenditure in France," p. 47; Gary Freeman, "Socialism and Social Security," in John S. Ambler, ed., *The French Socialist Experiment* (Philadelphia: Institute for the Study of Human Issues, 1985), pp. 95–97.

88. On this point, see Douglas E. Ashford, *The Emergence of the Welfare States*, pp. 116–17.

89. On the influence of the Bismarckian reform on Sweden, see Sven E. Olsson, *Social Policy and Welfare State in Sweden* (Lund: Arkiv, 1990), pp. 40–47. On the

impact of World War I, see Alexander Davidson, *Two Models of Welfare: The Origins and Development of the Welfare State in Sweden and New Zealand*, pp. 77–78.

90. On the impact of World War II on the development of the Swedish welfare state, see Alexander Davidson, *Two Models of Welfare*, pp. 138–45,; Sven Olsson, *Social Policy and Welfare State in Sweden*, pp. 110–17; and Dorothy Wilson, *The Welfare State in Sweden: A Study in Comparative Social Administration* (London: Heinemann, 1979), pp. 8–15.

91. Walter Rüegg, "Social Rights or Social Responsibilities? The Case of Switzerland," in S. N. Eisenstadt and Ora Ahimeir, *The Welfare State and its Aftermath*, pp. 182–99. On the extreme defensive measures taken by Switzerland in World War II, see Urs Schwarz, *Vom Sturm umbrandet: wie die Schweiz den Zweiten Weltkrieg überlebte* (Frauenfeld: Huber, 1981).

92. On the unique organization and effectiveness of the Swiss welfare system, see Ralph Segalman and David Marsland, *Cradle to Grave: Comparative Perspective on the Welfare State* (London: Collier-Macmillan, 1989), pp. 65–112; Ralph Segalman, *The Swiss Way of Welfare: Lessons for the Western World* (New York: Praeger, 1986).

93. Walter Rüegg, "Social Rights or Social Responsibilities? The Case of Switzerland," pp. 185–86.

94. Charles Tilly, *Coercion, Capital, and European States, A.D. 990–1990* (Oxford: Basil Blackwell, 1990), p. 51.

Chapter 6: War and the Totalitarian State

1. The Futurist movement in literature and art that flourished at the turn of the century has often been described as proto-Fascist in style. Its philosophy and spirit portended the militarism and glorification of war of the Fascist and Nazi movements; its rejection of tradition and bourgeois culture was cited admiringly by Leon Trotsky in *Literature and Revolution* (1922). The Futurist Manifesto was a list of theses published in 1909. See Marjorie Perloff, *The Futurist Moment: Avant-Garde, Avant Guerre, and the Language of Rupture* (Chicago: University of Chicago Press, 1986).

2. Hitler, cited in John H. E. Fried, "Fascist Militarisation and Education for War," in International Council for Philosophy, *The Third Reich* (New York: Howard Fertig, 1974), p. 769.

3. Cited in Philip Selznick, "The Combat Party," *Problems of Communism* 2 (1953):36.

4. José Ortega y Gasset, *The Revolt of the Masses* (New York: W. W. Norton, 1957).

5. Hannah Arendt, *The Origins of Totalitarianism* (New York: Harcourt Brace Jovanovich, 1973 [1951]), p. 329.

6. Martin Broszat, "Departmental Polyocracy and the Forms of Führer absolutism," Ch. 9 of *The Hitler State: The Foundation and Development of the Internal Structure of the Third Reich*, trans. by John W. Hiden (London and New York: Longman, 1981 [1969]); Peter Hüttenberger, "National-sozialistische Polykratie," *Geschichte und Gesellschaft* 2 (1976):417–42; Detlev Peukert, *Inside Nazi Germany: Conformity, Opposition, and Racism in Everyday Life*, trans. by Richard Deveson (New Haven: Yale University Press, 1987), pp. 67–86 and 101–44; and the historiographical essay, "Centralized or polycentric dictatorship?" in John Hiden and John Farquharson, *Hitler's Germany: Historians and the Third Reich*

(London: Batsford Academic and Educational Ltd., 1983), pp. 59–109. But as Peukert notes (fn. 15, p. 265), "Even in a theory of fascism which assumed 'polyarchy' among the National Socialist organs of authority (i.e., a theory which assumes that control in the Third Reich lay not with the 'leader' alone but with a variety of power blocs such as the Party and SS, economic interests and the military), the tendency for control over the population to become total must be recognised."

7. Frederic J. Fleron, Jr., "Soviet Areas Studies and the Social Sciences: Some Methodological Problems in Communist Studies," *Soviet Studies* 19 (January 1968):313–39; Benjamin Barber and Herbert J. Spiro, "The Concept of Totalitarianism as the Foundation of American Counter-Ideology in the Cold War," *Politics and Society* I (November 1970). For rejoinders, see Maurice Cranston, "Shouild We Cease to Speak of Totalitarianism?" *Survey* 23 (Summer 1978):62–68.

8. A somewhat different list of six fundamental features is found in Carl J. Friedrich and Zbigniew Brzezinski, *Totalitarian Dictatorship and Autocracy* (Cambridge, MA: Harvard University Press, 1956), pp. 9–10. For further attempts at a definition of the phenomenon of totalitarianism, and discussions of its nature, see Herbert J. Spiro, "Totalitarianism" in *The International Encyclopedia of Social Sciences* 16 (New York: Macmillan and Free Press, 1968), p. 108; Leonard Schapiro, *Totalitarianism* (New York: Praeger Publishers, 1972); Hans Buchheim, *Totalitarian Rule: Its Nature and Characteristics*, trans. by Ruth Hein (Middletown, CT: Wesleyan University Press, 1968).

9. See the discussion in Sigmund Neumann, *Permanent Revolution: Totalitarianism in the Age of International Civil War*, 2nd ed., (New York: Praeger, 1965), Ch. 8, "The Impact of Permanent War." "The dictatorial regimes are governments at war, originating in war, aiming at war, thriving on war" (p. 230). Ernst Nolte, *Three Faces of Fascism*, trans. by Leila Vennewitz, (London: Weidenfeld and Nicolson, 1965), pp. 110–13, 120–35, 409–410, likewise discusses the commitment of the Fascist movements to waging "eternal war."

10. Raymond Aron, *The Century of Total War* (New York: Doubleday, 1954), p. 88.

11. Sergio Panunzio, cited in A. James Gregor, *The Ideology of Fascism: The Rationale of Totalitarianism* (New York: The Free Press, 1969), p. 173.

12. Philip Selznick, *The Organizational Weapon: A Study of Bolshevik Strategy and Tactics* (New York: McGraw-Hill, 1952), pp. 17–73.

13. Cited in Alex de Jonge, *Stalin and the Shaping of the Soviet Union* (New York: William Morrow & Co., 1986), p. 230.

14. Alex Inkeles, *Social Change in Soviet Russia* (Cambridge, MA: Harvard University Press, 1968), p. 159.

15. On this point, see Werner Betz, "The National-Socialist Vocabulary," in *The Third Reich*, pp. 784–96, especially p. 792; and Ilya Zemtsov, *Lexicon of Soviet Political Terms* (Fairfax, VA: HERO Books, 1984), pp. 152, 247–49.

16. On the latter phenomenon, see Tony Ashworth, *Trench Warfare 1914–1918: The Live and Let Live System* (New York: Holmes & Meier, 1980), pp. 12–14.

17. James L. Payne, *Why Nations Arm* (Oxford: Basil Blackwell, 1989), pp. 103–121.

18. Eric Hoffer, *The True Believer*, reprinted in *Between the Devil and the Dragon: The Best Essays and Aphorisms of Eric Hoffer* (New York: Harper & Row, 1982 [1951]), pp. 236, 241; his comments on the parallels between mass movements and armies, pp. 236–41, are also recommended. On the totalitarian state as an

occupying army, see Hannah Arendt, *The Origins of Totalitarianism*, pp. 415–17; See also her comments, p. 373, on "the artificial creation of civil-war conditions" by totalitarian movements.

19. Cited in Hans Buchheim, "The SS—Instrument of Domination," in Helmut Krausnick, Hans Buchheim, Martin Broszat, and Hans-Adolf Jacobsen, *Anatomy of The SS State* (London: Collins, 1968), p. 201.

20. Hajo Holborn, "Origins and Political Character of Nazi Ideology," *Political Science Quarterly* 79 (December 1964):546.

21. V. I. Lenin, *Collected Works*, Vol. 28, p. 69; *Selected Works*, Vol. 7, p. 269; and Besançon, *The Rise of the Gulag*, p. 222.

22. Historical estimates on the number of fatalities suffered during this period are taken from Robert Conquest, *The Great Terror: A Reassessment* (Oxford: Oxford University Press, 1990), pp. 484–86. The earlier figures on casualties of collectivization are from Robert Conquest, *The Harvest of Sorrow: Soviet Collectivization and the Terror-Famine* (Oxford: Oxford University Press, 1986), pp. 299–304. Conquest's works are indispensable to understanding these two periods of Soviet history. On the nature and purposes of Stalin's terror, see also Hannah Arendt, *The Origins of Totalitarianism*, Chs. 12 and 13; and Alexander Dallin and George W. Breslauer, *Political Terror in Communist Systems* (Stanford: Stanford University Press, 1970).

23. Simon Schama, *Citizens*, p. 789. See pp. 781–92 on the casualty figures of the Terror and the revolt in the Vendée.

24. Lenin, cited in Alain Besançon, *The Rise of the Gulag: Intellectual Origins of Leninism*, trans. by Sarah Matthews (New York: Continuum), p. 222.

25. L. Trotsky, *The Defence of Terrorism* (originally *Terrorism and Communism*) (London: The Labour Publishing Company, 1921), pp. 47–48; see also pp. 61–64 on the influence of World War I on the Bolshevik use of terror.

26. Richard Pipes lays out the case for the origins of the Terror predating the Russian Civil War in his *The Russian Revolution* (New York: Random House, 1990), pp. 789–802. For comparative analysis of the Russian and French reigns of terror, see Theda Skocpol, *States and Social Revolutions: A Comparative analysis of France, Russia, and China* (Cambridge: Cambridge University Press, 1979) and Rosemary H. T. O'Kane, *The Revolutionary Reign of Terror: The Role of Violence in Political Change*.

27. Adolf Hitler, *Table Talk*, cited in J. P. Stern, *Hitler: The Führer and the People* (Berkeley and Los Angeles: University of California Press, 1988), p. 33; Himmler and Heydrich cited in Karl Dietrich Bracher, *Die Deutsche Diktatur: Entstehung, Struktur, Folgen des Nationalsozialismus* (Cologne: Kiepenheier & Witsch, 1976), pp. 448 and 463; V. I. Lenin, *Polnoe cobranie sochinenii*, Vol. 35 (Moscow: Political Literature, 1950), p. 265; Lenin, *State and Revolution*, cited in Lenin's *Collected Works*, Vol. 25, pp. 405, 413–14. Numerous similar examples of Lenin's thinking on violence can be found in Nathan Leites, *A Study of Bolshevism* (Glencoe, IL: The Free Press, 1953), pp. 341–67 and 379–416.

28. On the influence of Social Darwinism in Germany, see Alfred Kelly, *The Descent of Darwin: The Popularization of Darwinism in Germany, 1860–1914* (Chapel Hill: University of North Carolina Press, 1981), pp. 100–22, and Arno J. Mayer, *The Persistence of the Old Regime*, Ch. 5. The quotation from Wagner is cited in Hans Kohn, *The Mind of Germany: The Education of a Nation* (New York: Harper & Row, 1965), p. 280.

29. On this point, see Peter Emil Becker, *Zur Geschichte der Rassenhygiene: Wege ins Dritte Reich* (Stuttgart: Georg Thieme Verlag, 1988) and Peter Weingart, Juergen Droll, and Kurt Bayertz, *Rasse, Blut und Gene: Geschichte der Eugenik und Rassenhygiene in Deutschland*, pp. 114–20. Hajo Holborn in "Origins and Political Character of Nazi Ideology," pp. 545–46, discusses the Social Darwinist strain in National Socialism. See also Kelly, *The Descent of Darwin*, pp. 105–109, but note that Kelly minimizes the impact of Social Darwinism on Nazism (pp. 120–22). On the influence of Treitschke, see Peter Winzen, "Treitschke's Influence on the Rise of Imperialist and Anti-British Nationalism in Germany," in Paul Kennedy and Anthony Nicholls, eds., *Nationalist and Racialist Movements in Britain and Germany Before 1914* (London: Collier-Macmillan, 1981), pp. 154–70.

30. One nineteenth-century scholar, David G. Ritchie of Oxford University, saw the parallels and even tried to suggest some direct historical linkages. See his article, "Darwin and Hegel," in David G. Ritchie, *Darwin and Hegel with Other Philosophical Studies* (London: Swan Sonnenschein & Co. 1893), pp. 38–76.

31. Kelly, *The Descent of Darwin*, pp. 123–26.

32. V. I. Lenin, *Imperialism, the Highest Stage of Capitalism* (New York: International Publishers, 1939); Lenin, speech at the Third Congress of the Comintern, in Lenin, *Selected Works*, Vol. 9, p. 242 and Vol. 8, p. 297. The classic work by Georges Sorel, which greatly influenced the socialist movement of Europe, was *Reflections on Violence*, trans. by T. E. Hulme and J. Roth (Glencoe, IL: The Free Press, 1950 [1908]). Appendix 3 of the third French edition, "In Defense of Lenin," pp. 303–309, was a spirited defense of the violence attendant upon the Russian Revolution.

33. See Hans Kohn, *The Mind of Germany*; Fritz Stern, *The Politics of Cultural Despair* (Berkeley and Los Angeles: University of California Press, 1961); Friedrich C. Sell, *Die Tragoedie des Deutschen Liberalismus* (Stuttgart: Deutsche Verlag-Anstalt, 1953); and Woodruff D. Smith, *The Ideological Origins of Nazi Imperialism* (New York: Oxford University Press, 1986). For general histories of the evolution of German nationalism through the Nazi period, see Louis L. Snyder, *Roots of German Nationalism* (Bloomington: Indiana University Press, 1978); George L. Mosse, *The Crisis of German Ideology: Intellectual Origins of the Third Reich* (New York: Schocken Books, 1981); and Edmond Vermeil, "The Origin, Nature, and Development of German Nationalist Ideology in the 19th and 20th Centuries," in International Council for Philosophy and Humanistic Studies, *The Third Reich* (New York: Howard Fertig, 1975), pp. 3–111.

34. George Mosse, "The Mystical Origins of National Socialism," *The Journal of the History of Ideas* 22 (January–March 1961):81–96. See also his article, "Toward a General Theory of Fascism," in George L. Mosse, *Masses and Man: Nationalist and Fascist Perceptions of Reality* (New York: Howard Fertig, 1980), pp. 159–96. A thoughtful discussion of the role of right-wing nationalist groups in Imperial Germany, which emphasizes their traditional nature and downplays the link with Nazism, is Geoff Eley, "Some Thoughts on the Nationalist Pressure Groups in Imperial Germany," in Kennedy and Nicholls, *Nationalist and Racialist Movements*, pp. 40–67.

35. Roger Chickering, *We Men Who Feel Most German: A Cultural Study of the Pan-German League, 1886–1914* (Boston: George Allen & Unwin, 1984), p. 123. On the history of the Pan-German League prior to World War I see Mildred S. Wertheimer, *The Pan-German League 1890–1914* (New York: Columbia Univer-

sity Press, 1924) and Michael Peters, *Der Alldeutsche Verband am Vorabend des Ersten Weltkrieges 1908–1914* (Frankfurt am Main: Lang, 1992).

36. On the parallels and divergences between nationalism and Soviet communism, see Adam B. Ulam, "Nationalism, Panslavism, Communism," in Ivo J. Lederer, ed., *Russian Foreign Policy: Essays in Historical Perspective* (New Haven: Yale University Press, 1962), pp. 39–68. The frequent use of the term "socialist fatherland" in Soviet military literature is another, exceedingly un-Marxist example of the nationalist lineage of Soviet Communism.

37. Hannah Arendt, *The Origins of Totalitarianism*, p. 206. Arendt's treatment of imperialism in Part Two of *The Origins* is invaluable. On the African experience specifically, see pp. 124–57 and 186–221. On the reluctance of the Western powers to apply the international laws of war to the kind of partisan or guerrilla warfare that they encountered in the imperial era, see Geoffrey Best, "Restraints on War by Land Before 1945," in Michael Howard, ed., *Restraints on War: Studies in the Limitation of Armed Conflict* (Oxford: Oxford University Press, 1979), pp. 17–38.

38. Andrzej J. Kaminski, *Konzentrationslager 1896 bis heute: Eine Analyse* (Stuttgart: Verlag W. Kohlhammer, 1982), pp. 34–35; Byron Farwell, *The Great Boer War* (London: Allen Lane, 1976), p. 392; Peter Warwick, *Black People and the South African War 1899–1902* (Cambridge: Cambridge University Press, 1983), p. 150–52. See also S. B. Spies, *Methods of Barbarism? Roberts and Kitchener and Civilians in the Boer Republics, January 1900–May 1902* (Cape Town: Human & Rousseau, 1977).

39. Thomas Pakenham, *The Scramble for Africa, 1876–1912* (London: Weidenfeld & Nicholson, 1991), pp. 602–28; Colin Legum, *Congo Disaster* (Gloucester, MA: Peter Smith, 1972), p. 35.

40. The classic account of the pervasive militarism of Prussian and German history is the five-volume series by Gerhard Ritter, *The Sword and the Scepter: The Problem of Militarism in Germany*, trans. by Heinz Norden (Coral Gables, FL: University of Miami Press). The critical period prior to World War I is covered in Volume II, *The European Powers and the Wilhelminian Empire, 1890–1914* (1970). On Russia's rise as a military power, see Christopher Duffy, *Russian's Military Way to the West: Origins and Nature of Russian Military Power 1700–1800* (London: Routledge & Kegan Paul, 1981).

41. On the war's impact on German society, see Martin Broszat, *Hitler and the Collapse of Weimar Germany*, trans. by V. R. Berghahn (Leamington Spa: Berg, 1987), pp. 43–50; Gerhard Ritter, "The Historical Foundations of the Rise of National Socialism," in *The Third Reich*, pp. 381–416; Karl Dietrich Bracher, *Die Auflösung der Weimarer Republik: Eine Studie zum Problem des Machtverfalls in der Demokratie* (Düsseldorf: Athenäum, 1978), Chaps. 1, 2, 3. On the compromised status of the German trade unions, see Ralf Dahrendorf, "The Tragedy of the German Labor Movement," in Dahrendorf, *Society and Democracy in Germany* (New York: W. W. Norton, 1967), pp. 172–87. A good comprehensive analysis of the breakdown of the Weimar Republic is M. Rainer Lepsius, "From Fragmented Party Democracy to Government by Emergency Decree and National Socialist Takeover," in Juan J. Linz and Alfred Stepan, eds., *The Breakdown of Democratic Regimes* (Baltimore: Johns Hopkins University Press, 1978), from which the data in Table 6-1 is adapted.

42. Bernd Hüppauf, "The Birth of Fascist Man from the Spirit of the Front: From

Langemarck to Verdun," in John Milfull, ed., *The Attractions of Fascism* (New York and Oxford: Berg, 1990), pp. 45–76. See also George L. Mosse, "Two World Wars and the Myth of the War Experience," *Journal of Contemporary History* 21 (October 1986): 491–514, especially p. 495; and "Toward a General Theory of Fascism," in Mosse, *Masses and Man: Nationalist and Fascist Perceptions of Reality* (New York: Howard Fertig, 1980), pp. 170–74. Michael Geyer, "The Militarization of Europe, 1914–1945," in John R. Gillis, ed., *The Militarization of the Western World* (New Brunswick, NJ: Rutgers University Press, 1989), pp. 65–102, in a brilliant essay analyzes how the intense mobilization experience of World War I contributed to the ethos of militarization and violence that engulfed Europe, and especially Germany, in the interwar years.

43. Robert Ley in *Völkischer Beobachter*, January 27, 1934, cited in David Schoenbaum, *Hitler's Social Revolution: Class and Status in Nazi Germany 1933–1939* (New York: Norton, 1980), p. 62.

44. On the role of the *Freikorps* and other paramilitary organizations in Weimar Germany and in the rise of Nazism, see Nigel H. Jones, *Hitler's Heralds: The True Story of the Freikorps 1918–1923* (London: Murray, 1987); Peter H. Merkl, *The Making of a Stormtrooper* (Princeton: Princeton University Press, 1980); Dominik Venner, *Ein deutscher Heldenkampf: Die Geschichte der Freikorps 1918–1923: Söldner ohne Sold* (Kiel: Arndt, 1989); Richard Bessel, "Violence as Propaganda: The Role of the Storm Troopers in the Rise Of National Socialism," in Thomas Childers, ed., *The Formation of the Nazi Constituency 1919–1933* (London: Croom Helm, 1986), pp. 131–46; Richard Bessel, *Political Violence and the Rise of Nazism: The Storm Troopers in Eastern Germany 1925–1934* (New Haven: Yale University Press, 1984); Karl Dietrich Bracher, *Die Auflösung der Weimarer Republik* Ch. 5. On *trincerismo* and Italian Fascism, see Roger Griffin, *The Nature of Fascism* (New York: St. Martin's Press, 1991), pp. 63–67.

45. Adolf Hitler, *Mein Kampf*, trans. by Ralph Manheim (Boston: Houghton Mifflin Company/Cambridge, MA: Riverside Press, 1943), pp. 204–206.

46. Roger Griffin, *The Nature of Fascism*, p. 38, italics removed from original. See also Griffin's generic definition of Fascism and outline of this general theory, pp. 26–55.

47. Hitler, *Mein Kampf*, trans. by Ralph Manheim, p. 281.

48. Horst von Metzsch, *Krieg als Saat*, cited in William K. Pfeiler, *War and the German Mind: The Testimony of Men of Fiction Who Fought at the Front* (New York: Columbia University Press, 1941), pp. 45–46.

49. Moeller van den Bruck, *Das Dritte Reich*, cited in William Pfeiler, *War and the German Mind*, p. 42. Pfeiler cites numerous similar examples, pp. 38–57.

50. William S. Allen, *The Nazi Seizure of Power: The Experience of a Single German Town 1922–1945*, rev. ed. (New York: Franklin Watts, 1984), p. 73; Theodor Abel, *The Nazi Movement* (New York: Atherton Press, 1966), pp. 313–15; Daniel Lerner, *The Nazi Elite* (Stanford: Stanford University Press, 1951), pp. 12–13, 60–61.

51. Alistair Hennessy, "Fascism and Populism in Latin America," in Walter Laqueur, *Fascism: A Reader's Guide: Analyses, Interpretations, Bibliography* (Berkeley and Los Angeles: University of California Press, 1976), p. 257, discussing why the "total war" experienced by Europe made it more susceptible to fascism than Latin America, where war occurred less frequently and on a small organizational scale. On the impact of gender imbalances and other sexual factors, see also

Klaus Theweleit, *Männerphantasien*, 2 Vols. (Reinbek bei Hamburg: Rowohlt, 1980). On the use of deported labor in Germany during World War I, see Robert B. Armeson, *Total Warfare and Compulsory Labor: A Study of the Military-Industrial Complex in Germany during World War I* (The Hague: Martinus Nijhoff, 1964).

52. Alain Besançon, *The Rise of the Gulag: Intellectual Origins of Leninism*, pp. 256–57. William H. Chamberlin's classic account of the Revolution comes to a similar conclusion: "The national morale was completely shattered by the World War. No one, except under extreme compulsion, was willing to perform any state obligation. The old order had simply crumbled away; a new order, with new habits and standards of conduct, had not yet formed; very often the only way in which a governmental representative, whether he was a Bolshevik commissar or a White officer, could get his orders obeyed was by flourishing a revolver." William Henry Chamberlin, *The Russian Revolution 1917–1921*, Vol. 2 (New York: Macmillan Company, 1952), p. 81. A dated, but still useful, analysis of the impact of the war on Russia is a volume in the Carnegie Endowment series on World War I: Stanislas Kohn, *The Cost of the War to Russia* (New Haven: Yale University Press, 1932).

53. V. I. Lenin, "Our Revolution: Apropos of N. Sukhanov's Notes," in *Collected Works* 33 (Moscow: Progress Publishing House, 1965), p. 177. (Lenin did not know, of course, about a *second* imperialist war; either the Soviet editors later interpolated the adjective, or he simply assumed that other imperialist wars were inevitable.) An excellent analysis of how the traditional institutions of Russian society proved too weak to resist the totalitarian takeover is Marc Ferro, *The Bolshevik Revolution: A Social History of the Russian Revolution* (London: Routledge & Kegan Paul, 1980), Ch. 3.

54. Tony Ashworth's, *Trench Warfare 1914–1918*, the most comprehensive study of trench fighting in World War I, mentions the Russian front only in passing.

55. One of the best accounts of the Russian army in World War I and its disintegration is Allan K. Wildman, *The End of the Russian Imperial Army: The Old Army and the Soldiers' Revolt (March–April 1917)* (Princeton: Princeton University Press, 1987). On the radicalization of the Army, see also Marc Ferro, *The Bolshevik Revolution*, pp. 69–85.

56. Richard Pipes, *The Russian Revolution* (New York: Random House, 1990), p. 278.

57. On the role of the Red Guards and war veterans in the Russian revolution, see Rex A. Wade, *Red Guards and Workers' Militias in the Russian Revolution* (Stanford: Stanford University Press, 1984). On "Front Bolshevism" and the role of the Army in the Revolution, see Allan K. Wildman, *The End of the Russian Imperial Army*, Vol. II, *The Road to Soviet Power and Peace* (Princeton: Princeton University Press, 1987), especially pp. 36–72 and 262–349.

58. Quotations and information on the SS are from B. Wegner, "The 'Aristocracy of National Socialism': the Role of the SS in National Socialist Germany," in H. W. Koch, *Aspects of the Third Reich*, pp. 430–50, *passim*; and Helmut Krausnick, Hans Buchheim, Martin Broszat, and Hans-Adolf Jacobsen, *Anatomy of the SS State*, trans. by Richard Berry et al. (London: Collins, 1968). Though the SS undertook the most awful of Hitler's policies, it would be wrong to see the mainline army, the *Reichswehr*, as innocent of crimes against humanity. Omer Bartov, *Hitler's Army: Soldiers, Nazis, and War in the Third Reich* (New York: Oxford University Press, 1991) shows that the nazification of the army had inculcated

front-line soldiers with an exceptional degree of brutality and ruthlessness, and that this manifested itself in the atrocities and cruelties committed by the German army, particularly on the Eastern front.

59. Lenin reportedly told Chiang Kai-shek that after the debacle in Poland he had concluded that Soviet Russia should render assistance to wars of national liberation abroad, but "should never again employ Soviet troops in direct participation." Chiang Kai-shek, *Soviet Russia in China: A Summing-up at Seventy* (New York: Farrar, Strauss & Cuhady, 1957), p. 22.

60. Most of these are well known and amply documented in standard histories. On the lesser known but very important Green Movement, see Oliver H. Radkey, *The Unknown Civil War in Soviet Russia: A Study of the Green Movement in the Tambov Region 1920–1921* (Stanford: Hoover Institution Press, 1976).

61. Robert C. Tucker has argued that historically there were two Leninisms—the Leninism of the New Economic Policy and the Leninism of War Communism; Nikolai Bukharin was the heir of the first and Joseph Stalin the heir of the second. See Robert C. Tucker, "Stalinism as Revolution from Above," in Tucker, ed., *Stalinism: Essays in Historical Interpretation* (New York: W. W. Norton, 1977), pp. 80–82, 89–92. On the importance of the Civil War as the progenitor of Stalinism, see also Roger Pethybridge, *The Social Prelude to Stalinism* (London: Colliers Macmillan, 1974), Ch. 3, "The Impact of War"; Stephen F. Cohen, *Bukharin and the Bolshevik Revolution: A Political Biography, 1888–1938* (Oxford: Oxford University Press, 1980), Ch. 3, especially pp. 60, 78–80, 86–87; Moshe Lewin, *Lenin's Last Struggle*, trans. by A. M. Sheridan Smith (New York: Pantheon Books, 1968), pp. 12–19.

62. See Daniel R. Brower, "'The City in Danger': The Civil War and the Russian Urban Population," pp. 58–80, and Diane P. Koenker, "Urbanization and Deurbanization in the Russian Revolution and Civil War," in Diane P. Koenker, William G. Rosenberg, and Ronald Gregor Suny, eds., *Party, State, and Society in the Russian Civil War* (Bloomington: Indiana University Press, 1989), pp. 81–104.

63. Iakov Sverdlov, cited in Pipes, *The Russian Revolution*, p. 728; italics mine. See also Lenin's essay, "The Worker's Party and the Peasantry," in Lenin, *Selected Works*, Vol. II (New York: International Publishers, circa 1935), pp. 237–42.

64. N. Osinksy in *Deviatyi s'ezd RKP(b). Mart-aprel 1920 goda: protokoly* (Moscow, 1960), p. 115, cited in Stephen Cohen, *Bukharin and the Bolshevik Revolution*, p. 60.

65. See James Bunyan, *The Origin of Forced Labor in the Soviet State 1917–1921: Documents and Materials* (Baltimore: Johns Hopkins University Press, 1967). On the link between the war and the Red Terror, see also Chamberlin, *The Russian Revolution*, Ch. 23. On Trotsky's scheme for creating armies of labor and militarizing Russian society, see Roger Pethybridge, *The Social Prelude to Stalinism*, pp. 104–107.

66. Cited in W. Bruce Lincoln, *Red Victory: A History of the Russian Civil War* (New York: Simon & Schuster, 1989), p. 513.

67. I. V. Stalin, *Sochinenia*, Vol. 13 (Moscow: Political Literature, 1951), pp. 38–39.

68. Figures are from Alec Nove, *Economic History of the USSR*, pp. 228–229. These official figures almost certainly understate the actual extent of Soviet spending, but they probably reflect the approximate rate of growth of that spending.

69. Moshe Lewin, *Russian Peasants and Soviet Power: A Study of Collectivization*

(New York: W. W. Norton, 1968), p. 260. The hunt for saboteurs and wreckers in the cities played a similar centralizing function.

70. Scholars continue to debate whether totalitarianism was a modern or an anti-modern phenomenon. See, for example, Roland Sarti, "Fascist Modernization in Italy: Traditional or Revolutionary?" *The American Historical Review* 75 (April 1970):1029–1046; Geoff Eley, "What Produces Fascism: Pre-industrial Traditions or a Crisis of the Capitalist State," *Politics and Society* 12 (1983):53–82; George L. Mosse, "The Mystical Origins of National Socialism," *The Journal of the History of Ideas* 22 (January–March 1961):81–96; Michael Burleigh and Wolfgang Wippermann, *The Racial State: Germany 1933–1945* (Cambridge: Cambridge University Press, 1991).

71. On this point, see Jeffrey Herf, *Reactionary Modernism: Technology, Culture, and Politics in Weimar and the Third Reich* (Cambridge: Cambridge University Press, 1984), Ch. 8; Detlev Peukert, *Inside Nazi Germany*, pp. 38–40.

72. Cited in Stern, *Hitler: The Führer and the People*, p. 34; see also pp. 28–34.

73. Walther Funk, cited in William L. Shirer, *The Rise and Fall of the Third Reich* (New York: Simon & Schuster, 1960), pp. 259–61. On the development of central controls and planning in Nazi Germany, see Allan S. Milward, *War, Economy and Society 1939–1945* (Berkeley and Los Angeles, 1979), pp. 113–17.

74. The Ministry of Munitions was called the Ministry of War Production from 1943. Alan S. Milward, *The German Economy at War* (London: The Athlone Press, 1965) is a detailed account of German industrial production during World War II. Albert Speer, *Inside the Third Reich: Memoirs*, trans. by Richard and Clara Winston (New York: Macmillan Publishing Company, 1970) is a useful, if biased, inside account of the events of this period.

75. Richard Pipes, *The Russian Revolution*, pp. 671–713; Stephen Cohen, *Bukharin and the Bolshevik Revolution*, p. 78–79; Roger Pethybridge, *The Social Prelude to Stalinism*, pp. 104–107, 118–119. On both War Communism and the Stalin revolution, see Alec Nove, *An Economic History of the USSR* (Harmondsworth: Penguin Books, 1982), pp. 46–82 and 160–224.

76. Figures on the growth of the bureaucracy are from Jane Caplan, *Government without Administration: State and Civil Service in Weimar and Nazi Germany* (Oxford: Clarendon Press, 1988), p. 217. Wilhelm Frick, cited in William Shirer, *The Rise and Fall of the Third Reich*, p. 200. The subordination of the Länder was a long and complex process that began in 1933 and continued until at least 1938, with mixed results. For details, see Martin Broszat, *The Hitler State*, Ch. 4.

77. Pipes, *The Russian Revolution*, pp. 693–94.

78. Trotsky, cited in Lewin, *Russian Peasants and Soviet Power*, p. 483.

79. Lewin, *Russian Peasants and Soviet Power*, p. 188. On the development of this technocracy from the Revolution to the Civil War and from the Civil War to the industrialization campaign, and its importance to the latter, see Don K. Rowney, *Transition to Technocracy: The Structural Origins of the Soviet Administrative State* (Ithaca: Cornell University Press, 1989).

80. On the Soviet system of wartime control, see Sanford R. Lieberman, "Crisis Management in the USSR: The Wartime System of Administration and Control," in Susan J. Linz, ed., *The Impact of World War II on the Soviet Union* (Totowa, NJ: Rowman & Allanheld, 1985), pp. 59–76. On the Soviet Union as a highly bureaucratized state, see two interesting analyses: Bruno Rizzi, *The Bureaucratization of the World: The USSR: Bureaucratic Collectivism*, trans. by Adam Westoby (Lon-

don: Tavistock, 1985), and Maria Hirszowicz, *The Bureaucratic Leviathan; A Study in the Sociology of Communism* (New York: New York University Press, 1980).

81. Contemporary sociologists have argued that the structural organization of bureaucracy is uniquely suited for the perpetration of callous violence. See the sources cited in Eric Markusen, "Genocide and Total War: A Preliminary Comparison," in Isidor Wallimann and Michael N. Dobkowski, eds., *Genocide and the Modern Age: Etiology and Case Studies of Mass Death* (New York: Greenwood, 1987), pp. 112–13.

82. Carlton J. H. Hayes pointed out over fifty years ago that totalitarian rule rests upon on mass support, as much as any democracy. See Carlton J. H. Hayes, "The Novelty of Totalitarianism in the History of Western Civilization," in *Symposium on the Totalitarian State*, Proceedings of the American Philosophical Society 82 (1940).

83. Wolfgang Benz, "The Ritual and Stage Management of National Socialism: Techniques of Domination and the Public Sphere," in John Milfull, ed., *The Attractions of Fascism*, pp. 273–88.

84. Wolfgang Benz, "The Ritual and Stage Management of National Socialism," p. 273.

85. *Mein Kampf*, p. 177; see the entire chapter "War Propaganda," pp. 176–86.

86. Detlev Peukert, *Inside Nazi Germany*, pp. 148–49. In *Mein Kampf* Hitler stresses the importance of education in preparing young men for future military service, which itself he described as "the highest school of patriotic education" (p. 413).

87. The examples from the Nazi curriculum are from Geert Platner, *Schule im Dritten Reich: Erziehung zum Tod* (Cologne: Pahl-Rugenstein, 1988), pp. 49–58 and 241–80; the quotation from Ewald Banse is in Gilmer W. Blackburn, *Education in the Third Reich: A Study of Race and History in Nazi Textbooks* (Albany: State University of New York Press, 1985), p. 127; Blackburn also uses the term "apocalyptic function" (p. 34). On education in the Third Reich in general, see Karl Dietrich Bracher, *Die deutsche Diktatur*, pp. 284–98.

88. On the militarism of the pre-1914 educational system, see Ulrich Bendele, *Krieg, Kopf und Körper: Lernen für das Leben—Erziehung zum Tod* (Frankfurt: Ullstein, 1984). On *Kraft* as the central theme of Nazi physical education, see Hajo Bernett, "Das Kraftpotential der Nation: Leibeserziehung im Dienst der politischen Macht," in Ulrich Herrmann and Jürgen Oelkers, *Pädagogik und Nationalsozialismus* (Weinheim and Basel: Beltz Verlag, 1988), pp. 167–94.

89. Konstantin Hierl, cited in David Schoenbaum, *Hitler's Social Revolution*, p. 63.

90. Cited in James Riordan, "Soviet Physical Education," in J. J. Tomiak, *Soviet Education in the 1980s* (New York: St. Martin's Press, 1983), p. 175.

91. Harriet Fast Scott and William F. Scott, *The Armed Forces of the USSR*, 3rd ed. (Boulder: Westview Press, 1984), pp. 326–334.

92. David Schoenbaum, *Hitler's Social Revolution*, pp. 247–48 and J. P. Stern, *Hitler: The Führer and the People*, p. 169.

93. Robert C. Tucker, "Stalinism as Revolution from Above," in Tucker, ed., *Stalinism: Essays in Historical Interpretation*, pp. 101–102; Edward Keenan, "Muscovite Political Folkways," *Russian Review* 45 (April 1986):115–81.

94. See Gerhard Ritter, "Historical Foundations of the Rise of National-Socialism," pp. 394–97.

95. Bracher, *Die Deutsche Diktatur*, pp. 367–68.

96. Cited in Richard Grunberger, *A Social History of the Reich* (London: Weidenfeld and Nicolson, 1971) p. 236; see also pp. 233–50.
97. "It remains one of the oddities of this war that Hitler demanded far less from his people than Churchill and Roosevelt did. . . . The discrepancy between the total mobilization of labor forces in democratic England and the casual treatment of this question in authoritarian Germany is proof of the regime's anxiety not to risk any shift in the popular mood." Albert Speer, *Inside the Third Reich: Memoirs*, p. 214.
98. Max Seydewitz, *Civil Life in Wartime Germany: The Story of the Home Front* (New York: The Viking Press, 1945) is an interesting account of the impact of the war on the German population by a former member of the German Reichstag.
99. Pipes, *The Russian Revolution*, p. 706; see also pp. 702–708.
100. Soviet welfare legislation is reviewed in Mervyn Matthews, *Poverty in the Soviet Union: The Life-Styles of the Underprivileged in Recent Years* (Cambridge: Cambridge University Press, 1986), pp. 113–25.
101. Mervyn Matthews, "*Perestroika* and the Rebirth of Charity," in Anthony Jones, David Powell, and Walter D. Connor, eds., *Soviet Social Problems* (Boulder: Westview, 1991), pp. 154–71.
102. The allusion is to the Greek poet Constantin Peter Cafavy's "Waiting for the Barbarians," reprinted in C. P. Cavafy, *Collected Poems*, trans. by Edmund Keeley and Philip Sherrard, rev. ed. (Princeton: Princeton University Press, 1992), pp. 18–19.

Chapter 7: War and the American Government

1. A. F. Pollard, *Factors in American History* (New York: Macmillan, 1925), p. 31–32. See also pp. 33–44. On the American attitude toward state sovereignty, see also Gordon S. Wood, *The Creation of the American Republic 1776–1787* (New York: W. W. Norton, 1972), pp. 344–39.
2. Stephen Skowronek, *Building A New American State: The Expansion of National Administrative Capacities 1877–1920* (Cambridge, Cambridge University Press, 1982), p. 3; see his entire discussion of American 'statelessness,' pp. 3–10.
3. "Placed in the center of an immense continent, which offers a boundless field for human industry, the Union is almost as much insulated from the world as if all its frontiers were girt by the ocean." Alexis de Tocqueville, *Democracy in America*, Vol. I, Henry Reeve text (New York: Vintage Books, 1990), p. 172. See pp. 170–72 for the full discussion.
4. Hegel, *The Philosophy of History*, pp. 85–86.
5. Samuel Huntington discusses the Tudor origins of the American political system in *Political Order in Changing Societies* (New Haven: Yale University Press, 1968), pp. 93–133.
6. Montesquieu, *The Spirit of the Laws*, pp. 131–32. Hamilton cited Montesquieu's argument approvingly in *The Federalist Papers*, No. 9.
7. Preoccupied by the war with France and financially strained, England failed to provide adequately for colonial defense, thus making its royal governors in America financially dependent on the local assemblies for defense and even for their own support. As one writer says, this was "the stirrup by which the colonial assemblies mounted to the saddle." Douglas Edward Leach, *Arms for Empire: A Military History of the British Colonies in North America, 1607–1763* (New York: Macmillan Publishing Company, 1973), p. 508.

8. Geoffrey Perret, *A Country Made by War: From the Revolution to Vietnam: the Story of America's Rise to Power* (New York: Random House, 1989), p. 562.

9. Gordon S. Wood, *The Creation of the American Republic 1776–1787*. In a more recent work, *The Radicalism of the American Revolution: How a Revolution Transformed a Monarchical Society into a Democratic One Unlike Any that Had Ever Existed* (New York: Alfred A. Knopf, 1992), Wood takes a similar approach, but does briefly acknowledge that the Revolutionary War "had a profound effect on America's society and economy . . . it touched the whole of American society to a degree no previous event in American history ever had" (pp. 247–48).

10. Bernard Bailyn, *The Ideological Origins of the American Revolution* (Cambridge: The Belknap Press of Harvard University Press, 1967).

11. Robert Middlekauf, *The Glorious Cause: The American Revolution 1763–1789* (New York: Oxford University Press, 1982), p. 314.

12. Howard H. Peckham, *The Toll of Independence: Engagements and Battle Casualties of the American Revolution* (Chicago: University of Chicago Press, 1974), p. 132–33. Peckham's figures enable comparison with the losses registered in other American wars, most accountings of which also normally include noncombat casualties. As a percentage of the total U.S. population, Peckham estimates the losses in other major wars as follows: Mexican War, .06 percent; Civil War, 1.6 percent; World War I, .12 percent; and World War II, .28 percent. As a percentage of the number of soldiers who served, the Revolutionary War toll was 12.5 percent, only slightly behind that of the Civil War (13 percent).

13. Rosemary H. T. O'Kane, *The Revolutionary Reign of Terror: The Role of Violence in Political Change* (Aldershot: Edward Elgar, 1991), pp. 122–23 reviews several estimates of the émigré outflow.

14. See Chapter 2, "The Military Origins of the Revolution," of Don Higginbotham, *The War of American Independence: Military Attitudes, Policies, and Practice 1763–1789* (New York: Macmillan Publishing Company, 1971), pp. 29–56.

15. John C. Fitzpatrick, ed., *The Writings of George Washington from the Original Manuscript Sources 1745–1799*, Volume 6, September 1776–January 1777 (Washington, DC: U.S. Government Printing Office, 1933) p. 397.

16. From Washington's personal correspondence, in *The Writing of George Washington*, Volume 6, pp. 39, 110, 402. For other examples of his disdain for the militia, see pp. 5–6, 96, 111–12, or the more than two dozen citations in the index, p. 539.

17. On Charles Lee's political and military thinking, see John Shy, "American Strategy: Charles Lee and the Radical Alternative," Ch. 6 of Shy, *A People Numerous and Armed: Reflections on the Military Struggle for American Independence* (Ann Arbor: The University of Michigan Press, 1990), pp. 133–62.

18. Edmund S. Morgan, *Inventing the People: The Rise of Popular Sovereignty in England and America* (New York: W. W. Norton, 1988), pp. 153–73, discusses the myth of the yeoman militia among the landowning aristocracy of America and Britain; see also Lawrence Delbert Cress, *Citizens in Arms: The Army and the Militia in American Society to the War of 1812* (Chapel Hill: University of North Carolina Press, 1982), pp. 15–50.

19. Charles Royster, *A Revolutionary People at War: The Continental Army and American Character, 1775–1783* (Chapel Hill: University of North Carolina Press, 1979), pp. 48–51 and 62–69.

20. On this point, see Christopher Ward, *The War of the Revolution*, Vol. 2 (New

York: Macmillan, 1952), pp. 934–36. Charles Royster, in "Founding a Nation in Blood: Military Conflict and American Nationality," in Ronald Hoffman and Peter J. Albert, *Arms and Independence: The Military Character of the American Revolution* (Charlottesville, VA: University Press of Virginia, 1984), pp. 25–49, discusses the impact of the war on the shaping of American identity both during the conflict and in its aftermath.

21. Merrill Jensen, *The New Nation: A History of the United States During the Confederation 1781–1789* (Boston: Northeastern University Press, 1981), pp. 54–63; Charles Royster, *A Revolutionary People at War*, pp. 295–311.

22. Peckham, *The Toll of Independence*, p. 132–33. This ratio should not be confused with the number mobilized at any given time; that would have been somewhat lower.

23. Chilton Williamson, *American Suffrage: From Property to Democracy 1760–1860* (Princeton: Princeton University Press, 1960), p. 80. For specific examples of the impact of the War of Independence on the extension of the suffrage in various states, see pp. 79–80, 87–89, 92–112.

24. "The relations of social classes to each other, the institution of slavery, the system of land-holding, the course of business, the forms and spirit of the intellectual and religious life, all felt the transforming hand of the revolution." J. Franklin Jameson, *The American Revolution Considered as a Social Movement* (Princeton: Princeton University Press, 1926), p. 11. On socialization and social-levelling, see pp. 1–29; on the extension of the franchise, pp. 26–29 and 61–62; on the antislavery movement, pp. 30–39. See also Royster, *A Revolutionary People at War*, pp. 241–54.

25. The linkage between nationalist leaders and the Newburgh officers is discussed at length in Richard Kohn, *Eagle and Sword: The Federalists and the Creation of the Military Establishment in America, 1783–1802* (New York: The Free Press, 1975), pp. 17–39. Kohn emphasizes that the failure of the Newburgh conspiracy was a critical step in the development of a professionalized military and a proper civil–military relationship in the United States.

26. The critical period from the Treaty of Paris to the convening of the Constitutional Convention is treated at length in Forrest McDonald, *E Pluribus Unum: The Formation of the American Republic 1776–1790* (Cambridge, MA: The Riverside Press, 1965) and in Merrill Jensen, *The New Nation: A History of the United States During the Confederation 1781–1789*.

27. Merrill Jensen, *The New Nation*, p. 389. Jensen discusses at length the importance of wartime finance and debt in the formation of the American republic; see pp. 72–73, 302–26, 359, and 375–98. See also Richard B. Morris, *The Forging of the Union 1781–1789* (New York: Harper & Row, 1987), Ch. 2.

28. War debts contributed to the nationalist cause in other ways also. States that assumed the debts typically funded their obligation by the sale of land and the issuance of paper securities; the latter were prone to rapid inflation. The formation of a strong central government promised to solidify the value of paper securities, while enabling new landowners to obtain more secure titles. Forrest McDonald, *E Pluribus Unum*, pp. 205–207.

29. Edmund Randolph's address to constitutional convention, May 29, 1787, as recorded by James Madison, reproduced in *Formation of the Union of the American States*, 69th Congress, 1st Session, House Document No. 398 (Washington, DC: U.S. Government Printing Office, 1927), pp. 114–115.

30. Hamilton also argues the case for national taxation primarily on national security grounds in Numbers 30 through 36 of *The Federalist Papers.*
31. Richard H. Kohn, *Eagle and Sword,* p. 290. Kohn discusses the significance of the Northwest Indian battles and the Whiskey Rebellion in Chapter 8, "Two Uses of Force," pp. 139–173. On the development and rationalization of the U.S. military establishment, see Chapter 9, "Creating the Peace Establishment [1794–1798]," pp. 174–192.
32. Leonard D. White, *The Federalists: A Study in Administration* (New York: Macmillan Company, 1956), p. 147.
33. An excellent analysis of the military policies of the Federalists and their implications for American government is in Kohn, *Eagle and Sword,* pp. 193–273. See also Lawrence Delbert Cress, *Citizens in Arms: The Army and the Militia in American Society to the War of 1812,* pp. 111–49, and J. C. A. Stagg, *Mr. Madison's War: Politics, Diplomacy and Warfare in the Early American Republic 1783–1830* (Princeton: Princeton University Press, 1983), pp. 120–76.
34. Chilton Williamson, *American Suffrage: From Property to Democracy 1760–1860* (Princeton: Princeton University Press, 1960), p. 188; see also pp. 182–207, *passim.*
35. Chilton Williamson, *American Suffrage,* pp. 226–27; the earlier quotation in this paragraph is from p. 188.
36. "It is a myth that most obstacles to the suffrage were removed only after the emergence of Andrew Jackson. Well before Jackson's election most states had lifted most restrictions on the suffrage of white male citizens or taxpayers." Edward Pessen, *Jacksonian America: Society, Personality, and Politics,* rev. ed. (Chicago: University of Illinois Press, 1985), p. 149. Pessen also dispels the earlier notion, popularized by Frederick Jackson Turner, that the Western states had led the way in suffrage reform; in fact, the movement originated largely in the East. See pp. 150–52.
37. Samuel P. Huntington, *The Soldier and the State: The Theory and Politics of Civil-Military Relations* (Cambridge, MA: The Belknap Press of Harvard University Press, 1957), pp. 203–208.
38. Calculated from the Table, "Series Y 308–317. Paid Civilian Employment of the Federal Government: 1816 to 1970," in U.S. Bureau of the Census, *Historical Statistics of the United States, Colonial Times to 1970,* Bicentennial Edition, Part 2 (Washington, DC: U.S. Government Printing Office, 1975), p. 1103. On the U.S. administrative bureaucracy in this early period, see James Q. Wilson, "The Rise of the Bureaucratic State," in Nathan Glazer and Irving Kristol, eds., *The American Commonwealth* (New York: Basic Books, 1976), pp. 81–82.
39. Chaplain W. Morrison, *Democratic Politics and Sectionalism: The Wilmot Proviso Controversy* (Chapel Hill: University of North Carolina Press, 1967); James McPherson, *Battle Cry of Freedom,* Ch. 2.
40. Carl Sandburg, *Abraham Lincoln: The War Years,* Vol. I (New York: Harcourt, Brace, & Co., 1939), p. 34.
41. Figures are from Bureau of the Census, *Historical Statistics of the United States,* p. 1103. Total Federal employment outside Washington, D.C., in 1861 was 35,473; of this the vast majority was in the Post Office department. We can assume that many of those in the South (perhaps a fourth of the total) remained and joined the Confederate side.
42. The army grew by a factor of 62 during the Civil War and the national budget by a factor of 20. The percentage of the national population that served in uni-

form during World War II was higher than in the Civil War, but the proportionate growth in both manpower (a multiple of 26) and national budget (a multiple of 11) was less. The figures cited in this paragraph are for the U.S. Army only. The Navy also added some 50,000 sailors during the Civil War, a sixfold expansion in manpower attended by a massive increase in firepower; by 1865 the Navy had 671 warships, including 236 steam-powered craft built during the war. *Naval* expansion in World War II was proportionately much larger than in the Civil War: an increase of 21 times in manpower from 1940 to 1945.

43. On the "strong state" characteristics of the Confederacy, see Richard Franklin Bensel, *Yankee Leviathan: The Origins of Central State Authority in America, 1859–1877* (Cambridge: Cambridge University Press, 1990), pp. 94–237, *passim*.

44. On the modern features of the Civil War, see Edward Hagerman, *The American Civil War and the Origins of Modern Warfare: Ideas, Organization, and Field Command* (Bloomington: Indiana University Press, 1988).

45. James Huston, *The Sinews of War: Army Logistics 1775–1953* (Washington, DC: U.S. Government Printing Office, 1966), pp. 176–85.

46. Richard Bensel, *Yankee Leviathan*, p. 169.

47. The highest pre-Civil War figure was 29.7 percent in 1814, during the War of 1812. From 1847 to the Civil War, the federal government took in virtually no internal revenues. Figures on U.S. revenue receipts are calculated from "Series Y. 352–57. Federal Government Receipts . . ." *Historical Statistics of the United States*, Part 2, p. 1106. On the significance of this shift, see Harry N. Scheiber, "Economic Change in the Civil War Era: An Analysis of Recent Studies," *Civil War History* 11 (December 1965):396–411 and McPherson, *The Battle Cry of Freedom*, pp. 447–48.

48. McPherson, *The Battle Cry of Freedom*, p. 447.

49. Eric Foner, *Reconstruction: America's Unfinished Revolution 1863–1877* (New York: Harper & Row, 1988), p. 23; see also p. 22. Information on the fiscal measures is largely from Louis M. Hacker, *The Triumph of American Capitalism: The Development of Forces in American History to the End of the Nineteenth Century* (New York: Simon & Schuster, 1940), pp. 361–63 and 365–68, and from James McPherson, *Ordeal by Fire: The Civil War and Reconstruction*, pp. 202–205. On the historical debate over the impact of the measures on industrialization, see Scheiber, "Economic Change in the Civil War Era," in Note 47 above.

50. Mark A. Neely, Jr., *The Fate of Liberty: Abraham Lincoln and Civil Liberties* (Oxford: Oxford University Press, 1991), p. 53. Neely's book is the latest of several excellent studies on civil rights violations during the Civil War. The classic work is James G. Randall, *Constitutional Problems under Lincoln* (New York: D. Appleton, 1926).

51. John Whiteclay Chambers II, *To Raise an Army: The Draft Comes to Modern America* (New York: The Free Press, 1987), pp. 41–65; James M. McPherson, *The Battle Cry of Freedom*, pp. 600–611. The unpleasant memories associated with resistance to the draft during the Civil War were one reason why the United States did not resort to the draft again until World War I.

52. Memorial Day address, May 31, 1915, in Arthur S. Link, ed., *The Papers of Woodrow Wilson* 33, April 17–July 21, 1915 (Princeton: Princeton University Press, 1980), p. 288.

53. Hondon B. Hargrove, *Black Union Soldiers in the Civil War* (Jefferson, NC: McFarland & Co., 1988), p. 211.

54. On the impact of the Civil War on the labor and women's movements, see Foner, *Reconstruction*, pp. 30, 255–56, 446–49, and 472–73.

55. Eric Foner, *Reconstruction*, p. 469; see also pp. 469–70. On the war's impact on voluntarism and public spirit, see Morton Keller, *Affairs of State: Public Life in Late Nineteenth-Century America* (Cambridge, MA: Harvard University Press, 1977), p. 7–13. Keller also observes that the impetus that the war gave to local political activism began to ebb in the 1870s; see pp. 110–21.

56. Allan Nevins, "A Major Result of the Civil War," *Civil War History* V (September 1959): 237–50.

57. The Civil War pension system and its implications for the rise of social welfare provisions at the national level in the United States are discussed at length in a recent important study: Theda Skocpol, *Protecting Soldiers and Mothers: The Political Origins of Social Policy in the United States* (Cambridge, MA: Belknap Press of Harvard University Press, 1992). See in particular pp. 102–51. See also Ann Shola Orloff, "The Political Origins of America's Belated Welfare State," in Margaret Weir, Ann Shola Orloff, and Theda Skocpol, eds., *The Politics of Social Policy in the United States* (Princeton: Princeton University Press, 1988), pp. 38–52.

58. M. Slade Kendrick, *A Century and a Half of Federal Expenditures* (New York: National Bureau of Economic Research, 1955), p. 10.

59. Kendrick, *A Century and a Half of Federal Expenditures*, pp. 40–44.

60. Nor can it be seen simply as a by-product of industrialization, for considerable industrialization had taken place prior to the war, and at an even more rapid rate than after 1865, without corresponding effects on state spending. See Douglass North, *Economic Growth of the United States 1790–1860* (Englewood Cliffs, NJ: Prentice-Hall, 1960). See also Scheiber, "Economic Change in the Civil War Era."

61. Figures on troop strength are from James E. Sefton, *The United States Army and Reconstruction 1865–1877* (Westport, CT: Greenwood Press, 1980), pp. 260–262. Richard Bensel, *Yankee Leviathan*, p. 380, offers even lower figures, but these appear to be in error. Information on the size of the Freedmen's Bureau is from Foner, *Reconstruction*, p. 143.

62. On this point, see Foner, *Reconstruction*, pp. 438, 439–40 and 454–59. Only in recent decades have historians come to appreciate the degree of violent Southern resistance to Reconstruction. See Michael Perman, *Reunion without Compromise: The South and Reconstruction: 1865–1868* (Cambridge: Cambridge University Press, 1973); George C. Rable, *But There Was No Peace: The Role of Violence in the Politics of Reconstruction* (Athens, GA: University of Georgia Press, 1984); Michael Perman, "Counter Reconstruction: The Role of Violence in Southern Redemption," in Eric Anderson and Alfred A. Moss, Jr., eds., *The Facts of Reconstruction: Essays in Honor of John Hope Franklin* (Baton Rouge: Louisiana State University Press, 1991), pp. 121–28.

63. Richard Franklin Bensel, *Yankee Leviathan*, pp. 378–95. See also Phillip S. Paludan, *A Covenant with Death: The Constitution, Law, and Equality in the Civil War Era* (Urbana: University of Illinois Press, 1975), pp. 274–82; and Eric Foner, *Reconstruction*, pp. 425–59.

64. Stephan Skowronek, *Building a New American State*, pp. 16 and 37–162.

65. Jerry M. Cooper, *The Army and Civil Disorder: Federal Military Intervention in Labor Disputes, 1877–1900* (Westport, CT: Greenwood Press, 1980). A survey of federal military intervention in domestic disturbances was prepared for the U.S.

Senate in 1903 and contains much valuable information on this and earlier periods; see U.S. Senate, 57th Congress, 2nd Session, *Federal Aid in Domestic Disturbances 1787–1903* (Washington, DC: U.S. Government Printing Office, 1903).

66. Kendrick, *A Century and a Half of Federal Expenditures*, p. 46.

67. Sidney Ratner, *American Taxation: Its History as a Social Force in Democracy* (New York: W. W. Norton, 1942), p. 370. Figures on wartime governmental expenditure are taken from "Series Y. 457–465. Outlays of the Federal Government: 1789 to 1970," in *Historical Statistics*, Part 2, p. 1114.

68. On the impact of the war on the Federal Reserve, see Charles Gilbert, *American Financing of World War I* (Westport, CT: Greenwood Press, 1970), pp. 177–89 and p. 218.

69. Ratner, *American Taxation*, pp. 375–76; *Historical Statistics of the United States*, Part 2, p. 1110.

70. On the significance of the taxation revolution of World War I, see David M. Kennedy, *Over Here: The First World War and American Society* (New York: Oxford University Press, 1980), pp. 106–12. Statistics in this paragraph are calculated from Series Y. 358–373. Internal Revenue Collection: 1863 to 1970," in *Historical Statistics*, Part 2, p. 1107. The figures for the 1920s count only 1925–29, because statistics are not available for the earlier years. If anything, the figures would have been higher in the early 1920s, before the Internal Revenue Act of 1921 lowered wartime tax rates.

71. U.S. Civil Service Commission, *Thirty-seventh Annual Report*, p. vi.

72. Perhaps to compensate for granting such immense authority to the President, the Act included several provisions that showed continuing hostility to the regular Army: the incorporation over Army objections of the National Guard as an official reserve component of the Army; the formation of the Reserve Officer Training Corps (ROTC); and a provision mandating that no more than half of the Army General Staff could serve in Washington at any one time! See Perret, *A Country Made by War*, p. 311, and Huston, *The Sinews of War*, p. 314.

73. Robert Higgs, *Crisis and Leviathan: Critical Episodes in the Growth of the American Government* (New York: Oxford University Press, 1987), p. 136. Information on World War I legislation is taken from William Franklin Willoughby, *Government Organization in War Time and After: A Survey of the Federal Civil Agencies Created for the Prosecution of the War* (New York: D. Appleton, 1919), pp. 5–9, 92–95, 263–67; and from Higgs, *Crisis and Leviathan*, pp. 128–30.

74. Kennedy, in *Over Here*, p. 126, describes it as "a foundation on which future Presidents were to erect a more potent Executive establishment."

75. On Baruch's stewardship of the WIB, see James Grant, *Bernard Baruch: The Adventures of a Wall Street Legend* (New York: Simon & Schuster, 1983), pp. 156–79; Jordan A. Schwarz, *The Speculator: Bernard M. Baruch in Washington, 1917–1965* (Chapel Hill: University of North Carolina Press, 1981), pp. 50–108; and Robert D. Cuff, "Bernard Baruch: Symbol and Myth in Industrial Mobilization," in Edwin J. Perkins, *Men and Organization: The American Economy in the Twentieth Century* (New York: G. P. Putnam's Sons, 1977). For a survey of the agencies, bureaus, boards, and other governmental units created during World War I see William Franklin Willoughby, *Government Organization in War Time and After: A Survey of the Federal Civil Agencies Created for the Prosecution of the War* (New York: D. Appleton, 1919).

76. See Robert D. Cuff, *The War Industries Board: Business-Government Relations*

during World War I (Baltimore: Johns Hopkins University Press, 1973), pp. 241–64, for information on the postwar dissolution and legacy of the Board, and pp. 265–76 for a discussion of the overall impact of the Board on business-government relations in the United States. See also Gerald D. Nash, "Experiments in Industrial Mobilization: WIB and NRA," *Mid-America* 45 (July 1963):157–74, and Kennedy, *Over Here*, pp. 140–43.

77. John L. Heaton, *Cobb of THE WORLD* (New York: E. P. Dutton & Co., Inc., 1924), p. 270. This account was first written after the war, and there is controversy about whether or not Wilson in fact spoke these words. See Jerold S. Auerbach, "Woodrow Wilson's 'Prediction' to Frank Cobb: Words Historians Should Doubt Ever Got Spoken," *Journal of American History* 54 (December 1967):608–17; and a response, Harry N. Scheiber, "What Wilson Said to Cobb in 1917: Another View of Plausibility," *Wisconsin Magazine of History* 52 (Summer 1969):344–47.

78. The judge ruled that the film, produced *before* the war, could cause Americans "to question the good faith of our ally, Great Britain." Peterson and Fite, *Opponents of War*, pp. 16–17, 92–93, 146, 214–17; Kennedy, *Over Here*, pp. 75–88.

79. Geoffrey Perret, *Days of Sadness, Years of Triumph: the American People, 1939–1945* (Baltimore: Penguin Books, 1974), p. 357. General surveys of government repression in World War I include H. C. Peterson and Gilbert C. Fite, *Opponents of War 1917–1918* (Seattle: University of Washington Press, 1957); Donald Johnson, *The Challenge to American Freedoms: World War I and the Rise of the American Civil Liberties Union* (Lexington: University Press of Kentucky, 1963); Michael Linfield, *Freedom under Fire: U.S. Civil Liberties in Times of War* (Boston: South End Press, 1990), pp. 33–68.

80. It is noteworthy that Walter Lippmann's service in the army and War Department helped shape his views on the utility of propaganda and contributed to his classic work, *Public Opinion* (New York: Harcourt, Brace, 1922), which inaugurated the modern study of public opinion. Lippmann later commented that he wrote the book "as the result of my experience in psychological warfare and in seeing the war." Kennedy, *Over Here*, p. 91. The information in this paragraph is from Stephen Vaughn, *Holding Fast the Inner Line: Democracy, Nationalism, and the Committee on Public Information* (Chapel Hill: University of North Carolina Press, 1980); James Robert Mock and Cedric Larson, *Words that Won the War: the Story of the Committee on Public Information* (Princeton: Princeton University Press, 1939); David M. Kennedy, *Over Here*, pp. 59–63. Two firsthand accounts of the propaganda activities of the Committee on Public information are George Creel, *How We Advertised America: The First Telling of the Amazing Story of the Committee on Public Information that Carried the Gospel of Americanism to Every Corner of the Globe* (New York: Harper, 1920), and Alfred E. Cornebise, *War as Advertised: The Four Minute Men and America's Crusade 1917–1918* (Philadelphia: The American Philosophical Society, 1984). On the role of the Post Office, see Kennedy, *Over Here*, pp. 75–78, and Peterson and Fite, *Opponents of War*, pp. 95–99.

81. Kennedy, *Over Here*, p. 82; see also pp. 81–82. Peterson and Fite, *Opponents of War*, pp. 18–19.

82. Maurine Weiner Greenwald, *Women, War, and Work: The Impact of World War I on Women Workers in the United States* (Westport, CT: Greenwood Press, 1980), pp. 13–21.

83. Alison Bernstein, *American Indians and World War II: Toward a New Era in Indian Affairs* (Norman, OK: University of Oklahoma Press), p. 22; on black soldiers in the war and the legacy of their service, see Arthur E. Barbeau and Florette Henri, *The Unknown Soldier: Black American Troops in World War I* (Philadelphia: Temple University Press, 1974); on racial unrest after the war, see Warren Schaich, "A Relationship Between Collective Racial Violence and War," *Journal of Black Studies* 5 (June 1975).

84. As early as 1914, Wilson had lamented that American entry into the war would mean that "every reform we have won will be lost." Cited in David Kennedy, *Over Here*, p. 11.

85. Charles Hirschfeld, "Nationalist Progressivism and World War I," *Mid-America* 45 (July 1963):151. See the entire article, especially p. 141. A detailed study of the Progressive movement during World War I is John A. Thompson, *Reformers and War: American Progressive Publicists and the First World War* (Cambridge: Cambridge University Press, 1987). Theda Skocpol, *Protecting Soldiers and Mothers,* pp. 480–524, discusses the legislative history of the Sheppard-Towner Act in great detail, but does not note the possible linkages with the war (a puzzling omission, given her emphasis on the protection of soldiers after the Civil War as being critical to the rise of the welfare state in America). Skocpol also does not mention the work of Richard Titmuss, discussed in Chapter 5 of this book, though her work is a marvelous confirmation of his thesis that welfare reform originates with social concern over soldiers, soldiers' dependents, and their children. The impetus given to the Sheppard-Towner Bill by the war is noted in Walter I. Trattner, *From Poor Law to Welfare State: A History of Social Welfare in America,* rev. ed. (New York: The Free Press, 1984), p. 206, fn.

86. Walter Lippmann, "Mr. Wells at the War," *The New Republic,* March 17, 1917, p. 202.

87. "The Uses of an Armistice," unsigned editorial, *The New Republic,* November 16, 1918, pp. 60–61.

88. On the effort to preserve the war agencies, see Ellis W. Hawley, *The Great War and the Search for a Modern Order: A History of the American People and Their Institutions, 1917–1933* (New York: St. Martin's Press, 1979), pp. 45–48.

89. Hawley, *The Great War and the Search for Modern Order,* pp. 100–104, 199–206.

90. All quotations from Roosevelt are taken from Gerald D. Nash, "Experiments in Industrial Mobilization: WIB and NRA," *Mid-America* 45 (July 1963):158–74.

91. John A. Garraty, "'The New Deal, National Socialism, and the Great Depression," *The American Historical Review* 78 (October 1973):911; for further on the military features of the New Deal, see also pp. 925–26. More on the army and the CCC is in Arthur M. Schlesinger, Jr., *The Coming of the New Deal* (Boston: Houghton Mifflin Company, 1959), pp. 336–41; Charles W. Johnson, "The Army and the Civilian Conservation Corps, 1933–1942," *Prologue* 4 (1972):139–56.

92. *Hearings Before Subcommittees of the Committee on Appropriations, House of Representatives,* Vol. 25, 77th Congress, 2nd session (Washington, D.C.: U.S. Government Printing Office, 1942), p. 165.

93. Ibid. p. 370.

94. *Interior Department Appropriations Bill, 1944, Hearings Before Subcommittees of the Committee on Appropriations, House of Representatives,* 78th Congress, 1st session (Washington, D.C.: U.S. Government Printing Office, 1942), pp. 326–27.

95. The radical metamorphosis of the Civil Service Commission during the war is described at length in Gladys Krammerer, *The Impact of War on Federal Personnel Administration* (Lexington: University Press of Kentucky, 1951).

96. David Brinkley, *Washington Goes to War* (New York: Alfred A. Knopf, 1988), p. 111. Figures on Pentagon and buildings are on pp. 72–73 and p. 119.

97. This was the conclusion of the Joint Congressional Committee on the Reduction of Nonessential Federal Expenditures, which studied the phenomenon in depth. *Congressional Record—Senate*, April 30, 1946, p. 4210.

98. Robert Higgs, in *Crisis and Leviathan*, Appendix, pp. 272–73, provides a listing; see also pp. 196–236.

99. *New Republic*, May 31, 1943, cited in Richard Polenberg, ed., *America at War: The Home Front, 1941–1945* (Englewood Cliffs, NJ: Prentice-Hall, Inc. 1968), p. 80; see pp. 80–84 for more details.

100. Robert Higgs, *Crisis and Leviathan*, p. 204.

101. Bureau of the Census, *Historical Statistics of the United States*, pp. 1114 and 1117.

102. Tax return data taken from successive volumes of *Annual Report of the Commissioner of Internal Revenue* (Washington, DC: U.S. Government Printing Office, 1941–45) and from *Historical Statistics of the United States*, p. 1107. See David Brinkley, *Washington Goes to War*, pp. 217–19, on the origins of income-tax withholding.

103. Perret, *Days of Sadness*, p. 358. On civil rights violations during World War II and their constitutional and judicial implications, see Paul L. Murphy, *The Constitution in Crisis Times 1918–1969* (New York: Harper & Row, 1972), pp. 213–47, and Edward S. Corwin, *Total War and the Constitution* (New York: Alfred A. Knopf, 1947).

104. Information provided by Historical Division, Federal Bureau of Investigation, Washington, DC.

105. Arthur A. Stein, *The Nation at War* (Baltimore: Johns Hopkins University Press, 1980), pp. 38–53.

106. Richard Polenberg, *America at War*, p. 124.

107. Brinkley, *Washington Goes to War*, pp. 82–83, 246.

108. Richard Polenberg, *America at War*, p. 132.

109. Merlo Pusey, "Revolution at Home," *The South Atlantic Quarterly* 42 (July 1943):218.

110. Alison R. Bernstein, *American Indians and World War II*, p. xi.

111. Ibid., p. 40.

112. Perret, *Days of Sorrow*, p. 323.

113. The figure on defense expenditures is in actual dollars. Adjusted for inflation, it would be much higher.

114. William H. G. Riker, *The Development of American Federalism* (Boston: Kluwer Academic Publishers, 1987), p. 104.

115. Harold Lasswell, *National Security and Individual Freedom* (New York: McGraw-Hill, 1950), pp. 23–49.

116. David Cauto, *The Great Fear* (New York: Simon & Schuster, 1978), pp. 112 and 268–75. On security procedures in the federal work force, see Jeff Broadwater, *Eisenhower and the Anti-Communist Crusade* (Chapel Hill: University of North Carolina Press, 1992), pp. 85–96. Other studies of the federal government's repressive activities during the Cold War include Natalie Robins, *Alien Ink: The FBI's War on Freedom of Expression* (New York: William Morrow and Company, 1992);

Jerry J. Berman and Morton H. Halperin, eds., *The Abuses of the Intelligence Agencies* (Washington, DC: The Center for National Security Studies, 1975). A survey of civil liberties abuses that have occurred during war throughout American history is Michael Linfield, *Freedom Under Fire: U.S. Civil Liberties in Times of War* (Boston: South End Press, 1990); on the Cold War era, see Chs. 5, 6, and 7.

117. Aaron L. Friedberg, "Why Didn't the United States Become a Garrison State?" *International Security* 16 (Spring 1992):109–42.

118. *Statistical Abstract of the United States*, 1991–92, chart No. 537.

119. Welfare expenditures also reached nearly 50 percent of federal spending during the New Deal, but they were then less than 5 percent of GNP, whereas by 1980 they had reached 11.3 percent of GNP.

120. Edwin Amenta and Theda Skocpol offer another explanation—that the United States, unlike the U.K., did not have in place a national social insurance program funded by general tax revenues prior to either war; this made it difficult for reform-minded politicians to capture quickly the enhanced revenue base and bureaucratic structure engendered by the wars. See their article, "Redefining the New Deal: World War II and the Development of Social Provisions in the United States," in Margaret Weir, et al., eds., *The Politics of Social Policy in the United States*, pp. 81–122.

121. The explosion of new welfare programs under Johnson cannot be attributed solely to public pressure for their expansion; opinion polls show that public support for increased welfare spending peaked in 1961 and declined steadily thereafter in virtually all social classes; see Morris Janowitz, *The Last Half Century: Societal Change and Politics in America* (Chicago: University of Chicago Press, 1978), pp. 160–61. On the domestic political effects of the war, see Joseph A. Califano, Jr., *The Triumph and Tragedy of Lyndon Johnson: The White House Years* ((New York: Simon & Schuster, 1991); Chs. 2, 6 8, 10, 11, and 16; Stanley Karnow, *Vietnam: A History* (New York: The Viking Press, 1983), Chs. 13 and 14; David Halberstam, *The Best and the Brightest* (New York: Random House, 1972); John J. Broesamle, *Reform and Reaction in Twentieth Century American Politics* (New York: Greenwood Press, 1990), pp. 262–63.

122. Doris Kearns, *Lyndon Johnson and the American Dream* (New York: Harper and Row, 1976), pp. 299–300.

123. Statistics are from *Defense 92: Almanac* (U.S. Department of Defense: September/October 1992), p. 30.

124. Chester J. Pach, Jr., and Elmo Richardson, *The Presidency of Dwight D. Eisenhower*, rev. ed. (Lawrence: University Press of Kansas, 1991), pp. 123–24; Stephen E. Ambrose, *Eisenhower*, Vol. 2: *The President* (New York: Simon & Schuster, 1984), pp. 250–51.

125. Tucker and Hendrickson, "Thomas Jefferson and American Foreign Policy," *Foreign Affairs* 69 (Spring 1990):135.

126. Ibid., pp. 135–36.

127. *Statistical Abstract of the United States: 1992* (Washington, DC: U.S. Government Printing Office, 1992).

Epilogue: The Paradox of the State

1. G. K. Chesterton, *The Napoleon of Notting Hill* (New York: Dover Publications, 1991). It is possible that Chesterton's choice of the year 1984 may have influenced Orwell's timing of his own futuristic world.

2. Otto Hintze, "Weltgeschichtliche Bedingungen der Repräsentativverfassung," in Gerhard Oestreich, ed., *Staat und Verfassung: Gesammelte Abhandlungen zur allgemeinen Verfassungsgeschichte*, 2nd ed. (Göttingen, 1962); Barrington Moore, Jr., *Social Origins of Dictatorship and Democracy: Lord and Peasant in the Making of the Modern World* (Boston: Beacon Press, 1967); Brian M. Downing, *The Military Revolution and Political Change: Origins of Democracy and Autocracy in Early Modern Europe* (Princeton: Princeton University Press, 1992); Robert D. Putnam, *Making Democracy Work: Civil Traditions in Modern Italy* (Princeton: Princeton University Press, 1993).

3. A fascinating account of its spread is Samuel P. Huntington, *The Third Wave: Democratization in the Late Twentieth Century* (Norman, OK: University of Oklahoma Press, 1991).

4. Michael Doyle, "Liberalism and World Politics," *The American Political Science Review* 80 (December 1986):1151–69. Other scholars have also elaborated on this thesis; see, for example, Steve Chan, "Mirror, Mirror on the Wall . . . Are Freer Countries More Pacific?" *Journal of Conflict Resolution* 27 (December 1984):617–48; David A. Lake, "Powerful Pacifists: Democratic States and War," *American Political Science Review* 86 (March 1992):24–37; Melvin Small and J. David Singer, "The War-Proneness of Democratic Regimes, 1816–1965," *Jerusalem Journal of International Relations* 2 (1976):50–69.

5. See Raymond Vernon, *Sovereignty at Bay: the Multi-National Spread of U.S. Enterprises* (New York: Basic Books, 1971); Walter B. Wriston, *The Twilight of Sovereignty: How the Information Revolution is Transforming Our World* (New York: Charles Scribner's Sons, 1991). On the implications of growing and complex interdependence, see Robert O. Keohane and Joseph S. Nye, *Power and Interdependence: World Politics in Transition*, 2nd ed. (Boston: Little, Brown and Company, 1989).

6. Martin van Creveld, *The Transformation of War* (New York: The Free Press, 1991), pp. 192–227.

7. See, for example, John E. Mueller, *Retreat from Doomsday: The Obsolescence of Major War* (New York: Basic Books, 1989).

8. Nikolai Ogarkov, *Vsegda v gotovnosti k zashchite Otechestva* (Always ready for defense of the Fatherland) (Moscow: USSR Ministry of Defense, 1982).

9. Max Weber, cited in Youssef Cohen, Brian R. Brown, and A. F. K. Organski, "The Paradoxical Nature of State-Making: The Violent Creation of Order," *American Political Science Review* 75 (December 1981):901.

10. Erich Maria Remarque, *All Quiet on the Western Front*, trans. by A. W. Wheen (Boston: Little, Brown, 1975), pp. 117–18.

Index

Catalonia, 38, 84, 87, 88
Cateau-Cambresis, Treaty of (1559), 41, 63, 73, 85
Catherine II, Empress of Russia (the Great), 121
Caucasus, 224
Cavalry, 32
Cavour, Camillo Benso di, 122, 142, 143, 145
Censorship, 273
Centralizing effect of war, 12–13, 74, 88, 98, 102, 213
Cerdagne, 84
Charles I, King of England, 79–82, 123, 125
Charles II, King of England, 83
Charles V, King of France, 34
Charles V, King of Spain, 40–41, 44–46, 57, 69, 85, 86, 94
Charles VII, King of France, 30–32, 34
Charles VIII, King of France, 39, 298
Charles XI, King of Sweden, 92, 93
Charles XII, King of Sweden, 93
Charles the Bold, 29, 31
Chase, Samuel, 252
Cheka, 203, 206
Chesterton, G. K., 297
Chickering, Roger, 209
Chinese Cultural Revolution, 228
Chivalric warfare, 32
Christian IV, King of Denmark, 70
Churchill, Winston, 160, 170, 173, 178, 184
Civilian Conservation Corps, 277
Civilian population, restraints on violence against, 108, 109, 120
Civil rights movement, 285
Civil society, 213
  degnerative impact of war on Russian, 219–222
  failure of in Weimar Germany, 214–219
Civil wars, 2–3
  American, 153, 170, 245, 247, 257–264, 266, 291, 294
  effect on state formation, 13, 28, 74, 82, 258
  English, 29–31, 38, 39, 64, 79–83
  French, 29–31, 73–74, 77

linkage with international wars, 16, 38, 68, 201
  Russian, 203, 206, 210, 223–226, 237
  totalitarian states and, 202–204
Clemenceau, Georges, 164
Clémentel, Étienne, 165, 167, 174
Clinton, Bill, 295, 300
Cloots, Anacharsis, 137
Coalitional path of state formation, 50–57, 59, 94–98, 246
Cobb, Richard, 132
Code Napoléon, 135–136, 141, 146
Colbert, Jean-Baptiste, 109
Cold War, 1, 188, 240, 245, 247, 286–290, 294
Collectivist state, 8, 196, 229, 275, 276
  rise of, 149–193
Collectivization campaign (1929–34), 203, 226–228
Cologne, 111, 142
Colonial warfare, 211
Comintern, 202, 223
Command procedures, 65, 66, 110
Commonwealth and Protectorate (1649–60), 82–83
Communist Party of the Soviet Union (CPSU), 199, 200
Comte, August, 161, 193
Comuneros revolt (1520–21), 45
Concentration camps, 198, 211
Concert of Italy, 54
Condottieri, 54
Confederacy, 244, 258
Congo, 211
Conscription: see Military service
Constitutional path of state formation, 31, 33, 39, 42, 47–49, 59, 72, 79–83, 88–93, 103, 118–120
Constitution of the United States, 243–244, 294
  military and security origins of, 252–254
Continental Congress, 246
Continental path of state formation, 27–39, 52, 59, 72–78
Continental System, 135
Cook, Morris Llewellyn, 278
Cornwallis, Lord, 126
Corradini, Enrico, 158

CPSIA information can be obtained at www.ICGtesting.com
Printed in the USA
LVOW131501170213

320480LV00002B/382/A